Sally Belfrage is more than a reporter of genius. She needs to live her books before she puts them on paper, a process which can demand a good deal of courage; which is, no doubt, the reason why a small output has won her deep respect.

She has two passports, British and American, and chooses to live in London, where she has brought up her two children. She wrote her first book when she was twenty-one: *A Room in Moscow*, describing the six months she had just spent working for a Russian publishing house. Her next came in the mid-sixties: *Freedom Summer*, a brilliant account of her experiences when working in a civil rights project in Mississippi. Her third book, *Flowers of Emptiness*, explored the reasons why the teachings of Bhagwan Shree Rajneesh appealed to so many of her contemporaries.

By the same author

A Room in Moscow
Freedom Summer
Flowers of Emptiness

SALLY BELFRAGE

The Crack

A Belfast Year

GRAFTON BOOKS
A Division of the Collins Publishing Group

LONDON GLASGOW
TORONTO SYDNEY AUCKLAND

Grafton Books
A Division of the Collins Publishing Group
8 Grafton Street, London W1X 3LA

Published by Grafton Books 1988

First published in Great Britain by
André Deutsch Ltd 1987

ISBN 0-586-20355-9

Printed and bound in Great Britain by
Collins, Glasgow

Set in Sabon

Contents

Introduction

When I first thought of going to Belfast, it wasn't Northern Ireland itself that drew me. I had no image of Northern Ireland beyond the very black-and-white and bored one that outsiders tend to have of the place. What concerned me to begin with were various abstractions. War in the long term – how one can live, particularly how women could live, at such a pitch of constant antagonism and danger. Commitment to an idea – that dedication to an idealistic future which can transcend, or even forfeit, the real lives of those it is meant to benefit. This is a theme I have written about before; here was a place where – from a distance, anyway – people seemed to be willing to go so far as to kill one another for the sake of perfecting life. I imagined their struggle, when I imagined it, as similar to Beirut's, an unstoppable engine of tragedy, travelling on and on independent of its causes. But as I've said, I knew nothing about it.

As things worked out, these elements inevitably came into the picture, but what I hadn't reckoned on was the quality of life I found in Belfast: people who were warm and involved and alive, and whom I loved more than any group I had ever encountered. These particular people are sustained by stories: their talk is magical. More perhaps than any other society, they convey their histories through song, verse, and *crack* – an Irish word meaning the talk, or the ambience, or what's going on. They depend on their mythologies to explain themselves and their actions, and it soon seemed to me that hearing them speak was the best way to get near an understanding of the war. The fact that there are at least three conflicting mythologies may make their situation more deadlocked; it certainly makes the listening more extraordinary. In the end I learned more about the place from listening than from my two yards of books.

I spent a year travelling every month to Belfast from London, where I live, staying for a week or more with, and listening to, the families who were becoming friends. I have given some people different names, but what they said, they said – although what they said could sometimes depart widely from the objective situation. I travelled around their beautiful countryside and to other towns in Northern Ireland, but have restricted my book to Belfast, because I had to limit it somewhere and everyone everywhere seemed to have something important to say.

The issues involved in the Northern Ireland war are endlessly complicated, if only because a war can hardly stand still, and there have been nearly two decades of new twists and embellishments, atrocities and peace initiatives. Add to this the different interpretations given to each development, so that there is never a theme without a counterpoint. But the basic situation does not change. For those who approach the subject from scratch as I did, I have tried to sum up the issues at stake – in what must be a very oversimplified way – in an appendix (page 404).

There are many people to thank – most of all the ones in the book, the many more who are not because of space, and the people who can't be named at all. Those who can: Tony Gifford, Nan Fromer, Bill Pirie, Susan Griffin, Desmond Fennell, Eleanor Goldschmied, Helena Kennedy, Fred Wiseman, Sylvia Meehan, Liz Curtis, Gordon Heald, Ted Smyth, Bob and Decca Treuhaft, Frances Murray, the late Henry Nash Smith, Paddy and Teresa Devlin, Anne Cadwallader, Pauline and Donal Murphy, Eileen Evason,

Steven and Patricia Smith, Kate Kelly, Tony and Jean Lynch, Joanna McMinn, Marie Mulholland, Mary Clemmey, Steven Greer, Michelene Wandor, Alger and Isabel Hiss, Lynda Edgerton, Prof. John A Murphy, Alison Lurie, Richard Kershaw, Liane Aukin, Lin Solomon, Maria Empira and Rosmarie Epaminondas, Anthony Sheil, all the people at the MacDowell Colony and at Annaghmakerrig and the Kilburn Bookshop, the John Simon Guggenheim Memorial Foundation; and Diana Athill and Elisabeth Sifton.

This book is dedicated to the people of Belfast, with love and gratitude.

Glossary

Adams, Gerry: leader of Sinn Fein, abstentionist MP, born 1949.

Alliance: a non-sectarian, largely middle-class party.

Andersonstown: Catholic housing estate in West Belfast.

Anglo-Irish Agreement: signed by British and Irish governments in November, 1985, giving the Southern government some influence in affairs directly affecting the Nationalists of the North.

Armalite: US-made semi-automatic rifle used by IRA.

ASU: Active Service Unit, small fighting cell of the IRA established in late '70s to prevent infiltration.

'B' Specials: Protestant auxiliary police force, disbanded by the British government in 1971.

Broo: From 'bureau', colloquial name for social security.

Castlereagh: RUC station used for the interrogation of suspects.

Corrymeela: Christian ecumenical reconciliation centre.

Cruthin: pre-Christian-era inhabitants of what is now Northern Ireland.

Cumann na mBan: women's military wing of Provisional IRA.

Diplock Courts: the system of non-jury courts for paramilitary offences, following the recommendations of Lord Diplock's enquiry in 1972.

Divis Flats: high-rise complex forming a Catholic ghetto in the Lower Falls section of Belfast.

DUP: Democratic Unionist Party, founded by Ian Paisley in 1971.

Falls Road: main artery of Catholic West Belfast.

Fenians: derogatory term for Catholics, taken from 19th century insurgent movement.

Forum Report: study completed in May 1984 in Dublin recommending various possible solutions to the Northern Irish impasse.

Free Presbyterian Church: church founded by Ian Paisley in 1951.

Gardai: the police in the Republic of Ireland.

H-Blocks: HMP (Her Majesty's Prison) Cellular Maze, popularly so-called from the shape of the blocks.

HE: Northern Ireland Housing Executive, government agency administering all public housing.

Hume, John: MP, Euro MP, and leader of the SDLP.

INLA: Irish National Liberation Army; the armed wing of the IRSP.

IRA: Irish Republican Army; correctly the Provisional IRA, also known as the 'Provos' or 'Provies'.

IRSP: Irish Republican Socialist Party, which split in 1974 from Official Sinn Fein; colloquially known as the Irps.

Long Kesh: old name, still used, for the Maze.

Loyalist: generally the term for the more extreme Protestants.

Maze: chief men's prison, divided into HMP Compound Maze (for those remaining 'special category' – political – prisoners); and HMP Cellular Maze, known as H-Blocks.

Nationalists: term for those who desire a united Ireland.

New Ireland Forum: see Forum Report.

NIO: Northern Ireland Office; mainland administrative HQ of all Northern Irish affairs since 1972.

Noraid: Irish Northern Aid, US fund-raising organization for IRA.

ODC: 'Ordinary Decent Criminal', i.e. a non-paramilitary who is not subject to Diplock courts.

Official IRA: the original IRA, from which the Provisional

IRA split in 1970, and which declared a ceasefire in 1972. Also called 'the Stickies', they are now largely absorbed into the Workers' Party.

Orange Order: Protestant secret society founded in 1796 which claims to promote civil and religious liberty, 'the open Bible' (as opposed to Catholics who have the Bible interpreted by priests), and Protestant succession to the British throne.

OUP: Official Unionist Party, aka the Ulster Unionist Party, headed by James Molyneux; majority Protestant party.

Paisley, Rev. Ian: founder-leader of the DUP and the Free Presbyterian Church, born 1926.

P-Check: 'Person Check'; legal provision by which police may stop and ask their name, address, where they have come from and where they are going.

Peace Walls: 20-foot-high corrugated iron fences separating Catholic and Protestant streets.

Peelers: name for police, since the time of Sir Robert Peel.

Pig: one-ton armoured car used by British army.

PIRA: Provisional IRA, which split from the Official IRA in 1970.

PTA: Prevention of Terrorism Act, British emergency legislation first enacted in 1974 enabling *inter alia* the deportation of suspected terrorists from mainland Britain.

Rah: colloquial name for PIRA.

Republicans: militant Nationalists who use violence.

RUC: Royal Ulster Constabulary, the local police force which is 90 per cent Protestant.

Sands, Bobby: first of ten Republican hunger strikers to die in the H-blocks in 1981.

Saracen: six-wheeled armoured personnel carrier.

The Sash: unofficial Loyalist anthem and marching song,

name referring to the orange band worn diagonally across the chest by parading Orangemen.

SDLP: Social Democratic and Labour Party, the main Nationalist party, with non-violent policies, founded in 1970 and led by John Hume.

Shankill Road: main thoroughfare through Protestant West Belfast.

Sinn Fein: 'Ourselves Alone' (Gaelic, pronounced Shin Fane), IRA's political wing.

Six Counties: Republican term for Northern Ireland.

SLR: self-loading rifle used by British Army.

Soldier's Song: national anthem of the Republic of Ireland.

SOSP: Secretary of State's Pleasure – indeterminate prison sentence given to underage offenders.

Squaddy: British soldier.

Stickies: colloquial name for members of the Workers' Party.

Stormont: seat of government of Northern Ireland.

Supergrass: an informer against former paramilitary colleagues who in return for his testimony is granted some form of immunity or reduced sentence, sometimes with relocation and new identity to follow.

Taig: derogatory term for a Catholic deriving from the Irish form of 'Timothy'.

Tricolour: the green, white and orange flag of the Republic, the white originally meant to represent a truce between Catholic and Protestant.

Troops Out Movement: mainland supporters of British withdrawal from Ireland.

Twenty-six Counties: Republican term for the South.

UDA: Ulster Defence Association, largest paramilitary body in the North, Protestant, legal.

UDR: Ulster Defence Regiment, locally recruited regiment of the British Army, 98 per cent Protestant.

UFF: Ulster Freedom Fighters, cover name used by UDA when engaged in violent paramilitary activity.

Unionists: most Protestant political parties, and their voters.

UVF: Ulster Volunteer Force, illegal Protestant paramilitary organization.

Workers' Party: non-violent Marxist Party which developed out of the Official IRA.

1
Is There Life Before Death?

Like a room so untidy you can barely make out the furniture or even tell with certainty which room it is, Belfast on first sight offended my most basic domestic instincts: derelict buildings, bombsites, barricades, blowing rubbish, graffiti, corrugated iron, barbed wire, the smell of rot, and the final affront – men in khaki pointing guns at you. To see past any of this was at first beyond my capacity.

Within days at least half a dozen people had said in one way or another: 'I *can't* be anywhere else.' – 'This is the *only* place to live. I tried Australia but I come back 'cause I missed the crack.' – 'It's the greatest wee town in the world!' An Englishwoman even said she was 'terrified the trendies will hear about it and they'll all want to move here.' And within days the eyesores had already begun selectively to diminish, as scars on a face fade out when they belong to a friend whose eyes and voice are what count. Nothing about the initial impression, however, gave any hope of this.

The place was full of contradictions. There was a Bacardi billboard showing Telly Savalas surrounded with love, heat and prosperity, itself perched in a heap of debris among crumbling buildings with bricked-up windows. Lots of other buildings had cages around them, but the people were open and unprotected. Everywhere the eye fell, destruction co-existed with survival.

The idea was to walk up the Falls Road, the main artery of the Catholic ghetto of West Belfast, beginning at its most startling bit of architecture, the Divis Flats. Confronting the bleak blocks of high-rises set in a sea of rubble, I didn't feel too confident about this, but there was nowhere to go but in. One of those huge, hateful system-built estates that look the same everywhere – architects have been known to call them 'stack-a-prole' – Divis contained one tall tower and vistas of concrete in six storeys, with a little chipped plastic in primary colours thrown in for brighteners. Just beyond appeared the twin steeples of a large old church. The complex seemed big enough to be a city on its own, if only it had any amenities or made civic sense. It was built between 1966 and 1972 for the Catholics (as a punishment or a palliative, depending on whether you had to live there or not), replacing one slum area with a worse one. It had gone the way of other such developments from New York to Amsterdam and even to Moscow: pillaged and looted by the bored and alienated younger inhabitants who had only bits of flotsam on a defaced rectangle to suggest where once a playground might have been planned. The youngest ones were playing anyway, balancing on cliffs of concrete, throwing around what they could lift, swinging on a dangling armature, and skipping and laughing as if there were no greater treat.

In a corner of one building, from a makeshift trestle table, two women sold limp vegetables and fruit. This was their own project, they said, because there were no shops. Not even a bench, for that matter, not a vestige of landscaping. Graffiti covered the reachable walls (BRITS WANK; IF YOU WANT PEACE PREPARE FOR WAR), and passages reeked of piss.

The women had a raw way of laughing about it – and about the rats, the black slime that grew on the walls, which the Housing Executive blamed on condensation, the bugs that dropped on your face as you slept, the sewage that backed up into the baths, the broken lifts, the overflow of garbage that couldn't fit into the inadequate chutes, the exposed asbestos they all breathed, the children drowned or injured falling into holes . . . Divis also had over 80 per cent unemployment.

But beyond the endemic horrors of all such places, the women pointed out what put Divis in a class of its own: the top floor of the tower had been commandeered by the army as a lookout post, and from there the people were in constant view 'through a gunsight'. The one telling me this, who said her name was Moira, pointed, squinting, up to the nineteenth floor of the tower. It was blacked out as if pretending to be invisible, the way people wear dark glasses to hide themselves, black with slits. Nothing happened in Divis of which the army was unaware. To emphasize this, residents campaigning for the demolition of the whole complex had recently got word that two of the buildings were shortly to come down. The official reason was that the land was needed for a motorway extension. It was maybe a coincidence, Moira said, that one of the buildings happened to be the only structure invisible to the outpost.

I told the women I'd be back and walked on up the Falls.

Despite the weather being fine and warm, there was such an intrinsic chill that the sunshine seemed a mockery, like the smile embalmers stick on the face of a person who hadn't the muscles to make that particular smile. In the clear light everything looked dingy, dismal, scarred. The side-streets leading off the Falls were lined with tiny tumbledown terraced houses, droves of dirty kids playing on the cracked asphalt and the odd wino propped against the equally cracked walls. Shops on the main road were open, but their windows were boarded up or covered with dirty wire mesh, and the entry was through a dark hole. Greengrocers displayed a few potatoes and onions in boxes outside, as if ready for instant evacuation. All original surfaces were covered in corrugated iron, wire or graffiti. Only florists, with lavish displays of funeral wreaths, seemed to be making a go of it. The road and pavement were strewn with rubble, and enormous boulders surrounded some buildings and barricaded off some side-streets. The local Social Security office, which served many of West Belfast's 12,000 unemployed, was completely wired in and decorated with rubbish that had been hurled at it and stuck. Garbage everywhere; not a refuse bin in sight, or a public telephone. The only public facility seemed to be the occasional pillar box, its red paint sloshed with green, with a metal plaque nailed to its opening making it impossible to post anything more than 1/16th of an inch thick. Anything that could be broken, was – windows, signs, lamp-posts.

Then a *jogger* went by, and two boys in mohawks. As I watched all three of them draw scornful stares from a group of men lounging outside a betting shop, a huge army vehicle drew abreast. It had a kind of cowcatcher in front and tiny windows wired almost to obscurity; you could barely make out the driver through a lifted hatch. Two soldiers were poking through another hatch at the rear with plastic visors over their faces and bulletproof vests. Each pointed a gun, one up and towards the side, the other straight at me. My heart tripped. Another just the same came by, two more soldiers, two more guns. The passers-by paid no attention.

I couldn't remember feeling so demoralized: as if I'd had the air knocked out of me and the aggressor was still at large. There was something astonishing in seeing women push prams along, shoppers congested in doorways, friends gossiping. It was hard to meet people's eyes and I was beginning to wonder about the wisdom of the notebook into which I was copying graffiti. Then an old man passed and tipped his cap at me. 'Hello dear!' he said.

'Lovely, isn't it?' I smiled too and the air came back. I went on scribbling graffiti. 'IS THERE LIFE BEFORE DEATH?'

As well as the usual FUCK DICKY and MURPH AND BUGSY WERE HERE, Catholic Belfast was daubed from end to end with the message: BRITS OUT – IRELAND FOR THE IRISH – PROVOS RULE – UP THE IRA. If the form and content of the writing on the wall is a measure of public involvement, these attested to an obsession. In contrast I thought of the *only* piece of related spray-painting I had ever seen in London, confronting me daily and for years as I drove my children to school: STOP THE WAR IN IRELAND. At some point an alteration had been made in dark paint: STOP THE WAR IN   LAND. What did it mean? Was the war in Ireland over? What war, anyway? 'Troubles' were quaintly referred to, but *war*? How can you hide a war?

Like many Londoners, I knew and didn't know, cared and didn't care about Northern Ireland. Even an Irish holiday a few miles from the Northern border in County Mayo had never once been disturbed by mention of a 'war'. Too boring, too complicated, and most boring was the idea of uncomplicating it. Something to do with nationalism and religion, neither of which interested me. The eye developed the knack, so perfected as to become subliminal, of skipping any story in the paper with ULSTER or IRA in the headline. News of the worst outrage would sometimes leak irritatingly past the edge of my blinders, but generally I was a lot better at blue-pencilling the news than any police state censor. It was amazing how much news there was when finally I looked. How can a war be hidden? You do it yourself.

But here we had a message the size of a house, for on such it was, and quite beyond human powers to conceal:

The NAZIS had HITLER — The BRITISH have THATCHER
The NAZIS had AUSCHWITZ — The BRITISH have LONG KESH
The NAZIS had the SS — The BRITISH have the RUC
WELCOME TO NAZI OCCUPIED IRELAND

The paintwork told the story of the years of fighting. GIVE THEM THEIR RIGHTS NOT THEIR LAST RIGHTS (sic) was left from the 1981 hunger strike, when ten Provisional IRA men imprisoned in the H-blocks of Long Kesh starved themselves to death to protest their 'criminalization' and the withdrawal of their status as prisoners of war. STATUS NOW – STOP THE TORTURE/H-BLOCKS – BREAK THATCHER'S BACK. But Thatcher said: 'The hunger strikers are taking the whole cause of Irish Republicanism with them to the grave,' and let them die.

INFORMERS BEWARE, and SHOW TRIAL NO TRIAL referred to the trials that had been going on since 1981 in which those known as 'paid perjurers' to their victims, 'converted terrorists' to the authorities and just 'supergrasses' to everyone else, had betrayed their former paramilitary cohorts (on both sides) and agreed to testify in exchange for immunity or reduced sentences, resettlement in some faraway country, and money. One Raymond Gilmour was singled out for extra (mis-spelled) treatment: GILMORE WILL BE GOT SOONER OR LATER. GILMORE ROT IN HELL.

Repeated everywhere, STOP THE STRIP SEARCHING referred to the women in Armagh jail who were being undressed for examination even on the way to and from hearings at the local courthouse where smuggling opportunities were minimal; as far as the community was concerned it was pure harassment.

Divisions of opinion were advertised. RISE WITH YOUR CLASS NOT OUT OF IT looked like the Workers'

Party. Anything in Gaelic or featuring the green, white and gold tricolour was Sinn Fein. TIOCFAIDH AR LA, 'chocky are la', Our day will come. Rivalry between Sinn Fein and the moderate Social Democratic and Labour Party had led representatives of the former to reuse the latter's initials all over the place in STOOP-DOWN-LOW PARTY. Once the IRA's initials had come in for it too: I RAN AWAY; but this message was old and quite unearned now.

Nobody bothered to get at the Protestants: their ideas were irrelevant here even if they ventured to this part of town. But there were words for the army, from the weary to the angry:

> WHEN YOU CAME TO THIS LAND
> YOU SAID YOU CAME TO UNDERSTAND
> SOLDIER WE'RE TIRED OF YOUR UNDERSTAND-
> ING TIRED OF BRITISH TROOPS ON OUR SOIL
> TIRED OF THE KNOCK UPON THE DOOR
> TIRED OF THE RIFLE-BUTT ON THE HEAD
> TIRED OF THE JAILS AND THE BEATINGS
> TIRED OF THE DEATHS OF OLD FRIENDS
> TIRED OF THE TEARS AND FUNERALS
> THOSE ENDLESS ENDLESS FUNERALS
> IS THIS YOUR UNDERSTANDING?

and:

SOLDIER, DO YOU THINK THAT YOU HAVE GOT AWAY WITH THE MURDER OF OUR POLITICAL PRISONERS AND INNOCENT CHILDREN ON THE STREETS?
WELL,
THINK AGAIN FOR YOUR NAME IS
ENGRAVED ON THE FREEDOM-FIGHTER'S
BULLET!

These were not the relatively slapdash work of the aerosol artist but huge murals carefully composed and rendered. Most had been splashed with dollops of white or black paint which looked thrown and had dried in drools. Some murals had been retouched back to their original state; one was a meticulous painting of three armed women, apparently African, Palestinian and Irish, with the motto:

> We must grow tough
> but without ever
> losing our tenderness.

Sometimes it was only the picture that counted, like a strange fallen Christ figure on a gable end. Sometimes it was the message.

> THE GREAT ONLY APPEAR GREAT BECAUSE
> WE ARE ON OUR KNEES
> LET US RISE

And one that seemed to sum up the others:

FOR THOSE WHO BELIEVE NO EXPLANATION IS NECESSARY	FOR THOSE WHO DON'T BELIEVE NO EXPLANATION IS POSSIBLE

There is a more permanent kind of graffiti, carved in the stone of graves. A walk up the Falls ends in Milltown Cemetery where are the plots of the Republican dead. IN PROUD AND LOVING MEMORY OF ALL THOSE WHO GAVE THEIR LIVES IN THE CAUSE OF IRISH FREEDOM. There followed twenty-four names, two of them women's, of some of the dead from the first decade of the current Troubles. Another tablet read PLEASE REMEMBER OUR FRIENDS WHO WERE BRUTALLY MURDERED, with five men's names, two women's. A short distance away the graves of the hunger strikers were in a long plot ringed in green. There were many empty places waiting. I saw a middle-aged woman standing nearby at a conventional grave. As I passed she said, not so much to me as to the air: 'I hate seeing the Republican plot. There are so many names you can put faces to.'

Up Glen Road past the cemetery is Turf Lodge, a newish estate of small drab houses and vandalized, bricked-up shops, where lived Kathleen Stewart, whose son Brian had been killed by a plastic bullet in 1976. Mrs Stewart's case against the British army, fought ever since, had just been turned down by the European Court of Justice in Strasbourg, which had decided that despite fourteen deaths and countless injuries, plastic bullets were 'less dangerous than alleged'. I had a letter for her from her London lawyer. Without it, or even so, I wasn't sure I had the stomach to pry into her tragedy; in the event, she wanted to talk about it – the first of many.

She was a warm welcoming woman with a most beautiful face. Those of her seven surviving children who had left home spent their days there anyway. Everybody, including her husband, was unemployed, and the place was full of the generations. Mrs Stewart's children were as handsome as she was, but thin as wires. We sat beside the fireplace opposite a wall covered with a big TV, pictures of Jesus and the Pope, and a glass-fronted cabinet containing knick-knacks and a shrine to Brian with his portrait in the middle. He had a sweet child's smile and long blond hair, which dated his death. On the floor was a huge flowering busy lizzie. Everything was very clean.

I suddenly remembered how when I had had one child I wanted another in case anything happened to the first. Of course it turns out not like that at all. Seven living children in no way dulled Mrs Stewart's pain about Brian. But her voice was always soft, no matter what the stress of the situation she was describing, the obtuseness of her interviewer or the number of times she must have said it.

She read the letter from the lawyer and told me what had happened. 'The day Brian was killed, I had made the children's dinner early and afterwards Brian was sitting beside me and I was helping him with his English homework.' When her daughter Marie arrived home at ten past six she offered to take over with the homework if her mother would put her dinner out. In the kitchen Mrs Stewart heard a knock at the door and when she came out saw that Brian was answering it – a next-door neighbour wanted to borrow a tin opener. Brian then went out, walking up the street to the shops. Within three minutes he was in an ambulance, mortally wounded with a shot in the head. He died six days later on his thirteenth birthday.

On television an army spokesman claimed 'that Brian was the ringleader of a rioting mob of four hundred, that they'd watched him for a considerable time, they'd fired at a specific target, and their men were restrained if anything.' But there had been no riot, Mrs Stewart said – if there had been, 'I never would have let my children out. My children used to say to me it was like a prison. Whenever the army came into the area I used to bring them in and close the door.' What happened was that a riot had begun *after* Brian was shot and as a direct result. But by the time the case came to court for the first time, the army's version had changed: only 150 rioters this time, and soldiers had aimed not at Brian but at 'a tall youth with a blue and white striped jumper'. In any case, it was self-defence.

Her own witnesses had another story: two girls who had been standing in the street said Brian had come up to them and 'the next thing there was a bang and Brian fell to the ground,' Mrs Stewart said. 'Then two soldiers ran over and grabbed Brian by the heels and tried to pull him down the street. In court they said they were going to render first aid to him, but you don't pull anybody down the street if you're going to render first aid to them. But one of the girls held on to Brian and he was brought in to Margaret McGee's house and Margaret rang for an ambulance.

'The judge said the girl was a vicious liar to say that the soldiers would act in such a callous manner. But I know, I live here, and I have seen the soldiers and I understand what they can do and what they have done; for I have seen them pulling fellows into Saracens and tramping on them, I've seen them making men lie down in the street and running up and down their bodies, and jumping on their hands. I have seen them doing this with my own eyes, it's not hearsay. But them judges and all the people have to do with the law, they don't live in these ghetto areas, they live away out in private dwellings and the army never goes round to bother them.'

She nodded towards the window and, turning, I saw a soldier running past, rifle at the ready, then another. Across the street were several more. Bringing up the rear was another squaddy walking backwards. It was over so quickly I couldn't believe it. 'How often does that happen?'

'Two or three times a day. But some days they step it up.'

She went back to her legal difficulties. After the judge dismissed the case, she appealed, but the army kept vanishing. The soldiers actually involved in Brian's death – the private who shot him, the lieutenant who gave the order, and the major who had issued the first statement, were promoted: 'I don't know why.' When she needed the major to testify about his initial statement, since it contradicted a later one, he was unavailable, transferred elsewhere.

Couldn't he have been subpoenaed? 'I don't know about the law,' she said. 'It was the first time I or anybody belonging to me been in court, and we didn't know what way things were worked. I thought, When you go to court you get justice, and if you're telling the truth they know you're telling the truth. You have nine witnesses and the Ministry of Defence has one – the soldier who shot your son – but everything he says is the honest-to-God truth and nine witnesses is all telling lies.'

On another level she was able to be amazingly philosophical about the army. 'Every country has to have some sort of riot control and I understand that. But when innocent children are being killed, justice should be done. My case was already pending going to the European Court when Julie Ann Livingstone was killed, Carol Ann Kelly, Stephen McConomy – their brains blown out by soldiers when there was no incident or cause. I don't believe in that. But you take these young fellows, only eighteen, ninteen years old, the government has taken them children and trained them to go out and kill to keep us down; and they're patrolling these streets, some of them's bound to be half crazy.

'At the beginning I was angry and very frustrated about it, but if anybody had put a gun in my hand and set that private in front of me and told me to shoot him I couldn't have done it. It wasn't in me to do that. My husband would've shot all round. No matter if he would've been killed or not. If it was women that was in power there would be no sons changed to kill mothers' sons. I don't like somebody taking children and making them into murderers.'

But the pressures on her own sons were hard even to hear about, let alone for them to live with. She told about the time that Gerard, when he was fifteen, had been standing outside when the army had come along and the last man in the patrol, walking backwards, bumped into him. Mrs Stewart was just coming home from the shops and witnessed what happened. 'The next thing the soldier had Gerard pinned against the wall with his rifle, and I came over and said, "That was only an accident, why are you getting so angry?" And the soldier says to me, "Go and mind your own f–ing business." I says to him, "That's my business because that's my son and it's outside my door and," I says, "that's an accident, you were walking backwards and he had his back to you and the two of yous bumped together." And he called this other tall soldier over to him, very swarthy with a black moustache, and this one was clickin' his gun and all, and I was afraid of them shooting Gerard. Brian was killed and I was afraid of Gerard getting shot. And I told this other soldier that it had been an accident, and I says, "I don't want my son hurt because I had a young son killed four years ago." And this soldier says "Good, f–ing good, they don't kill enough of yous f–ing Bs." And I says to him, "That's your opinion and I can't change it, I hope to God nobody ever goes into your country and does the same things that is happening in these streets." And this other soldier says, "Yous f–ing Bs want us to bow down and honour yous." Then Gerard says, "No, we don't." The big soldier lifted his fist and he hit Gerard in the nose and the blood was running out and he was falling. I caught him like that there and the soldier came over and he punched me in the face. Me and Gerard ended up in the hospital. I had to get all my teeth extracted. They paid me £500 and they paid Gerard £250 so we wouldn't bring it to court.'

Her son Seamus made us tea and there were more stories about the army – how they had come into the area 'in their hundreds' after the Queen had visited the province in 1977, because 'the IRA was supposed to have put out a statement that they were going to do something, and they said the Queen was insulted, so they were in to give us a hard time. But I mean it wasn't the ordinary people that threatened the Queen, it was the IRA.' Nevertheless they went into houses and wrecked furniture, beat up old-age pensioners ('Mrs Malone was standing doing her washing and they upturned her washing machine and kicked the legs off her') and stole money ('Jimmy Monaghan had £300 upstairs in the wardrobe, his daughter was getting married, and they stole the £300 on Jimmy').

I had the feeling of stones being added to my stomach with each new story. But 'it's something you have to live with,' said Mrs Stewart. 'The people know there's nothing they can do about it. The only outlet is for the young men to join the IRA to avenge all these things. That's the reason I think most of them join, because they know that this is all wrong, this here shouldn't have happened. There's nothing else for them to do. There's no jobs, there's nothing.'

As for her own attitude to the IRA, 'the Loyalist politicians say everybody in Catholic areas is IRA and controlled by the IRA, but it isn't so. We might sympathize with them and their cause, and we would like to see a united Ireland. Because until there's a united Ireland we're going to have this conflict on and on and on. It has gone on hundreds of years and it always returns to the British army on the streets.'

I asked if she had any Protestant friends. Not only friends, she said – two of her brothers and one sister were married to Protestants, with some of the children brought up one way and some another. The Protestant halves of these marriages had a good understanding of what it meant to be Catholic, especially the wife of one of Mrs Stewart's brothers who had been interned without trial for three and a half years, though 'he never even threw a *stone*'. They occasionally all met in town 'for dinner and a good laugh' but they couldn't visit each other's homes for fear of paramilitary violence in the ghettos. 'The divide has really broadened now, whereas before this all happened the people were really happy together, lived and worked together. Now I can't see any way they're going to get back together with the army here, because there's no room for negotiation.'

She had grown up in a mixed neighbourhood. 'The people used to sit in the street, Protestants and Catholics, and play music till one o'clock in the morning. We had a lovely time. It was very simple, and everybody loved one another. If something happened to one it happened to the lot of us, it was that kind of community.' Violence was unknown; 'you never heard of murders here.'

Mrs Stewart walked me to the nearest cab rank, past the corner where her son had been shot. 'See where those railings are? Brian was standing beside that there. And the soldier was behind a car. He shot Brian from there.'

Then one last human detail: what Brian had been doing that day. He had asked her for twopence before they had begun on his homework. When she collected his clothes from the hospital the twopence was gone and there was a cigarette in his pocket. His last words to the girl on the corner were: 'Have you got a light?'

'Friend of Mrs Stewart, are you?' said the taxi driver to me suddenly. I said I had been doing an interview with her and was writing about the place. 'Here's something for you,' he said, as up ahead a roadblock became visible. Soldiers wearing jungle camouflage were random-checking cars. 'They're not supposed to be here doing that there,' the driver said. 'That's the UDR.' Seeing it was a taxi, they waved us by. The driver didn't react to this as anything out of the ordinary; the last time I had seen a roadblock was a couple of decades ago in the Sinai Desert.

'There's no way round it,' he said. 'This is the only

entrance and exit to this housing estate. They were all built this way so that we can be cut off at a minute's notice like. But the UDR are supposed to keep away from this, it's usually the RUC. Not that what anybody's supposed to do makes a difference.'

Then the driver told me he had a sister doing time in Armagh jail; she'd been caught with some guns. She was the brightest in the family, he said, had done brilliantly at school, and now was enrolled in an Open University course. She was only twenty-two, and he hated the idea of her being locked up 'till her life is away.' He wished he could be as cheerful about it as she was.

When we got to the end of the ride he refused to take any money. He wouldn't even argue about it.

The sky next day was still clear blue, the temperature Mediterranean, and you could hear people commenting on how unusual it was. 'In this heat, we'll have to start having siestas,' one woman said to another on the grass in the Botanic Gardens. All around me the green was dotted with semi-naked tanning flesh. Meticulously tended and with a great glasshouse like the one at Kew, the Gardens seemed far from Troubles or trouble. After a while the other woman commented: 'The unemployed can have a permanent siesta.' Looking again after this remark, I realized there was an unusual aspect to the view. The prone bodies belonged not to the mothers and small children normally found in a park on a weekday, but almost all to men.

On the way to West Belfast, beginning to be able to increase the depth of field beyond the nearest pock-marked wall, I could see how abruptly the ugliness ended at the edge of a steep row of mountains, green and sloping like a long reclining body curled beside the city for protection. Belfast's setting, with its slash of river through the centre and the Lough beyond, and patchwork hills on the other side too, was as lovely as any. As for down here, the bright light again seemed strangely offensive on the Falls.

The entrance to the Sinn Fein office was on a brief row of shabby terraced houses off the main road. Thigh-high boulders were placed strategically around the building to ward off car bombers. A huge mural outside was splashed with paint but this affected only its aesthetics, not its message, which was to advertise *An Phoblacht/Republican News*, the Sinn Fein weekly newspaper. The paper and other Republican literature were on sale in a pleasant bookshop just around the corner in the Falls itself, with a one-way mirrored door – you had to ring a buzzer to get in after being given an invisible once-over. Although known to everybody as 'the Sinn Fein bookshop' and with no other pretensions, cheques for books bought there had to be made out to 'The Art Shop'.

Sinn Fein itself didn't run to mirrors. The two outer doors were covered with protruding wire cages, and the once-over, after buzzer-pushing, came through a peephole augmented by two closed-circuit video cameras. After the sunshine the place felt like a cave. The windows were either boarded or wired over, the main light sources a few bare bulbs. One or two friendly bruisers manned television screens on a broken desk at the 'reception'. Upstairs were warrens of dark corridors, scruffy offices, worn furniture. Only the posters on the walls were fresh, such as BRITANNIA WAIVES THE RULES, or one showing Margaret Thatcher WANTED FOR MURDER.

I was looking for Chrissie McAuley of the Women's Department and had been vaguely gestured to the back to have a look. Once admitted, I wasn't challenged again and got lost. In one room a wide-set man with a scraggy brown beard said, 'I saw you walking up the road yesterday and I thought, "There's a stranger, she looks lost".' He wasn't very helpful about getting me unlost, however, and a few minutes later I bumped into him again downstairs among half a dozen men. I asked them the way out. 'She's looking for Chrissie,' said brownbeard. 'She must be a feminist. She'll break you in two if you look at her the wrong way.' They stood there scoffing and chortling. Then one among them who hadn't seemed to find it funny either, a tall nearsighted man with another brown but trimmed beard, gestured and opened a door for me. 'That's our commander,' said a small fair fellow executing a mock salute towards the man holding the door, who was Gerry Adams.

Chrissie was at home a few numbers down in the terrace opposite – one of the tiny houses built up to a century ago in the old Belfast style for the mill workers who once populated the area, made to be a slum from the start. The McAuleys' place was an improvement on the original insofar as a back room had been appended to house both a kitchen and a lavatory, in such conjunction that, as Chrissie put it, 'you can sit on the bog and stir the food at the same time.' We were in the more hospitable front, with the television on silently, many small clothes drying over the backs of chairs, papers on tables, books on shelves. On top of the shelves were two wooden harps and a Gaelic cross carved in reddish wood, made in Long Kesh. In Catholic houses there were either carvings from the prison or religious images or both.

Chrissie was familiar: I had seen her on television, in some programmes about the Troubles I had borrowed on videotape. Most British television coverage of Northern Ireland gave short shrift to Sinn Fein, but now and then in an attempt at 'balance' there was a brief interview with leader Gerry Adams, publicity director Danny Morrison, or Chrissie. Sometimes she was to be seen on a dais exhorting the people, or at a funeral glimpsed in the background wearing dark glasses. An intense, slight, good-looking woman of twenty-eight, she had that Irish combination of very black hair and very white skin, and her own way of flaring her nostrils to signal an important point, or indignation or, most often, laughter. There was a quality of contained ferocity in her dry manner which gave it its edge – a tiger bred small, a wildcat in kitten's clothing. She was also half-Protestant.

The ferocity was less than contained when it came to her politics. More than half her life had been spent in the Republican struggle, three years of it in jail in Dublin on an explosives charge, and now besides Sinn Fein work she covered news stories for *Republican News*, gave at least a day every week to visiting friends locked up in Armagh, as well as taking care of two pre-school children – a girl of four and a boy of two. She was pregnant with a third and, having trouble, was often off to hospital. Her husband, Richard, who had to fill in then, had spent five years in prison himself and now was in charge of the Sinn Fein press department.

Some of Chrissie's wrath was reserved for the Housing Executive, who spurned her appeals to get her family rehoused properly. This place was condemned, she said, and they were squatters. All her appeals were met with one response: since they shouldn't be living there in the first place they must go back where they came from – Richard's parents' house – before the Housing Executive would consider their case. But the parents weren't well and couldn't put up with 'screaming kids': they still had three of their own at home anyway. 'There's many more in the same boat: this area has the highest proportion of so-called squatters – something like a hundred as opposed to ninety-odd legal tenants.' But it was better than Divis, where her sister survived on dreams and rumours of possible demolitions.

The 'screaming kids' now materialized: a little girl came in from playing in the street and started rummaging in her mother's handbag. Soon afterwards a small, snuffling boy leaned around the door. When he had been out in the street too he had been 'bold'. 'You were bold, weren't you?' Chrissie railed at him. 'You ran out in front of a black taxi, didn't you?' He had been shut up in his room. She agreed to his release now, but shook him as he sobbed and said, 'You know what I will do if you do that again? I'll give you to the Brits and they can keep you!'

Meanwhile her daughter, Bronagh, who had the same blue-dark hair as her mother, was silently smearing eye make-up all over her face, gauging the effect in a small cosmetics mirror, pleased with the result. Her cheeks were soon a strange dark mauve.

Chrissie talked about life at Mountjoy Prison in Dublin, where throughout her three-year term she had been isolated from other Republicans but had managed a good many conversions. The women there, 'the most decent people I ever came across in my life,' were caught in a poverty trap of drugs and prostitution and continual imprisonment, and she had pushed to get a remedial teacher in and tried to encourage them out of their illiteracy and hopelessness. 'All of them got dead interested in the struggle up here. They'd never heard any other version than the media one, which is as distorted in the Free State as in Britain.' I found this surprising, but, she said, 'The Free State is just as oppressive as the Brits: you better believe it.' The state television company in the South is not permitted to give broadcast time to Sinn Fein; and the security forces there hound Republicans as hard as their Northern counterparts do. But it was the North that concerned her.

'Constitutional politics is a joke. We've had constitutional politics since this state was founded. We've had a one-party state in the Stormont. What did the Unionist regime ever offer the Nationalist people? There's no way I would even dream of stepping back an inch, never mind a foot, on the principle of what I want now, and I have two kids and another one coming. We have to keep pushing ahead. It can get no worse.'

'What do you want now?'

No pause: 'A united socialist democratic thirty-two-county republic.'

'What are you going to do with those people down there?'

She thought this very funny. '"Those people down there", our fellow Irishmen and women, our country-people' – lots of nostril flaring – 'will gradually see, as the structure in the Free State starts to break down – and it *is* breaking down: there are less jobs, the economic situation is deplorable, they're up to their necks in debt – and with Sinn Fein's message getting across to working-class people, you'll see the dividends over several years. It will be a hard slog, we know that, just as it'll be hard to convince the Protestant population up here that Sinn Fein or Republicanism doesn't pose any threat to their welfare. The Protestant people have to understand that they are part of this nation, that a united Ireland won't threaten their heritage or their lives. They'll simply be entitled to no more and no less privilege than the people next to them.

'A lot of the Protestant hysteria is whipped up by the politicians. Paisley and Smyth and Robinson say "Go into a united Ireland and you'll lose your Protestant heritage and be swallowed up in this Papist state." But I mean the Protestants in the twenty-six counties have never faced that problem; they're free to practise their religion and run their education the way they want it. There is a stranglehold of the Church down there, but as Republicans we believe that church and state should be totally separated. It will be a while. Nothing's going to be achieved overnight. I mean this phase of the struggle has gone on fifteen years; we've been struggling for eight hundred years just to get rid of British imperialism, never mind starting the day with our own problems as Irish people. But nothing can happen until the Brits get the hell out.'

I asked Chrissie how they were planning to persuade the Protestants to get in on this. She started with what I learned was a frequent observation: 'We've probably more in common with the working-class Protestant people in the North than with the working class down in the twenty-six counties.' Because of distortions in the media, she said, Republicans had been presented as 'sinister-type people who front for the IRA. A lot of them still believe it, but our vote throughout Ireland has shown there's a lot of support for Sinn Fein, and we can grow on that. There's no way now for the Brits to say there is no support for a thirty-two-county socialist republic, for there is, a hell of a lot of support. They can see SDLP [Social Democratic and Labour Party, the moderate Catholic party] voters shifting to Sinn Fein, people who support the idea of a united Ireland and see the IRA as patriots.'

This conversation was by no means uninterrupted, which made Chrissie's ability to stick to the subject the more impressive. The kids were in and out with scraped knees and thirsts and short-term boredoms; and Richard McAuley came home briefly looking for something – as young, dark-and-light and handsome as Chrissie, more contained but just as tired. Her sister from Divis came by for a cup of tea. And Danny Morrison dropped in with some chore for Chrissie. He looked at me and the tape recorder, and Chrissie solemnly explained I was a social worker.

When the coast was clear again I asked her about the Protestant part of her family. 'My father's a Protestant; he comes from County Down. He married my mother in '54. People tend to think that this is the only phase of the struggle where there were Troubles between Catholics and Protestants – but you can go right back to the inception of this state, and there were always pogroms against Catholics, in the city and in rural areas, by Protestant people. Heinous murders were carried out by Protestants to keep down Republicanism and to retain the state at all costs. My father met my mother at a time when there was internment. And when he came to the Falls Road courting her, he was a bit dubious about it but he still kept coming on, and he eventually became a convert to the Catholic religion.'

'Is that what she required of him?'

'That's what the Catholic Church required. And so the two of them were married, right? But I never knew that he was a Protestant. I *never* knew he was a Protestant until '69! We used to go down to my granny Graham and religion was never brought up; we were accepted as her grandchildren and that was it. We lived here in the Lower Falls and when the Protestants burnt Bombay Street down, my father was away in England. He could never get work here; I didn't understand about it then, but he was always victimized because he was a convert. He used to work in the shipyard with Protestants, you see, and that's taboo. As far as they're concerned a dead Catholic's okay but a dead convert's even better. He got death threats, open threats from Protestants he worked with. You're looking to be killed, like. So he had to go to England and move around all the time, as a sheet metal worker. He wasn't here in '69 the night they burned down Bombay Street. We all had to evacuate. He heard about the Troubles, and he came straight home. We – I was the eldest of five kids – were staying first of all in a school, then in some people's house in Andersonstown. Everyone who had wheels or could get wheels, left the area or got out any way they could – put their stuff in prams and moved up the road.

'Then we moved back down. I'll never forget that day. It was like something in outer space, seeing all these British soldiers in riot gear and rifles and barbed wire and smoke – there was just a stinking atmosphere, some of the houses were so burnt. Our house was still standing, but it had been looted, they'd broken in and thrown our things into the street, everything all over the place.

'It was then that my daddy sat down with me. I was saying, "Who done this? The Protestants – they're *bad* people." And he said, "Chris, love, it's not. It's the way this country is." He says, "I'm a Protestant." And I couldn't – these Protestants come and burn us down, and he says "I'm a Protestant." I just couldn't – relate to it. There was never politics talked in our house. I didn't know what Republicanism was. I'd seen graffiti on the walls, IRA, stuff like this, but the IRA was never talked about. Because the IRA's last campaign before that was in the fifties. And you read about what the IRA did in 1916, that was part of your history in school but there was never any strong feeling about it, a united Ireland or anything.

'So we sat down and that was the first time we ever talked about the different traditions. But then, a few weeks after that, sure there he goes out, fighting off the British soldiers, protecting the area, along with everybody else, against CS gas [used for riot control before the introduction of rubber and plastic bullets], against the curfew that was imposed.'

Chrissie said she had had no contact for years with her Protestant uncles and aunts. One uncle used to drive a bus up and down the Falls and gave her free rides. He had a daughter she played with, who now was 'grown and has a family and I couldn't tell you where she is. I'm always curious. But I'd never feel – inclined, even . . . and they've never tried to contact me. And especially with my Republican background, people know me. I'm sure they have me well-branded. But I'm prepared to talk to them, no problem.

'The problem is that this is made out to be a religious war, that it's this religious difference, which it isn't. It's a political war against British occupation. Personally I think the Brits are very blind, they really are. How long are they going to stay here and try to keep this thing going? The longer they stay the worse the whole damn thing is for everybody. I mean let's get it over with once and for all. Do they want another eight hundred years? In every generation there's going to be people who oppose the British presence. And there seems to be a blockage with them, they just can't seem to get it into their heads. They're just prolonging the whole thing, for the Protestants as well as Catholics. I'd rather have it all over with. *And if I die I die.*'

'What about your kids?'

'*If they die they die.*'

It took me a minute to take in not only what she had said but how she said it. When her anger was released, it was hard not to take it personally. But she went on:

'I was a kid when the Brits came over here. I was only thirteen, in my first year in secondary school. Now my daughter's starting primary school. We've got nothing to lose. Seen too much suffering, seen too many failed British bloody initiatives in the Six Counties, and the effects they've had on our people. You know, not only the high unemployment, the bad housing, but all the different issues which arise from British occupation – the shoot-to-kill policy, the internment policy, plastic bullets, and the whole way the judicial system is geared. There's a total erosion of civil liberties here.

'Honest to God, sometimes it depresses you. And you can get very very frustrated. There's times when I can go about for weeks and pass British soldiers in the street and

I don't see them. Even though I am looking at them. And then there's other weeks or particular hours or minutes, when I look at one, and I tell you, I would just love to say to him: "Would you go and get your fucking self out of our country? Leave us alone? For I am *sick* looking at yous!" There's times you just feel like that. But I have had arguments with British soldiers, with RUC men.'

'Did you pick them?'

'No, they've picked them. I'm very quiet. But – you know, when you're taken in and they try to draw you out and all the rest of it, they have no answer. They definitely have no answer. They have nothing to offer me. To me, an RUC man is only an Orangeman in uniform, a bigot. At the end of the day, they're working-class people, and I feel sorry for them to be so corrupted and to have no give. At the end of the day I'd have give. I'd be prepared – not to compromise my country – but to say to him, "Right, I can understand your point of view, and have every sympathy. Let's try to avoid as much bloodshed as we can." That's what I want. I'm not a warmonger. But they will hold on to this Union until every man, woman and Catholic child is dead.

'On the other hand, if it came to the Brits withdrawing, I'd say sanity would prevail among the Protestant working class. We know they have a lot of weapons. They have the UDR, for a start, who replaced the "B"-Specials; the RUC; plus the various shades of paramilitary organizations. But let's just see what will happen. I don't think that they will. There might be skirmishes in the cities, or the more hard-core rural areas, but they'll get a fight, because we're not going to lie down either. I mean I'd defend my family with a carving knife. You have to do something. Is that all being taped?'

'Yes. Want me to rub it out?'

She started laughing again, listening to herself. 'It's just that some of that I'm talking as a mother, and some of it I'm talking as a Republican, for Sinn Fein.'

'Well, who wouldn't be out with a carving knife to defend their family?'

She seemed positively amazed at this. 'Would you?'

'I know where mine is.'

'What?'

'My carving knife.'

'Oh Lord.'

From Chrissie's I went to the centre of Belfast in one of the many 'black taxis': superannuated London cabs revived sufficiently to make it up and down the Falls all day, and with meters removed and an extra seat installed where the front luggage space used to be. They stopped when hailed and were usually full, passengers getting in, getting out, for thirty-five pence a ride – cheaper than the bus and far more convenient. The drivers would drop you where you liked, help women with their shopping and get out to stow pushchairs or large bundles in the boot. Most drivers were Republican ex-prisoners, and it was a Republican profit-making enterprise. Loyalist paramilitaries, who had seized on the idea, ran the same service with their ex-prisoners up and down the Shankill Road.

The taxi I hailed had three teenage boys in the back. From my drop seat I studied them: they wore impressive suits and very chic Italian shoes. The effect was somewhat marred by long bulky khaki jackets which in any case were absurd given the weather. At the last stop I asked them the way to City Hall, and they offered to show me. As we walked I commented on the unusual clothes.

'We're *mods*,' one boy said proudly. We passed some girls also wearing unseasonal knee-length khaki, who smiled at the boys. 'Those are mod girls,' said the spokesboy, even more proud.

'How do you know who's a mod and who isn't a mod?' I asked. 'What do the other people look like?'

They grimaced: '*Skinheads.*' These, it seemed, wore Wrangler jackets, jeans and Dr Marten's boots. Then there were the 'heavy metallers' who were covered in leather and studs. Vast disapproval, boo, hiss, sneer.

'Do you fight each other?'

They did, three heads nodded in unison.

'But isn't there enough fighting around here?'

They stared at me.

'So why do you fight?'

They looked as if I were the last simpleton on earth, and shrugged. 'Have to, don't we?'

2
Troubles

It was interesting to return to London and find everyone there completely indifferent to what I had just seen. People displayed an extraordinary knack for changing the subject. If I persisted they'd say, 'How *boring* it all is, the way the Irish go on and on and on' – as if they were having an endless hole drilled through a tooth, excruciating but not fatal, boring and boring.

Not having thought about Northern Ireland before, much less the history of Anglo-Irish relations, I hadn't paid attention to English racism towards the Irish either. In addition to the endlessly unfunny Paddy jokes, suddenly I heard English people talking about Paddies whenever they meant anyone or thing particularly pea-brained, clumsy, or weird. My watch, for instance, is upsidedown and backwards and runs counter-clockwise. An ingenious device. 'That must be an Irish watch,' people were prone to say.

The stereotypical Irishmen of my childhood in America were poets, leprechauns, policeman, and owners of bars called P. J. something. Once a year on St Patrick's Day they painted the line down Fifth Avenue green and drank too much. At my school on March 17 *everyone* wore something green. To Americans the (mythological) Irish contributed a lovable, quaint heritage worth protecting and valuing, despite their supposed feckless streak. There was a ghastly kind of sentimental fondness in this common to most patronage, but it was quite different, as images go, from the English one.

To the old colonizers the Irish are 'thickies and brickies'.

They cost money individually because they take work from the English and do it for less, or live on 'our dole' when they could perfectly well starve at home. They cost even more money collectively because they will keep fighting their tedious war and we have to protect them from a 'bloodbath'. Although – as a newsagent said, following my vain request for the *Irish Times* – why not get out and leave them to it? 'We'd be well rid of both lots of Paddies, say I.'

One thing clear was that English and Americans, who share so many prejudices, completely misunderstand each other where the Irish are concerned. In the US, endless extradition hearings involving alleged IRA terrorists highlight the romanticism attaching to their cause; the English continue to fail to grapple with the contradiction of seeing the Irish as too retarded to sort themselves out the way decent people do, and at the same time as capable of a singularly treacherous and cunning kind of villainy.

Frequently in the English news at that time was the fiend Martin Galvin, head of an American outfit called Noraid which helped to finance the IRA. Galvin had been barred under the Prevention of Terrorism Act from entering Northern Ireland. He said he was going anyway, with his delegation, to the commemoration of Internment Day on August 9. On that day in 1971, 350 men had been arrested and interned: it was the day that had started the crisis that in turn had led to the imposition of Direct Rule. The London tabloids were full of the OH NO YOU DON'T, OH YES I DO byplay which precedes (and often provokes) an Incident. Instead of ignoring Galvin they sneaked around after him, building him up into a kind of Pimpernel.

* * *

I arrived on 8 August in time to see, all over West Belfast, the bonfires of Internment Night being assembled, huge teetering stacks of wood and old furniture, two or three storeys high, some with Union Jacks perched on top. They would be set ablaze at midnight, and at 4 A.M. – which was the hour in 1971 when hundreds of houses were raided simultaneously and the arrests made – the women traditionally banged on the pavements with bin lids.

This intelligence came from Chrissie McAuley when I called on her. She said Belfast was full of 'revolutionary tourists'. Last year she'd put up a British rock group in her attic, for instance – using the derisive tone reserved for the subject of foreign voyeurs – and what they had done was try to catch some sleep before 'the 4 A.M. crack'. But at 4 A.M. they had refused to get up. Chrissie was outside later, talking to an elderly woman who lived opposite, when a pig (a one-ton armoured car) drew up and beamed them with a spotlight – 'so they were well aware it was an old lady with a young girl talking.' Then a soldier opened up with a plastic-bullet gun. 'When they shot I felt a thud, even though it didn't hit me. You could see sparks coming out of the gun. The old lady fell right down: I thought she'd fainted. People were running all over the place trying to get inside. Some of them were even running on top of *her* trying to get into *her house*. I shouted, "Stop, help me, she's fainted!" When I picked her up I saw that her leg was just dangling, the whole bottom part just hanging off at right angles. The *blood* coming out of her! I panicked.'

'*You* panicked?'

'The *blood* coming out of her! It was just spurting! I ran up and down shouting, "*Doesn't anybody in the fuckin' street have a fuckin' phone*?" Finally a phone was found, the ambulance came and they stopped the bleeding, saving the old woman's life. In wild agitation Chrissie returned to her attic and screamed and shouted at the rock group, until they woke up. '*Then* they went outside! They joined the rioting and two of them got lifted!'

'How do you join a riot?' I asked.

This seemed to strike her as just as sensible as asking, How do you eat bread? or How do you go out the door? I had to rephrase it several times before she took it seriously. She said you threw bottles.

Danny Morrison came in with a sheaf of papers, glanced at me and said, 'Oh, the social worker.' He gave the papers to Chrissie, very excited about them: some newly unearthed material written by Bobby Sands in Long Kesh. I had seen a short diary Sands had written during his sixty-six-day hunger strike before his death on 5 May 1981: these were typical of the 'manuscript', Chrissie said, each signed 'Marcella' (his sister's name) and written on lavatory paper in a hand too microscopic for me to read. The fragments of paper had been mounted tenderly, like ancient papyrus scrolls. 'Tell the typist to give up her *life* before these,' was Morrison's message.

Chrissie said that when they had first started the *Republican News* much of the raw material was such 'comms' from the prisons, and deciphering them nearly ruined her eyes. The paper was on the run, the Brits in pursuit, and they produced every issue from a different location. 'Bobby's first comm was about rats. I have a phobia about rats. Someone else had to do that one.'

In the whole day preceding Internment Night, I hadn't seen a single British patrol. Were they keeping a low profile for Noraid? A taxi driver said they were just getting in some sleep before the long night. We drove up through Andersonstown past the massive estate's cul-de-sacs, to a stranger each one the same as the last, each with its own towering heap of wood waiting to be lit. Hundreds of children milled about, heaving anything burnable on top of the nearest pyre, all so tall that the heave needed to be mighty and often missed. Then another child would fling it back, with luck hitting the top, with even more luck missing again so it could be thrown another time. With the air thick with flying debris it was better to be helmeted in a taxi.

Destination Ryan. The Ryan house was a stopping place for many a revolutionary tourist. It was quite normal to find a Flemish-speaking journalist downing a vast plate of food in one corner, a bellicose Irish-American in town to seek his roots and making inflammatory 'Up the Rah' remarks in another, as well as processions of local people in all kinds of trouble which required the ear of Rita Ryan, mother of eight children all of whom were there as well. The living room where this took place was the right size for about a quarter of its occupants at any given time, but the fire was always lit (when they could afford the coal or turf) and the tea constantly coming (whether they could afford it or not).

I had met Rita and her husband Dermot on my previous trip the month before. She did volunteer work for Sinn Fein; he worked irregularly at whatever he could get. They had had their share of Troubles: Rita's Aunt Emma was blinded by a rubber bullet (plastic's predecessor); Dermot had been interned for fifteen months in the early 1970s; Rita's sister was killed by CS gas; the family's previous house in a mixed area had been booby-trapped and destroyed by Loyalists. 'And then,' Rita said, 'you get a lot of foreign journalists coming along saying, "But how can you support the IRA?" I think it's dead easy to support the IRA.'

Like others I was meeting, Rita seemed beyond exhaustion, annoyance, or the remotest possibility of self-indulgence. They believed so vehemently in their cause and had lived at white heat for so long that their thresholds of dissatisfaction were by now unidentifiable. It was impossible to imagine them in a 'normal' life.

The eldest child, Mairead (pronounced My-rade), a wildly bright elfin creature who did much of the housework and cooking, was left to babysit while we walked down to the 'PD', a local club originally set up for Prisoners' Dependents. It was nearly dark. An army helicopter kept an eye on things, an annoying bee. Bonfire after bonfire waited for a match. Few cars on the roads any more: the danger of hijacking was too great. As we neared the PD a great feather of black smoke was visible in the twilight over the rooftops: 'What's *that*?' – 'That'll be a bus,' said Dermot. On the Falls just beyond, the carcass of an overturned bus lay burning brightly with teenage boys cheering it on. To Rita and Dermot there was so little novelty in this spectacle that it was hard to extract an explanation of it from them. Boys would get on the bus, order everyone off, sprinkle it with petrol, then fire it, though how they turned it over remained a mystery. It wouldn't be the only one that night: either the only mystery or the only bus.

The PD entrance had the usual wire cage to keep out the unwelcome and, inside, two very large cosily lit rooms crammed with people drinking to ear-splitting music. A man who greeted the Ryans was introduced as a grandfather, although he looked about thirty. 'Watch the paint,' he said as we shook hands, 'I'm doing the double' (on social security and working illegally as a painter at the same time). He bought us drinks and moved on; Rita said he'd just been released after eight years in Long Kesh. She pointed out others to me. 'That man is a solicitor. His father was killed. His son's in prison.' – 'That's Hugh,' she pointed to another. 'One of his brothers was shot dead in a bus and the other was beheaded by a cheese wire.' Or four women together at a table, all in their thirties: 'Those are the merry widows.' Their husbands had all been killed and they liked to stick together. They were having a terrific time, bellowing out 'The Boys of the Old Brigade'.

The song changed to 'Four Green Fields'. Rita said: 'This song was playing when my aunt was blinded by the rubber bullet.'

Rita's Aunt Emma had worked in the mill from the age of fourteen and even after some of her eleven children were born. One day the estate where she lived was sealed off by paratroopers who were raiding the houses. There was nothing to do but wait it out and as she stood at the window there was a shot and both eyes were gouged out of her head. Her youngest child was eight. 'She's coped extremely well,' said Rita, 'she's a great person. Washes, does her own cooking, minds her grandchildren. And she's campaigned endlessly; she's been in America and spoken at conferences about plastic bullets. She's just fantastic.'

Our conversation was taking an enormous effort, with many shouted repetitions, to overcome the music. Soon the singing was such an uproar that nothing else was possible except drinking. People kept buying us doubles. Rita stuck to lemonade but others were soon in a state of concentrated and applied inebriation that I hadn't seen this side of Moscow. This night was obviously a special one, but she had talked about what a problem drink was becoming in the area: not just the men, but women secretly drinking at home, with their children going from glue-sniffing to drinking themselves in their teens and ending up as 'hoods' to pay for it, preying on the poor. When we got up just before midnight to go to see the bonfires, getting up was just about all that some customers could accomplish.

The streets outside were glittering with tiny sparkles from minute shards of broken glass. We walked from fire to fire, meeting their friends everywhere and standing in the hot light circles being given more drinks and admiring the blazes. All the children were out, from babies in prams on up, but older boys had taken over the night. Gangs of them ran rowdily around the fires. Bottles smashed. A car full of more boys, glimpsed briefly, careered past us at terrific speed, mounted the pavement, and was out of sight over a hill. Joyriders in a stolen car. 'Can those kids drive?' I asked; they had just missed my foot. 'It wouldn't matter if they could,' said Rita. 'The idea is the danger.'

There was less judgement in the atmosphere than anxiety. Joyriding was becoming an epidemic. Some of the boys were being killed by the RUC at roadblocks: that seemed to be the law's only response. Otherwise the community had to police itself, and 'the army' (not the British army) would be warning those boys, doing more to recidivists – a beating with hurley sticks or kneecapping, maybe.

We stayed clear of the main roads where the Brits were patrolling in their pigs and Saracens. 'No point in getting shot just for looking at a bonfire.' You could hear shots. At the first commemoration of internment fifteen people had been killed, I was told, including two priests. (I could find no record of this but people believed it.) We had gone full circle and now were back near the PD where people were still lurching around, including a couple so drunk that when one fell down the other fell too and they just lay there moaning and thrashing in the parking lot in their best new clothes. An alley leading to the main road was filled with boys running in and out as the police and army screeched past firing at them. The boys threw bottles back, behaving as if the armoured cars were the bulls at Pamplona, taunting them, fearless and mad. In the darkness I could make out a huge khaki vehicle roar past the alley, boys rampaging in away from it, shots. From the broken glass and rubbish in the alley one boy plucked a plastic bullet for me that had just been shot at him: it was still warm. He said I could keep it and picked up a bottle instead.

The bullet was not at all what I'd expected. 'Plastic bullet' had conjured up a regular-sized bullet made of plastic, and I had been unclear how it could kill. This was a dense off-white tube, four and a half inches long, similar in size and shape to a cardboard toilet paper roll but heavy enough to hurt if you dropped it on your knee. These bullets, officially known as 'baton rounds', are fired from a special gun at 160 miles an hour. The British police have said, 'It's like being hit by a cricket ball hit hard by a good player.' Cricket didn't seem a useful analogy when it came to fourteen deaths. Many rounds were fired that night but so far as I knew no one was badly injured. It's hard to find out, though, Rita said, as anybody wounded by a plastic bullet avoids hospital, where he has to be reported for riotous behaviour to justify having been shot.

The Internment Day commemoration – a parade and rally – was held not on 9 August but three days later, on Sunday. Why it was put off, in a predominantly unemployed community, was unclear. I went to see Rita's Aunt Emma.

It was impossible to believe that this tall, slim and dignified woman was sixty-four and had produced eleven children. She must have been very beautiful before she lost her eyes. Plastic surgery and dark glasses now hid the damage. She sat quite straight and with great composure and stillness – her handicap only evident when she needed to feel her way to the door – in an extremely handsome drawing room, all dark green and beige (even her glasses the one, the Labrador guide-dog the other). Her distinguished old house at the top of the Falls Road was bought with the compensation money she received for being blinded. 'I cried the day I got that money. I was broken-hearted, because there's no way thirty-five thousand pounds could find me back everything I lost. There wasn't a happier woman alive in the world than myself till the morning I was shot.'

This was in spite of great poverty. She talked about her childhood in the Lower Falls where the tiny houses had outside lavatories and 'three girls in one bed and three boys in another.' There was nothing to cook on but two hobs, one on each side of an open fire. Not that this mattered, since 'you didn't need a lot of facilities to cook potatoes, cabbage, soup. You made bannocks and soda bread on the griddle. Enjoyable, you know. And you got porridge in the mornings with salt. Tea was a luxury, not very often did you have tea.

'I hear people say now, "Oh it's terrible", but I lived through the hungry Thirties. Things were very bad. We had riots. People got what you call outdoor relief, but they couldn't live on it like. But when you're young, if you're getting enough to eat and you've a bed to lie on that's about as far as your imagination takes you.'

At fourteen she had to leave school and was 'very lucky' to get a job in the spinning room of the mill, working beside her grandmother who had brought her up and was 'of all the people I've known in the world, the wisest, nicest ever I met.' They worked from eight in the morning to six at night and until one o'clock on Saturdays, stood barefoot in water all day, and walked to work bare-legged in the rain or snow. 'But it was the only way of life that you knew, so you just got into the mood of it. And I would say the happiest days that I spent, I spent in the mill.' What she remembered was the friendship, the way they 'all came down the Falls at night after a hard day's work singing', and dances ('gettin' to the jig was two pennies, and you had a big problem gettin' them') and the love affairs, which were very innocent, because 'sex, we didn't hardly know the meaning of the word.'

She married in 1944. Although there was no conscription in Northern Ireland, her husband joined the forces. 'A lot of people joined up because it was a means of living. It was mostly Catholics, too, because Protestants had work in the shipyards.' She continued to work at the mill while Belfast was bombed and until after the birth of her second child, when her husband came home for good.

'Even if you had a good education, when you were being sent for a job, you knew that a Protestant would get it. Stormont was definitely a Protestant parliament for a Protestant people. Housing was the same. The Catholics were all struggling in wee small houses and whenever the housing programme did get going, the Protestant people could pick and choose where they wanted to go, while the Catholics had to take what they got. You were always and ever a second-class citizen, but you were conditioned to that. You knew not to expect to get the best house or the best job. You knew it'd go to your Protestant friend – neighbour, you didn't have very many Protestant friends: you worked with them, yes, and you got on all right with them until such time as the Twelfth of July come round. And then they'd nearly fall out with you like, or cool off, and they'd decorate the whole mill with Union Jacks and streamers.

'You just stayed home on the Twelfth. The Twelfth was very important – that was their victory over you. The Eleventh night, they danced like wild Indians round their bonfires, screaming and cursing the Pope, and "hang the Fenians". And on the Twelfth they'd bang their drums and light their bonfires and sing all their Orange songs and they paraded and they dominated. On the Twelfth they took over the whole of Northern Ireland with their bands and their banners. You know. They still do, only on a quieter scale now 'cause the world is watching them like. But when I was a wee girl it wasn't quiet. That was their day to let us know that they reigned supreme and we had to do as we were told.

'There were Protestant workers in our mill, yes. God help them too like, looking back, they were being used as much as we were being used. Their conditions might have been a wee bit better than ours – they had a choice – but they were working hard for what they got.

'Now in the 1940s there was kind of an uprising. The IRA became active. There was internment brought out. My husband had an uncle Albert – he always and ever was connected, very much involved all his life. He was interned. He did seven or eight years. For thinking. For *thinking*. He never was caught with a gun or a rifle or a bomb. And many's the time I'd say, God forgive the Stormont government, because all those men who were interned were badly beaten and starved, no parcels going up like there was in this internment in the Kesh.

'And then of course you had the "B"-Specials, which go under the new name now of the UDR. They were disbanded as the "B"-Specials and brought back as the UDR. Now the ordinary British people mightn't know that but we know that. You see, we were always and ever a police state.

'I would like there to be some way to stop the violence. I hate violence. I think it's a very sad thing. But at the time it all happened I think it was necessary. Because the civil righters got on to the streets and were beat into the ground. And there *was* no IRA then. There might have been people still sympathetic towards a united Ireland, but quite honestly there was no IRA. And then of course they re-formed into the army they are now. In those days the Protestants were literally coming down and murdering the Catholics like, and burning them out.

'In the 1940s it had faded away because we weren't strong enough. They had lifted all the known activists and raided the houses and terrorized the people. Even if you had a wee bit of sympathy for them you were afraid to show it; nobody was strong enough. It was nearly like the French resistance movement under the Germans: same feeling. Every decade you'd get these wee outbreaks and revolts, but they didn't last long, because they were always nipping it in the bud. Until 1969, when people got a wee bit more agitated, students became aware of what was happening: fifty-odd years of the same Unionist rule; and there definitely was discrimination. The IRA was formed again. Not that anybody wanted it, but quite honestly it was necessary. And I think everybody that's been killed or hurt – British soldiers, Protestants, RUC, Catholics and all – that the blame lies with the British government. For every death in this country in these Troubles I myself put the whole blame on the British government. Maggie doesn't seem to care. There's nothing we can do because if the English people can't stand up til her how can we stand up til her? If Maggie can have a wee flag flying over the Falklands and a wee flag for the royal family, that keeps 'em happy.'

I picked up an official tourist board leaflet about Belfast. 'A Hibernian Rio,' the city was styled, 'ringed by high hills, sea lough and river valley, Belfast's magnificent setting certainly deserves the epithet.' That copywriter had had his work cut out for him. 'Keep a sharp eye out for Belfast's rich street architecture,' he advised, in 'this vigorous seaport, city of some 360,000 people.' Among the recommended sights were Queen's University, 'modelled on Magdalen College, Oxford,' and Belfast Cathedral (no sect mentioned), not to speak of the 'Rose Trials every July' ('always at least 100,000 blooms to see'). I looked to see if the writer had given a notice to the Forum, the city's only top-class hotel, and how many times it had been bombed, but he must have thought better of it.

At 'the magnificent City Hall (opened 1906) . . . an impressive building full of civic pride,' a parade was in progress that Sunday morning. Many ranks of men in bowler hats and with fringed orange collarettes over their dark suits trod sombrely and in time to the beat of a big drum: Protestant World War II veterans laying a wreath of poppies for their fallen comrades. There was not a soul in the streets to look at them. But parading is a commonplace in Belfast, the local pastime, and on a Sunday the Orangemen liked particularly to parade to church, morning and evening. Belfast is rather famous for its Sundays. The great feature of 'the Belfast Sunday' is that nothing is open and there isn't anything to do. Watchful fundamentalist Sabbatarians fight to maintain this situation in the face of wicked Catholics who want to play games in the parks or buy something to drink. That way you may as well go to church, or parade, or better yet parade to church.

At 2 P.M another parade began up the Falls Road. Besides the police who lined the street, there weren't too many spectators at this one, either: everyone was marching. Hundreds of families had made an outing of it, bearing banners and waving Irish tricolours to the beat of sprightly bands playing flutes, drums and bagpipes. Before joining in myself, I watched the American Noraid contingent go by. Martin Galvin was not among them, though according to rumour he might turn up at the rally after the march. Some of the Noraid team wore IRA T-shirts, and all of them nearly drowned out the flutes with cries of 'I-R-A! ALL THE WAY!' No one else took up the chant. 'It's only the Yanks who'd have that nerve,' a bystander commented. 'Sure they can go home after.'

Most parades have boring bits, long stretches between floats or bands when all you can do is trudge, not necessarily in step. This one, despite its serious purpose, was irrepressibly merry, melodic and bright. Only when we got near Connolly House, the Sinn Fein headquarters in West Belfast where the rally was to be held, were there signs of trouble. A helicopter flying low was said to be photographing everybody. A score of grey armoured RUC Land-Rovers was parked in a U as if to catch us as we came. Some boys, bunched on the roofs of the shops opposite Connolly House, began throwing stones, and without a second's pause the police responded with plastic bullets. A *cataract* of boys spilled off the roofs, while panicking and screaming onlookers fled wherever they could. I ran up some stairs because everybody else did, and only when I stopped to try to take a picture and two large men stepped on me before a third knocked me down did their real fear come through. The shooting seemed to be coming at us, and I had the sensation, This Can't Be Happening. All my life I'd been to demonstrations where people had been herded away, dragged off, arrested – but shot at?

Gerry Adams' voice came amplified from the rostrum to plead for peace and calm. The police lowered their guns and the marchers dribbled back into the street. A moment later Adams asked for first aid assistance. Two bagpipers had been hit. An ambulance arrived and a wounded teenage girl in a band uniform was carried past.

Though depleted, the crowd still filled the square. The people had recovered in a second; even the little children weren't sent home. Adams asked everybody to sit down to show their pacific intentions and to provoke no more reaction. They obeyed immediately and became a sea of sitting families, ringed around entirely now by armed and helmeted police backed up by their vehicles. The policemen had been allowed to take their jackets off in the warmth and to roll up their white shirtsleeves, but they all wore thick bulletproof vests, plastic visors and neckties. They looked like prop soldiers, since you couldn't see their faces, and within the amphitheatre made by their Land-Rovers it almost seemed to be some special sort of performance. The press alone had ignored Adams, and photographers stood beneath him clicking their gadgets: they were hoping that Galvin would show.

Gerry Adams introduced a speaker from the English Troops Out Movement, then Chrissie delivered a message from the women prisoners at Armagh and the men at Long Kesh. And then – after a final plea to the police to understand from the nature of the seated people that their purposes were peaceful – Adams introduced Martin Galvin, who strode out of Connolly House at the rear of the platform. As Galvin took the microphone, the police charged.

They came in from all sides, ramming and running into people with the armoured cars, bludgeoning them with truncheons, loosing hundreds of plastic bullets point-blank into the crowd. The air was full of puffs of smoke and cracking reports as spectators went down. There was nowhere for most of them to run, and they were beyond screaming: it was a matter of huddling in knots and praying and crying. Television cameras recorded the brutality. John Downes, attending the rally with his wife and eighteen-month-old baby, was shot in the heart in full view of the lens of the man from the *Daily Mail*. The press people themselves were manhandled, threatened and hit. One had his film taken; all were stampeded and pushed aside in the frenzied rush for Galvin, who escaped in the mêlée into Connolly House. He had never said a word.

In moments the square was still but for the police with their smoking guns and knots of hysterical, weeping people who were shot at if they tried to move. The injured lay bleeding everywhere. One man had a gaping hole in his cheek which spurted every time he breathed. A seven-year-old bled heavily from one ear; an elderly man lay unconscious, shot in the back of the head. Medics were frantically trying to revive John Downes, but he had already turned blue.

Rumours about Galvin's miraculous escape circulated for days. He'd been passed overhead, with the help of two lookalike Sinn Fein decoys (one of whom was arrested). He had been disguised as a policeman in a red wig. Sinn Fein wasn't telling.

The RUC issued a statement so at variance with the witnessed, documented, photographed experience of the world's press that you could only wonder at the effrontery:

> They [the police] were attacked and obstructed by groups within the crowd, which numbered in excess of 2,000, obviously determined to prevent Galvin's arrest and who had been instructed from the platform to do so. To protect themselves from those throwing missiles and to effect entrance to Connolly House, the door of which had been barricaded after Galvin had entered, a total of 31 plastic baton rounds were discharged – a number of them in the air to disperse the crowd . . . Initial reports indicate that 20 persons were taken to hospital, and a 22-year-old man, who was identified as a rioter, was found dead on arrival at hospital.

The following day the RUC's chief constable, in ruling out an independent enquiry of the incident, went into more detail:

> Before Galvin appeared stewards positioned women and children outside the railings in front of the platform . . . The decision to intervene and arrest Galvin was an operational decision taken with regard to the circumstances existing at the time, based on the principle of speed using minimum force. Twelve baton rounds were fired at this time in the air to disperse the crowd and one to

force the door of Connolly House. Baton rounds were not discharged into groups of bystanders, as has been alleged . . . One man died and police have evidence as to his actions prior to his death. He was clearly identified as a member of the party who were rioting and his actions were also clearly witnessed.

John Downes' death was briefly featured in the British press, but only as a stick to beat Sinn Fein with. There was outrage at SF's 'propaganda victory', 'propaganda harvest', 'propaganda martyrdom', though buried at the bottom of some stories was an observation from Shirley Williams, president of the Social Democratic Party, that 'not since Peterloo in 1819 have British police shot anyone dead at a peaceful meeting.'

The main thing was to blame somebody. In Belfast the (Protestant) *News Letter* blamed Galvin, the (Catholic) *Irish News* blamed the police, and the (Protestant) *Telegraph* blamed Sinn Fein. In Britain the press mostly blamed James Prior, Secretary of State for Northern Ireland, for banning Galvin in the first place. Prior tried to cool things down by accepting all responsibility. Nobody bothered much about the RUC except Sinn Fein, who issued another WANTED FOR MURDER poster with a picture of the victim and perpetrator at the moment of the shot. A little too late to recapture the media's ephemeral interest, the RUC also issued photographs of the same moment, theirs showing John Downes bearing down on the guns brandishing a slim stick.

In September 1986, RUC Reserve Constable Nigel Hegarty was tried in Belfast Crown Court for the manslaughter of Downes, and was acquitted. The judge said, 'I think it is probable that the accused did act almost instinctively to defend his comrades without having time to assess the situation in the light of his knowledge of the police regulations.'

The SDLP MP Seamus Mallon thought the decision

'amazing by any standards' and said it would 'rank with hundreds of others which have brought the process of justice into disrepute, and which have diminished respect for the process of law in Northern Ireland.'

John Downes' father Gerry said he had 'never expected any other verdict.'

3
Flags for Breakfast

I wanted to meet Protestants. It seemed an absurd problem, given that they were the majority. I had the address of a woman who ran a supergrass committee, but she had no phone and I had been advised to 'try about teatime'. Tea is the evening meal in Belfast, eaten about six o'clock, so I had some hours to kill. I thought I'd go and look at the rich Protestants who lived, it was said, in the Malone Road. So I got the 71 bus going south, rode it to the end and walked back.

Old mansions, each one different, set among old trees, old gardens. Malone Road seemed to be the Park Lane or Park Avenue of Belfast, but as Park Lane and Park Avenue once were. Even the pillbox at the corner of Windsor Park was a discreet stone muffin; you'd hardly notice the little slits for guns. The UDR base behind it was nicely landscaped and invisible among mature trees. The spacious, gracious, well-kept properties rolled by. What a dappled green and golden city Belfast was for the well-off! Supergrasses, shoot-to-kill, plastic bullets, kneecapping – such things belonged to a different world.

On the long walk back I overtook a couple of rather haggard women walking along ahead and asked them lamely and foreignly the way to City Hall. They weren't going that far, they said, or they'd take the bus, why didn't I? I'd rather walk. They were cleaners, it turned out, going from one job to another, but they lived in Ardoyne. Theirs was a 'dolly mixture' area cut up by peace walls (twenty-foot high corrugated iron 'environmental screens' dividing street from street), and what a place! 'They' were stoning the children; 'they' broke all the windows the minute you got them fixed; 'they' were trying to run us out of the area.

Who was 'they'? One of the women, a reedy redhead, said, 'I understand in America the people think that the Roman Catholic people are being squashed down daily. But it's the other way around, the gospel truth, it's the other way around.' She offered me a cigarette, and one to her friend.

By now they were so excited about setting me straight, especially after I produced my cassette recorder, that we ended up walking quite a long way together as they struck off their list of grievances. The redhead did most of the talking. Her name was Mrs Binstead. The children had nowhere to play, she said, and whenever they were sent to the shops they got beaten up. They were beaten up trying to get on a bus or walking in and out of the area, and they were picked on by the police. 'There used to be a local cricket pitch but with the Protestant people getting squeezed out it's now a hurley – ' (she didn't know the word for where the Irish sport was played). The local school had to close down but she had heard that a *Gaelic* school had opened in Andersonstown. 'They get everything they ask for, oh aye, no doubt about it.' There were so many peace walls in their area now that to go a few yards to the shop you had to walk a half mile around.

The other woman, Mrs Crocker, a small stiff person with hair like a white carnation, had a problem with broken windows, and in between Mrs Binstead's itemization of sundry injustices broke in with, 'Not a week my windys aren't put in left right and centre' – 'Billy said to me, Come out of work. I couldn't come out of work 'cause I couldn't live there day and daily with the windys comin' in' – 'I would say forty to fifty times I come home from work and my windys was gettin' put in by the opposite side.'

Mrs Binstead meanwhile was trying to tell me about the overall deterioration of their neighbourhood. 'I'm not saying there was nothing for the Roman Catholic people – they preferred their areas that they wished to live in. You always had this. Maybe it's not right but that's the way it was. But then a few moved up and then another lot moved in and gradually the Protestant people were squeezed out.'

I asked them if it didn't make them want to move. 'But where are you going to move to?' said Mrs Binstead. 'I come from Sandy Row – it's pretty well known. And where I lived, there was no Catholics and Protestants, I wasn't brought up that way. When I moved the children up to Ardoyne, they asked me, Is the Pope a Catholic? So you can guess my children weren't brought up knowing which foot people dug with. Until I came to Ardoyne. And then I realized what the people were fighting for, you know?'

'Which foot?' I was stuck back there.

'Haven't you heard that?' said Mrs B. 'We say they dig with the wrong foot. Roman Catholics. The left foot.'

'What do they say?'

'Sure I don't know . . . But there's nowhere in Belfast at the minute that the Protestant people aren't being squeezed out,' she continued. 'Jobwise, everything. See Shorts' – they make airplanes and different things, you know, missiles.' Apparently Shorts' was due to take over the old DeLorean factory in Catholic West Belfast where the workforce would inevitably be Catholic, although Shorts' had always been a Protestant plant. 'And see DeLorean. Our Betty has a friend' – she was saying this more to Mrs Crocker than to me – 'who worked there in the office. And she said she watched Republican people on night shift *smash*ing those cars, breaking the windscreens, all to destroy the firm.' She turned back in my direction. 'And this is what gets me. Your man [Danny] Morrison can stand and talk about being in all-Ireland: I mean, they're starving to death down there! They're *starving*. They come to *shop* here. I don't know if you know anything about their economy, but I mean you couldn't live down there! And this is what they want us to go intil!'

She stopped to catch her breath and Mrs Crocker pursued the thought: 'See my brother, they were down there one weekend. And they went into a hotel – not a big fancy hotel now. Four vodkas and four wee lemonades: eleven pounds twenty! You couldn't survive down there, love, so you couldn't.'

'Well this is it, Margaret,' said her friend. 'They are getting supplementary benefits for their large families. They don't want to work, and that's the truth of it. They get more from the public assistance than if they're working.'

'If you came and looked at the house I'm living in,' said Mrs Crocker, 'now both Billy and I's working, my windys need badly replaced, and they are moving into brand-new houses that are being built over the back of me, *they're* not working, so their rent's being paid, their rates, their heating. I have all that to do. *And* payin' for the windys.'

'Have you tried laminated glass?' I said.

'Well the new one that the Housing Executive rehabilitated, it was in that wired glass. But they actually come up round the front and just stood with big bricks till they smashed it in anyway.'

Mrs Binstead nodded. 'They must be sick in their mind. They can't be anything else, dear. They must be sick in their mind. I mean, I don't understand the mentality of why this is going on. I mean they've got children, and they're rearing them up. But the way we were brought up was, you don't hit your next-door neighbour, you live with him. But to me these children are being tutored.'

We had reached the place where they were going, it

seemed, but they wanted to keep talking. 'What I mean is, if there's a riot, and stone-throwing, what I do and what the rest of the mothers do, you go and bring your children in. But they are inclined to throw their children out to stone-throw. And this is why they talk about rubber bullets and children being hit – if they weren't there, they wouldn't be hit by rubber bullets! This is what I can't understand.'

I was so saddened suddenly by the image of Brian Stewart's face that I said I had to go, and wouldn't they be late? Mrs Crocker was still talking about her windows as Mrs Binstead led her away.

The squaddies in the British Army are supposedly issued with tribal maps of Belfast coloured green and orange, so they'll always know where they are. One of those would have come in useful. Rather soon, however, you learn which areas and streets are Catholic, which Protestant. This helps you avoid making appointments requiring you to go directly from one to the other, entailing impassable 'peace walls' and circuitous routes on public transport (which doesn't cater for this need), or else two separate taxis, one of the tribe you are leaving and another of the one you are entering.

The Ormeau Road, or sections of it, presented no problem: it was mixed. The only trouble was, I was supposed to see a woman named Joyce McCarten and didn't know what her religion was. The subtle local techniques for worming out this information (from the name, address, the school attended) were unavailable to me – and even if I'd known the questions, what could I have made of the answers? In the event, religion made no odds: she actually didn't care. Her marriage was mixed; her friend Mrs Rice (present also) was of 'a different', unspecified, religion; and the very point of Mrs

McCarten's life was to disregard sectarian differences, not so much to rise above them as to go beneath, to the issues of poverty, housing and welfare affecting the whole working-class population. She resisted politics so entirely that she would have no truck even with that breed which shared her concerns, the Workers' Party; and theories of proletarian politics were alien to her. What mattered was the Women's Information Group, women 'from all the ghettos in Belfast, both sides of the hard-line areas,' who got together once a month to help each other deal with the practical problems of poverty.

Mrs McCarten must have been pushing sixty but with her hair dyed black she showed that effort still counted. She smoked one cigarette after another, dropping ash around to join the other dust. This was obviously of no account to her; it was people who mattered, and any who came by (the traffic was constant) got her whole attention and care.

She and Mrs Rice made something of a team. Mrs Rice was a graceful white-haired granny. She always called Mrs McCarten Joyce. Mrs McCarten always called Mrs Rice Mrs Rice. They had been best friends for twenty years.

Mrs McCarten began her activist career in 1971, provoked by Mrs Thatcher, who as Minister for Education was practising for Prime Minister by abolishing free school milk for schoolchildren. Thatcher the Milk Snatcher, everyone had called her. 'We borrowed two big cows, with big tits like *that*, from a farmer, and we walked them to the City Hall.' They laughed and laughed; ash went everywhere.

'There's different wee bits over the years. I've stood up against the organizations two or three times. There was a lad shot here in the road, and in retaliation they opened up shooting at soldiers. But you shouldn't be shooting at anybody. I don't believe in soldiers getting shot or policemen either, because they're somebody's son. I went out against the IRA when they kneecapped my son about two years ago.'

SB: 'Is he all right?'

Mrs McCarten: 'Well he's all right.'

Mrs Rice: 'He's never been the same, love, since it.'

Mrs McCarten shuffled through a pile of clippings and produced one for me. 'He'd been baby-sitting with his girl. There was another wee lad, a Protestant, shot too. I think it was mostly about religion. You know, going about together.' (So she was Catholic, or at least her son was.) 'Read all down that, that's the letter we put into the paper. I warned them to lay off.'

'On the night of Saturday, April 3rd, a gang of armed and masked men entered two houses in Ormeau Road, shooting and wounding a youth in each house before disappearing. No organization has claimed responsibility for this act. Nor have the victims or their families been given any excuse, however unreasonable, for the action.

'As the mothers in this district, we wish to make known to those responsible, that this community, Ormeau Road, has had too much death and destruction in its midst. We make no distinction between either those who fell victim to gunmen, whatever uniform or whatever cause they claim to be advancing, and those who carried out the deeds. We want an end to death. We want to live in peace with one another and nearby communities. We want to try to provide a better life for our young people, so that they can feel wanted, so that they have self-respect, a place in the community. We want to see their idealism and energy being used in the service of the people, not misguided by cynical fireside generals.

'The brutal treatment to these young people causes us not just immense sadness, but anger. On whose authority did those responsible commit this act? What rights to trial or jury did these youngsters have? Was no humanity to be extended to those deemed to have offended against those anonymous organizations who behave exactly like the Ayatollah's regime in Iran? We suspect that sectarianism might have been a principal factor in the incident. Whether it was or not we have this to say: we welcome anyone to this community regardless of creed, who is interested in establishing contact, discussing common problems, making friends. The only precondition is that they come in a spirit of peace. They have more to offer us than the self-appointed armed gangs who cripple and maim young people who, whatever their faults, cannot be held responsible for the decaying physical environment they have lived in for their short lives. To those others we say we want no part of your actions: you have nothing to offer.

'We have had to make public our feelings lest anyone should think that our silence in any way constituted consent. Yours etc., Angry Mothers, Ormeau Road.'

She said the letter was printed in all three local papers but there had been no answers. She'd gone to 'several places on the Falls and they couldn't give me a reason why they done it': it seemed simply a case of shooting both boys because of their friendship. 'But oh! That night I run up that Ormeau Road and I bust into the bar and I said *everything*. You know it's an awful sensation. I can't run very well, but I was *something* up that Ormeau Road, and if I had got them I'd have died in their grip. They're bullies. And the majority of people don't support people like that. They say that Sinn Fein has a lot of support: not from ordinary women like myself, they don't have. You know, fear has a lot to do with it. People are afraid to voice their opinion. But I think the more you talk the braver you get.'

Mrs Rice came in: 'Twenty years we lived as neighbours. Terrific area this was. You never heard religion. It was just the scum we let get in that destroyed it, on both sides. In the hard-line areas you get the intimidation. But to neighbours here, whether the bands went up the road or they went down it, made no difference. Joyce would keep an eye on my children, and I kept an eye on hers. In fact her young ones was practically reared in our house.'

Mrs McCarten had eight children; Mrs Rice four.

'One of mine's married on to a Protestant girl,' said Mrs McCarten. 'Another one's going with one out of the village. You'd get the slagging now and then, but they don't take any notice. They get stopped by the police and they get, "Why are yous two together?"'

Mrs Rice: 'The police, instead of encouraging these children, seem to have a suspicion about them.'

Mrs McCarten: 'My grandchildren are going to a mixed school, because I don't agree with the Catholic schools. Children now are brought up with bigotry and hate. To me if we can get children growing up understanding both sides, its half our battle; you know, there's a bit of a chance for the future.'

Mrs Rice squeezed my arm. 'Do you know who you're meeting?' she said. 'You're meeting the troublemakers.'

Mrs McCarten: 'On one occasion I was invited to a women's conference in Dublin. I didn't know who it was, I just thought it was an ordinary women's conference. Little did I know Sinn Fein was there. And this woman Rita O'Hare was the guest speaker.'

Mrs Rice: 'She lured the British soldiers to their death.'

Mrs McCarten: 'Never rung a bell with me, you know. But she got up and she started about Northern Ireland and how she wanted violence and all this. I sat for a while and I let her carry on. When she was finished I said, "Here, there's another side to the story. What are we going to do with a million Protestants? Are we going to bomb and shoot them all? Let me tell you," says I, "the people of Northern Ireland are browned off with the Troubles, we're sick of violence. We want an end put til it."

'Oh my God, didn't your woman come down on me! Now, because I got my say at the meeting – I didn't give a damn who they were or what they were – do you know what they branded me? They called me a Communist. "A

Communist supporter disrupted the whole meeting." You know our group had a great laugh.'

The Women's Information Group was four years old, and the 'wants and needs' of women were so great it was expanding to Carrickfergus, to Downpatrick, to Antrim, throughout the province. Now they had even received a tiny grant from the Northern Ireland Office.

Mrs McCarten: 'We have phone calls from all over. People want to know how it's run and could we advise them setting up their own. We tell them both sides of the community has to be in it. It's funny how keen they are on it.'

Mrs Rice: 'They learn in it. The way the politicians have them believing, the Catholic community in these hard-line areas thinks there's no poor Protestants, that all the Protestants are working. In the Protestant hard-line areas, they think the same of the Catholics. When you hit the Women's Information Group, you discover that we're all in poverty. Let me tell you, when I rise in the morning, my first thought's not what religion I am. A bag of coal's £7.40, that's what I get up thinking about. I forget about my religion. Fact I very seldom think of it.'

Mrs McCarten: 'I meet so many women, young women with wee families. They're sick of it too.'

Mrs Rice: 'You've no idea. It's only the real hard-line people here. These people who are out about trial without jury. The reason why it's trial without a jury is because if there was a jury, they would shoot them. Or if you went as a witness you'd be shot. So what do they expect? If you suppress justice you have to take the next best thing. Now I don't believe in these informers either, because it would be awful if there was one innocent person convicted. But if there was no organizations there would be none of that. But I mean there's so few people like Joyce who can go out and meet both sides. You know, there's a fear. It's not everybody has the courage. It takes a lot of courage.

'See the politicians, the people on television: you would think listening to the Unionist politicians there that they were always at the beck and call of the Protestant people. They are if you have money. But the working class – they don't know we exist.'

Mrs McCarten: 'The Unionist politicians, the Nationalist politicians are not fighting for what we want. What they're talking about is an all-Ireland or a divided Ireland. To hell with Ireland. None of my sons will die for Ireland, I'll be quite honest. I don't think Ireland is worth dying for. My sons feel the same. They couldn't care less.'

Mrs Rice: 'The truth is it suits the politicians to keep the people at one another's throats. People then are that mixed up in the violence and trouble they forget about their real needs. The politicians don't want us to think about the unemployment or the poverty. They just keep us fighting and electing them in.

'The way I live: this is God's earth, there's none of us has any claim on it. You only get a life span in it, and at the end of that you get six foot. Ireland, England, Scotland – it doesn't matter. I don't believe like the Yanks, a flag in your hand at every opportunity. A flag makes a very poor breakfast.'

Mrs McCarten: 'That's true. There's not two flags you can fry them and eat them.'

Mrs Rice: 'Flags don't interest me nor never did. Now you've met both sides. Joyce is one side and I'm the other, and believe me there's hundreds like us. If you went out the door with a flag in one hand and five pound in the other, they wouldn't notice the flag, you take it from me.'

The traditional way to find out what's really happening is to interrogate the taxi driver on the way to the hotel bar where the press hang out and where, if they haven't got the story they can just as well conjure it up. It didn't seem necessary to resort to the hotel bar but that was no reason to neglect the taxi driver. If you asked: 'Have you ever been hijacked?' you could bet on a story or two.

'. . . three guys, see, wantin' to go to a bar on the Falls Road. When I pulled over the one in front got out and the one behind got out and I just turned to see what the third guy was doing. Well, from under his duffle coat he pulled out the biggest, blackest gun that I ever seen in my life. All I could hear was "*click*". And it was put to the back of me ear there. And he just asked for me driving licence – '

'What for?'

'Well it means if they're caught they know who you are and where to go look for you. That's the very first thing they do. So they took me into the bar and I was locked into a back room. And they said, if they done the job, I wouldn't be gettin' the car back; if they didn't get the job done, they would be back in half an hour. They must have got doin' what they were settin' out to do because they were back in an hour's time. I asked the guy for me licence and he said, It's sittin' in the front seat.

'He told me not to report it. So to me the most sensible thing to do was not to report it. See, most of this is organized crime like. It's organized by different organizations, IRA or UVF or UDA. We all know that. It's not as if you're goin' to be takin' on a coupla guys, it's an *organization*. I'm probably one of these people who would have said, If it happened to me I would do this or I would do that. You do absolutely *nuthin'*, you just do what you're told, it's as simple as that.'

Caroline Newell ran a Protestant support committee to fight the supergrass system: 'supergrass' referred to any former paramilitary who turned Queen's evidence and informed against his erstwhile colleagues in return for immunity or favoured treatment. She lived behind the Shankill Road in another fairly new development of small identical two-storey houses. Her own address was on a square decorated in red, white and blue bunting left from the July Twelfth commemoration of the Battle of the Boyne. Even the curbs were painted red, white and blue. A group of little boys were marching around the street beating sticks on cardboard boxes covered with paper Union Jacks.

She was at home, her kids were out, and her husband George was working that night at a club where he poured drinks. He had been named by a supergrass and arrested in the autumn of 1983, and it was unusual that he had been granted bail; but the charge against him, 'Conspiracy to murder person or persons unknown, date unknown,' was outlandish even for a Diplock court – though presumably he had UVF membership counted against him as well.

The Newell house was another sort of place from the Catholic houses I'd seen (although as in every house, the telly was on in the corner). Sleek, new, and spacious, it had everything but a telephone. They had moved there recently, after their last address had been published in the newspaper 'and we decided it was safer'.

If Caroline Newell had been sitting in Schwab's Pharmacy in Hollywood fifty years ago she would have been discovered. She had the kind of blonde tall glamour that thirties' movie queens were made of, a glowing, even smile and a voice like crushed velvet; and three weeks earlier she had given birth to her third son. She had begun Families for Legal Rights after George's arrest, organizing the wives and mothers of named men, and her politicization had been quick and brutal. She was twenty-seven.

Families for Legal Rights 'never started until I started it, if you know what I mean? The supergrass thing was going on and on, and there was ones sentenced and there was ones getting arrested but there was never a group nor nothing in the Protestant community. And then the day my husband was charged, I stood up in court and asked the judge why was he getting took away from me and my children on the word of an alleged murderer. George was supposed to have walked into a room and said he wanted somebody killed and the informer John Gibson was supposed to have overheard this. There was nothing else against George at all. My husband's never been in trouble, only driving offences and all this carry-on.

'Well it was a very understanding judge. Travers – he was shot there too, so he was. Him and his daughter, coming out of church – the daughter was dead. Well that was the same judge that let me speak that day, and he says, "I understand and I'm sure your husband will be granted bail." Right enough the next week he was, so he was lucky enough. But John Gibson hasn't even been sentenced yet – he's admitted to two murders and about thirty-odd other crimes – so the trial won't go on for at least a year or a year and a half yet. And a good lot of men are inside that didn't get bail so they'll have to wait those two years or more on remand.

'Then the next day after the court carry-on – och, there was press and all wanting to speak to me and everything was new to me and I was all flustered and didn't know what to do. I have a sister down the street and I got a friend, and the three of us made placards and stood outside the Crumlin Road jail. There was about thirty or forty women in the court that day and I knew only a few of them, but we were able to get them out and have a big giant protest. And within days the group was formed – I think everybody was just waiting for the opportunity for to form something like that. And we started writing letters. Flip, I wrote to everybody, all I do is write letters, introducing the group and asking for donations, asking for help from MPs. So we've slowly got on our feet, money-wise, and we've been able to provide wee things for kids and all. There's a wee trip goes Thursdays for the prisoners' children.'

Her baby needed attention and she left me with a scrapbook of newspaper clippings (unattributed: I couldn't tell which papers any of them came from). One story dealt with a press conference held jointly by the Families for Legal Rights and a similiar Catholic organization, Relatives for Justice: 'The groups said they had found enough common ground between them to join together in public protests against the use of uncorroborated informer evidence.' A joint statement was quoted: 'We believe that established politicians ensured and fermented the divisions among people to consolidate their own positions of power and now stand idly by while the very basis of any civilized society, the law itself, is destroyed.' Another clipping read: 'KILLINGS BOON TO TRIALS? Ironically the news that the UVF has renewed its assassination campaign has been well received in certain quarters of the Northern Ireland Office . . . Officials were concerned about the joint action of Loyalist and Republican relatives of prisoners held on supergrass allegations. But now the killings have started again, the men at the top know that the fragile unity of the anti-supergrass committee will quickly fall apart, thus destroying an important propaganda weapon.'

When Caroline returned, with the baby in a bundle and a warmed bottle, I asked about the Catholic connection. 'Have you met anyone on the Catholic side of the community?' she asked, and I said the problem had been more in meeting Protestants. 'You'll always find that,' she said.

'Why?'

'Och, we're just a wee bit more suspicious than the Catholic community.'

As for joint efforts on the supergrass front, various difficulties had arisen, none of them to do with the women themselves. 'The first time some of our group met some of their group we found that so-and-so's mammy was from the Shankill and so-and-so's granny was from the Falls, you know all this carry-on? That's what I thought at first: women could sit down and discuss all this. But then when you come up against the politicians, politicians that know you need them, then that's the end of it all.'

Caroline had had more or less to reinvent political lobbying. They were given support almost immediately from the middle-of-the-road Alliance and the Catholic SDLP; and the Rev Ian Paisley's Democratic Unionist Party had proved less difficult than expected because Paisley himself happened to have been in the area campaigning for votes for the European Parliament, 'so we chased them up and down streets and got them.' There was more of a problem with the most powerful Protestant party, the Official Unionists, and here was where their nonsectarian approach hit a roadblock. 'See we definitely need the OUP, no matter what way you look at it, and they know it and this is why they're dangling us on a string. It all lies in their hands. So for us to stand with the Catholic women, they won't help us. And there's other conflicts too: we need the support of, say, the woman next door, and the woman next door mightn't like the idea of us going with Catholics. So we decided to stay on our own. Although everything we have, it's all one thing, you know? They're all the same as us. I still see them in court and all, and we speak like, we don't walk by each other nor nothing, so we don't.

'It's been hard work, I can tell you. Writing letters and getting letters back and trying to hold the women back from protesting – they want to go down to the Official Unionist headquarters and wreck the place. But we don't want them to have an excuse not to meet us, so we're trying to hold the women off. I'm expecting a meeting soon, and if it doesn't come we're going to put it into the press that the Official Unionists don't want to know their own voters. You have to do that.'

She had not only to attempt representations to politicians on every level, but to educate herself and the others in welfare rights and different aspects of the legal situation by calling in experts to speak at their Monday evening meetings. Fund-raising was time-consuming. She was no slouch at public relations either. 'There's just not enough hours in the day like, for to do everything.'

She and the baby made primitive coos at each other. 'We were all just ordinary housewives and it's hard to believe that a year ago we were just doing our dishes and changing nappies and now we can approach politicians and state our case that we have been denied every human right.' She was changing a nappy now. 'I swore I'd never have any more kids in this bloody country. But like here's another one. 'Cause like what are they growing up to? If things get worse God knows where they'll end up.' What about leaving? She and George had left when they first married, she said, 'to Scotland, really to get our head shot from all this . . . But he got homesick and I got homesick and we come back here to live. I love here, so I do.

'I'd like it all to come to an end. Although I wouldn't like to live in a united Ireland either, so I wouldn't. But I'd like everybody to be happy. No matter what woman you talk to in our group, she'll tell you the same thing. Everybody's totally disgusted. And I'm sure there's a lot of women in the Catholic community feel like that too. It's so hard on the women, this is what gets me. See, when you look round and you see some of the women in our group, I could just sit and cry for them. Ones that are really hard hit – about six kids and no money and no bail for their husbands. There's about sixty women in our group and I can guarantee you there's only about ten that's quite normal. The rest are all on nerve tablets, some of them's turned into alcoholics and all this carry-on. All because of this. There's one woman in particular has three jobs and five children and her husband's in jail, and she is a nervous wreck. She cleans in the morning, she cleans in the afternoon, and she washes glasses in the bar at the weekend. Her eldest daughter takes care of the kids. That woman, if you just look at her she bursts out crying, so she does.'

I asked her what, after all this, she felt about the British. Would she too like them out of Northern Ireland?

'No, I think we need the army. I would think that, whereas Catholic women wouldn't think that. But when we speak to Americans and they say that their law is based on British law and they wouldn't let this go on over there, you say, Well damn British law then. But we're still British, like, you know what I mean? We carry on our placards WE ARE BRITISH CITIZENS GIVE US BRITISH LAW.'

She talked about lobbying MPs in London who claim that the people of Northern Ireland *are* given British law. 'We were there for five days and in that five days my tongue was sore, telling the same story.' Caroline invited some of them to Belfast 'and it's, "Right, well, I'll think about it," you know, "I'll keep in touch."' The MPs 'hadn't a clue what an informer was or why he was granted immunity,' and some refused to believe the charge against her husband until she showed them the charge sheet. 'Isn't it awful to think your life is lying in the like of their hands? When we went to the House of Commons we nearly passed out to see *that's* what your life's resting on. I just sat and I looked and here's me: My God that's a disgrace. They're all sitting laughing and bloody snoring –

the people here if they seen all that they'd say, Och to hell with 'em!

'Whenever we met people in London, they seemed to think that the Nationalist community was the hardest hit. But that's definitely wrong. We've had to thump it into whoever we've met, Americans and all, that the Protestant community is as hard hit as what the Catholic community are. But the Official Unionist politicians portray this upper-class thing, that the Protestant people aren't scroungers, that they don't diddle the broo and all this carry-on, the way the Catholic community would; little do they know that the Protestant people are as bad off as the Catholic community and they *have* to.'

As I was leaving, I asked her about the flags and bunting decorating her square. 'They're mine,' she said – she had made the flags herself and got the men in the square to put them up, where they would stay until after another two parades next month. 'My other sons are in the band. Och they're real wee boys and I just let them walk away there, so I do, in their uniforms.' There seemed to be no connection in her mind between such displays of sectarianism and the other things she had said.

One of Caroline's committee members was Dora Bingham, wife of another supergrass victim who was serving twenty years. The 'paid perjurer' in his case was one Joe Bennett – 'the type who,' Dora said, 'if something came up he'd say he'd done it and name lots of others, even if he'd actually been in jail at the time.' Dora had a deadpan drollery combined with a very winning gentle shyness. She lived in Ballysillan – what Mrs McCarten and Mrs Rice would call a 'hard-line' area, in this case UVF – with her two school-age children and the remains of her husband's champion pigeon collection.

'John was charged in October 1982 with possession of

a rocket launcher. Well, supposedly he stole that from the Provisional IRA. The British *army* can't even get one from the IRA, but they say he could go in and steal one. Also possession of warheads – five hundred detonators and seventy-three guns of all sorts – which they never recovered any.'

'Don't they have to produce something?'

'Not if Mr Bennett said he'd seen them. When John was in Castlereagh [the main RUC interrogation centre] they never even asked him about them. You'd think that would be important, to find out where they were. Bennett said that John got these guns by mail order. Said John's uncle in America got them and sent them to another uncle here that owned an engineering firm. John has no uncle in America, and he hasn't got an uncle here that owns any type of firm. It's unbelievable like what's actually happening when you have a look at this. Politicians know. And they agree that it's wrong, but "We're not going to stop it." I know the Unionist Party's for internment – they just want people put away – but since they can't do that any more, they have internment with another name. Even the people who are on remand at the minute, if their cases fall through they've already served their purpose – been put out of action for eighteen months or two years on remand. It's even longer for Republicans. The main purpose is just to get them off the roads, you know. So they're happy with that. I'm not saying that everybody in these cases is innocent, not at all, but I'd say the majority of them are innocent of the charges put against them.'

Luckily she had and continued to hold a full-time job, at a cigarette factory (free samples chain-smoked and offered in handfuls). 'But it's frustrating, so it is. Knowing you could be living your life like anybody else till someone called Bennett come along. I did meet him once, he come to borrow a tape. But according to the evidence he was up at my house every week. With John and I working, the only time we spent together was weekends. We'd go to the country with friends or John spent the day about the shed or with his pigeons. He'd had pigs, and a goat that cut all the neighbours' grass, and a dozen horses, then the pigeons – breeding the bloodlines. When he was arrested he'd just won his first cup.

'So he was busy like. And the kids were always here so. One of the charges put against John was that Bennett was up here on a Sunday afternoon with about eight or nine of them and an M-60 machine gun. But they don't give specific dates so you can't provide an alibi. And Dessy Boal, the barrister who took all sixteen of the accused men in the Bennett case, could only fight it on the credibility of the witness because to claim innocence for two or three of them would shed doubt on the others. In the appeal the judge found twenty-two reasons for not believing Bennett. But John's still inside.'

There was also tremendous resentment at the conditions of imprisonment. 'I don't like the IRA. I detest them, but at the same time they're not ordinary criminals. It's the same with the Loyalists. They believe in what they're doing, you know. Although a lot of the things they're doing *I* don't agree with, so I don't. But they're not the same as ordinary criminals. They can't be treated the same.

'You always had in the North *I'm British, I'm British*. Now my kids are growing up hating the British. They took their daddy away. It would be different if he had done something, you'd say "Well, he did this and now he has to be punished." John's own daddy was a policeman. My kids never had any problem with policemen but now they just hate them. You can't talk about law and order now; the police are bent, that's my opinion like. You had it demonstrated in that shoot-to-kill case of Seamus Grew.

You know, the murder the policeman was up for? He pumped thirty bullets into Grew. Now Grew was a terrorist suspect, but at the same time the police said that he drove through a roadblock, which he didn't. It just shows you what they're prepared to do. And the judge – the judge is human. He has his own political beliefs. And the judges sitting in these cases being mainly Unionists, they can't tell me that they're not biased. They're bound to be. They say law is above politics but it's not.

'See if there wasn't any Troubles this would be the nicest place in the world. When I was brought up we had the Twelfth of July parades, but there was always Catholics lived here and there in the same streets, and you got on with them, you know? In Belfast everybody was the same: the working-class people were poor and the rich people were rich. It didn't matter whether you were Protestant or Catholic, you were all out of a job. And then the civil rights come in – I could understand that, people fighting for jobs and votes – but Republicanism crept into it, the riots, and things happened during the riots you'll never forget. People getting killed. You never forget things like that. There was ten of us including my mammy and daddy. Mammy's dead, that was brought about by the Troubles. I come from the Shankill. We lived facing an army barracks and there was riots one day. And there must have been hundreds of those tear-gas canisters, just firing up the street. My mammy had a bad chest, and the CS gas killed her.' The same as Rita Ryan's sister.

Her family is largely dispersed now – four sisters married to soldiers stationed elsewhere and a brother who had to emigrate. 'He's an asphalter. It's mainly Catholics working in that. So they told him they'd shoot him if he didn't get out. Well he had no other trade so he went to Australia.' She hadn't seen him in twelve years.

'We'd like to see peace one day, but there doesn't seem

to be any way. I think there's too many people making too much money out of it. But I don't want my kids to grow up hating Catholics. I hate what the IRA is doing but the ordinary Catholics don't have horns. Only you can't distinguish the difference to two kids.

'But I wouldn't go into a united Ireland for the simple reason that their laws are too oppressive at the minute. Anti-abortion laws, anti-birth control, no divorce, things that affect mainly women. But Britain doesn't want us either. If another Labour government were in tomorrow, they would say, Right, pull the troops out, yous are on your own.

'You see with your accent, no matter where you go you're branded. You go to England and it's not like you're from Ulster – you're a Paddy. You go to the Free State and they're very wary of you too. It's baffling. Times when you feel you've had enough, like.

'We went on holiday the August before John was arrested, to Spain, and it's funny when you're away, you don't think anything about . . . We met a few fellas, we were very friendly with them over there. They were from the Falls Road. And here we'd be at each other's throats, like, you know? You have to go away to get on with it. And another couple we met on the way home, we sat and drank with them and they were a Catholic family called Breige and Paddy. People wouldn't believe it like.'

There was a chance for a close-up on the supergrass phenomenon at Crumlin Road courthouse, where the preliminary enquiry of William 'Budgie' Allen's case was going on. Budgie was an ex-Ulster Volunteer Force man. Having pleaded guilty to fifty-two charges, including conspiracy to kill, he turned informer and named forty-seven people who stood to serve terms of seven to twenty years apiece if Budgie were believed. He was the latest of twenty-seven 'reformed terrorists' who had named four hundred and fifty people; their evidence was often too fantastic to credit, so the conviction rate was less than a fifth – mostly Republicans. The rest of the arrested men, if not acquitted, had been released after the supergrass 'changed his mind' and retracted his testimony, but they might have spent two years or more in prison awaiting trial.

The courthouse was a magnificent Greek revival structure painted peach and white and topped by a gilt Justice with her blindfold, scales and sword. From most angles, however, the building was so fenced in and festooned with barbed wire that a clear view was unavailable. Across the wide street was the Crumlin Road jail, its dirty Corinthian columns obscured by more wire. An underground tunnel joined the two together for the convenient transfer of prisoners.

At the courthouse entrance men and women were separated and I passed through a cubicle where my name, camera and cassette recorder were taken and two women constables administered a frisk. Further in, past the main lobby, the procedure was repeated but there was nothing left to take except my name. The enquiry had been due to start at 11 A.M. but in the court no one was yet present except at least three dozen policemen and those seventeen of Budgie's victims who had been granted bail, and who were hooting and catcalling as I entered. The delay was explained to me by a neighbour in the press bench. 'Trouble in the prison. Some people have been hurt.'

The culprits already in court presented a plug-ugly picture: yobbos with tattoos and skinheads exchanging loud banter and wisecracks with each other and with their guards. My neighbour, who said he was the judge's bodyguard, was talking about the violence of the prisoners. 'Last time there was one of these trials, it took them *three days* to wipe the blood up. Isn't that right?' he asked a cop in front of us.

The cop shook his head in disagreement. 'Four,' he said.

'They've probably had a punch-up in the prison,' the bodyguard went on. He wore a badge to identify himself as a 'Royal Greenjacket' and was miffed I'd never heard of them. 'They'll probably limp in with bleeding noses and black eyes.'

At this point the prisoners entered, up some steps in the centre of the court which apparently led from the tunnel to the jail. They seemed neither bloody nor bowed, though how could you tell with such raw material? There were so many of them that no dock could be capacious enough, so they were spread around the court, surrounded by RUC and prison staff. Everyone was smoking. Courtroom decorum was neither here nor there; the prisoners shouted and brayed among themselves, threw more smokes around, and rained insults on the bench. A shout ran out: 'Higgins! Are you circumcised?' Raucous laughter. Mr Justice Higgins, who was trying the case, was not there yet. His bodyguard bridled, but I couldn't bring myself to ask him about the significance of the insult. Maybe it had to do with Higgins being one of only two Catholics on the bench.

At a sudden signal for the court to rise the defendants put out their cigarettes and stood soberly. Judge Higgins took his place and there was silence. He either hadn't heard the scurrility or was ignoring it. A defence lawyer pleaded that one of the prisoners had had his congenital heart condition 'exacerbated by an altercation with a number of police officers' and was unfit to attend. The judge acceded to a request for an adjournment and left the court. The instant the door shut behind him the uproar resumed. One prisoner leaned out of his pen as he was being let out and waved a pair of handcuffs he was holding, shouting: 'They used *these* to beat us!'

The congenital heart condition must have cleared up next day when I came again. This time the tiers of the public gallery were full of wives and mothers, and many bewigged personnel filled the centre of the courtroom; only the prisoners were absent, all of them.

'They have gone for a pee break,' explained the judge's bodyguard. 'I don't know, Republicans must have stronger bladders. This never happens with them.' In yesterday's 'altercation', it seemed, one prisoner, in getting handcuffed, had 'got nipped' and hit out. 'Then six or seven joined in, and you know our police don't take kindly to that, so they stuck into them.' The men had then refused to go to court and the idea of carrying thirty-one of them had been a bit much. 'But their legal man had a yarn with them and said it was better to adjourn.'

The prisoners now returned. This time the possibilities for mayhem had expanded to include the public gallery. Not only words flew around, but packs of cigarettes, sweets, newspapers, and one woman flung an opaque plastic bag to a prisoner which could have contained absolutely anything. As a courtroom spectacle it all seemed rather unusual, I commented to the judge's bodyguard. 'We've got to give them a little leeway or it would be worse,' he said.

Budgie appeared, surrounded by five guards. A slight, blond-bearded fellow in a grey suit, he mumbled inaudibly in a rehearsed monotone in answer to questions from the prosecutor, who had it all down in front of him anyway – the deposition had been typed like a script with the parts distinguished in red and black. The lines had been well-learned. The defendants now listened as one by one Budgie did them in. You could tell who was being named not by hearing it, which was almost impossible, but by looking for the nudging and poking on either side of the blushing and smirking prisoner. The men so mentioned in this catalogue of crime appeared more pleased with the attention than troubled with its implications. But they had a long way to go: the trial proper, as opposed to this preliminary enquiry, wouldn't be starting for months.

When the trial did begin, there would be no jury, just one judge. This was how the Diplock Courts had operated since 1972, an 'emergency' policy which also relaxed the normal rules and safeguards regarding the admissibility of confessions and the use of uncorroborated accomplice evidence. If the judge (as jury) believed Budgie's testimony against his former friends, he (as judge) was supposed to warn himself (as jury) not to put too much weight on that testimony before he (as judge) put everyone away for as long as possible.

The whole process was summed up by a sign I saw scrawled on a wall later that day: WHEN THOSE WHO MAKE THE LAW BREAK THE LAW IN THE NAME OF THE LAW THERE IS NO LAW.

4
True Blue

The supergrass people, the Women's Information Group and the cleaners mostly saw themselves as near the bottom of the heap. Several layers up was Dorothy Elliott, the ex-principal of an ex-school in Ardoyne, a mixed area which was increasingly Catholic: the same area the cleaners came from. A state school, Finiston had been attended by Protestants – virtually all Catholic children throughout the province went to Church schools. Because of the demographic changes, those Protestants remaining in the area lacked sufficient numbers for a school and the place where Finiston had stood until three years ago now looked like a bomb-crater.

Mrs Elliott, the trim, energetic widow of a UDR man, now worked for Save the Children Fund, and with an SCF sticker on her car and a little poodle in it, she darted about everywhere, even delivering me up the Falls to the Sinn Fein office – but drew the line at the posh Forum Hotel in the centre of town, for fear of car-napping joyriders.

She also didn't bother about who was listening, but talked in her wry, lively way in the middle of a full coffee shop or any kind of crowd, happy to cut up everyone, but particularly the people with 'caveman attitudes' on her own side: like the Orangeman she was trying unsuccessfully to get on the phone – 'he's probably out airing his sash.' Or her neighbours' automatic way of voting – 'Someone said to me the other day, "If there was a wee pig up for the Unionists I would vote for it".' Or the people in the Finiston area who called Catholics 'animals', such as the man who had said to her, 'I know you're an educated woman, Mrs Elliott, but I don't understand how you can call an animal a friend.' He had trained his dog to bite Fenians, though how the dog was to recognize one without being able to enquire about his school was moot.

I particularly relished her pedagogic asides. We were walking along past a greengrocer's advertising FRESH PEA'S next door to a shop selling FISH & CHIP'S, and she mentioned the time when Loyalists had taken to the Republican idea of barricading off their ghettos to outsiders – making them No-Go areas – and she'd seen a sign on the Oldpark Road: THIS ONE COME'S DOWN WHEN THE ONE'S ON THE FALL'S COME DOWN. 'Belfast is *very* enthusiastic about apostrophes. You can't have too many apostrophes.'

They used to call Finiston School 'Silver City' thanks to all the corrugated iron around it, and 'Dodge City Academy' for more obvious reasons. A company of one hundred and forty men of the British Army was stationed there with a gun emplacement on the roof, and soldiers acted as 'lollypop patrol' to escort children there and home again. 'I have had to go out of school in a flak jacket with the boys driving a pig in front, just to buy cigarettes.'

Mrs Elliott was as sardonic about the army as about everyone else: 'Two things come from the sky, paras and birdshit.' When the British decided to reduce the numbers of troops in Northern Ireland Finiston was left to fend for itself. Thereafter attempts were made thirteen times to burn it down. One way and another a Finiston education seemed a fair preparation for Belfast life. 'Miss, Miss, we better get down on the floor, that's an Armalite!' – 'It's all right Miss, it's an SLR.' She herself could never tell the difference. 'We were shot at more times than I can think. I have had to lie under my car to get away from the bricks and bottles flying overhead. And I have found that one's veneer of civilization is very thin. There could be real excitement in the air, the adrenalin rose, and I wouldn't have minded throwing a few things myself.'

The warfare in Ardoyne had been so unpredictable that Mrs Elliott had an arrangement with the Catholic headmaster of a nearby school that, depending on who was attacking that day, she or he would rescue the children out of the mixed local nursery school. She often had to deliver the Finiston students home. 'There is nothing more frustrating than being under attack in your own car, diving in among the missiles and delivering kids to a house where the mother doesn't even bother to come to the door, just curiously looks out at you as if she's saying to herself, I wonder why they are home? And you just think, Bugger you. And you've got to go through all this again but you do it, again and again and again.' Then she'd finally get home to her own safe and untouched part of Northern Belfast to find the neighbours discussing the greenfly on the roses. 'I wished they knew there was a *war*.'

Talking about her national identity, she said, 'I regard myself as British. I was educated in the British way. I was brought up to feel the wee hairs on the back of my neck prickle at the very mention of Trooping the Colour, or the Battle of Trafalgar. You don't learn Irish history. Children have one term of Irish history up to age eighteen. But to be very honest we have far more in common with the South. I have always had the view that I would quite happily go into a united Ireland, but now I'll be damned if I'll be bombed into it. So I think myself British until I go to a rugby match. And then I'm shouting for Ireland.'

'Even if they're playing England?'

'Oh yes!'

'What about your friends?'

'Every single person I know.'

But uniting Ireland was obviously more complicated than a rugby match, and she had other objections than the violence being used in its name. 'I no more agree with the Catholic Church in the South than I have ever agreed with the influence that the Protestant churches have tried to have in Northern Ireland. To my mind church and state should be totally separate. It horrifies me to see people who claim to be religious becoming politicians. I don't see Paisley or Smyth (Grand Master MW Bro Rev. W. Martin Smyth, BA, BD, MP, MPA, who divided his time among the Orange Order, Westminster, and St Anne's Cathedral) as being Christians, whatever "Christian" means in this context. But I think the word "Christian" makes me feel uncomfortable. Because people who claim it here always seem to have a set of Noes, a whole catalogue of things you can't do. It doesn't seem to be a list of things that you should do. And therefore people who use it here generally make me want to go exactly the opposite way.'

Mrs Elliott saw the 'Protestant work ethic' as 'just a social-work term, which is equally applicable to lots and lots of Catholics. I don't think there's such a thing as one section being work-shy. If you advertise for a volunteer, for every hundred volunteers you get, ninety-eight of them will be Catholics. And who are the people who are most interested in further education? It's Catholics. My experience is that Protestants in working-class areas are far more likely to sit back. I don't think Catholics have ever been handed anything, and therefore they reckon they've got to work for it.

'At the moment I really do feel quite bitter about English politicians making decisions about something they're not very well informed about and aren't even interested in becoming better informed about. England has always been a thorn in the flesh of the Irish.'

Her husband Bob, who had been director of an electronics firm, had joined the UDR part time 'because he felt he needed to make a positive contribution to the country to get law and order back,' and was against any and all paramilitary forces. 'He didn't believe in yahoos ruling no matter what side they were on.' It meant staying up every fourth night to do 'unpleasant and boring' guard duty, but 'it was important to him not just to sit in the golf club or the bar but to go out and do something. I must say I felt very proud of him. In the training camp they were told, "Already the IRA will know that you've joined and your troubles at home will start now." He had to take a different route to work every day, vary the time, and wear a coat over his uniform.

'Then the phone calls started. "Your husband will be going on duty tonight. Kiss him goodbye because it's the last time you'll ever see him." – "Well, your husband's away and there's a bomb in your back garden." – "Your husband's a UDR bastard and I'm coming to shoot you because you organize the orgies in your school between the children and the army." – "I'm coming up to rape you, Mrs Elliott" – I thought that one was my husband's nephew playing a joke. "Great! When?" So I got a string of abuse. For some reason I felt quite cool and I said "Well, I do hope you feel better having got all that off your chest." Then I hung up and poured myself a huge drink.

'Or I'd say, "Would you phone someone else, there's a good TV programme I'm watching." Believe you me I didn't take it as casually as that but I thought if they didn't get a rise out of me . . .'

The Elliotts made elaborate contingency plans for what she was to do if she were kidnapped, say, with a bomb put in her car, and told to drive into the school. 'We decided that even if he were held hostage I'd phone the authorities. Because we were older and we had had our lives.' They rigged an electronic warning device in the lavatory, special locks were put all over the house, and to this day she never went out of a room without locking it or into a room at night without immediately closing the curtains and blinds, never opened the front door without turning on an outside light first. 'We had to balance living that way against his making a contribution to his country's security.'

But Bob became 'bitterly disillusioned' at the way the UDR men were used. It was 'more important than anything to have your drill right and your buttons brassoed. Bullshit Baffles Brains, he'd say. There were certain Republican areas where he was instructed never to drive because it might be seen as provocative. They were used to quell disturbances in the Protestant estates. They felt they should have been used impartially. According to press reports now, some UDR men, particularly in the country, are also in the paramilitary. But when he worked in the UDR it was made up of men with a social conscience who wanted to get the country back to normality, respectable men who by no stretch of the imagination wanted to put people away or victimize anyone. Not one of them I knew was bigoted. I can only speak about the area he was working in. The UDR has an image as a Protestant force, but there were Catholics in it, though they were in the minority. In his group there were two Catholics, neighbours of ours.' (Two per cent of the UDR overall are Catholics; and UDR men have been convicted of paramilitary offences.)

Mrs Elliott loathed the paramilitaries on both sides because of her work with young people. 'They have robbed them of their youth, they've segregated us. It's no longer possible to see youth as a time of experimentation and experiencing everything, because it's too dangerous. When I was young you went everywhere – I knew more Republican songs than they did from going to all the singsongs in the pubs.

'Few people are in the paramilitary organizations for idealism. There's a lot of money to be made. At the beginning it was a matter of self-help, people offering to look out for each other's houses. Then they started organizing and coming round and saying, "We thought if everyone contributed 10p a week we could make sure your windows aren't broken." Entrepreneurs ganged up and enlarged their areas. There are flourishing protection rackets. And now little men with power from the Troubles don't want to relinquish it to return to being merely little men. They're a major or some other bigshot in a paramilitary organization: why go back to being someone of no consequence? With the money they've made some of them have started legitimate businesses – video centres, pubs, bookie shops, drinking clubs. It has damn-all to do with idealism. At Finiston there was a man who kept his kids out of school in order to be summonsed, because if you are arrested you go up a rank in the paramilitary organization and your salary rises. *Any* offence.

'Oh yes, it's quiet lately, really. Apart from the shootings and the bombings there's no trouble.'

The subject of Finiston came up again in conversation with a friend of Mrs Elliott's, Betty Emery, who had taught there and now had a class of eight-year-olds at another school. 'Sure when I was in Finiston the kids were never done running to the doctor gettin' tablets – all their wee nerves were away. Most children would have been on Valium. To keep them quiet.'

It was different at her current school: the children had no contact with Catholics at all. 'The only thing that will ever solve this is desegregated education,' she said. As it was, 'the bulk of the children here think that Roman Catholics are another race. Like your Pakistanis. Half their parents are in jail for some trouble or other, connected with the UVF. They're bringing it into the classroom, so the other decent children are hearing it. Roman Catholics are just aliens to them, that's what's so tragic. I know from teaching religious education – if they're talking about being a Christian I would say "Who are Christians?" and then I always add about the RCs. And they say, "Don't be *silly*, Miss, don't be daft!" And I'd say, "But we all believe in the same – " "Oh, you're daft." And coming up to the Twelfth I take great delight in telling them that King Billy was financed by the Pope. Well they all nearly have a coronary on the spot. I'm waiting for somebody to come up and do me.'

We were about to leave her empty classroom and she was looking around for something. 'Kids here have no respect for the law. I leave money lying around, I suppose because I've always been intrinsically honest and it annoys me to think anybody would steal from me. My kids get a lecture on the first day: if anything goes missing from my room I'll break their arm. That's child psychology. Something was gone once and one wee fella stood up and said, "Miss, I didn't take it, but if the police come and hear my name, they'll immediately think it's me." He has that attitude, because his whole family are always in trouble. He's growing up with that and he'll probably end up in crime himself. What do you do? I think the only way it'll ever change is if there's co-education, Prods and Catholics together.'

Betty's parents, Austin and Molly Ardill, were Unionist politicians – her father had retired and her mother was now active as a local councillor in the nearby town of Carrickfergus, where she was touted to be the next mayor. We met Molly Ardill for lunch. A pastel lady with an almost English accent, she had perfectly coiffed white hair and smart clothes. Her highest accolade was 'perfectly charming'.

The mother and daughter talked about mixing: how groups of young people got on well when they were taken away from the environment, but immediately on returning home started throwing things at each other again. Her constituency in Carrickfergus 'would be very predominantly Protestant', Mrs Ardill said, though she came in contact with Catholics. 'When I look back to when I was a little girl, you were either very definitely Catholic or very definitely Protestant. Everyone knew what everyone else was. I never played with Roman Catholic children.

'I would have nothing against anybody who's a Catholic – not in the wide world – provided they're loyal to the state and respect the state. After all, the state's providing them with so much. A lot of these people who are crying for a united Ireland don't really want it. I mean who would want to live in Eire – the cost of living! They're nearly almost bankrupt! And they don't have anything like the social services that we do.' On the other hand when her husband had been a Northern Ireland Parliament member they had often gone 'down there' and 'they treated us gloriously' and 'were perfectly charming in every way'.

She had served on her council for eight years, 'trying to stem the tide' against changes that 'weren't in keeping with the historic character of the place. It wasn't politics that brought me in, definitely wasn't. Although I've strong views on politics, you'll have guessed. I mean I'm not anti-Catholic or anything like that, but I don't want a united Ireland until a majority of the people democratically want to go into a united Ireland. I've been talking to Margaret Thatcher about it quite a lot. And she assures me that while she's Prime Minister, or has any power, she will not work to put us into a united Ireland until the majority of people want it. And I believe her. I think she's a woman of her word, don't you?'

I asked her about the rumour that she was to be mayor of Carrick. 'Well, a lot of people say that. But nowadays you're getting people coming up and looking for positions in order to boost their own ego. They haven't got any social background or educational background. Loud-mouthed people, very ungrammatical and all that kind of thing. It's nothing to do with money – it's to do with – oh well, you know yourself. There is a difference, isn't there?'

What about the Unionist party's position on violence? Did they consider concessions to Catholics? 'You can't make a concession to terrorists,' she said. 'That's the trouble.'

'But that aside,' I pursued it, 'there is a lack of faith in the institutions of society in the Catholic areas.'

'This is Sinn Fein. I'll send you a copy of the oath that the members of Sinn Fein take. You'll see there the basic principles of their organization.'

Since 'concessions' was a dirty word, what about 'power-sharing'?

'My husband can tell you a lot about that. As a matter of fact, at one point Austin invited John Hume and Paddy Devlin [both then leaders of the SDLP] to come down to our house, and they came every week for about six weeks, and spent all morning, and I gave them lunch, and into the afternoon, discussing. And when they were with us, they agreed. There was a lot about power-sharing. But Paisley intervened and blew the gaff, that these people were meeting in our house. They could have agreed with us. And you know they were perfectly charming to me: they never would leave without coming into the kitchen to thank me.

'It may be too polarized now. Certainly I wouldn't agree to having Sinn Fein or Republicans in such a government. But they've got to take the SDLP in somehow, in order to take the power away from the Sinn Fein. But how to get a formula they can all accept is the thing. Too many people in politics at the moment are making too much out of it for themselves, and they don't want the thing to settle. It's terrible. My husband is so annoyed about it – even the way our party is going – their intransigence, not talking, that kind of thing. You'll *never* get *any*where if you don't keep on talking.'

As promised, Mrs Ardill sent me a copy of a document headed 'THE SINN FIEN OATH':

I swear by Almighty God, by all Heaven, by the Holy and blessed prayer book of the Roman Catholic Church, by the Holy Virgin Mary, Mother of God, by her bitter tears and wailings by Saint Patrick, our blessed and adorable Host. The Rosery, to fight until we die wading in the fields of red gore of the Saxon tyrants and murderers of our glorious nationality, if so fated, to fight until not a trace is left to tell that the Holy soil of Ireland were trodden by these Heretics. Also these Protestant robbers and brutes, these unbelievers of our faith will be driven like the swine they are into the sea, by fire, the knife, or by poison cup, until we of the Catholic Faith and avowed supporters of all Sinn Fein action and principles clear these heretics from our land.

Age is not to be considered in our blessed deeds of extermination of brutes who in the past ages robbed many of our Churches. We must shed streams of blood of these tyrants to again claim our Holy places. Report to our blessed priests regularly upon all works and business transactions of any kind.

At any cost we must work in secret, using any method of deception to gain our ends towards the destruction of all Protestants and the advance of the Priesthood and the Catholic faith until the Pope is complete ruler of the whole world.

Our beloved Ireland has been held in chains by these cursed foreign tyrants for ages. Now we can see the end of their power. We must strike at every opportunity using all methods of causing ill feeling within the Protestants ranks, and in their businesses. The employment of any means will be blessed by our earthly Fathers the priests, thrice blessed by His HOLINESS the Pope.

Scotland must be swept clean of their accursed beliefs, by the extermination of all Masonic and all such bodies as do not accept our creed must perish, as before the days of the accursed Reformation. So shall we of the Roman CATHOLIC Church and faith destroy with smiles and thanks givings to our Holy FATHER the Pope all who shall not join us and accept our beliefs.

So help me God.

At the bottom of this duplicated typewritten page was a note: 'This is a Copy of the original which was found outside the Chapel in Dungannon.' Apart from the sentiments expressed, which seemed distant in the extreme from the concerns of Republicans I'd met (who seldom if ever mentioned Protestants), the illiteracy of the document was nothing if not anomalous from the people who wrote very intelligent English indeed in the *Republican News*. Only one enquiry was necessary to establish that the document, worthy of the authors of the Protocols of the Elders of Zion, had almost certainly originated in the British Army's Lisburn headquarters in 1969, perhaps properly spelled then; perhaps not. As early as the 1820s similar Irish Catholic organizations had been accused by the British of pledging themselves 'to wade knee deep in Orange blood.'

The next time I was in Belfast the Ardills invited me to dinner in Carrickfergus. They had recently moved from a very large house to what they called a 'modest bungalow', though it was more a ranch-house, filled with antiques of the massive China urn variety, with designer bathroom and kitchen and many doors off the long central glassed-in hall. They chose to sit in a small cosy room with a smoking fire and a TV on silently in the corner. The TV and the fire, the dimensions of the room and its large-patterned carpet made the ambience curiously like the only room in all the other houses I'd been to; and in the same way, we ate there too – though with cloth napkins (theirs in silver rings) and fine china. They offered nothing stronger than orange juice and gave off a teetotal impression; the grace Austin said before the meal requested the good Lord to see to the needs of those less fortunate.

The Ardills were quintessential Unionists, the people who have run Northern Ireland for decades. They made me think of an advertisement for life insurance showing confidently smiling gran and grandpa, fulfilled in their old age not least because they had made provision for it. He was tall and muscular and firm-chinned, and had chopped all the firewood himself, very neatly. He talked in a low, deliberative voice, full of authority. While she organized the food he began with chit-chat which almost immediately became vituperative about 'the iniquitous system of unemployment' and the dole: 'too many look upon it as a payment for a life of doing nothing.' Because his wife had mentioned his expertise, I asked him about the Protestant paramilitaries.

'When the Troubles were starting off in the early 1970s, the British government adopted a most peculiar attitude: they fell for the Republican propaganda, like so many others, and they said, "Oh these Protestant Unionists over in the North of Ireland, they haven't been fair to these people, they've discriminated against them, we'll have to teach them a lesson." And they did away with the "B"-Specials, they civilianized the RUC, and they opened the police barracks and said, "Oh these are community stations, anybody can walk in at any time" – you know, be all palsy walsy. Of course the Republicans lapped this up. They rubbed their hands and said "This is great" and they walked into the police barracks and blew them up. The Protestants were blamed for everything, of course – and these Republicans were running throughout the city. It's not very far from a Republican area to a Loyalist area. As a result a lot of the Protestant people who lived in the Shankill Road and the east of Belfast were terrified.

'Well a lot of men then said, "If the police and the army aren't going to do anything about it, we'll go out and patrol the streets," and they started vigilante groups – two or three men would walk round, maybe with a stick or something like that, just patrolling their areas and protecting their own wives and children. This is what it started as. There was no UDA or anything then, just the local vigilantes.

'Well the Troubles went on unabated, and nothing was done to curtail the shooting. Then the vigilantes began to get a bit more organized and, being ex-service and whatnot, I used to get called in to talk to them. I met many groups of men and talked to them about the dangers of taking the law into their own hands, and yet advising them how to be prepared and equipped to handle their own areas. Then they formed the UDA out of all these groups, set up on paramilitary lines. And as so happens in all walks of life, some of them thought, This is a good racket to get into, and they began to look for hardware here and there. Then the shooting started on both sides.'

The pudding trolley was brought to Austin to serve. 'And that's how the UDA got a bad reputation. Now I'm not condemning the UDA by any means (would you like some fruit with it?). They went from one thing to another (would you like the juice over it? It helps it) and got involved in a whole lot of things they shouldn't have been involved in, largely because some of the fellas cashed in: some of them were making very well out of it.'

SB: 'Who was paying the money?'

Mr Ardill: 'That's a bit of a mystery. But they got it.'

Mrs Ardill: 'Didn't they steal things off lorries and things?'

SB: 'People talk about protection money.'

Mr Ardill: 'Yes, there were protection rackets and all sorts of things. Worked on both sides, you see. And that's how they were getting money, big money. And the heads of these organizations have done very well out of it, like the trade unionists and some of the socialist members of parliament. I mean Jim Callaghan has a big farm and has made a lot of money out of being a socialist, you know?'

SB: 'Actually I don't know.'

Mr Ardill: 'Well so I'm told anyway. Unfortunately the UDA went off the rails a bit. People condemn the UDA for being gunmen and being as bad as the other side – well they're not as bad, because if the Republicans weren't carrying on the terrorist campaign the UDA wouldn't be involved in it. Theirs was largely a defensive role. Supposing one of your children was blown up. You'd say, "I'll get those boys for that." Just the same as when Hitler invaded Poland and Britain said, "Oh well you can't do that and we're going to fight you for it." For the unenlightened that's their natural reaction, to have a go themselves rather than negotiate. And you can have a lot of sympathy for them because we have had it now for fifteen, sixteen years and there has been an awful lot of talking, and where are we? We're worse off than a few years ago.

'If the British government had had an ounce of courage, when the Troubles started they should have stopped it. They should have put the gunmen out of the way. There are only a handful of them. Whereas they've allowed them to go on increasing, become part of world terrorism . . . Admittedly the politicians here didn't make it easy. But they've shilly-shallied and they've hedged about and och! they've made an awful hash of it. Margaret Thatcher is the one to blame now.'

Mrs Ardill: 'Well I don't blame her, she's got an awful handful – '

Mr Ardill: 'All she has to do is let the security forces wipe out the IRA. I fought during the war with an Irish regiment, and you couldn't ask for better men – if you lead them. But they're no good without leaders. The IRA is just the same. If you take the leadership out of it, the rest would fall away very quickly. The UDA and UVF – that'll all go by the board if they wipe out the IRA. When Merlyn Rees was here as Secretary of State, I said to him one day,

I said, "Merlyn, until you really carry out what you know and believe to be right, and that is that these IRA should be taken out, you're never going to get anywhere. There are a whole lot of good bogholes here, and you should make use of them." He said, "What do you mean?" I said "Merlyn, you really say you don't know what I mean? Because if you don't, I'll tell you." But that's what he should have done! If he had taken out two or three now and two or three the next night – say nothing about them, they just don't come back – '

Mrs Ardill: 'They're terrible cowards, you know.'

Mr Ardill: ' – no enquiries or anything like that, just Paddy here and Seamus there, nobody knows where they are. And if they did that, the boys will soon take cold feet. And you may get one or two wrong ones by mistake, but what is that among so many? That's the only way to do it.'

SB: 'What about internment?'

Mr Ardill: 'Oh! That was only nonsense. A charade. There were far too many in prison; we can't afford to keep them. Look at those two fellas that were shot yesterday [two shoot-to-kill victims at a roadblock]. That's the only answer to them.'

The news came on the television and Mrs Ardill turned the sound up. 'Twenty-six people charged with terrorist offences on the evidence of the supergrass Raymond Gilmour have been acquitted . . . biggest trial in our legal history . . . the Lord Chief Justice said Gilmour was "entirely unworthy of belief" . . . "a selfish man to whose lips a lie came more easily than the truth".' To shouts of cheering prisoners being released in the Crumlin Road the voice continued: 'Gilmour's evidence could have virtually demolished the IRA in Londonderry . . .' A BBC reporter asked one of the released men about justice. Furious, the man replied 'No, it's not justice! How could two and a half years in prison be justice? I'm innocent!'

'Look at that,' said Austin Ardill, very annoyed. 'Now you *think* of what that has cost the country! The Lord Chief Justice has been presiding for six months over that, and all the barristers, solicitors and whatnot involved, and today he's thrown out the case! They're all out on the street, they're all Republicans they say, and they're more bitter than ever. And they'll go back and get involved. After what that has cost the country!'

Mrs Ardill: 'And they're going to get big compensation because they've spent two and a half years in prison.'

SB: 'I thought they couldn't get any compensation for that.'

Mrs Ardill: 'Well I don't know.'

Mr Ardill: 'No, I don't know they'll get compensation. But the thing is, it's scandalous.'

SB: 'But the whole supergrass thing is scandalous, as a structure.'

Mr Ardill: 'Yes, as a structure it's not good.'

Mrs Ardill: 'How are they to catch these people?'

Mr Ardill: 'In any case the police have to get bits of information if they're going to catch anybody.'

SB: 'But it's so unreliable, that kind of information.'

Mr Ardill: 'Well some of it shouldn't be, if they did it right. But it's like everything else, they're paying money. They're treating them too well.'

Mrs Ardill: 'Well I mean he couldn't do anything else. He's a very honourable man, the Lord Chief Justice. He wouldn't have done that if he felt Gilmour was truthful. You know Robbie Lowry, Austin. And you wouldn't say that he would be unjust. As a matter of fact he would *want* to convict them.'

Mr Ardill: 'In a war situation it's the survival of the fittest. And having courts of enquiry, bringing a wee nineteen-year-old soldier up for shooting some fella, and giving him a life sentence, I think they're scandalous! [A court in England had just convicted a soldier of the shooting-in-the-back murder of a youth in Belfast who was the road manager of the pop group Bananarama.]

Mrs Ardill: 'I thought that was very tough! He was only doing his duty!'

Mr Ardill: 'That was ridiculous. But it's a very difficult situation. Are you Catholic or Protestant?'

SB: 'Well, I descend from a long line of C of E clergymen – '

Mr Ardill: 'Oh that's not so bad. I like to know what I'm talking to. The Roman Church here in Ireland is quite different from the Roman Church anywhere else. They say it's Catholics fighting Protestants, but it's not really a religious war. It just happens the Catholics are on one side and the Protestants another. And you know the Roman Church, by and large, are at the back of the IRA. The two fellas that were shot dead up at Gransha Hospital the other day, when they went on a motorbike to shoot somebody and the security forces were tipped off and shot them dead [also in the back] – those two fellas got state funerals as far as the Roman Church was concerned! They had masses for them, they were heroes!'

Mr Ardill: 'A number of priests have been openly supporting them and working for them; would you have some more coffee? Journalists usually drink coffee and smoke cigarettes or cheroots or something, don't they? Wait'll I get something more on the fire. 'Cause I like to keep the heat up.'

As he loaded up the fire I asked him if he had given up hope of a political solution.

'No, no,' he said, 'there could be a political solution if there were somebody strong enough to bring it about. I have put forward several suggestions to various Secretaries of State as to how it should be done but och! no.'

He mentioned the episode his wife had spoken of at lunch, about meetings between himself and Martin Smyth and John Hume and Paddy Devlin to discuss a document for change: 'We went right through it and by and large they agreed with it. They were realists. We could have had a peace settlement in '74. Things were coming round. We had told Paisley, I should say, that we'd been asked to meet the SDLP and conduct discussions behind closed doors. And Paisley said, "You'll never do anything with those boys but if you can, God bless you" – that's just what he said. When we were getting very close to a settlement we informed him and he said, "I knew nothing about this, this is all behind scenes, making deals behind my back." He blew it all up, and that ended it, of course. He has such a big voice and he commands a lot of support, he can present a thing in a sensational fashion – if he was able to come out and say "Austin Ardill and Martin Smyth are making a deal with the SDLP behind our back," then the UDA and the Loyalists are up in arms. From that they've just been going from bad to worse. Now the SDLP are a broken body, and Sinn Fein have come up and there's just no dealing with them.

'Sinn Fein and the Provisionals are one and the same thing. There's no doubting that Gerry Adams and all are members of the IRA. The Sinn Fein is only a ruse to bluff the British government that they are a legitimate political organization.

'What we need is somebody now of statesman's stature: we virtually need a dictator. Northern Ireland's only a wee tuppence-halfpenny place, million and a half people, no size of a place at all. It's a very important little place nevertheless. I would run it the way you'd run a business. I don't think we need a cabinet structure. You see, the bone of contention between the Nationalists and the Unionists was that the Nationalists are in very much a minority, yet wanted a say in government, what they call power-sharing. Well now, power-sharing just doesn't work. We've tried it; it wouldn't work. You see, if you have a cabinet structure, the cabinet ministers are all privy councillors. Now how can you have a cabinet structure – with rebels in it? How can you discuss a security issue if you know that one or two of your colleagues are spies? So my idea would be to run the country without that. Have an elected body over at Stormont, and have the committee system, and the Secretary of State and two people elected from the Assembly who would act with him as advisers – and they would form the top management.'

SB: 'And these would all be Unionists?'

Mr Ardill: 'Well, they'd be elected from the House. Most likely they'd be Unionists or Alliance.'

SB: 'But there still would be no voice for Nationalists.'

Mr Ardill: 'No, but there'd be no voice for the masses of Unionists either, and the Nationalists would all have an equal say in the committees. You know what galls me so much – they talk about the unfair treatment and the iniquities of the Stormont government. That was a perfect system! As far as I was concerned everything was above board, and they all got a fair crack of the whip.'

Mrs Ardill: 'But you see, the Catholics wouldn't cooperate. In the 1930s and even later, the Catholics were not encouraged to go to university. The Church wanted to keep them down, to keep control, and they controlled the Catholic population in a very massive way. Then the Cardinals began to see that if they were ever going to get a united Ireland they would have to get their people educated to be able to take positions in the country. And then they started, and John Hume, Austin Currie, Bernadette Devlin, all that lot, those were the first to have further education.

And then they started agitating, and sitting down on the floor in the House of Commons, and going out and saying about discrimination against Catholics – but actually they discriminated against themselves! Isn't that correct, Austin? And I have seen the children brought to the opera house to see a Shakespeare play, and I have *seen* – before, always they sang the national anthem at the end, but now they would get up and walk out! Every time!'

Mr Ardill: 'Northern Ireland is part of the UK, full stop. No ifs, ands or buts. It's not up for sale or negotiation. And any citizen that wants to live in Northern Ireland is part of that state, and that's not an Irish republic, it's part of the UK. Cut out all the flannel and fluff and compromise and set up an administration to run the country fair and free for all.'

Mrs Ardill: 'A lot of the Catholics would dearly love to have it back the way it was before. It's the IRA that's keeping – '

Mr Ardill: 'People are very fickle. Over in the mainland, one election they'll vote Labour and the next they'll vote Conservative or whatever – they'll vote any way. But here the gunmen are in charge. And until the British government have the guts – excuse the expression – to deal with the gunmen, we're never going to get anywhere. I firmly believe that the masses of RC people would sing the national anthem if they got peace restored and the gunmen taken off their back.'

Mrs Ardill: 'Oh I think they would too.'

5
Crack

'The Ulster accent has always been an effective cordon sanitaire around the province,' a British critic wrote with some hauteur under the heading 'Wurr are they nah?' Some of the conversations I had in Belfast were by no means as simply heard as they may read – although generally people made allowances for me and saved the poetry for each other. But the accent alone could be no end of a mystery. It's simple enough to come to terms with feg and geg for cigarette and joke, but some of the pronunciation foxed me for months, and even then I couldn't get a foothold on some accents. People speak differently, I was told, even in this part of Belfast or that. Nothing to do with Protestants and Catholics, who talk alike despite little opportunity to hear each other. Film is fillum and flowers are flahrs without regard to tribe. But Catholics from the Falls swore they could tell a Catholic from the Short Strand, a mile away, by the accent. I couldn't distinguish, I was just banjaxed, as they say, by the vowels, whoever was using them, especially 'ow'. 'The Clyde has lifted,' someone said, then lost me for paragraphs as I tried to work out how. Mound is mind and now is nigh and sound is signed and I'll never live it dine. High nigh brine cie. For that matter, wise is ways and time is tame, and there is thar so whar is up the stars? Sammy is Sommy and Barry is Borry and he's hoppy as Lorry. Poor is pure. The unemployed, I was told, 'indulge in the purest kind of sex.' Purest? 'You know, in the ditch,' was the answer.

Many Cockneys think that Northern Irish is the ugliest

English to be heard, but that may be to draw attention away from their own. I found Belfast English lilting and lyrical, inventive and funny – and optimistic, because of the upward inflexion, suggesting doubt or paradox, at the end of most sentences. Threats or imprecations are less than convincing when the tune is so opposed to the message, and it's even hard to sound grossly pompous – despite the hideous overwork given the clichés 'grasping the nettle', 'taking the bull by the horns', 'standing up to be counted', and 'nailing his colours to the mast'. (Of these, the first two often tended to be what Catholics said other people ought to do, and the latter two what Protestants said they themselves did.)

One of the commonest words is 'crack'. There is no direct translation, which is what makes it such a good word.

'What's the crack?'

'You know the crack yerself.'

'He was sayin' til us about the Chinese, and all this here crack.'

'Then yer mon joined in the crack.'

'This is deadly crack.'

'The crack was 90!' (best crack; no one knew why it scored 90).

Or, as one of the incredibly rude horoscopes that are printed in one Sunday paper had it: 'If an affair is more complication than crack, then find some friends who are as shallow and insincere as yourself.'

The crack in Belfast (the big smoke) is *magic*. (The opposite of magic is *desperate*.) People greet each other: 'What about ye?' and sign off 'Alla best!' or 'Safe home!' 'C'mere till I tell ye,' starts the yarn. 'What do you reckon – the carry-on in this dunderin' place we live in! Sometimes it sickens the heart outta me' (or makes me heart-feared, or heart-scared). All right, nothing too complicated about that. But what's 'on the pig's back'? 'Doing fine.' Right. 'Wee buns'? 'No problem.' Yes. 'Looking away'? 'Doing a line.' Eh? 'Having a bit on the side.' Got it. How about 'a looter'? 'A dig.' A dig? 'You know, a swipe in the gub.' Oh.

Some people lived in kitchen houses, but the kitchen was the living room and the place where you cooked was the scullery or working kitchen which contained the jawbox (sink). He hopped himself well up (dressed warmly) to go out for the messages (shopping). Then one thing led to another and all this caper and carry-on and whenever he stopped at the pub, he hoovered up five pints and got poleaxed (jarred, puddled, punctured, paladic, plucked, blocked, blitzed, snattered, stocious, steamboats, elephantsed, arsified, blootered, lockjawed, or merely full). 'You know what yer mon's like, like.' – 'Och aye. Not a titter of wit.' 'Did you get the sausingers but?' – 'I'm only after goin' til the shop so.' ('But', 'so', and 'just' perch on the ends of all kinds of sentences. 'To' is nearly always 'til', 'when' is 'whenever' and 'them' is often 'them'uns'.) 'Catch yourself on! Go you back now.' 'I'm busy at the minute but.' 'Man dear, I seen the day you hadn't a knicker on your arse and now you got some money you're drinkin' it!' 'I could see you far enough!'

A child is a wain, which just has to come from 'wee one', yet you often hear 'wee wain'. 'He's a boul' wee divil, right enough. And he's always gurnin' (wailing). 'Sure your hands are absolutely mingeing, go you and wash! Would you stop runnin' around like a clarty wee gyp or I'll give you a looter, so I will.'

'Lord fuckin' love 'im like, he's a decent spud, he's dead sound, dead on, he's beezer (brilliant).' 'He's a Billy Whizz, a real gamester.' On the other hand he's a sleekit, narky, culchie tulip, a gansh or a glipe or an aleckadoo, in fact he's beezer (an eejit – idiot). Wait a minute, someone on the other side of town said beezer meant 'brilliant'. 'See, we can't agree on anything.'

When you are on the broo (unemployed) what is there to do but dander about? To be arrested is to be lifted or nathered or knollered or pranged or scooped – 'and then the peelers dirty-Joe'd him' (the police promised him a deal, then reneged). 'You're a-wantin' – someone's calling for you. 'I'm wearin' up til it' – getting ready.

There are more ways to question someone's sanity in Belfast than anywhere I can think of: he's a loop, a balloon, he's as odd as a nine-pound note. He's wired, a spacer, he's not the full shilling. He's as queer as a bottle of chips. He's wired up but not plugged in. He's a header, a headbin, a headbanger, a head-the-ball, his head's a marley. 'He took the head-staggers.' Och he's just not wise, so he's not.

What with all the ways of being drunk, crazy, or arrested, you'd think there would be more words for 'rain'.

Some mysteries just had to remain private. What's 'griskins'? 'It's horrible wee creatures which have never been described,' I was told, 'but when people use the term they know what they mean.'

Sitting in a house in Andersonstown, a huge Catholic housing estate in West Belfast, you are never in doubt about where you are. A helicopter hovers overhead and its clatter is the Belfast musak. Little time goes by without the soldier patrol – a 'brick' of four – passing by a few feet away, first three of them in riot gear clutching their SLRs as they steal forward; moments later a fourth treading backwards, alert for snipers. Sometimes the squaddies of a second brick or a third lurk furtive and terrified behind the walls and hedges across the road. Occasionally a six-wheeled Saracen, an armoured personnel carrier, whines slowly by, or a pig with two soldiers, pointing guns at angles to each other. Both the locals and the army call it a pig, but it doesn't look like a pig, more a strange sort of square-snouted reptile with lots of flaps and hatches. The locals don't often call these vehicles much of anything: when any of this goes by, they don't react at all. At any rate the conversation doesn't flag and nobody refers to the signs of war and occupation out there. To me each khaki person was a shock. It seemed worth mentioning, acknowledging. I thought of Kurt Vonnegut's 'So it goes.' I wanted to say each time they punctuated the day, so they go.

In the tiny snug living rooms, each with turf or coal fire and Sacred Heart on the wall, the sofas and chairs were constantly filled with people and more on the floor, together often with a horrible old dog; the television was on in the corner but no one was looking: there was too much to say, and the humanity of the atmosphere was as warming to some chilly part of the soul as the fire to the sodden feet. Children catapulted about the room and told you things and sat in your lap. The tap of the mail slot meant another caller with news of some tragedy or triumph. No one ever went off alone or sat in their own rooms, because those had space only for beds and were meant for sleeping; they were unheated and clammy but most of all there wasn't anybody else there. People wanted to be together and to talk.

At first I couldn't stand staying in such houses: no reading light, nowhere quiet to read anyway, the smell of damp and unbathed cur and rank old boots, the fug of smoke and heat building up, the chaos of all those people coming in and out, the tatty plastic imitation of luxury that is poverty, the constant explosion of emotion that is the real thing. And the guns going by. So they go.

At the Ryans' the atmosphere was always this way, if even more populous than most because of the eight children competing for attention. In so big a family it is necessary to work out your own stratagem to be noticed. One may do it with smiles and charm; another with earnest conversation; a third with cunning and a certain underhandedness; a fourth with showbiz skill at mimicry and joke-telling; another with hugs and cuddles; one just by sitting still and being very beautiful. Pairs of them had old rows to fight and there were also obvious lifelong alliances, but always conflicts broke out over what was whose, his turn or hers, or just for space on the couch or the nearest lap. A mini-eviction usually settled the quarrel. '*Move!*' said Rita. In and out they all trooped on errands: if you had no fridge and no money for quantities of goods, anything needed was bought on the spot. A child would be sent to deliver a message for lack of a phone. Someone had to go out back to fetch more turfs for the fire. Another was entrusted to take somewhere a plastic-wrapped parcel the size of a thumbnail, a letter for Long Kesh. Meanwhile the several conversations never faltered. At some point plates of food appeared; the tea never stopped. The only time that motion froze and talk stilled was when the television news came on with a local item. Afterwards, everything picked up exactly where it had left off. One evening of this and I was destroyed. The strange thing was that after a week of learning to accept it, getting to expect it, and then coming even to need it, leaving Andersonstown invariably felt like being orphaned. I felt as if at home I lived in an old cold stone castle just because it had rooms enough for everyone to be in another one from me.

Rita Ryan, as if she hadn't enough people to mother, took on as well the billeting of visitors among her friends. Delegations were always arriving from England or America. Homes were opened to all, though it meant the chosen family having to double up in their few beds. Having given over a whole bedroom to a Noraid American who came for Internment Day and stayed for months, she assigned me to a young couple nearby called Brendan and Kathy Mullin. Nobody seemed to know about the arrangement until midnight of the day I arrived, but if the Mullins minded they put a fine grace upon it.

Their place had just the same layout as the Ryans' and as everywhere on the estate: front living room, back kitchen, bedrooms above, bathroom at the top of the stairs; but theirs lacked one small extra room on top and had a mere four children, though these created just as much uproar. The fifteen-month-old baby stampeded in unpredictable directions babbling and spilling things; the three little girls, like Chrissie's daughter, were fond of smearing makeup around and showing off – that was what they were doing, except that they did it with a sort of delicacy, amounting to deference, new to me: they even shut up when asked, which was before I was ready because their act so beguiled me. 'Shall we dance? Shall we sing you a song?' and they were off on a trio: 'I look in the mirror and what do I see? Two eyes and a nose and a mouth and that's me – ' while their parents tried to tell me stories of raids and riots, encounters with Brits and Irish derring-do. While the feeling here, as at the Ryans', was of competition, it was of such a generous kind that the *spirit* of competition was missing.

It seemed constantly amazing how quickly one could adapt to the lack of almost everything. But there was little point in talking about this to people who hadn't a choice – just as congratulating oneself on being indifferent to nation and nationalism would mean nothing to someone who has the first not at all and the second only as a frustrated but sustaining dream. In the end poverty and discrimination mean *no choice*.

Coping with the no-choice of poverty with any sensitivity was not at all easy. It was one thing to suggest eating healthier food than chips and sweets, but how could they afford it? 'I forgot to bring a towel,' I said to Kathy Mullin, who instantly fetched me one. Only when I returned it at the end of the week did it dawn on me I had seen no other towel there: it was the family's towel. The teapot was battered, blackened and lidless. Since it worked harder than anything in the house I could buy them a new one; but how could I buy them a new everything? What about the other people I was getting to know down the road and for miles around? It wasn't luxuries that were missing but the simplest necessities. But whatever they had, they shared.

The political no-choice created an enviable solidarity and sense of purpose in Andersonstown. Hardly a household had no casualty of the Troubles. It was standard to find an extra child around whose mother was visiting her husband (or brother or sister) in jail, or both of whose parents were out on Sinn Fein business. Party work seemed an ingredient of many people's lives. And the children's political education was not neglected for a moment. One of the Ryan boys made a crack about Orangies and Rita slapped him. 'They're not the enemy! The Brits are the enemy!' Like a catechism all small Ryans were put through their paces: 'What did the Brits do?' – 'They blinded me auntie.' 'What did Maggie Thatcher do?' – 'She let the wee boys die' (on the hunger strike). The youngest one was encouraged to tell about the nice Provo who had lifted her on his shoulders at a demo. There was Irish dancing and singing and rude ditties about the Brits, which everyone howled together. But while conscious of and fighting racism against themselves, they indulged in their own, as in Dermot recounting with indignation a story about a West Indian in London telling him to go back where he came from. 'Black as the ace of spades! Telling *me* to go back where *I* came from!'

Dermot seldom had work. He was often to be found in

a demolished torpor on the couch staring at the television. When a job came along the change in him was drastic: his movements brisk, his smile ready. The best job was at a local Republican club running the bar. The story was never available except in small pieces, but it seemed he had kept accounts more scrupulously than custom allowed. Since drinking clubs are a big source of IRA revenue, you'd think he would have had strong allies. But there was of course no full explanation of what had gone wrong: only a few weeks after beginning, Dermot was out of work again and more depressed than ever. The reason given was 'a row'. Subsequently he found occasional jobs as a bricklayer, which he hated.

Once in a while it was possible to get him talking, and then it was hard to get him to stop. Tales of internment: how initially in Castlereagh his interrogation had resulted in broken ribs on both sides, a permanently damaged kidney and concussion. He had been questioned round the clock for seven days, and in between made to sit six inches from a painted silhouette, spattered with blood, with a beating if he moved. Once he had been taken up in a helicopter and, hooded, thrown out. The fact that the chopper was only feet above the ground and he wasn't hurt hadn't affected his fear. What had kept him going was anger. He had already decided he would die, so 'I wasn't going to give them satisfaction first.' And he'd got off very lightly: he knew men who had had sensory deprivation techniques done on them – hooded, starved, and spreadeagled against the wall unable to hear anything but white noise. Most of them had never recovered, he said.

The hardest torture to endure for him had been the time they came into his interrogation cubicle and asked him to 'Sing "The Sash".' He didn't know it, he said. 'Then sing "The Queen".' When he refused, they'd gone to the next cubicle and savagely beaten an old man, returned and asked Dermot to sing 'The Queen' again, repeating the process until the old man was nearly dead.

Internment in Long Kesh itself had been quite enjoyable after that and an intermediate stage in Crumlin Road jail, where he couldn't even get treatment for his injuries. For nearly a year and a half he'd been locked up in a long hut with three dozen friends, eating food that their wives somehow got for them, and refusing cooperation if their guards didn't call them 'Mister'. They had a radio and their wives' knickers hanging over their bunks. In the end they burned the hut down. Long Kesh had changed since then.

Once I asked him whether, with all the awful things that had happened to him and his family, he'd thought of leaving Belfast. 'I couldn't do it really,' he said. 'I'm too much a part of the place. It's not as if I have anything to give up. I don't own a stick of Belfast. Not one blade of grass. Not that it minds, ya know. But . . . although I haven't travelled the world, I have met people. And there's people in Belfast which – this may sound a wee bit ironic – the world should take their example from. When the madness clears. You know, in their sane moments. And I have lived through the sane moments. I'm very grateful for it. I have seen people at their best. You don't often get that opportunity.'

Around the streets when the weather made it possible the children played and the young men loitered. There was nothing else to do. In the house where I was staying, Brendan Mullin had nothing to do either. He had worked for an English firm which installed heating and treated walls for damp. The firm had gone bust two years earlier. Although there wasn't a radiator in Andersonstown and every other wall had damp patches, such work was not being done 'because the Housing Executive said it was too expensive.' Brendan had been paid £80 a week, in a firm which he said hired men for the same work in England for £125. He was now living on the dole without hope of finding another job but making himself busy doing housework.

Kathy carried most of the burden of the three children and had that woebegone image of herself that afflicts young mothers who never get enough sleep, whose entire intellectual sustenance is the chatter of illiterate innumerate sweeties, and whose time is divided among cleaning the house, dressing the little ones, undressing the little ones, and the next meal. She never complained. The downtrodden part of her was visibly thin in any case: the moment she started to tell a story of the past the lively vivid girl came back. And when one night we went out to a ceili (an Irish square-dance) she spent all her attention for hours on looking beautiful, succeeded, sprang to life, danced, laughed, sang. Next morning she was back on the sofa slouched into the posture of the defeated, covered with kids, and suddenly as two-dimensional again as the picture of Christ on the wall behind her, the picture that Brendan had trained baby Sean to point at when asked 'Where's God?'

There may have been nothing to do, but there were always stories. Both Brendan's and Kathy's fathers had been interned, one in the 1940s, one in the 1970s; Brendan had been jailed himself for a year; Kathy had grown up being raided by the army every night; both had been arrested too many times to count; all their relatives seemed to have gone in for exploits of the most improbable kind and suffered for them; their eldest daughter had been hit in the foot by a plastic bullet in this very room. There was just no end: as long as you could sit there, the stories kept coming, both adults talking at once and the children too, the whole atmosphere a running cabaret of the grotesque – because as dreadful as the details often were, the outcome often evoked laughter or a kind of wry triumph.

The latest outrage had as yet no conclusion, however. The Sunday after John Downes was killed by the plastic bullet in the 'Galvin demo', Kathy's brother Kieran had been shot in the back by a policeman, 'a peeler that was out after him'. Kieran had been beaten up earlier in the year by this policeman, it seemed, and had fought back; the RUC charged him with assault and he counter-sued. In court the judge had thrown the case out, but 'the cop told Kieran that he would "get him back" so he *shot* him in the back, with a plastic bullet at point-blank range.' This from Brendan. Kathy took up the tale: 'My sister was there too and when Kieran was shot she went into high-sterics. She asked the peeler why he shot my brother and he just turned round and says "He was riotin'." Riotin'! He was buyin' chips from a caravan! And then the peeler tried to make out Kieran was an informer, because he knew him by name you see.'

'He was in the hospital two weeks,' Brendan went on, 'and from it his nerves are wrecked. He imagines he's walkin' down the road and this peeler's going to shoot him dead now, you know? He's a carpenter you see, he's always using his hands, but now if he's in the pub he can't even lift a pint without the beer just spilling out of the glass, you know? He can't even write his own name. But there's worse cases, you know.'

'See where Kieran's concerned,' said Kathy, 'him and that wee boy Brian Stewart were friends. They was together the night before Brian was shot dead. I think all this still preys on him as well.' This led to stories about plastic bullets, including the charge that British soldiers sometimes doctored the bullets to make them more lethal, embedding bottle tops, batteries and razor blades in them.

Of most interest was their own experience as active Republicans – or what they would say of it (slightly more each time I came), including how they had met. Brendan had been in jail with Kathy's father, but hadn't known her then. 'The first time we met she threw a pint of beer over my head.'

'We went to this club one night,' Kathy amplified. 'I had to bring over this – stuff, you see. We didn't know each other, but all I knew was I had to bring – gear – to this club for somebody to pick up. And he didn't like using girls. So while I was waitin' on some stuff to take back, he's sittin' with his mates and I heard him say he had no money left and that was the only pint of beer he could have. And the sly remarks is coming over towards me. Then he said somethin' and I got the pint and poured it over his head. So I did. Here's me: "You'll say nothin' more about *me*."'

Brendan was laughing. 'My last pint. And then I got married til her!'

They brought out their wedding album, by far the most lavish thing in the house, with padded embossed covers and vast colour enlargements of them and the wedding party all beautifully dressed. Talking on top of each other, and baby Sean reeling around with excitement, they told a not altogether comprehensible story about the caterers at the wedding having difficulty getting through (through what, it was not clear) and the British Army having sprung to the rescue to escort them in. But the punch-line was audible enough: 'And we had *wanted men* at the wedding!'

Kathy grabbed Sean and took him upstairs for a bath, so Brendan could talk. He went back in time to a period of having been arrested 'for four hours twice a week for a couple of years. I was too young to be interned, so they just kept lifting me. Used to throw you in a cubicle of breeze-blocks and make you stand there with your fingertips against the wall, and if you moved they'd beat you with a baton on the back of the leg. Never questioned me. Just harassment. Used to get me in and I'd refuse even to give my name, say nothin' til 'em. 'Cause I knew what was comin' anyway, goin' to get a beatin' anyway, so you were better sayin' nothin'.' Finally, 'because I was a known Republican,' they accused him on the word of an RUC man of having been in possession of a weapon. 'No weapon was ever found. No witness. I applied for bail but I was remanded back in custody. But they dropped the charge at the end of it. Insufficient evidence. It's a good case of internment, you see, that's all it was.

'There was a mentally handicapped guy in with me. Nice guy from Derry. He was charged with murdering a soldier. No witnesses again. Never any evidence against the young fella. That guy was fifteen when the offence was supposed to have happened. He should never have been in there. But he got Secretary of State's Pleasure, which means he just stays there, no sentence. May never get out. That was 1974.'

'But there had to be a trial, no?'

'Oh there was a trial. But sure nine times out of ten you know the verdict before you go to court.'

'But if they had no evidence against him why did they continue with it?'

'Because in the Republican movement at that time, you recognized the court until the day of your trial, when you dispensed with counsel and refused to recognize it. So far as the Republican movement's concerned, the courts are illegal. They're a farce. So you didn't recognize them. So your man, once he refused to recognize it . . . although he's innocent, not involved or anything, nothin' to do with it. He wasn't even a member of the Republican movement by the way. He surprised everybody by refusing to recognize the court.'

It had got dark by now and six-year-old Josephine had come in from playing outside and wanted to sing me a song. Very lively and bright, she was dressed lovingly by her mother and usually the same as Teresa, who was a year younger, and Breige, a year younger yet. This day they were wearing pink and white frilly dresses – though by now the colours were more mud on mud – with their long brown hair done up in top-knots. Because her sisters were at an aunt's house, Josephine was eager to use the opportunity for a solo. First she sang a song, then she told her story.

'I was sittin' over thar' – she pointed at the couch, Kathy's station – 'and the Brits was outside' – she pointed out the window – 'and I was just sittin' over thar, and I was only three, and the Brits shot me on the foot, and it was *awful sore*.'

'What did you do?' I asked.

'I fired a stone at them. I did, I fired two stones at them.'

'Did you hit somebody?'

'No. I hit the Brits.'

'Ah.'

'And I had dreams about the Brits and I thought they was comin' in to raid the house. 'Cause they come into here the last time and Mammy was only here and I was havin' a ride in my uncle's car and I come back and the Brits was in our house. They was searchin' the place. They was searchin' under our beds and searchin' everywhar. And the beds was wrecked.'

'What happened to your uncle?' I asked, meaning the uncle with the car.

'He had to go to the hospital 'cause he was shot all over,' said Josephine. Maybe it was the same uncle.

'He wasn't shot all over,' Brendan said.

''Cept in his belly – '

'He was shot in the back,' corrected her father.

Josephine said: 'With a plastic bullit.'

'What were you shot with?' I asked.

'A plastic bullit.'

'What happened to the bullet? Did you keep it?'

'No, Daddy hit the Brit in the face with it.'

'What?' I turned to Brendan. 'You threw it at him?'

Brendan said, 'He was standin' in the middle of the street and I walked out right up to him face to face and I slapped him in the face with it.' Josephine started singing me another song. 'Well it was only the natural anger of a father,' Brendan said.

Brendan: 'I was born up the Shankill in '59. Up to '68 it was fifty-fifty. Then in '69 the Catholics started to pull out, you got threatenin' letters and things put through your letterbox. But my father was a staunch Republican and he wouldn't move. He said, "I live here, I've reared my family here and I'm not movin'." But then August '69 they came round the house and they dug up the back garden and they found rifles – old rifles, 1916 and that, probably UVF gear from years and years ago, you know? Either that or IRA gear, I don't know. But then we had to get out.' The night they moved, the house was burned down, though the family had left the curtains drawn so it would look inhabited. 'It was the first house on the Shankill to be raided by the RUC and army combined. They just surrounded the street and went for our house. They lifted me, my father, my two brothers. They held me four hours. They held my dad seven days and then they couldn't prove anything so they had to let him go.

'The housing conditions on the Shankill Road were even worse than they are here now, and they're still as bad. It's not just us, the Protestants have bad housing too. I can't understand them. They suffer the same as we do. I grew up with Protestants. I'd rather have Protestant neighbours than Catholics. They were great. I played football with a Protestant team. Followed the bands on the Twelfth of July, kick the Pope up and down the street. Nobody cared then, that was the early '60s, just children enjoying themselves, that was it.'

Another night after the children were in bed we got some alcohol in – beer for Brendan and Pernod for Kathy, who mixed it with fizzy white lemonade. (White lemonade is mixed with everything in Belfast, from Scotch to Southern Comfort to port to Cointreau and white wine.) She told me tale after tale of her life before marriage, the various (brief) employments which the Troubles had finished. Serving in a bakery she had been held up by hoods, one of whom she recognized despite his mask. 'Jesus, Joseph and Mary, the manager started murder over that' – her having given them the money – even though the hood 'wouldn't have shot me 'cause he knew me. But if I hada let on I knew *him* then the boss would have reported it to the army and the army would have taken me in for questioning.'

The job didn't last long in any case: 'This time a whole lot of hoods attacked the poor fella that was bringin' in the bread and buns. And there was only me and this other girl there. She gets the keys to go and lock the door and here's me: "We can't leave that wee fella out there on his own!" so we run out til him. We were murdered like, they nearly killed us that day. They got a load of firelighters and were firin' them into us, but we got the delivery fella into the bakery. And we phoned the boss to come up, and it was as if nothin' had happened! He just told me, "Can you open the shop now?" Here's me: "You're foolin'." I got my coat and I walked out.'

I asked her what the boss ought to have done.

'He shoulda closed down the shop and sent us home! That wee fella was in a terrible state. That wee fella's face was tore off him! And the boss expected that fella to get into his van and go for his next delivery, which was ridiculous. I closed the shop.'

Another job she'd had was in an art supply store downtown. 'There was a Protestant manager. He just thought he was the cream. You know, the top of the cake. I was upstairs on my own one day servin' this woman – the boss had said just before, "I'm goin' next door if there's any phone calls." And the next thing, *Bang*. A bomb. And here's me: Sacred Heart of Jesus! You could see nothin' because the shop was all smoke. But the customer was still there with her children. I got a towel and I wrapped the towel round them, you know, and they got downstairs. But I was still up the stairs. And they had just got away when the stairs came down. So everyone's out of the shop bar me and I had no way to get out. This fireman in the end climbed up the wall to get me to jump down into this big white thing two floors down. I'm terrified of heights. Here's me: "You've *no* hope, Charlie! I'm dyin' *here*." So he said, "You're goin' to have to get out, this place is gonna fall down wi' you." Here's me: "*No!*' And he got behind me and he just shoved me. I called him everything when I got round.

'Then I found out the bomb had gone off in the shop next door. I says, "My boss was in there!" Then somebody says to me, "There's three bodies in there, could you identify them?" And I thought they meant *bodies*, you know, a person, but dead like – not bits and pieces. Now the boss was sittin' under the bomb – not a mark on him. A girl on the second floor – I couldn't identify her. They only knew who she was from the ring on her finger. And the man who owned that shop, blown to pieces too.'

'Whose bomb was it?'

'It was the Provos'. It was meant for the bingo hall, but

it went off early. The fella that was droppin' it worked next door.'

'Was he killed?'

'No.'

'Was he caught?'

'Nope. They got another fella, and he wasn't the one that done it.'

'Why would they want to bomb a bingo hall?'

'I dunno what the reason was. Like it didn't make any sense to me to blow up a bloody bingo hall.'

Most of our conversations skirted around the law: whose law, who was breaking it, what became of them. Kneecapping was a touchy subject brought up more than once but usually deflected. One day I asked Brendan about something I'd heard on the BBC, that the punishment often involved not actually shooting through the kneecaps but immobilization with a shot in the thigh muscle. He said the BBC had been misinformed, that it was the kneecaps. Later someone else told me that it came in various degrees: for severe crimes, a .45, shot from the back, left a large exit hole, blowing off the cap entirely with nearly irreparable damage. Lesser criminals had their knees shot through the side. For the least serious it was just through the muscles. The worst offenders – informers, those who killed civilians – were executed.

I said to Brendan it seemed to me that punishment shootings created the same problem as 'British justice' in that, being summary, they too often could catch up the innocent.

'And there has been a lot of innocent people punished by the Irish Republican Army,' he said, just as 'the Brits get away with a lot in the name of putting away who they construe to be baddies by framing them for something they didn't do.' But the hood problem was a serious one and the RUC didn't react to it: 'If the RUC catch them, they let them go again because the hoods do their work for them.' In a general sense, he seemed to think that anything involving the oppression of Nationalists was encouraged by the law; but also the police recruited them as informers.

'We don't like to call them hoods, anyway, because it gives them character – "*We're the hoods*," you know – we'd just prefer to call them anti-social wee boys. They're criminals. There's never a weekend over at those shops that somebody's not given a hidin' by these wee lads. And the volunteers risk their lives if they're going to deal with it; if a volunteer gets a gun out of a dump he'll get ten years if the British Army catch him – for possession with intent to endanger life, right? Or if they see him with a gun, they open fire and they kill him. There's them two possibilities. It's not worth it. Over these wee gangsters. People are screaming to the Rah "Do something about the hoods", right? And then, if they kneecap somebody, "You shouldn't have hurt that poor child!" How do they win? I mean they've got no jail to put anybody in. They have to find some form of punishment.

'Gerry Adams went to a meeting last week, and there was this fella saying, "The IRA should do this and Sinn Fein should do that." And Gerry says to him: "If you had a gun, what would you do?" "I would do this and I would do that." So Gerry takes a notebook out and he opens it and he says, "What's your name? What's your address?" Your man starts to panic. "What are you taking my name and address for?" Gerry says, "I'll tell the IRA to supply you with a gun and you go out and do it." The best answer.'

'But it's gettin' beyond a joke,' said Kathy. 'See my brother I'm tellin' you about who was shot by a plastic bullet?'

'He's a fuckin' hood too,' said Brendan.

'He's a hood too,' Kathy confirmed. 'And if they come in to kneecap him I wouldn't stop them. He's up in court soon for joyridin'. And he's lookin' five years in front of him, and I hope he gets it. He was caught in a stolen car, goin' up the M-1 tryin' to kill himself.'

'See they get up in the morning,' Brendan went on, 'they sit about the house, they run wild, they stand at the street corner, they dander about. They're on the dole, they've no money to go anywhere except maybe once a week when they get their dole. So this is our problem.'

'Years ago we didn't have this,' Kathy said: 'not so much unemployment.'

Brendan disagreed. 'No, I think they feared them more.' The hoods feared the IRA, he meant.

'How did it change?' I asked.

'See, years ago, your record couldn't have a blemish on it, or the Republican movement wouldn't touch you. But a whole lotta fellas died, and many fellas went inside who got that discouraged and when they come out of jail didn't want to get involved again, you know? Because of the supergrasses. Years ago you could walk about these districts carryin' a gun, but if you're seen with a gun nowadays it's a cert the army'll be knocking the next morning. Touts.'

Kathy said, 'I was beat up one time by the army. I was at a disco and they pulled us out. The army raided the place every day, but this time they brought policewomen to search us. And no way was she searchin' me. Nobody touched me. Well me and my mate got stuck intil it. We had a big fight and all. At the end they took us and gave us a hiding. They took us in the jeep to arrest us, and halfway up the road they stopped, opened the door, threw us out, and beat the shite out of us. About four of them. Male and all. And we went home, and when my ma seen us she cracked up. And her and my mate's mammy marched down to Fort Monagh, and yer man – army intelligence – sat them down. Says, "Missus, you're here about your daughter Kathleen what didn't do nothin' and she's a wee innocent, right? C'mon til I show you her file." Well, my ma says he knew *every*thing I was up to. They were just waitin' on me to put a foot out of place and they had me.'

'How did they know?'

'People gettin' lifted,' said Brendan, 'and scared of bein' beat up in the barracks, told the Brits and peelers everything. But they wouldn't sign statements. So therefore you couldn't be brought to court and charged. They needed a witness, like you have with the supergrasses.'

'The support for the Rah isn't there any more anyway,' Kathy said. 'Not the way it used to be.'

'The Republican cause is a good cause,' Brendan qualified. 'But it takes a big thing to get the Nationalist people to do anything, you know. It took the hunger strike and Bobby Sands to die before they come out on the street in strength. And then it took the likes of John Downes murdered by the RUC for them to come out again, you know? It takes a tragedy to bring the Nationalist people out. Which is a terrible thing. But that's the way it goes.

'I'm a staunch Republican and I'll support them the whole way, but I definitely disagree with some of the things they do, some of the atrocities. But that's not going to change my opinion about Republicanism. Besides, our whole family, right to the time of my grandfather and all, were all Republicans from his age' – he nodded at the photo of his son which hung over the mantelpiece.

There was suddenly an almighty cacophony of dog-barking outside in the darkness. 'What's going on?'

'Army patrol,' Brendan said, drawing back a corner of curtain, and there they were, crouching, the menacing silhouette of guns.

'How do the dogs know?'

'They see the uniform. Dogs have sense, you know?'

In Andersonstown the dark is very dark. In December it begins before four. The street lights, if not broken, are too high up, out of scale with the houses – though there was an intact bicycle tyre around the base of one lamp-post for months, which got there, one of the Ryan children said (shrugging), because 'someone just shinnied up to the top and slipped it over.' As in all cheaply built estates there are no mature trees, only a few scrawny hedges encircling front gardens, so against the night sky one sees only a ragged edge of chimney pots and television aerials. Splodged wall murals, mostly to do with the hunger strike, stick out at you. Walking along in the long shadows with footsteps echoing behind you it's easy to dramatize yourself into the state of The Ancient Mariner:

> Like one, that on a lonesome road
> Doth walk in fear and dread,
> And having once turned round walks on,
> And turns no more his head;
> Because he knows, a frightful fiend
> Doth close behind him tread.

But the footsteps, passing, turn out to belong to an old woman in a hurry, and despite the fact that I am allegedly in the thick of terrorist gangsters, and certainly armed troops, I feel safer than on my own street in London. It is a community with everyone known and accounted for, and even if you have no specific role you belong to someone who does. I was on my way to the Ryans'.

I never took a trip to Belfast without making at least a brief visit to the Ryans and Mullins. But since neither family had a telephone, these were no-warning visits, with some more convenient than others.

The week before Christmas I turned up suddenly to find Rita in a dither, saying, 'It's a complicated night.' Nevertheless from my Christmas bundles she immediately assumed I'd come to stay and stretched a meal for ten – stew, boiled potatoes and Brussels sprouts, mostly potatoes – to feed an eleventh. As she and Mairead dished it out, she explained that a volunteer had been shot dead by the RUC after a failed ambush at the border, and because he came from Andytown his body had been brought home to lie in state at his family's house around the corner. There was going to be a hero's send-off that night, with a Guard of Honour of masked IRA men at his wake. At one point the body would be carried outside for the black-dressed men to shoot ceremonially over the coffin. 'Have you got a camera?' she asked. 'Oh, too bad.'

One 'complication' was that she had spent the day shopping, not for Christmas presents like everyone else, but for uniforms for the Guard of Honour. I was dying to ask where you shopped for IRA uniforms but she had other concerns: men would be coming by that evening to dress in them.

The same evening, they decided to decorate the Christmas tree. After tea Dermot brought in from the back yard a tall fat conifer and the furniture was moved around to accommodate it. He lay on the floor mending lights and Rita hung decorations in the windows. When Dermot got the colours to come on suddenly, the kids burst out cheering: 'Daddy does it again!' They each loaded the branches within their reach with little items they had made themselves, while Dermot adjusted the angel on top and Rita got out some decorative beads she remembered buying with her mother thirty-five years ago. In the pandemonium there was the occasional flap of the mail slot, signal that someone had arrived. Mostly the visitors were friends who came to cheer and advise, but sometimes no one came in from the entryway. If it was the odd volunteer come to pick up his uniform, presumably he was let in and ushered upstairs.

While the decorating continued I thought I'd use the chance to go to see Brendan and Kathy's children before they went to bed. They were still up, but Brendan was out, Kathy said, delivering presents to a relative. I had a roll around on the floor with the children, a cup of tea with Kathy, then got back to the Ryans' in time to see the lights glinting from the tree in the glowing firelight and the children singing songs. Nine-year-old Peter stationed himself in front of the television (still on, sound off) to sing *The Dying Rebel*:

> My only son was shot in Dublin
> Fighting for his country bold
> He stood for Ireland, and for Ireland only,
> By the harp, the shamrock, green, white and gold.

He sang with great passion and seriousness, and I thought (as some of them must have done) of the dead volunteer around the corner. The littler ones wanted to do numbers too: 'I had a wee dog and his name was Jack, he piddled all over the Union Jack, rinky dinky parley voo.' A version of Mary had a Little Lamb: 'Hurrah for Mary, Hurrah for the lamb, Hurrah for the Provos who didn't give a damn. And everywhere that Mary went the lamb was sure to go, Shoutin' out the battle cry of free-eedom.' Or, with regard to the season, 'Jingle bells, Santa smells, a hundred miles away. He did a fart behind a cart and blew up the UDA.' Everybody was giggling and the decorations tinkled on the tree.

Time passed and an idyllic (if eccentric) family Christmas scene played itself out; nothing more was said of uniforms or Guards of Honour. I was staying elsewhere that night and worried about being late. Finally I said that

I hoped the ceremony would be happening soon because I had to leave. 'Oh it happened already,' said Rita. 'While you were out.'

I was fed up and ashamed of it, but there was nothing to do about such bad luck. On the way to get a black taxi, I passed by the Mullins' to say good night. Brendan still wasn't there.

Thinking about it later, I wondered if it had involved more than bad luck. Suddenly one of the few allusions Brendan had made to his life as an active Republican came back to me: he'd been involved in some street violence wearing a balaclava, and when he'd got home his mother had given him a thrashing. 'She'd seen me out there,' he said, 'and she knew me from my dander.'

6
The UDA – Everything to Lose

Now and then the way we've got used to the world's ratcheting madness is still amazing – some flash in time and a distant sanity is recalled, re-called, as if still operative. It seems to happen in big and trivial moments indiscriminately – when you suddenly catch yourself having the loony idea that this bus-ride, which came to forty pence last week and fifty pence this, can still be had for the twopence it once cost *all the time*; and then the jolt back from reality to 'reality'. Or for some silly reason you become unhinged enough to assume it's still a life where food is not routinely sprayed, irradiated or polluted with poison, or where what the 'leaders' say is even partly true.

Walking into a Belfast department store where the windows displayed T-shirts stencilled MENTAL BLOCK and BRAIN DAMAGE and where, just inside, a plaster mannequin (nattily dressed) was balanced on its head, I met, as well as the usual wall of very loud pop music, a young man running a metal detector over everyone. It gave a low moan as it met my bag but he showed no interest and waved me through.

On the up escalator I had the jolt: I have come in here in the usual way, finding it not even worthy of note to be tested for guns and bombs before being allowed to look at shirts advertising cerebral deficiencies (anyway I was after socks). In Belfast, after all, people are searched even before admission to the airport, let alone a plane, and only very recently did they suspend security checks of everyone going into the city centre – the gates and security sheds are still there. But what kind of place is it where the children grow up believing that hitting even this boutique must be seriously guarded against, with no cause for surprise, never mind dismay, and we won't even consider outrage? When will this be standard everywhere?

Retreating out again I took another look at the fellow with the metal detector. He was actually a boy, and his eyes didn't match, giving him rather a daft look. His machine was a grey box with a silvery loop protruding, and as he waved it casually over incomers, he looked near death from boredom.

'What does it do exactly?' I asked him.

It perked him up, being addressed as if he were there. 'It's supposed to pick up different kinds of metal,' he said importantly, out of the side of his mouth.

'Why does it go off for everyone?'

'Well,' he explained, 'keys, money – everyone's got some metal on them.'

'But if it always goes off, isn't it sort of pointless?'

Suddenly it was as if his life were passing before his eyes and they actually matched. 'You're right!' he said. 'It just goes off, right enough! It goes off if you push the button!' He showed me the button under his index finger and demonstrated that it went off even with no metal in view. 'It's a complete waste of *time*!' he nearly shouted, alarming two women coming in as he waved his wand over them without pushing the button: nothing happened. 'It's useless! *Useless!*'

I left him there either less or more happy than when I came in.

Jolt and double jolt. You are supposed to become used to being checked although since you are not really being checked, in fact you are supposed to become used to the *idea* of being checked, not to being checked. And since everyone in Belfast to whom I mentioned this anomaly

was aware of it, it seemed likely the bombers were too.
'Anyway it's employment,' several people said.

It's impossible to give a picture of Belfast: the best you can do is represent it as a collage, jumbled scraps which closer up have little relationship beyond their contiguity. Seeing the city suddenly as you approach over the hills from the airport it seems whole enough, if slashed through with new motorways: the giant cranes and gantries of the shipyard, like a centrepiece on a dinner table, hovering above the seemingly compact mass round the harbour and the winding river Lagan. Down below, when you are there within it, the first impression each time is of some hideous strain of military-industrial leprosy, excrescences of war and decay. Although the place is by no means all or even half that way, enough of it is to give a shock that numbs you at first to the rest. Later, further, past the blight, it begins to seem more than any other city a collection of alien villages whose occupants meet only in the centre, anonymously, in the universal truce of consumerism. The residual civility of the British and the traditional kindness of the Irish mask a multitude of feelings. Crowds pushing among Marks & Spencer, British Home Stores, Boots, Burton, Dolcis, make it seem like any biggish British town – if you keep your eyes averted from the security gates on all sides, the flak jackets worn by the law, or the fellow pointing his gun at you out the back of that jeep. But the people start to sort themselves out like some great unwinding Maypole at the City Hall, ringed round with parked buses waiting to head east (the ones on the west), south (on the east) and so on. (Apparently a German called Werner Heubeck was imported to organize the buses, and by some playful whim decreed that contact be kept up to the last tangled minute of parcels and shoppers. The buses south don't leave too often, giving you lots of time to wonder at his inscrutable scheme.)

The buses south don't leave too often because the people there have cars. But servants travel on them, the elderly go one route to a hospital, and twice a day thick mobs of uniformed schoolgirls crush inside and flash their passes without a let-up in their giggling and gossiping. Queen's University, kempt and green, goes by, an advertisement for tradition and civilization, and you can see some of its eight thousand students strolling about untroubled, un-Troubled. The lovely park in which the University is set is merely an intro to the foliage which is the main feature of life further south, where nothing but the occasional ramp in a side road or a yellow metal barricade (open but ready) reminds you where you are. Nobody here would be so petty as to fuss about sectarianism. They are mostly Protestants anyway.

But the majority of Protestants can't afford to rise above such considerations. The buses east, where the body of them live, pass through a barrier at Donegall Place where there is a stop for a security check – someone in uniform boards and marches perfunctorily up the aisle and back again. The guard seldom glances at the passengers or at anything else except down, but not with care enough to find a bomb, and what else could it be about? Across a gash of motorway, over the river, the bus passes outside the Catholic enclave of Short Strand. Beside it, nothing. So much of the city seems unused – either derelict buildings or littered wasteland. The Bronx. In the largest cleared spaces the new estates sprout. Brick two-storeyed houses, terraced and semi-detached, with small front gardens and net curtains looped in picture windows, the square flickering blob of the TV visible through many. Encased in new brick or old brick, life seems a contained business, the only view out through that small ever-on box with its plastic beauties and comics, catastrophes and politicians.

The Newtownards Road provides glimpses of the rows of ancient miniature houses which help give Belfast the reputation, so proudly proclaimed by its natives, of having the worst housing in Europe. By now there are inside toilets in most, but the effect is narrow, crowded, sordid.

But looked at more carefully the old houses give another impression. There is something warmly human-sized about them, like the houses children draw and feel comfortable with, tidy and pleasantly proportioned and with an attention to detail which differs from street to street – plaster or tile fringes, or rounded windows or fan-shaped brickwork above the doors. They have a mellow ageless solidity (despite some bricked-up windows signalling their demise) lacking in the utilitarian products of the last two decades, plunked around insubstantially as if about to blow away. Above all there is the care they have been given by their occupants. The windows sparkled, the paintwork and curtains were fresh, and the greatest sign of how cherished they were was the absence of that overwhelming sign of human disaffection, graffiti. The newer estates were blotched and scrawled with initials and nicknames – DAZ, SOUP, WONKA – and the odd UVF or FTP for seasoning. (FTP, the Protestant counterpart of FTQ on the other side of town, displays the local unseemly attitude to Pope or Queen.) 6 INTO 26 WON'T GO, an old byword by now. Major political decoration in Protestant Belfast takes the form of elaborate, unspoiled murals on gable-ends, low on mottoes (ONE FAITH/ONE CROWN, IN GOD OUR TRUST, NO SURRENDER, or just 1690 – ULSTER), with a big King Billy on a white horse, or a crown on a Bible, or the Union Jack and the flag of Ulster indissolubly linked. There have been Protestant murals marking territory in East Belfast since the 1920s, long pre-dating the Nationalist ones.

The shoppers on the Newtownards Road look unhealthy and wear the bright synthetic clothing that the poor wear everywhere. If you smile at them they smile back, and nod and wish you the time of day, not like the English who tend to look affronted by such behaviour, if not terrified. Above the heads the signs on the shops and frequent churches say FRESH MEAT CENTRE; PAULS BIG SAVINGS – ABC REGALIA DIVISION; TRY CLARES HOME COOKED SAVOURY FOODS: ROAST KNEE; John Armstrong Ladie's Wear; JESUS CHRIST IS LORD, Dallas Hot Food Bar; Bible Christian Union and, above PICK 'N PLAY and the 5p SHOP, It Is Appointed Unto Man Once to Die, After This The Judgement. The Westbourne Glentoran Supporters Club and a firm of coach builders have closed-circuit cameras aimed at the entrances. So does the UDA.

The Ulster Defence Association's office was not unlike Sinn Fein's. Besides the camera to identify intruders, there was a fine-mesh grille inside, open but presumably useful for sieges, and an array of cruising bruisers suggesting a readiness to meet trouble with trouble. They were not short of camaraderie and good humour, possibly filtered down from Supreme Commander Andy Tyrie whose door had a sign reading 'SHORT KESH'. Another notice on the stairs begged those brutes trooping up and down to refrain from throwing butts on the floor: 'You are giving the cockroaches cancer.'

In a tiny reception cubicle with the switchboard and TV monitor sat Hester, whom I'd come to see, with as many people lounging around as space permitted and a constant commotion of bells and buzzers. Apart from another woman who made tea, the atmosphere was heavily male, and male heavy at that. Hester was obviously more than a mere receptionist – she appeared almost to choreograph the place, to know everybody's business and, with an effective blend of chiding, wisecracking and mothering, to take on and tame the more threatening of the species. The tough streak was the more engaging considering her small size and prettiness, her provocative clothes, obvious warmth, even more obvious energy, and tiny hands with bitten nails. Before all this began, she had been a cabaret dancer. She still moved like one, and with the kind of confidence that reassures rather than undermines. She fixed whomever she was addressing with huge hooded eyes that seemed to be the same unlikely shade of blond as her hair, and talked with gusto and profanity, giving off the sense of being alive to her limits.

She took me into a quiet room to talk, where we hovered over an electric fire. Great big men peeked around the door now and then as we talked, ostensibly seeking something. One of them actually was: his raincoat. The others just looked nosy, or maybe they didn't know what to do without Hester to ask.

I began with a question about the Protestant women – why they seemed to be so inert, with no visible activity coming from them on any front, local, feminist, or international, apart from those married to supergrass victims.

'The women are changing over here but very very gradually. With social issues they're probably more inclined to complain among each other than actually stand up and be counted. If you talked to them about nuclear war – even if they felt strongly about it, because of the Troubles it would be very secondary. If people are being shot down in your own home town and your country's being held to ransom, if you're wanting to do something it's a case of starting at home.

'I don't want to appear hostile' – there had been a certain caginess about setting this interview up – 'but quite a lot of the media do a one-sided thing, and it's more than unfair. Here we're doing our best to try and cope with things, and you come across some programme and it looks as if everything you've tried to do – why, why have you even tried? These people are brainwashed before they even come to Belfast. This is what made me hesitate. But there are all sorts of levels here for such a small place, and I would like you to see a good broad view.' Then she began her own story.

'Well, '68, '69, those sort of years. I came from East Belfast, from the suburbs. I was the eldest of seven, and I was the only one who went across to West Belfast – and that was by accident. I got married and I put my name down for a council flat, and you had to name the area of your choice. At one point they said, "Look, the areas that you put your name down for, there's a long list, but we can move you to a place called Suffolk." I'd never heard of Suffolk except as a place in England. But Suffolk was beside Andersonstown; and I decided to go up and have a look. It was lovely – maisonettes and flats and houses. So I went back to the housing authority and put it down as my number one choice.

'Most Catholic people would say when you're Protestant and you live in Belfast, you've automatically got a house. I had a hard time getting my house, just as they would have had. But I got it and I moved in two or three weeks before Christmas. I was expecting Maria. There were quite a lot of young couples around there, and you got on pretty well. It was a mixed area. I got to know my neighbours and I absolutely loved Suffolk.

'I don't think I was terribly socially conscious, because I'd been a dancer, but I did notice a very big need for a pedestrian crossing. A youngster just a couple of doors from us was knocked down and killed. People said they'd gone to different authorities and I couldn't accept the answers they were given. That was my downfall. I went to a Unionist meeting and created merry hell; and they agreed there was a need. They did this, that and the other thing, Stormont, Police Authority, but there wasn't much movement. And I says "Right", and I go to the women and I says, "C'mon with your prams and we'll block the road, we'll get a pedestrian crossing." And we got one!

'I'd started to look round and see what was needed. To my mind Unionists were wee fuddy-duddies, like the Conservative Party, the fur-coat brigade, and I didn't want to have anything to do with them. But at their meetings most were just the ordinary people of the area, and I started to get to know them. Then they asked me to be the secretary of the small local branch. I said, "No way, I'm a dancer and there's no way I could be in an office doing officey kind of things." And they said it's not like that, it's part-time etc., and I said all right, I'd give it a bash. Well it worked out okay. But it got me into looking and reading and getting myself informed. And I saw things I didn't like.'

One of the things Hester didn't like, when the Civil Rights Movement brought it to her attention, was the voting system. Apart from some very obvious gerrymandering to keep the Catholic vote down, there was a property qualification in Northern Ireland up until the late '60s which operated against the poor. Those with nothing to their name could not vote at all; those with two or more properties were allowed two or more votes. In 1968 the first marchers took this, together with housing and unemployment, as one of the issues. But unpoliticized as she was then, it was news to Hester: 'I mean it didn't enter my head that people didn't *have* one-man-one-vote! And when I found out, I nearly went mad – WHAT? And there was a lot of arguing with my family: I was going to march.

'"They're a pack of rebels," I was told, and I said I

don't give a damn. My husband thought I had turned funny in the brain because he was a real pacifist and he was studying hard, didn't care about all these things that I got angry about but if it kept me happy . . . I was warned and told that you don't trust Catholics. And I stood up for them and I said, "Some of these people happen to be my friends. Some are Protestants and some are Catholics but they're good people." "Ah well, you'll soon learn," this kind of attitude. But it turned out I had a strep throat the week before the march and it got really bad so I didn't get to go.

'After that there were a few social things but no bad hassle. But internment morning did make a change in my life. I heard a lot of noise and I went to the door and there were lorryfuls of youths flinging bottles, shouting "Get out, you Orange Bs," all sorts of abuse. God almighty, what the hell's happening? A couple of neighbours said it was internment. I said, "What do you mean, internment?" – "They're lifting people and no one can get to work, can't get through" – all this carry-on, really bad, you know? All I could think of was Maria and Campbell, the wee ones – I felt really vulnerable with them – and at breakfast I asked them how they'd like to go to their Auntie Patsy's for a week. I had no idea how I was going to get them over to East Belfast: the phones weren't working, the security forces were practically non-existent, it was absolute madness. People termed as friends suddenly counted me as their enemy, and it was frightening. But I threw things in plastic bags quickly for the kids and got them out – that was a big relief.

'Little groups of people were standing about, people were burning buses down at one end, a lot of women were banging bin lids. I thought it was mental. You see, though I had gone into politics on the fringe I was still very naïve. I didn't know what lay behind most things. All I knew was that what they were doing was wrong. You were hearing rumours about people being thrown out of their houses and I thought it was just gossip. But three hours later I believed it, because Catholic people were coming round (I didn't say Republican people then, where now I'd be inclined to say Republican or Provisional IRA) – not all of them would have been my friends but they'd have known me, known I wasn't a bad cat or something – and putting people out of their houses, saying, "Just get the fuck out of the road now! We're taking this area over, this is our area." There were varying degrees of intimidation – some at gunpoint, others with threats, others who didn't need to be threatened because they knew their next-door neighbour had been so that was enough for them.

'Within a week seventy-nine people were put out of their houses in that area. I wanted the people to stay and say, To hell with ya, this is our country as well as yours, and we have a right to live here. But when people are panicking . . . It was a very traumatic time.

'With the help of a few others I got the school opened and at least got a couple of hundred kids in out of the road and things like that. But the whole thing was opening my eyes. First of all I was very very bitter. I says, My mammy's right, me da's right: these people that I'd counted as friends and stood up for against all in my family are treating me as if I were some sort of an alien. I says to myself, Right, we're not going to take any more of this. And I went up to them and said, "Right, this is as far as yous are going. You're not coming down to take any more houses." Some of the Catholic people were willing to talk, but others were throwing stones and all the rest. By that time other Protestants had come round, so it was one mob against another. And the buses were burning on the roads – the place was an absolute mess.

'Anyway I got a phone call from my family. They're

living in a completely different world, remember: over where it's nice and safe. And they heard there was trouble and they wanted me to move. I says, "No way am I moving. No way, for a pack of rabble who are trying to put me out."

'But I'd started to change my views. I'll give you an example. My young lad – who's grown up now, he's eighteen – had a very deep voice for a kid, and there used to be a song called "I Was Born Under a Wandering Star". Well, with his voice he was asked to sing, you know, as a party piece. He was only about four. There was a family two or three doors down from us, a Catholic family, Devlins they were, and the old woman used to bake home-made bread, and she used to ask, "Come on in" and put him up on the table and, "Come on, sing Wandering Star" and Campbell would get the hot bread with the butter on it. It was just, you know, a game. She was like an old granny to him, you know. Two days after internment, Campbell was out on the street, and she just walked right by! Now that might sound petty, but it hurt me – because the child couldn't understand.

'Well, about four months later the Republicans had got themselves organized and then maybe sent out a dozen youths to stone people's houses. Now maybe ten houses are stoned – it would only take two people to move to frighten others. And the rumours.

'The intimidation was on all kinds of levels. For example Maria and Campbell went to Sunday School, and before that I'd send them round for the newspapers and a packet of smokes. One Sunday they were beaten with sticks – now not hard, but they were frightened. And that happened because they belonged to me. I was known – I have a bad temper and when I see something wrong, I can't shut my mouth.

'Places where I'd gone on walks with the kiddies I could

no longer go. There was a local class for Irish dancing – which to me is very attractive. When Maria went there, she was sent to Coventry. I thought it was bloody rotten. Through all this I tried to shield the children. I didn't blame the Catholics; they were still the age where you could say, "That's the bad boys doing that." Like the bogeyman.

'Meanwhile there was sporadic gunfire and bomb attacks at the local shops or the local British Legion Club. The houses kept emptying. Lenadoon Walk became Catholic, Doon Road totally Catholic, half of Horn Drive, where I lived, became Catholic – which meant that you were living on a border edge, right?

'One night in November, about tea-time, I'd done the dishes and thought I'd go out and get the paper and some sweets for the kids. There was a river with a little bridge at the corner of Horn Drive, and when two or three long-haired lads came along in the dark, saying "Hiya Hester," I just thought it was Protestant fellas. In the minute or two that I'd said "Hello" – or seconds – they'd grabbed me and said, "We know you've been helping them, now c'mon," and pushing and shoving. I had high boots on, platforms at that time, and one of the heels broke. Whether they had any intention of throwing me into that river I don't know, but you could hear a foot patrol coming, heavy army boots, and I heard them saying, "Okay they're coming, right, get under." I still didn't think of anything sectarian: I was frightened to hell's gates, I tried to shout but it wasn't a scream that was coming out, it was "Mammy!" – which was stupid, you know, and it sort of come out like a croak. I got pushed right underneath this bloody bridge. It was all muck at that time of year, sodden with muck. And I realized then that one had a gun with him. "We know you've been helping them. What have you been telling them?" I didn't know who or what they were talking about, and even if I had been helping anyone, my mouth wasn't working for me. As the foot patrol was coming up – must have been high on the bridge and we were right underneath, you see – they threw me hard, I hit a sort of rock, and they ran across the river – I could hear the squelch of their feet – and they disappeared. I was frightened to get out. I didn't know whether they had gone for good. I don't know how long I lay there before I came out. I knew I was wet and sore and I tried to walk but there was no heel on my boot.

'I knocked at the first house. The woman screamed when she saw me: I think she thought I'd been tarred and feathered, I was so covered in muck. They sent for the security forces. I only told them what I've told you, I couldn't tell them a lot. So they went out hunting but I don't think –

'Well after that I started to get pretty bitter towards the Republicans, so I decided, Right, am I going to sit here or do I stand up and be counted? So I decided to leave the Unionist Association because they weren't doing anything. I put that in writing to them and gave my reasons. You see if you're under threat, under siege, to my mind you needed to get yourselves together, needed to help the community, and not just on Sundays. I decided to work to help people. Gradually with doing that I came in contact with the Ulster Defence Association.

'I became very aware of my own identity, what I felt I belonged to. Not so much with my family, who were very respectable Loyalists, but when I would come to doing anything, they said, "Oh no, you don't do that, you'll get yourself known." I says, "I'm already known." "Well then you're going to get yourself murdered." Here's me: "Don't be talking rubbish." Looking back, they were sensible.

'My husband was out of all this. He'd be sitting reading a *Which?* magazine in the back of the house with the bullets flying off the walls. We grew further apart. I think I might have grown apart from him anyway, but he was a decent bloke, great father, should have been put in charge of about two hundred kids. We had a good talk. I knew I was going to leave in the end – I was there solely for those kids. We had the one thing in common – we both loved the kids.

'I was really worried about this bitterness starting inside me against the Republican movement – if the kids started to ask questions, how to answer them. It's a very big responsibility: because I started to almost hate the Provisional IRA. Most people would pass that on to their kids without a thought. They were getting past the stage where you could say "That's the bad boys."

'Well, with the marriage breaking down I went out socially, maybe once a week. I went out for a bit of a giggle every Monday night with about five girls to the Lisburn Hotel where they had a cabaret and discotheque. One time on the way I met a foot patrol – it was the Green Howards, and one of them, you called him Decker, says, "Is that you going out to enjoy yourself, Hester?" I says, "Too right."

'Around ten there was a phone call for one of the girls with me. She came back in an awful state, saying "We're needing to get back" – her baby sitter was ringing to tell her that Lenadoon was burning. We got home about half ten to eleven and there were clusters of people and all the lights out, but no burning that I could see. I came in and my husband says, there was trouble over there, you know, but the kids were all right. It turned out that a Loyalist mob had gone mad and had started to retaliate by putting Catholics out of their houses.

'A couple of days later the police came and interviewed me. About a month later they interviewed me again. Then I was washing the windows about a week after that and a policeman came along and he says, "Hiya Hester, you all right?" I says, "Yeah." He says, "Would you like to come down to Lisburn?" I says, "The kids come out of school at two, I'll have to be back." – "Oh we'll have you back by then." I says, "What for?" And he says, "We want to have a chat with you." Well I didn't really want to go but I went. And they charged me! They charged me with intimidation. I don't know what all, leading a hundred men up Lenadoon and burning, all sorts of bloody things. I couldn't believe it like, you know? So here's me: fuck it, I know where I was, everybody knows where I was.

'Well I was eleven months on bail, in which time I'd been in the papers and on the news. I had dozens of obscene threatening letters from Republicans. I was really angry by this time – anger that doesn't go away for a while.

'When it came to my court case, this Catholic woman stood up and said she'd seen me leading men up Lenadoon. That was a bloody lie for starters. The Green Howard regiment were serving in Germany by then, and they flew three Green Howards the whole way back to say they had also seen me! I couldn't believe this! I had been good to these men! All I could think was I knew one of the fellas' names was Decker, but he wasn't called. These three others stood up and said they'd seen someone answering my description doing these things.

'Well I got the girls to speak up for me, but that didn't do. And here's me: "Right, there were military police there and one of them was named Gary." They found out where he was, at Aldergrove. They were willing to fly three Green Howards from Germany to speak against me, but that MP wasn't allowed to come from Aldergrove, which is only twenty–thirty miles away! This is what made me think it was a set-up job, that I was being framed because I had started to become an embarrassment to the authorities.

My solicitor had to subpoena his commanding officer. To this day I haven't seen that boy to thank him: he told the truth. Only for him that I got off.

'I had a lot of threats after the court case, and the marriage was real shaky. I had a lot of thinking to do. So I decided I would try to live away, go to Scotland, because I could think and look at things a wee bit more. I lost the Suffolk house anyway because they put a bazooka through the roof. Like a doll's house, the roof was just peeled off.

'Then I met John in Scotland – probably at a very vulnerable point. I have two wee boys by John now. I stayed in Scotland for a year and a half, but I was constantly feeling as if I'd ditched a sinking ship: my roots were here, and what the hell was I doing over there? But I decided second time around, I'm not going to make a mess of it, I don't care what happens, I'm not going to get involved, and I'm not going to stick my neck out for people who . . . if you've been in the news, that bit of dirt always sticks.

'But I'd become friendly over the years with different UDA people – some whom I respected, who'd try to do the decent thing. So now and then when something was wrong in the Protestant community I'd go down to UDA headquarters and say, "What the hell is happening?" Gradually the bitterness wore away and I started to think a wee bit more constructively, I hope, about the country. I'd been bitter, you see, because I'd been wrongly accused. But gradually I started to see that everyone was not to blame for that. I was living in the suburbs of East Belfast in Dundonald, and it's different there – most of the murders and the atrocities take place either on security forces or sometimes in bombing, but there isn't an actual threat to your life when you're sitting in your Dundonald living room.

'The only people that I could see was doing anything

was the Ulster Defence Association. I started to think, if my court case had gone wrong and I'd been put in jail, who would have looked after me? The Ulster Defence Association. Then Andy Tyrie asked me did I want to work on a part-time basis. He'd seen me writing in, calling in to ask what's going on. I'd had several long talks with Andy and from what I could find out, he seemed to want a better society and to try and help people.

'Of course you'd have the odd stupid ones that would go out and do something that was completely against what the UDA stood for, a murder or robbery, then say, "I'm in the UDA" and the press would latch on to it. There's quite a lot of things they did in the past. But there's no way Andy would condone murders of Catholics just because they're Catholic. No right-thinking person would.

'Andy has been working very hard to pick and choose who is accepted now. Trying to restructure, train and reorganize, get rid of rabble. It's a slow process. A lot of in-depth interviewing. Then there's a period of training. Communications, first aid, a general run of everything – to have a bloke you could rely on if there's an emergency.

'What people forget is that when law and order broke down, in the early '70s, they left us to our own devices. They allowed the Republicans to have barricades in the streets. Now you don't need to have a brilliant imagination to know what was going on behind those barricades, that they were actually going from strength to strength. They were running their own radio station – I didn't realize then the importance of a good propaganda machine. The Protestant community were always way behind in that.'

A head came round the door, one which had been there before.

'Hello Andy,' said Hester.

The Supreme Commander was a pleasant-looking man in his late forties who looked as if his face, under its moustache and blue-tinted glasses, wasn't quite finished. He said now that he had an appointment soon, so if I wanted to talk to him this was the only chance. I hadn't actually asked to talk to him.

Andy Tyrie brings to mind the old idea that real strength lies in resilience. He might bend to stress but not break. His longevity as top man of the Ulster Defence Association – the largest paramilitary organization in Northern Ireland and the only one never proscribed, with a membership varying from forty thousand in the mid-70s to about ten thousand now – has been remarkable in such a boiling world. Since 1973 he had seen it past many changes, inheriting a loose confederation of local vigilante groups formed on an ad hoc basis to defend their areas – with some members, generally using the name Ulster Freedom Fighters, responsible not only for random sectarian murder but also for sadistic torture first. Under his leadership the UDA became more disciplined and centralized; went through a period of politicization when the organization championed an independent Ulster with Catholic participation; and has now geared itself to prepare for Doomsday with the Ulster Defence Force, an elite fighting body. It has an unsavoury reputation, not only for the enormities committed by its members in the past, but for alleged protection racketeering and the involvement of some of its members in embezzling and extorting. These were 'the rabble' Hester had alluded to, and the idea now was to clean up and clear them out.

Allusions were very nearly all you got, however, around the UDA. Any questions about what went on elicited altruistic speeches on welfare work or, at the outside, on the current training courses which sounded more like overgrown-boy-scout stuff than anything nasty or lethal. Tyrie himself is far too affable for conversational wave-making, and he does more than tell you what he thinks you want to hear: he believes it.

It was his idea now that I had come to hear about the women – which he pronounces 'wee-men' – and in his very neat office, with the radio playing pop music and the large desk ornamented with a huge polished bullet like a copper dildo and a pen holder made of a rifle butt, he expounded. Even five-minute interruptions for the telephone never made him break his stride. The talk was about the low opinion held of women and their use almost exclusively to make tea; but now he had a plan to create a women's auxiliary, so that they would develop politically along with the men. It seemed to be news to Hester. And although he talked of 'moving very rapidly within the new year' to implement the plan, nothing had come of it two years later. Meanwhile, the other woman in the office brought us tea.

In any case there were obviously more promising lines of enquiry: the UDA's independent Ulster programme, for instance. In 1979 they had sponsored the publication of *Beyond the Religious Divide*, a remarkably enlightened document which proposed a full bill of rights for all citizens in a free and sovereign Ulster, in an attempt to fairly cut across national loyalties to both Britain and Ireland. A detailed constitution for the new state was drawn up and distributed with, on its back, the message:

TO THE PEOPLE OF NORTHERN IRELAND – we commend the words of Bacon:

> He who cannot compromise is a fool,
> He who will not compromise is a bigot,
> He who dare not compromise is a slave . . .

The very fact that this was addressed to the people of *Northern Ireland*, not *Ulster*, illustrated its own spirit of compromise; but the political party set up to promote the concept was called the Ulster Loyalist Democratic Party, automatically sacrificing nonsectarian support on two semantic counts. In any case the idea failed to catch on and how much potency it retained might be gauged by one of the signs on Tyrie's wall: KEEP ULSTER BRITISH. 'Not so sure about that,' he said when I pointed to it. 'It was sent by the Young Conservatives over in England. Propaganda value.'

'I'm very interested in the independence idea,' I said.

'So am I,' Tyrie answered. 'Really. I am an Ulster nationalist. Nothing else counts to me. The British government's only secondary. Our problem is that through the different generations of British people being involved here, we actually sold our birthright; we stopped realizing that we're Ulster people, and we gave away all our traditions, feeling that being British was a better form of protection than being on our own.

'See, the problem here is not religious: we've come to believe that it's really territorial. There are people in this island who see Ulster as a prize, and that they need to have it. But in fact this island has *never* been united except under the British government. Even within ourselves we feel different – our attitude and our approach is totally different in the North and in the South. Even back til this fella here' – he pointed to a tinny bas-relief on the wall behind him – 'Cuchullain: he's an ancient mythical figure, the warrior from Ulster who fought against all the men of Ireland, and he always won. But even he divides the two communities now. The IRA uses him as *their* sort of legendary hero. This goes back long before Christ; the group who lived here were called the Cruthin – an ancient British race of warriors who were the same stock as the Picts in Scotland, and different from the Gaels who were invaders from Europe.'

He and Hester began burrowing through the bookshelves to find me a book on the subject, plus a copy of their 1979 manifesto. Of the latter, he said, 'An awful lot of political parties have adopted things out of that. What we're talking about is an Ulster national identity. Which we do have. You know, it's madness.'

'How can you get the Catholics in on this?' I asked.

'Sure they are part of it,' said Tyrie.

'But how can you promote that?'

'See, I think we need to sort our own problems out first – and realize who we are. Because we do a very bad impression of an Englishman. And that's what people think we are. But I'm not a second-class Englishman, I'm a first-class Ulsterman. We all need to realize that. If we do we'd win. It's sorting it out in our own minds.'

Win what? 'But if you don't all come along together – just as you put it before about women – I don't see how you can get their support.'

'But you'll not get your support until the people who live here realize who they are. That's the Ulster Prod. They're not sure. They simply identify themselves as British. It's not as simple as that. When you say you're British, it lets people know you're not Catholic and you're not Irish, in a sense. But when you say you're an Ulster person people start: "Well where's Ulster? What is Ulster?" Then you have to start explaining all about that. We gave so much to everyone else, we've just failed to establish ourselves properly. We can't even deal in normal politics here. We should be a labour-minded community here; we're not allowed to. We vote Unionist and people think that makes us Conservatives, but we vote Unionist as a form of protection.'

Someone else came in then – John McMichael, Tyrie's second, to say their meeting was about to begin. I was invited to return another time and given some back copies of their monthly magazine, *Ulster*.

Ulster turned out to be a sometimes more, usually less literate concoction of pros and cons summing up the UDA point of view. They were against rather more than they were for. Exhortations for Protestant unity were the central theme, and attempts to make their constituency conscious of an identity around which they could pull together. There was a fair ambivalence towards the British government and its security forces: the alleged shoot-to-kill policy was a good idea since it was aimed exclusively at Republicans, but the supergrass system was not. The Falklands War had been a fine thing, but any moves Britain made together with Ireland were viewed with disgust and disdain as based on misinformation and/or a fundamental betrayal of a sacred trust. There was one proposal for repartition of the North to exclude Nationalists 'apart from West Belfast'. Not much was said about the independent Ulster idea. In any case how such an entity, with these people promoting it, could have any Catholic support was arguable, since all things Catholic from the Vatican on down came in for blanket disapproval. Also viewed negatively were Sinn Fein and all Republicans, the SDLP, the Gaelic Athletic Association, Irish-American institutions, ecumenism, most Unionist politicians, the *Daily Mirror*, the PLO, and such disparate characters as Neil Kinnock, 'Col. Khadafyi,' and 'Robert Mugabwe'.

The most interesting article developed Tyrie's idea that 'the problem here is territorial.' The unsigned piece was obviously the work of an outsider, since it referred to the UDA's 'sinister side' (though the UVF was called 'even more sinister'), but its appearance in their own magazine presumably constituted acknowledgment, if not endorsement, of its contents. The UDA was said to have discontinued 'criminal' business activities and 'random sectarian killings' in favour of legitimate businesses and direct strikes against 'militant Republicans' – the latter policy leading to 'UDA members being involved in a number of murders, for example of Maire Drumm [vice-president of Sinn Fein] in Belfast's Mater Hospital in March 1976; Irish Independence Party Councillor John Turnly in Carnough in June 1980; and in the attempted murder of Bernadette Devlin McAliskey and her husband at their Coalisland home in February 1981.' But:

> The UDA cannot really be referred to as a 'terrorist' organization, in the accepted academic definition of the term. The use of the word 'terrorism' implies a strategy of a sustained and systematic campaign of violence, whose overall object is to promote widespread terror. Furthermore, 'terrorist' groups are usually engaged in attempting to build some kind of desired utopia. This is something the UDA is hardly engaged in, for their actions are motivated more by attempting to maintain the status quo.

Therefore at most the UDA could be called a 'secondary terrorist organization'. UDA activities were shown to be largely reactive. In political crisis, whenever the Protestants felt a threat to their security from either the IRA or the British government, they responded with massive recruitment first into local 'defence' groups and later, when these were centralized, into the UDA itself. They were 'defending their own territory', it said.

The definitive populist success of the UDA was in 1974, when Britain tried to institute Protestant-Catholic power-sharing at Stormont, together with a Council of Ireland that was intended to involve the South in the North's affairs. With the Ulster Workers' Council, and in the face of procrastinating politicians, the UDA called virtually all Protestant workers out on strike. The article failed to mention the significant role of intimidation in the strike's success; nor did it say anything about the resulting withdrawal of foreign business which had since brought the unemployment and deprivation levels of UDA members almost into line with the Catholics.

The article ended: 'The only solution will be one the Protestants will not regard as a threat, if it is possible to find such a thing, whilst accommodating Nationalists.'

The motivating force behind the UDA might be summed up in a sentence from another article in *Ulster*: 'Though we may not have much to gain, we have everything to lose.'

7
A Blotted Copybook and Three Bowls of Soup

Belfast in the snow – deep drifts in Turf Lodge and soft wads of it still falling. Someone on the phone from the Newtownards Road said it was merely raining there: 'God is a Protestant,' he explained, as matter-of-factly as another time he referred to a long, new, finely pointed pencil: 'Now that's a Protestant pencil.' But the snow was a matter of altitude: Turf Lodge adjoins Andersonstown on the slopes of the western hills.

The city is ill-equipped for cold, let alone blizzards. But for once Belfast was entirely beautiful: even more monochrome, but with the signs of fighting softened, the debris under cover. Inside, everyone huddled by their fires. The bedrooms are freezers: without many-to-a-bed and hot-water bottles, half the population might expire in the night. Awake, they had nothing but complaints. Even the children couldn't have the riotous time they'd have made for themselves with the right coats and boots; and though the hills made perfect sledding, who could afford sleds? The best they could do was make brief forays out to throw snowballs or improve a treacherous hilly path into an ice slide to skid down in their slippery shoes.

The moral climate in Northern Ireland is cold the year round. This time I bumped into it with bruises. There was a woman I wanted to interview whom I hoped to stay with. She worked in a peace organization and seemed exceptionally enlightened. Staying with her was out this trip, I was told on the phone by an intermediary, as she was busy with meetings. Later I learned it was just *out* and that she never wanted to see me again. I'd 'blotted my copybook'. When I learned how, the first response was laughter, then disbelief. Apparently it had to do with a conversation we had had a couple of months before, about marriage. Once upon a time, I'd told her, I had married a Palestinian to help him get to the United States. I didn't actually remember having told her this, nor why. Over the years others have taken this information as a matter of passing interest, little note. But what I had done, it turned out, was to *desecrate a sacrament*.

I didn't know what a sacrament was. It happens there are seven of them, but I was unlikely to desecrate the others (as well as matrimony: baptism, confirmation, communion, confession, ordination, extreme unction), though that made little difference since I was already condemned to purgatory, no way out. The woman concerned works with reformed paramilitaries, i.e. killers, but murder doesn't involve a sacrament and you can always confess and receive absolution. 'Besides,' a lapsed Catholic friend explained to me, 'it's okay to hobnob with murderers because it's a good Christian act – you have a chance to save their souls. Who'd try to save yours?'

This was not, it turned out, even a matter of tribe. A Protestant peace colleague of the Catholic was equally shocked and wouldn't talk to me again either.

When it comes to sin, the two groups who fight about so much else are in agreement. It was the Unionists who were most vociferously anti-abortion in Northern Ireland so that unlike anywhere else in the UK, it is illegal, and over two thousand Northern women travel annually to the mainland for the purpose. Both sides opposed change in the homosexuality legislation – though it was Ian Paisley and his Democratic Unionist Party who came up with the slogan 'Save Ulster from Sodomy' – and liberalization came only after the European Court of Human Rights found against the government. All are great sticklers for the rules, both in a trivial sense (e.g. on a Northern motorway nobody ever drives in the fast lane except to overtake, and then only after signalling) and in a sweeping moral sense. In a recent worldwide Gallup poll, people were asked with which of the two following statements they agreed:

A) There are absolutely clear guidelines about what is good and evil. These always apply to everyone, whatever the circumstances.
B) There can never be clear and absolute guidelines about what is good and evil. What is good and evil depends entirely upon the circumstances at the time.

More of the Northern Irish – 42 per cent – agreed with statement A than any other people in the world (34 per cent of British and Americans concurred, and an average of 26 per cent in Europe as a whole).

In any case, I went to stay with Mary McMahon, one of the leaders of the Workers' Party.

A couple of blocks from the Sinn Fein office is the headquarters of the group they vilify more even than the British Army. The Workers' Party is sometimes called the 'Officials' because, as the Official IRA, they were the original inheritors of the fighters of the 1920s. In 1972 they chose to fight nothing but sectarianism itself, to dissociate themselves from paramilitarism and to deal in class politics. But their past reputation so dogs them that Protestant recruits are few and Catholics none too numerous either: their poll in elections has seldom exceeded 2 per cent. If they are really that meaningless, why does everybody hate them so much? Sinn Fein people and others who particularly loathe them call them 'the Stickies' or 'the Sticks', a name which began on the Easter when they changed their traditional fund-raising lapel lily from something you attached with a pin to something on sticky paper. An innocuous enough origin for a name; but '*the Sticks*' could be hissed with a terrible venom. 'What I like most,' said Mary Mac, 'is being called "a despicable Sticky" by the Provos, because that means we're hurting them.' The two groups have spent much time and energy hurting each other, as it happens, in mysterious traditional feuds which are described ideologically but which often seem something else. The fighting ended, legend has it, after the day six were killed on either side and they decided to call it quits.

Not only are the Officials severely stigmatized by their past, but their present isn't always thought to be entirely consistent with their idealistic views – there is a nearly universal belief that their guns have only gone under the floorboards. It's their claim to purity which is riling. Prejudice against them is generally directed towards their supposed hypocrisy: they may say they believe in non-sectarianism, bread-and-butter issues, social and economic justice, but this Official was involved in a shootout and that Official is corrupt. What is normal to the point of banal in others is held against the Workers' Party. They are the kid in the crowd who says the king is naked.

A frequent campaigner for office and an obsessively hard worker for the WP, Mary Mac is a young woman who seemed to have nothing else in her life. She had a soupbowl haircut over her broad face, and the widest, greenest and most honest eyes I ever saw. What in others would be called 'compassion' is for her automatic – she was the one politician I met in Northern Ireland who shared the poverty of and worked unremittingly for the lowliest of her constituents, whether they voted for her or not. She had a great deal to say to try and persuade the unbelieving; but in a place where many parties and people purported to be socialist and almost all were in reality nationalist, the words at Mary Mac's disposal had almost been bled of their meaning. The fact that she didn't care two figs for the glorious Irish cause and thought the priorities were employment and an equitable distribution of wealth, peace and social justice, struck most people as treacherous, barmy or at best utopian. Anyway, 'in Northern Ireland,' as a moderate Protestant put it (who 'would vote for the WP if it wasn't so pointless'), 'everyone votes against, not for. When it comes to it, you can't afford principles.' Mary Mac had principles, there was no one who didn't admit that; but wouldn't it be a waste of a vote if what you were trying to do was defeat SF/SDLP/OUP/DUP? (The other non-sectarian party, the Alliance, usually dismissed as 'hopelessly middle-class', didn't do much better – another victim of the mentality which drives people, *when it comes to it*, to vote for their tribe.)

Mary Mac lived in a bleak Turf Lodge flat on the second floor of one of the few buildings to rise that high; all the others were terraced or semi-detached cottages. Having lived on the ground floor in the past, with windows broken and hate-slogans daubed on the walls – especially in 1981 when she refused to hang a Bobby Sands poster in her window in support of the hunger strike – she felt safer upstairs.

Her flat was basic: a few Native American posters, a Soviet calendar, bare lighting, rudimentary furnishing. There was nothing to eat in her kitchen; she subsisted on the poorest diet of tinned spaghetti and a bit of bacon. The austerity of her life was emphasized by a bad case of flu which she refused to coddle, going out to the WP office or to help people all day, including Sunday, whatever the state of her fever or the dampness of her feet, resisting even sleep if anyone needed her (someone usually did). The only concession she made to illness and the weather was to refrain from a daily run up the snow-covered hills which could be seen from her back window (hills which Hester had complained she could no longer climb because 'they belong to the Catholics now'). From this way of life and because of public appearances in which she was rarely less than deadly serious, Mary by reputation was somewhere between Mother Teresa and Rosa Luxemburg. But when she relaxed with a pint in her local – a place where she was loved and revered – she could be merry and witty, given to deep belly laughter.

Still, her views on almost any aspect of the situation offended pretty well anyone, the other Catholics of West Belfast most of all. 'A lot of people tend to think that somehow the revolution will happen without them making it happen or contributing to it. But this place is going to change because people like us are going to plod on to the end of our lives telling people that they are exploited and that who they worship is irrelevant. They are fighting over nonsense. They are used and abused by sectarian bigots on both sides. The only people who can change that is the working class, not Dublin and not London. Union Jack or tricolour: fuck yous all.' The solid support for Sinn Fein in her Andersonstown constituency was just about impossible to combat, but in her view intimidation was as responsible for that as tribal feeling. 'In an area where the Provos expect solidly to pick up votes, they believe as part of their whole philosophy that if they physically batter the opposition out of the way, then that secures victory. The first time the Provos stood there was an enormous amount of bad feeling, fisticuffs, fights and rows, simply because they couldn't come to terms with the fact that we were prepared to run against them.'

As far as she was concerned Sinn Fein were national socialists. Sinn Fein's slogan in the EEC elections, she said, had been ONE PEOPLE ONE VOTE. 'All they left out was ONE VOICE, and then it would have been identical to the Nazi motto. If you don't conform, you will be severely punished.' Forty-four people had been vigilante victims in the last six months, she said, and 'a number of them are still trying to find out what they were supposed to have done wrong.' Anyway, did kids actually deserve to be bumped off or crippled for joyriding? The least they could expect at this point was 'breeze-blocking' – cement blocks dropped from a height on their limbs until the break was audible. 'It's cheaper and easier than bullets.'

She thought the Church deeply complicit in the mess they were in. Especially she felt that the great block to any progress was the lack of integrated schools. 'The Church isn't prepared to surrender control over anything that dominates here. And I wouldn't go so far as to say that segregated education is the cause of the division in this society, but it's the biggest single institution that maintains it and substantially protects it.'

A recent initiative to unite the two teacher training colleges, Catholic and Protestant, had failed largely through Catholic Church opposition. Pressure had been exerted on children to get parents' signatures opposing it; petitions were passed down pews at Mass. A first step towards integrating education in general, the college merger was 'portrayed by the Church as an act against Catholics, another attack on the Catholic religion.'

Attempts at reconciliation earned both praise and scorn from her. Corrymeela, a Christian ecumenical centre on the north coast ('I have a lot of time for them because they're based here'), invites groups from each side, often women and children who live possibly feet apart divided by a peace wall, to spend weekends together to thrash out differences. In contrast there was an American group which 'takes the kids away every year – so many Protestants, so many Catholics. They'll all love one another and come back and all the divisions will be overcome: a farcical notion, and very patronizing. You just think, what are these fuckers doing in the States then? What about the ghettos there? If they have so much money to throw about, why is there so much poverty in their own country?'

Other local organizations were doing a more realistic job, in Mary's view, particularly women's groups. 'There's an emerging force of working-class women who are organizing themselves in very mundane ways; they decide not to get involved in party politics but they *are* involved in politics. People need to rethink their definitions of politics. A vast majority of women are pissed off by what passes for politics here: what relevance has it to the lives they're leading? How does it put food on the table and clothes on the kids?'

Late one Saturday night, after she'd put in a full day of work with a high fever, Mary met me at a Workers' Party club that was celebrating its last fling: it was about to be torn down and replaced by another. The club was in a Catholic area in the middle of a wasteland of snow and new building, and I got the impression that the people there were all Catholics too, although the music was straight disco without the moving Irish laments that characterize the drinking clubs of Sinn Fein. The evening was just getting going as we neared midnight; Mary was very ill, but the only way to get her to go home was to plead my own exhaustion. She was angry at my faint-heartedness and refused to let me pay for the taxi. On the way we passed a British army patrol and started talking about 'Brits Out'. The conversation began amicably enough.

'When you send military people in to hold the fort,' she said, 'when you say that ideas can be imposed by physical force, effectively what you're saying is that you have failed politically. What we have always said is that the British Army have no role in the streets, they are not a police force, and they should be withdrawn to barracks. But don't forget that the UDR is a regiment of the British Army which is locally recruited, and what do you do with them?

'The theory has been that if the army was pulled out, there would be a bloodbath. I personally don't think that would happen.'

The taxi arrived at her small block of flats and our feet skidded as we gingerly made it up a path of sheer ice. The subject of the British view of the Northern Irish situation preoccupied her, and she talked about having attended a conference in London not long before when, during a factual rundown of what was happening and the forces people fought, 'this wee bitch stood up and said she had spent four days in Derry and she had seen the British oppression. She ranted and raved for about twenty minutes about her four days in Derry.' Mary was sick of four-day wonders, she said, 'fucking wee Brits who come over here and tell us what to do.' The British Troops Out Movement was full of such well-intentioned people who were unable to understand.

We'd got back upstairs by then. I mentioned the name of a member of Troops Out who had dedicated all her life and energy to persuading the British to change their policy. 'She's hardly a four-day wonder.'

'No,' said Mary, 'but she's not Irish. I'm just *sick* of Brits telling the Irish about the Irish revolution, and telling the Brits how they are oppressing the Irish.'

'But she feels responsible for it – '

Mary was spluttering with rage. 'Why? Why? Why does a member of the British working class assume the sins of the British ruling class? First of all she is assuming that a national identity overrides class, and therefore her analysis is suspect. Secondly, no member of a working class that has not achieved its own liberation – most of all, the British working class – has *any* right to assume the sins of the British ruling class. I don't assume unto myself the sins of the Irish ruling class for what they have done internationally. I don't assume any responsibility for de Valera's position of neutrality in the fight against fascism. Because I was a member of a working class that was not and is not in power, and I had no responsibility for that decision. My task, my principal and foremost task is not to cringe over it and cry over it and say to people "I'm terribly sorry"; my responsibility is to liberate and be part of my class and free my class from *my* ruling class. Then I can talk on equal terms with working-class people in their countries.'

I said, 'Do you think the British should have no opinions about what goes on in their government?'

'They should have class-based opinions.'

'I don't know where class comes into the Falklands, for example, but obviously a lot of people were opposed to any British intervention there. That doesn't mean we should have been minding our own business, fighting for the British working class, and letting those people do what they wanted in the Falklands – '

This was getting as overheated as Mary's fever. Neither of us was talking any more, just interrupting. 'If the Labour movement of Britain had fought for itself against its own enemies instead of dabbling and fucking *whingeing* around the world about the sins of the British ruling class for the last sixty years,' Mary said, 'they wouldn't have *had* a British ruling class that would have gone to war in the Falklands – '

'Never mind what would have happened, it happened! You think we should have stayed at home and talked about the miners and forget the Falklands – '

Mary interrupted. 'The whole thing happened because the British working class are not in charge of their own – '

I interrupted. 'It doesn't matter why it happened. While it was happening, should we not have said anything?'

'I didn't say that.'

'That is what you're saying, that we should not comment on injustices committed in our name!'

'I didn't say that.'

This was obviously quite out of hand now, and I couldn't remember any more how it had begun. What next, 'a lackey of British imperialism'? No: Mary merely dismissed me with, 'I will not be interrogated in my own house!' and I slunk off to bed under all my clothes, considering the further decline in the state of my copybook.

In the morning I had an appointment with one of Mary's constituents, a woman who she had told me had been jailed for three bowls of soup.

It was so cold in the little house that you could see your breath. Unploughed snow was piled in steep banks in the roads outside, and Maggie McAteer sat huddled by one electric bar in the living room taking care of two of her twelve (or fourteen? – she wasn't sure) grandchildren. They were little girls, neither talking yet, both in nappies; their mother was in hospital having just given birth to a son. The father of the house was Chuck, the only one of Maggie's five sons who had never been in trouble, the only one who had a job, as a painter and decorator. Because of the third baby the Housing Executive was installing heating and as we spoke workmen pounded and hammered until it was their dinner time, when they said they would be straight back. (I found out three months later that they never returned. Still no heat.)

Maggie looked to be around seventy, wizened, very thin, colourless, half-toothless – so that it was a shock when she revealed she was in her mid-fifties. According to local scuttlebutt she hung out with winos and underwent a complete change of personality when she drank: fighting irrepressibly, stealing – once, for instance, walking off from a gathering with all the coats which, when intercepted, she said were for her sons.

The house was the same as all the others but barely furnished and reflecting more than the usual poverty. Maggie herself lived on £22 a week social security but somehow had managed a spread for me – having invited me for 'a cup of tea and a wee yarn' – of biscuits and cakes, from which the little girls ate the icing, smearing it all over the room and over Maggie's clothes. She ate nothing, but kept dabbing at the spots, lighting cigarettes, ineffectually attempting to soothe the cold, bored, whining babies. Her thoughts came out chaotically and constantly reverted to her eldest son Michael's suicide.

'Michael was at the Adult College of Further Education at St Louise's. He was very socialist-minded – och, took all the cares of the world on him really. He was so well-liked at that school. They have a Michael McAteer Cup for creative writing there now. But – too much pressure, I don't know. And then he'd been interned, when he was a student, and spent eleven months. He was one of the first on the prison ship *Maidstone*. From four o'clock in the morning of the 9th of August, 1971, within a matter of hours there was five hundred picked up and Michael was among those five hundred.

'This prison ship – God, will I ever forget that. See when I went down to that quay, somewhere down at the docks, it was the first time in my life I was ever at the docks. And never was on a boat in my life. I looked up at that boat and here's me: "God, he just *couldn't* be in there!" I read about it in the 1920s and 1930s but I didn't think it could ever come to Ireland again. That my son would actually be on one!

'He was just picked up, there were no charges against him. It was Brian Faulkner [then Prime Minister of Northern Ireland] called internment. He signed: Your son

Michael Gerard McAteer has been considered a threat to the security of Northern Ireland and I have no further ado sort of thing than to sentence him to internment. Like many others – he wasn't on his own. They were herded in like cattle. And I remember, they were walking down the gangway and the paras were that side and the paras were this side, and I stood and I cried. You should have seen them and their SLRs. Those lads got murdered either going down or coming back again. We stood – not only me, there was other mothers as well – and cried.'

Like many other families, the McAteers were subject to army raids in the early hours of the morning, often with the house torn apart in the troops' search for something incriminating. 'And from the word go – I was the first family to actually be raided in Ballymurphy. At that particular time we didn't know anything about raids. They just came out, the para regiment, and they cut the street off. And if you'd gone outside your door: "I'll count three, and see if you're not in through that door I'll blow your brains out." This was the army tactics. Och the very dogs were lying dead that morning. I was raided fifty-nine times.

'Then the prison ship was closed down. They opened a camp – it used to be an army camp during the war for the Americans. Michael was sent there classed as an internee. Well, their internee – but *you* had to keep them, *you* had to feed them. You brought them their food, you half-cooked their meats, you brought them their tea, their butter, their sugar. You fed them and clothed them, took their dirty wash home, took it back again. One visit a week. Away in Magilligan it was, almost ninety miles to get til it. There was no roads intil it, you simply went through all these fields, jagged up to there with nettles. It was cruel. And we got to this camp, all you could hear was the dogs. They were training Alsatians. I don't know, it was a terrible, terrible experience. I just couldn't handle it, I was shattered. And every other day the army was raiding me, all hours of the night, banging "Get up," – "You stand here," – "You stand there," separating you all in the house. It was then that I started on Valium tablets.

'Michael was the eldest, he was seventeen then. Vera must have been seven, she was the only wee girl I had. Denis was born in 1962, so he was very young. During these years each of them were getting to the age of leaving school, with the result I would say, "This is going to be another Michael." It happened to Kevin then. Picked up in the night, picked up and what have you. It just went on and on. There was seemingly no end to this. For myself, I love my children that much, I figured maybe everybody else could cope. But maybe that prison ship did a terrible lot of damage to me. How cruel everything was to him. You know, he didn't seem to get any enjoyment out of his youth. He became interested in so many different things at the end, CND, poetry, Marxism. But I think he felt the pressure on himself. He used to say to me, "You worry too much." I used to say, "I don't know, but Michael, what did you get out of life? From sixteen and a half you were in the prison ship, prisons and what have you." Because of the short life that he had, and there was nothing – except the education and maybe the laughs that he had at St Louise's. Apart from that I don't think you could say there was any part of his life that he lived.

'He got married. She ran off with another man. As a matter of fact she became pregnant to another person. Her child was born just after he died. And he had two children of his own – he loved them. She has them, and I have never saw them since.

'Then Desmond. He was eleven and he was picked up and given one-to-three years for "riotous behaviour" – for something that there was thousands of other people doing, adults doing. Belfast was an inferno at that time, there was no let-up: you had bombings, you had shootings and killings every night. Michael was interned at this time. Kevin was in. He was fifteen. He ended up getting time. I was going round three different prisons in Northern Ireland. I'd never survive it again. Definitely I'd never survive it, love. See me going to those prisons, away to Magilligan, cup of tea maybe, and not a bite in your inside. And maybe not the money or the wherewith when you come back.

'Well I just said to myself, "There's another one out of the house." But I fought then so hard for Desmond. I said to myself, Desmond got one-to-three years and now he's there already *four* years. Their excuse was "He's at school here and he's very much settled at school" – St Patrick's Training School. I said, "That's not the thing. For I can settle him at what sort of school I choose to put him in."

'So it went on to five years and I took a mad notion one night and stole him out of St Pat's. I went up on a visit. This is how I felt at this time: full of venom. I took a private taxi and said "This is it." They were out in the yard playing football. And I said to this other woman, "Listen, I'm taking Desmond out of here tonight. And if the Brothers are looking for him, don't say you even saw me here."

'I was a bit scared, now. But I had his clothes and all with me. Left the taxi at the bottom of the lane. Went in, saw Dessy. Said, "Right, see that ball? Kick that ball over to those steps. There's a taxi waiting for you at the bottom of the avenue. Now, I'm not going out with you. You get into the taxi, get on the clothes – throw those prison clothes in the grass, wherever you like, put them under a tree."

'So I stole Dessy out. I took him home with me. I had a job waiting for him. I couldn't let him sleep in my house. He slept in some neighbours' of mine. And I woke him up every morning – I woke them all up every morning for work – had them lovely. He had almost a year out. What happened? The military stopped him. "Desmond McAteer." So he was lifted again, and got a further three years for absconding from the school. *They* classed it as absconding.

'You know what I did at that court? I said "No, my child did not abscond!" I could have got three years meself. My solicitor said to me, "Margaret, just say nothing." But I got up and said, "I beg your pardon, my son did not abscond. I was the one. You were the magistrate who sentenced him to one-to-three years; but he already did four and a half, almost five. My son did nothing. I should be charged with kidnapping. I took him from it. This is an injustice of the highest order. If a magistrate puts out a court order on you, surely to God they should comply with the laws, if there's such justice in Northern Ireland." Well the judge just waved it off.

'Desmond then started to fight the establishment. He knew that injustice was done on him. And he made it very hard on himself. He did everything bar the right thing. He was the youngest prisoner, and they had no youth facilities then, and they put him in the back of the hospital. And he broke out to get on to the roof – they got the army to hose him down. He got five years again. I don't know how he's still sane. I simply don't know how Dessy's still sane. They never ever ever let up. All his life, the whole time just a vicious circle surrounding him. First the four and a half, then the three, then a further five years. Only one Christmas was that boy at home in eleven years.

'The Workers' Party did a great lot for me then. We got in touch with the NIO [Northern Ireland Office] and put it on television. I did a programme called The Borstal Boy. I told everything, how I felt about how Dessy ended up. This was still a *child* like. This is the torture he had to go through.

'So between one thing and another – Michael's internment, and Desmond, Kevin – I ended up in the psychiatric hospital. I knew I needed treatment, I needed something: I don't think I accepted all this. But my sons – who'd go and visit them? Nobody would do that for me, I had got to be out to do that. I managed quite for a time. I fell apart many times but.

'Then Kevin got shot. One thing after the other. I had the dinner all waiting. Kevin hadn't been in, he'd been downtown. He'd been in and out in the meantime. I'd said to Kevin, "I have your dinner ready there"; he says, "I have to go down to Armstrong's." "Well," I said, "I'm going to wash my hair but if you're back your dinner will be in the oven." I went and had my hair in the water and I heard the shooting. Just round the corner from where we lived. He was hit five times. He's not dead but one of the bullets hit him by the spine.

'The other side shot him – The Provisional IRA. I was a supporter of the Workers' Party, very much so at this time. The Workers' Party was a socialist thing – not involved with guns or anything like that. And here was I fighting the system, but I was also fighting the PIRA as well. I was very much hated in the area, me and another few, even Mary Mac. I was getting quite a lot of torture from them: I couldn't go into a shop, couldn't get served; even if I was first in the queue they'd bypass me. Now you see those people before the Troubles? They were so nice. It was just something hateful. Taxis that were empty went past me. They still do.

'Then a Provo was shot in our street. I wasn't there that particular weekend: I was in Omagh. The Provos came looking for Kevin, thinking he had done the shooting, and held my Vera as a hostage. She was fourteen years old, and alone in the house. Lucky to God, Kevin was out, and a woman who was a supporter of the Officials spied the two men going in; she saw Kevin in time and gave him taxi fare and said, "Get out of the road as fast as you can." That was the second attempt on his life. He'd already been shot, but they didn't get him with the right bullet.'

When Mrs McAteer came home from Omagh, Mary Mac told her what had happened, and she went downtown with a friend to look for Kevin. 'I saw these three Provos come along with this woman – she was the sister of the man who had been shot in our street. I saw them sorting out something like money – I thought they must have a drink on them and either they're counting their money to get chips or they're seeing if they have the price of another drink. Then the woman walked over to me and said, "*You Sticky bastard, you killed my brother!*" and she just went *BANG*. I got a double fracture of the jaw, teeth out, and seven stitches.' She showed the scars and further demonstrated her toothlessness.

'I got to the Royal Hospital and the doctor says to me, "A woman? Mrs McAteer, a woman couldn't have done that on you. She must have been *massive*!" But she wasn't. She was my size. How did she do it? I suddenly realized she'd had a weapon: the silver I thought they were counting – she had it in her hand between her fingers! "*You Sticky bastard, you killed my brother!*" And I wasn't even there when her brother was shot! I was in Omagh!

'I was still looking for Kevin. The doctors wanted to keep me in – I had to feed through a straw – and I was sorry to make so much trouble but I says, "My son – the Provisionals have already shot him and I have to get out of the hospital *today*!" So I got out, and I ended up getting Kevin to England – through Mary again. It was terrible. Terrible, terrible: I had to get him *arrested*. You know the fine for the car? I had to get the RUC to pick him up and arrest him. Just for safety's sake. I knew he'd only be in for a day or two, twenty pound or something. Just so the Provos wouldn't get him. Then to England.

'It all came out in the open then. I got on television, Mary got me on, and I said to the Provos, "Right. If you want to shoot someone, I have enough harassment from the British Army, but when it comes from both sides, from you people," I said, "that's it." I said, "Listen. If you want to shoot anyone you can shoot me because I have my life led, right? My sons have got to lead their lives yet. You take me. For any of my sons, I don't care which of them. Because," I said, "I don't know what Kevin's done on yous. I am a supporter of the Workers' Party but surely to God that's no reason for shooting my son." MOTHER OFFERS HER LIFE FOR HER SON: that was the headline.

'Their father. He was there. Very much a silent character. Didn't get involved. I ended up getting rid of him, because he was no help towards my sons. He never visited them in prison, he gave them no support. Now he says about beating the cops, doing this, doing that. *Now* he would say it. But he didn't do it when they were needing him. I haven't seen him. It's nine months since I saw him. And I walked past him in the street. Can't bear to talk to him, honest to God I can't.'

Racking coughs interrupted her then. Both children were moaning and wailing, having eaten or spread around the icing from the cakes; she stopped long enough to find them their dummies, and settled them down, one beside her and the other on her lap, where they fell asleep. Then she continued.

'I had five boys, and those boys just suffered. Right down the line. With the exception of the fella that lives here, Chuck. Chuck was very much a loner. Very quiet. He had a terrible accident when he was young, and had brain surgery. And I didn't want him to go to an ordinary school. You know, rough, he might get knocked about and all this. So I sent him to this beautiful school, Cedar Lodge. It was mixed, interdenominational, on the Shore Road. And maybe, you know, this played a part. Chuck was at that school till he was sixteen. He mixed with Protestants and Catholics. And he had only one half hour a week of religion. Whereas in the other schools they have maybe an hour's religon *every morning*. I think it made him very broadminded, being at that school. To me he turned out the best of the heap.

'When I look round me now I say God no, religion doesn't come into me at all. My mother was a Protestant herself. And I have a sister a Protestant. No, I think if they had rid of religion we mightn't have all this carry-on today. I'm more maybe Marxist than anything. I think if we were all Marxist the world would be a better place to live in.'

This was when a workman stuck his head round the door to say he was off for his dinner and, 'I've a new fire ordered and I have to pick it up at two o'clock.' – 'That's okay love,' Maggie answered, 'right love, thanks Jim.

'There's a terrible bitterness in my heart. Towards the Provos, towards the British Army, the RUC, the heap of them. I could write a book for all the wrongdoings they done my children. I just sit and go back over everything. The prison ship, the Kesh, being hospitalized, fighting for Dessy, fighting for Michael, fighting for them all, fighting the system, fighting the Northern Ireland government, fighting the British Army and then fighting the Provos. At times I think if I hadn't taken the Valium, or taken the drink – I had to take a drink or I wouldn't survive, love. Because there were times I definitely had a block-out, I went out of my mind. I think I should have ended up in the sea. There were weeks you were making up parcels . . . one Christmas, I had no Christmas dinner because my parcels cost me all my money. I ate chips on Christmas Day. But I was happy to eat those chips. As long as my sons were all right.

'Mary Mac was a great standby for me. Mary had this wee club round here and God help her I was all my time there to get talking to her and get my mind lifted away from everything. Many a time we've had all these discussions.'

Mary and Maggie had gone canvassing together for the Workers' Party too: a risky business. 'Door to door, and we went to this door. And God, your woman answered with a big knife. A big breadknife. Mary had said to me, "Don't bother with that door." Here's me: "They came to *my* door for *their* crowd, so I intend to go to their door, Mary." And I went. God I tell ya I'm lucky to be alive love. She'd all these posters of Gerry Adams in the window. I just did it like. To let them know I wasn't a bit frightened of them.

'You see the Provos? May God forgive me but they're as bad as the paras! They caused more deaths than the British Army. Maybe they have the quantity but they haven't the quality, of Irishmen, as such. You give any man a gun and he can shoot it for you.'

In this history of her problems, she had not once mentioned the three bowls of soup. When I asked her about it, she sighed.

'Three alcoholics,' she said, 'and they were just simply starving. All I had was forty p. I knew these people, they were dead decent people, didn't matter to me if they were alcoholics. Everybody's the same to me. But wait'll I tell ye. We went to the café: it wasn't a bad place we picked like. Three bowls of soup. And I swear to God it wasn't even soup, it was dishwater. I think they got a wee bap type of thing with the bowl of soup. Anyway the girl left me the ticket. It amounted to eighty-odd p. And I hadn't got eighty p, and they hadn't a penny. So I says to the girl, "Go ahead, there's forty p, you can take it or leave it." And I says to the men, "See yous later," and they says, "Thanks very much Maggie, that was great."

'Never thought of another thing, love. But the owner, that old dog – these are your own people, Catholics. This was a Catholic woman from Turf Lodge but. She knew that they were alcoholics that were getting the soup. These are the ones at the altar rails, like. Go to chapel every morning. What have you.

'That was about eleven o'clock. Half past four the police pulled up. "Mrs McAteer?" I said "Yes." "Would you like to come with us?" Here's me: "Beg your pardon, what for?" He says, "We just want to speak to ye down at Musgrave Street."

'So I goes down to Musgrave Street. I says, "What's it all about?" He says, "Come up the stairs." I goes up the stairs, he opens this door. "Oh my God," I says, "what are you doing here?" Opens the next door: "What are you doing?" The three that I got the soup for were lifted! Says I, "What are you doing here?" "Soup, Maggie." "Ach, my Jesus Christ! Soup! You're jokin"!

'I got charged with three bowls of soup, and I got a month's imprisonment. The men were all right, it was me that they ordered. I was the culprit. Did you ever hear the like of it? Dickens couldn't beat it: Oliver asks for more.

'I went to Armagh prison. You know how you go to the governor and he looks at your chart. He looks at me and he says "Three . . ." – he just couldn't believe it. I said, "Yes, three bowls of soup, and I have to do one month in your establishment."'

'Did they strip-search you?'

She was uncharacteristically speechless. Then, 'God, love, you want to see, your pants in a heap and all! Terrible, really is, swear to God. Really wicked that. Oh

Jesus, you've no idea what it's like! Although I hate the Provos and they're very much agin it, it is – very degrading.'

'Were you in with the Provos?'

'Aye! All in. Nobody spoke to me, dear. But you learn a wee lot in prison too, you know. You just be a good listener. I would say it's an education in itself. The different classes of people you'd meet. Some up for fraud, what have you. There was a policeman's wife, and her and I got on great. Course they found out she was a policeman's wife and she was just simply ignored. *Spat* on. But she and I were very great. "Let me tell ya something," I says to her, "I'm in here for three bowls of soup. What are you in for?" "Well," says she, "I just converted twenty thousand pound to my own use. For a firm I was working for." And she gets six months for twenty thousand pound, and I get a month for forty p. *And* she got to keep the twenty thousand! It was over a period of two years that she done it. "Well," I said, "I really think that I should have done something like that there too, seeing I come in within these walls. I should have maybe something to show for it." I said, "I have nothing to show for three bowls of soup, dear. Not even a full stomach."

She caught herself laughing and stopped as though that were impermissible. Her eye drifted to the single-barred electric fire in the fireplace and she said: 'Michael did some marvellous poems. There was a beautiful one, *Clown on the Mantelpiece*.' There were 'delf' figurines of clowns on either side of the mantelpiece above the electric heater. 'He wrote a poem before he died, know what he called it? *In to Eternity*. If you'd read that poem you'd say to yourself, "If I had saw it then, my God." Maybe he just wrote it in that morbid state. But it was Michael. And it was Michael's death. Dying alone. Found alone. Everything was in the poem, and it actually pointed to his death. How he died, no one near him.

'He was found on the grass. It was a very warm day, and he must have just took a dander. He was outside the College of Art, and he'd a book with him. He was to start teaching at the London School of Economics in eleven days. He'd been studying economics for a long time.

'The cop that was in charge said to me in high court, "You know, it was a beautiful day, and everybody was there. But come nine o'clock, the people all disappeared. And I was patrolling round, patrolling round, but I saw this figure lying on the grass for a long time. I was going off duty about half past nine and decided to have a look – because that fella seemed to have been lying in that same position from when I came on duty. And," he said, "I went over on the grass, and he was lying face downwards, clutching this book, and I turned him over. I realized he was dead." He'd been dead for two and a half hours. And yet how many people passed him by and passed him by and passed him by. See this is life in Belfast again. You could just be lying dead, nobody to care.

'I went mental after Michael died. I'm very discontented yet with life. And I think if Michael had had a different chance, hadn't been interned and all this . . .'

At St Louise's they remembered Michael McAteer with great love and sense of loss. 'People leaned on him even though he was someone who needed to lean himself,' one teacher said. 'But he never showed it and we didn't understand until his death.' They spoke of him as someone of great talent, particularly as a teacher, and when the creative writing cup was awarded in his name later in the year they put together a collection of his poems for his mother. One of them, called *Mother's Day*, she had never seen before:

The long arduous years of struggle
Are etched deeply on her saddened but radiant face
Her entire body a bitter reflection of loss of self
For she did lose self, many years ago
When her love for her offspring
Defied all common laws of rationalization and logic
When she fought, desperately at times
To shield and protect her weakened young
And even in later, recent years was able still
To summon untold strength and courage
And to practise the preaching of love . . .

The last word for the Workers' Party came from one of their voters, a very tiny, ancient man in a pub. First he told me a story. 'King William was being rowed across the Boyne,' it began, 'and the poor wee boatman looked up at him: "Excuse me sir, do you think we'll win?" There was no answer. "Excuse me sir, do you think we'll win?" And King Billy put his hand on his head. "My dear man, win or lose, you'll still be John the Boatman."

'But there is an answer,' he went on: 'the workin' people united together. If the people were all together and lookin' for better livin' standards, they would soon remove the politicians, wouldn't they? Now the politicians divide them and they allow them to do it, and until they stop it they'll always be divided. But that doesn't say there isn't a way out and the people won't take the way out. If the masses of the workin' class people unites together, there's no hard or big to surmount.'

8
Republicans in an English Court

Hearing the evidence, you'd think it was murder by dustbin. First of all, two dustbins full of guns, bomb-makings and documents found in a forest in Oxfordshire ('the Pangbourne cache'); more buried dustbins in Nottinghamshire and Northamptonshire, adding up to 'the most sophisticated terrorist arsenal ever found in Britain'; then 110 dustbins of debris collected by the Anti-Terrorist Squad after explosions in London in late 1981. Two culprits sit heavily guarded in the dock at the Old Bailey. One is dark, one fair; one clean-shaven, one bearded; both twenty-nine, Catholics, from Belfast. They are Thomas Quigley and Paul Kavanagh, and they have sat it out in custody for over a year while the contents of dustbins were sifted and linked to each other and, maybe, to them.

There are ten charges: three of murder, one of attempted murder, two of causing explosions, and four of possession of explosives and firearms. The events happened immediately after the end of the hunger strike in 1981 and within five weeks of each other, therefore presumably were the work of a single Active Service Unit. First there was a bomb made of thirty pounds of gelignite and a thousand six-inch nails which was intended to hit a vanload of soldiers returning to Chelsea Barracks in the Ebury Bridge Road. Instead it killed two pedestrians, one of them Irish. A Wimpy Bar in Oxford Street went up nine days later and a bomb disposal expert with it: the mechanism was booby-trapped. Then there was a car bomb that nearly finished Sir Steuart Pringle, Commandant General of the Royal Marines: his right leg had to be amputated. Finally, an attempt was made on the life of the Attorney-General, Sir Michael Havers, but while his house was partly demolished, he wasn't in it. Whoever performed the jobs, you couldn't say any of them had achieved anything, even its object.

But that might have been that, had not two forest rangers kicking around in the leaves in October 1983 tripped on a bit of plastic and, curious, dug out the Pangbourne cache. On the 112 pounds of explosives inside, the long-delay timing fuses, radio control units, wire reels, hit lists and false documents, were several sets of fingerprints, among them Quigley's and Kavanagh's.

Now everyone is ready to play some part in the antique ritual of British justice. Enthroned above sits the judge in his scarlet robe trimmed with ermine. Above him on the wall hangs a gold sword. Below him, the Court Clerk, and ushers who call the occasion to order and close it again with 'Be upstanding in court!' and 'God save the Queen!' To the left, at a long desk, the prosecutors and defence lawyers, ready to insult each other 'with the greatest respect'. All these people wear wigs of various sorts, and the lawyers have on black gowns with odd pockets over the left shoulder blade – ('for the discreet presentation of gratuities', apparently, 'some time ago', though when exactly none of those who sport one knows). To the right, the jury box and, directly over it – making them mutually invisible – the public gallery. To the rear of the whole tableau are fifty blue plastic boxes of prosecution exhibits piled on trestle tables.

The jury is being selected: twelve men and women out of ninety-six, who pile into the courtroom taking every inch of aisle. They are asked to disqualify themselves if 'yes' is the answer to any of three questions: Have you or a close relative or friend served in the armed forces? In the security services in Northern Ireland? Been directly affected by a bomb explosion? It's no surprise that most men over forty are out because of question one, but strange how many of all sorts say yes to something – what? They don't, though, have to tell, and many may be using this as an expedient to opt out.

There are peremptory challenges from both sides: the prosecution doesn't like long hair, the defence distrusts *Daily Telegraph* readers. Nothing much more to go on, not even an occupation or the sound of a voice beyond its 'Yes' or 'No' to the three questions. But there are very few spares left when the twelve – half men, half women – are eventually selected. The 'mems of the jury,' as the judge addresses them, look varied enough, but who any of them are or what they stand for no one will ever be legally allowed to learn.

They'll have to reach two verdicts, one for each man. The cases are different. The dark one, Quigley, has nothing against him but fingerprints on some of the items in the cache. He'd told the police when they brought him over from Belfast that he'd never been in England before in his life. But the blond-bearded one, Kavanagh, was actually trailed to the woods where the dustbins were found, together with a third Irishman with the unexpected name of Natalino Vella, who has spilled beans in custody and is pleading guilty (which means his case will be heard after the others).

An Irish nun known to one of the defence counsel apparently told him, 'That Vella is a wicked fella.'

'He's not so bad,' the lawyer replied.

'He talked,' said the nun. '*He talked to the police*.'

'Well,' said the lawyer, 'but he'll probably go down for twenty years.'

'That's about right for talking,' the nun said.

Twelve English faces, serious and sincere, furrow up as

they listen to interminable details about Memopark TPUs, mercury tilt switches and battery intersects; and scrutinize photos of the bits and pieces of exploded debris to find a match with the contents of the cache. (Other photos they may disregard, says the prosecutor: the ones of bits and pieces of human people. But the photos are there). The stuff obviously ties in to those 1981 bombings: among it are keys to exploded cars, ends of wire that match other ends. The question is, does it connect to Q and K? The forensic people are so delighted with themselves and their gadgetry – including a new laser fingerprint finder – that much less time is spent on this main (and only important) point than in showing off their sleuthing skills.

Attention returns, for lack of much else of interest, to those twelve faces, and the question of how they are to pass judgement on two Irishmen who are at war with them. If they see no war, believe that they are not at war, and are told there is no war, the charge amounts only to some disgusting and fanatical criminality directed at their own good selves. If a jury of peers means a jury of equals, it's hard to think how there can be justice here. 'I swear by almighty God,' they have been required to say, 'that I will faithfully try the prisoners at the bar and give a true verdict according to the evidence.' Assuming they perform their duty conscientiously, what can it mean – evidence involving more than a week of forensic minutiae about transceivers, limpet magnets and command wires, with nothing about having your house raised by the security forces time and again from early childhood? Or about having a brother shot dead by the British Army (true of both men)? How can Thomas Quigley's use of false identification papers in his own home town – where his brother Frankie is one of the Ten Most Wanted Men – make sense to twelve law-abiding Britons who know little if anything of constant P-checks?

Tommy Quigley, when he finally gets to the stand after a numbing succession of experts, tries to explain about Frankie. If he gave their common surname, he says, the police took him in, simple as that – for four hours, or three days, or seven days. Arbitrary police behaviour of this sort is a concept quite alien to the twelve, who don't even bother to give Quigley a glance as he amplifies. Nor do they view with sympathy, if view at all (since the placement of the witness box, just beside them, means they must crane their necks), Quigley's tears as he talks about his other dead brother, and his continuing anguish over Frankie, who is doing eight years now in Portlaoise jail in Ireland. According to Tommy's story, it all goes back to Frankie anyway: Frankie was in hiding just over the border in Dundalk where Tommy went to visit him and, being left alone one morning, opened the door to a girl who handed him a bag to give to his brother. He was 'nosy' and looked in the bag. He found things that looked like radios, or walkie-talkies, and a roll of wire cable and a thick bunch of papers. He'd gone through all this and put it back in the bag, and that is how his prints were found.

Tommy has alibis for the bombings too. October 10th, the date of the first one, is his mother's birthday; they always had a party; and he especially remembered it in 1981 because he and Geraldine couldn't get a baby sitter so they'd had to take the kids, including their newborn baby, to the party. And he remembered well the second explosion, a week later, because he and Geraldine had specifically decided not to go out, as they normally did on Saturday night, after the news of that very bombing: it was the one meant for Pringle, whose regiment was on duty in Belfast at that moment, so Tommy had expectations of trouble from the soldiers in retaliation.

There it is again: the suggestion that punishment may possibly be meted out in these British Isles to those who don't deserve it. In our society we have action and reaction, cause and effect, crime and punishment. Soldiers don't just run amok. Things don't happen without a reason. All comers to the Bailey are being body-searched for the duration of this trial: there must be a need for this. A helicopter flies above the prisoners' transport to and from Brixton jail and, it is said, there are police snipers hidden on all the nearby rooftops. Why? It is obvious: these men must be dangerous. See how foreign they are? Nobody can understand a word Quigley says. The defence counsel has tried unobtrusively to translate, repeating all the answers to his questions. He manages it without sounding patronizing, but the judge is impatient and keeps rolling his eyes in despair and asking the witness to slow down. It doesn't do a bit of good. The words come out just the same, only now with gaps in between. 'He-kmin-tilla-hahs-baht-nahr-lehter,' repeats Tommy painstakingly. But after half a day of this, much of the court seems to have given up even trying to make sense of it.

Unlike the sneering countenance in the police photo that the papers reproduce, Quigley looks very shy and vulnerable, with soft dark eyes that cry easily and a sweet smile when he can muster one. His story is unshaken by cross-examination and seems convincing. Is it true, or did he do it? That is the only question, not: If he did it, why?

The other man, Kavanagh, has a fanatic's eyes. They remind me of someone – full of holy zeal, intense righteousness, a complete absence of compassion or humanity. All day I ponder who else it is who has that look. Finally I have it: Mrs Thatcher.

The trial continues. All of Tommy's family has flown in to give their versions, and all of them support his story – with small emendations and elaborations, some of which prove contradictory. But we are relying on memories of events three and a half years ago, and none of the disagreements is substantive.

First to appear is Tommy's girlfriend Geraldine. The reason they never married, it has been explained, was that Geraldine's first husband was killed and his family owned the house where she and their child lived: if Tommy moved in, then the family, still in mourning for their own son and out of respect for his memory, might have made difficulties about the house. So Tommy officially only lived there on weekends and otherwise with his mother.

Geraldine has streaked short hair and is very attractive, soberly dressed in a black suit and black patent high heels. Her composure gives her words an extra ring of truth, though there is still a problem with that accent. Most of it is comprehensible enough, if quaint in the high-falutin ears beneath the wigs, but now and then a phrase baffles them. 'He stayed a wee while and then he went out, so he did. We decided to sit in and get carry out.' 'Is that like "take-away"?' They have to sort out that she means drink. People whose furnishings obviously include a permanently stocked drinks cabinet have some trouble with this concept; and the judge, who is writing everything down, makes a big show of tolerant patience as she exceeds the limits of his comprehension. 'When you say your "sister-in-law *and that*", whom . . . precisely . . . do you mean?' 'Betty, Roy's ex-girlfriend,' she explains levelly. Both His Lordship and the prosecutor are scandalized by Geraldine's rather easygoing approach to her children. When do they go to bed? 'When they're tired.' Eyebrows rise wigwards.

At least this time the jury is looking at the witness: they take, it would seem, a more relaxed view about life than the judge and are less likely to find her ways so peculiar, and besides she is so pretty. Perhaps too some of the quality of life in West Belfast is beginning to filter through.

Geraldine is led through an explanation of the P-check, how the police are entitled to stop you and ask your name and address, where you're going and where you've come from. There are four or five army foot patrols in the area all the time, Geraldine says, and 'if there's more police, there's more patrols guarding them.' On the Shankill, a policeman can walk about alone without the need of his own army guard, but it's not like that in their area. The patrols stop and check you as an everyday occurrence, and 'if you're from a known Republican family you get a terrible lot of hassle.' They stand you against the wall and search you, and if they're not satisfied they take you away to the nearest barracks. It meant if Tommy was going down to sign on he'd run into them all the time – which was why he didn't collect social security, it wasn't worth it.

Geraldine's husband had been killed in 1976 in an explosion: 'Bombs he was making.' Yes, he was a member of the Provisionals. No, Tommy was not. 'What did you feel about your husband's death?'

She paused before her answer, which must have moved everyone. 'It's hard to forgive him for it . . . For leaving me.' Her turn was over. She exchanged small smiles with Tommy as the lawyers dismissed her.

Tommy's mother is next, an auxiliary nurse, plump and maternal in a pale green cape, clutching her bag to her chest as she testifies. That party for her birthday: why did she remember it that year especially? Because of the hunger strike – 'It was a bad time and we didn't think there was going to be a party. The boys were dying every week.' There were riots, burning buses, no transport, you couldn't get to work, stones and petrol bombs thrown at the soldiers, and the boys dying: how could they have a party? But the hunger strike had ended in time, so they went ahead.

The guest list is reviewed, and the subjects of conversation at the party enquired into. The judge seems consumed with curiosity over what they'd talked about. They all say that while they can't exactly remember, they probably would have talked about the hunger strike. What seems to astonish the judge was that they hadn't been more interested in the London bombing that day. In fact the bombing seemed not to have concerned them until their Tommy was eventually accused of it.

The prosecutor, a rather Dickensian figure with a wagging finger and sanctimonious air, catches the mother out in a mild inconsistency to do with the guests at the birthday party. A defence lawyer tells me they'd pointed out the discrepancy to Mrs Quigley since it was a matter of no importance, to see if it might affect her recollection, but 'I won't lie,' she'd said to them. Mother and son just remember events slightly differently – natural enough, but it leaves a bad impression. The jury never knows she said 'I won't lie.'

'Mrs Quigley, is your son Frankie in the IRA?'

'Yes.'

'And Tommy?'

'No.' The face of the Belfast mother comes over her, resigned and set. 'After Frankie, they all promised me they would never get involved.'

Processions of sons follow, four of her original seven, then their wives or girlfriends. In a typical exchange Christopher is asked about a contradiction in his initial statement with what he is saying now: it turns out to be a grammatical point of ludicrous unimportance, easily unravelled, but the judge belabours it. 'I am *inviting* you,' he says pompously, 'to be *kind* enough to *read* it to me.' This brother, like the others, is neither impressed nor rude. What does the jury make of it? They are one big blank, cardboard silhouettes at a shooting gallery. People are talking out of their truth here, *the* truth as certified on the Good Book, though what truth it is, the twelve show no sign of caring. Of course the truth is getting rather boring by now through repetition: nevertheless here are successions of men and women in extremis, and it is the job of their attackers and defenders to goad and taunt them even further like banderilleros and picadors. The Quigleys are remarkably composed, considering: they just get on with the job of defending Tommy who, throughout the day – gazing at his entire family one by one coming to support him (except the only one who really could, Frankie) – looks transported with love.

Dropping into the trial again, I wonder how people who have to go through this sort of thing every day endure it. The price is right, I guess, one way or the other. Your money or your life. Identified, gone over and searched downstairs, I show my pass at Court 2. One of the three hefty guards at the door breaks the ranks of silence to ask if I'm 'with the PA.' No, what's that? 'Well,' he says by way of answer, 'if you ain't got no socks you can't pull 'em up.' True.

The day's business starts with two last witnesses for Tommy. There is an ex-soldier who, when he was on duty in Belfast, had had more or less to memorize the Wanted photographs at the barracks, so he was pretty sure about the faces. It so happened he'd been in the Ebury Bridge Road shortly before the blast there, and had identified Frankie, not Tommy, as the bloke he'd seen hanging about. The jury asks to see the pictures and two large sheets wholly covered with portraits are produced – the same sheets which the soldiers were required to study daily (the *Most* Most Wanted were apparently displayed even inside their lavatory doors). The images of Frankie and Tommy are clipped out, mounted on blue card and passed around and the soldier says Frankie was 'definitely' the man he saw.

Next the puzzle of why Frankie isn't here to exculpate his brother if the bag story is true: a solicitor from Dublin is sworn in. She visited Frankie in Portlaoise, she testifies, and he said – 'Matter of order!' shouts the prosecutor, the jury has to file out and this line of examination is, His Lordship agrees, inadmissible: hearsay. All she had been going to relate was that Frankie was willing to help but there was no mechanism for leaving an Irish jail to testify in a British court. He also would have had a bit of a self-incrimination problem. Nonetheless the solicitor's testimony might have stilled some doubts, and members of the jury show what might pass for impatience.

That is that for Tommy, anyway, except for his barrister's finale. Now, because these things are staged so badly, without a programme or a pause for breath, it is suddenly time for Paul Kavanagh. Nothing marks the change of focus on his stolid face. In no time we're back in the dreary land of multi-strand conductors and Memopark TPUs. As well, the fingerprint expert is recalled for some reason never obvious as he is inaudible: but since it is English inaudibility the judge accepts it and refrains from doling out the small-child treatment given to the Belfast natives.

Where did the phrase 'courtroom drama' come from? Apart from the occasional showmanship of some hyperbolic barrister, it all seems like the Boring Department in Hell, with little relationship to the passion behind the acts being scrutinized, let alone the broken bits of bodies which were the results. No witnesses are called for Kavanagh and before you know it, the prosecutor is on to sum up the Crown's case. The entire catalogue of technical details is brought out yet again, as if the cache were on trial, not the men. The prosecutor's smarmy voice drones on, drilling holes in the brain. 'Unusual porosity beneath the surface ... characteristic air bubbles and extrusion marks ... number eight aluminium L-series electric detonator ...' The only people conceivably interested in wading once again through this dense thicket of trivia must be the men in the dock – if they were involved, the reconstruction of the finer points of their deeds must be at least tantalizing; if they were not, it all constitutes a first-class bomb lesson, how to go about it another time.

As for Quigley's alibi, 'that cock and bull story,' sarcasm takes over. The prosecutor's favourite phrase is 'how *convenient*'; his second favourite is 'what a *coincidence*'. After all, those relatives *would* rush to Tommy's defence: hard-core Republicans, what with Frankie in the IRA, his brother and Geraldine's husband dead, and Tommy doing 'voluntary work for Sinn Fein, the political wing of the IRA – you'd expect a family of *that sort* to gather round at a moment's notice to give support to one of their own.' Tommy Quigley behind all his guards is looking decidedly drawn by now, his smooth brow furrowed, and by the time it is punched home that 'you couldn't *want* more compelling evidence!' his goose seems fairly cooked.

But that's before Tommy's defence lawyer Mike Mansfield mounts his charger. First of all, how *dare* it be suggested that Sinn Fein is the political wing of the IRA? 'It seems to me that that is a serious allegation to make about a recognized political organization, particularly as there is not a *shred* of evidence to support it.' The jury has been dismissed for a little discussion here; we suddenly find ourselves in a high-class debating society, the House of Commons, for example, with cries of '*Withdraw!*' The prosecutor comments: 'I have no intention of withdrawing and I shall bear Mr Mansfield's criticism with fortitude.' It is really his best moment; however, the jury misses it.

When finally Mansfield confronts them on the issue ('It's like saying the Conservative Party is the political wing of the SAS!') the judge is smiling.

Mansfield asks the twelve to bear in mind the resources of the prosecution – months and years and fifty crates of evidence – tons of dustbinfuls of evidence: is this the best they can do? Despite it all, what have they got against Mr Quigley? – half a dozen fingerprints! He asks them to disregard both the most horrible aspects of the case ('You don't protect anybody by putting the wrong people away') and 'the myths and legends of Irish politics', prejudice, press pressure; and to remember the problems of living in Belfast, where 'the conditions are not like Bexleyheath.' Above all, they should consider that of all the mountains of evidence, nothing proves that Tommy Quigley was in London or not in Belfast: considering the prosecution's resources, in fact, it is remarkable that no eye witnesses of any kind have been produced to identify him as crossing the border, being in England, or purchasing or ever using any of the vehicles in the case, let alone at the scene of the cache or the crimes.

Finally, 'What evidence have they put before you that this man is a member of the PIRA? What have they got? Nothing. A *paucity*, a *dearth* of evidence. I suggest to you that he is not a member; and don't convict him because he's Irish and because of his brother.'

I reel out into the street in a daze, determined never to go near the Old Bailey again. I'll read the verdict in the paper; it's better than being toyed with any more by these actors in their eighteenth-century fancy dress. Approaching the underground in the early rush-hour crowd, I notice two people chatting together who look absolutely familiar: I know their faces by heart. Who are they? I'm about to greet them anyway, if only to find out, then the flash: mems of the jury! Not just wooden profiles but people who walk and talk. It's just as well I said nothing to them: they are not to be interfered with, according to various dire judicial directives.

But have they been interfered with anyway? Later I bump into someone I hardly know at all, who politely asks what I am doing and I mention the trial. He surprises me by saying he is aware of that trial: he knows one of the jurors. 'She has been followed everywhere by two detectives,' he says, 'and her telephone and messages interfered with. It puts a lot of pressure on them for a certain kind of verdict.' Questioned, he refuses to say more; in fact he obviously regrets having said that much.

This possibility of hanky-panky revives my interest sufficiently to return for the judge's final speech – or some of it, since it continues for two and a half days. His Lordship addresses the jury in a convivial, leaning-forward style as he goes through the indictment. A shorthand writer, absent for the adversarial summing up, is back to take it all down. The veins stand out on Tommy Quigley's forehead; Kavanagh is as impassive as ever. The prosecutor picks his nose discreetly, with his thumb. Everything down to the last scrap of wire is being again unearthed from the multiply disinterred dustbins, and heads both in and out of wigs can be seen snoozing forward, jolting upright again. In the press section bits of desultory dialogue keep some people awake.

'A Yank, are you?' says a woman to me.

'In a way.'

'In a way?'

'Well I'm also British, and I've lived here for thirty years.'

'*Thirty years?*' She looks at me hard. 'But what about that accent?'

'What about it?' I say.

Her gaze is full of pity. 'Oughtn't you to do something about it?' she commiserates.

Considering this suggestion relieves me of the judge's entire rehabilitation of the Memopark TPUs. But I really want to have another look at the jury in light of that conversation. They are being kept jumping by constant references to different parts of documented evidence, each having to locate the right page in the right folder of the right stack before him/her (the judge's tail-coated flunkey hands him his). It is the six women on the jury who are now of most interest to me: who could 'she' be? They are all as impassive as Kavanagh, deep in a stupor of monotony, with the judge's speech by now showing all the properties of an anaesthetic. While accepting that 'the observation evidence was unchallenged' he nevertheless clearly intends to catalogue the whole thing yet again.

Such a fiendish system, justice – it seems to boil down to looking at a given, contained set of facts from one angle, then another, with then an ostensibly impartial overview; the story told, amplified, illustrated, repeated, repeated again, summed up until it is washed and rinsed and dried of all the filth of emotion and human frailty, humane conviction. How many times can you hear the same funny story and still call it a joke? How many times can you relive a tragedy and still find it moving? I once knew a man who listened over and over to music he loved with the idea of conquering any passion that could interfere with its pure intellectuality. Perhaps some similar principle is operating here – remove all emotion, become bored enough to be dispassionate and dispassionate enough coldly to interpret 'the facts': deny and eliminate, through repetition and dissection, any humanity that ever came into it. Thus the jury's feelings are bludgeoned out of the way of their impartial, rational analysis of Whodunnit. There is an Irish proverb: If you go to court, leave your soul at home.

His Lordship would continue the following day, Friday. But late on Thursday an event is headlined which might have more influence on the jury than any of his speech: an IRA action in Newry, Northern Ireland, had taken nine RUC lives as home-made mortars fell on a tea hut at a police station.

His Lordship finished his summing up on Monday morning, timing calculated to prevent the jury having to be sequestered over the weekend. By Monday the vast collection of prosecution exhibits in their blue plastic boxes has been removed, leaving lots of naked-looking trestle tables: as soon as this trial goes out, another is to move in. But mems of the jury are still being invited to 'examine exhibit 1222' and '110-S' in their folders; and every inch of the progress of a white Rover – in which Kavanagh and Vella were seen casing various forests – is mapped out despite the fact that the defence never had reason to contest it. Then we go over once again, lest anyone missed it the last time or the time before that, which was surely the hundredth time anyway, the contents of the dustbins, together with pirate-style map-marks to their original location (pale tree, bare stump, twenty paces, X marks spot).

Pretty abruptly, it seems to me, after forcing them to endure what they have, 'Well there you have it, mems of the jury,' says the judge. If there had been any air left in the balloon, this certainly constituted a deflationary finale. I had been to less than half this trial and my sense of suffocation was as real as if I'd been buried in a dustbin in a forest.

But then the only unrehearsed, spontaneous outburst of the entire event almost made you believe in courtroom drama again. 'I'd like to say something here!' shouts a voice from the dock: Tommy Quigley has got to his feet and is calling to the jury as they leave to decide where he will spend his life. 'I had nothing to do with those bombings!' he leans out of the corner of the box and points with his index finger: 'Nothing whatsoever! *And that's the truth!*' Shock horror! He said it too quickly to be stopped. Now he is ushered out. The collective adrenalin in the room is almost material, the quality of the air changed as if lightning has struck and changed the ions.

But in no time all that is expunged as ritual returns. A couple of ushers hold up the Holy Book in turn and mumble how they swear not to 'suffer anyone to speak to them' as they lead their twelve charges off to be safely stashed until they have been delivered of a collective opinion.

Everyone involved, and a lot of journalists besides, must wait. Not His Lordship: a rape case is starting immediately in Court 2 and he is presiding over that as well. Everybody else sits in the second-floor cafeteria drinking coffee and speculating about the outcome. Of the Quigley defence camp, two predict acquittal, two conviction, two a hung jury. The latter would mean having to go through the whole thing again from scratch.

They're a little worried about the influence of the nine deaths in Newry. One of them had gone down to the cells and seen Vella, asking him 'What about this Newry business?' 'Well, you know,' Vella had said, 'life must go on!'

No end of coffee has gone down various legal and journalistic hatches before the day is out and we're summoned, hopelessly, back to Court 2. The wigged ones discuss His Lordship's proposition: 'I had in mind to ask them whether there was any count on which they had reached agreement.' The defence is opposed to this so the jury are simply summoned back to be put away for the night. When they appear it is in a different order – as if their deliberations had shaken them up as a whole as well as individually. Then I realize it is because they have finally chosen a foreperson: a plump blonde in her late thirties who had looked throughout the trial like the front-runner in a zombie contest. But unless they'd merely drawn lots, she must have proven her worth to them.

'Mems of the jury,' the judge addresses them, 'you will have to go to an 'otel. There will be toiletries and suchlike provided' and so on: messages would be delivered to their homes; they are not allowed to talk to *anyone*.

Quigley and Kavanagh in their old places look not so much as if they are sitting there as growing there, and have been mown down by a giant steamroller.

Tuesday. I don't know why I keep turning up at this place. I care about the verdict, but there are plenty of ways of finding that out. There is just something fascinating in this awful process. Members of Quigley's defence team, over their coffee, have been reduced to trying to guess his astrological sign. A trip to the cells is called for. Leo, it is announced portentously, though what it portends is not immediately obvious. Much more coffee is drunk, the relativity of hangovers discussed. Every time the public-address system crackles the whole room sits up an inch or two, but there is no summons to Court 2 until noon, and even then only 'for a question'.

The jury has sent in a note. 'Could you kindly confirm,' the judge reads it out, 'is it a correct interpretation of the law if an accused person is found guilty of possession of explosives subsequently used in bombing incidents leading to loss of life, are they guilty of murder?' Since the Pangbourne cache must contain explosives put there after not before any 'bombing incidents', the meaning of the 'subsequently' comes in for a deal of guesswork. It is a tricky business to ask them to clarify without revealing 'how far they've got, which we don't really want to hear' says the judge, speaking for himself. Nitpicking time. The defence wants it made clear that it must be proved that 'the particular defendant was present taking part in a particular explosion.' The prosecutor thinks it must mean 'present at the preparation of the device whilst in this country with the knowledge of how it was to be used.' Even His Lordship is getting bored by this. 'Anyone might prepare a device in *Northumberland* and just send it by *post*,' he points out. They work out something they can agree on, the jury returns and gains some sort of enlightenment from the directive that 'the defence say it is not an essential step to take – to conclude that possession equals murder – and they invite you not to take it.'

That's cleared up, to anyone at any rate with a legal training. Hours later, after everyone has spent the afternoon in the cafeteria drawing up their wills (the place being infested with solicitors) we are recalled. I am full of high hopes but no one else has any; they all seem to know instinctively that it's just to tuck the jury in again. An usher in the lobby outside the court is beefing about it: '*Used* to be the rule was: trial lasts a month, or no 'otel.' He can't make out, it appears, why these jurors are being treated to Her Majesty's hospitality after a trial of a mere two and a half weeks. 'And a second night! Shockin'!'

As we enter Court 2, the prosecutor in the rape trial is deeply engaged in perorating, and our judge appears loath to break his stride. 'She said that her stepfather indecently assaulted her by pushing his penis into her mouth.' A sinister-looking old codger in the dock is peeking out from under hooded eyes at his jury, another jury. 'What does he say with regard to her allegations of continuing sexual relations in the kitchen?' demands the prosecutor. 'And what of his wife's remarks: "You dirty bastard, I knew something was going on."'

At a convenient break, the judge adjourns them until the

morning. That jury leaves the way we had come in; our jury, for which there are presumably higher security arrangements, files in as usual from the rear to take their places.

They have reached no agreement on anything, they announce.

Wednesday. The jury has another question. Actually it is the same question, requesting 'further clarification of the question of possession of arms in the Pangbourne cache and their eventual use in the autumn of 1981.' Before the twelve are admitted the counsel hammer it out, with the prosecutor attempting, it would seem, to shift the basis of his case, and the judge getting snappish. When he finally addresses the jurors it is unlikely that their confusion is seriously diminished. 'Mems of the jury, may I make this plain: if in respect of either defendant you were to come to the conclusion that the prosecution case on counts 7 and 8 was not proved, then you would have to acquit him not only on counts 7 and 8 but also counts 1 to 6 because the case depends . . .' The only people in the courtroom who even attempt to follow all this, it would seem, are the two whose lives depend on it and possibly the prosecutor, who is silently gnashing his teeth, assuming he has any (they have not been revealed).

The press benches are packed, and the reporters are in a state of terminal exasperation as they head for the coffee again. Late in the morning their stint is partially rewarded. The jury is summoned and as if to reflect the swinging fortunes of the accused they have entirely reshuffled this time, with the women in the front row and the men in the back. 'Members of the jury,' the Court Clerk addresses them, 'with respect of the defendant Quigley, have you reached a verdict, unanimous, on all of the counts?'

'No,' says the foreperson.

The question is repeated for Kavanagh and, *mirabile dictu*, the answer is *yes*. Unfortunately, however, they 'left it in the other room' because they haven't quite finished it yet. Five minutes, they promise, and re-exit. The courtroom's atmosphere turns to adrenalin again as, in complete silence, a hundred or more people wait.

When they come back it strikes me that for them, the courtroom is always exactly as they'd left it earlier, and earlier still, and yesterday, and the day before, and last week – everyone in their regalia and places, as if none of us had ever moved but just sat there forever waiting for them.

'Do you find Paul Kavanagh guilty or not guilty on count 1?'

'Guilty.'

And so on, for ten counts, with only count 3 (the attempted murder of Sir Steuart Pringle with a car bomb) unaccountably collecting a Not Guilty. That won't make much difference to Kavanagh. He sits in his box rigidly with a glassy, unblinking stare.

'You find him guilty and that is the verdict of you all?'

'Yes.'

At last the journalists have some copy to file and they push and shove each other to the telephones. For the Quigley camp, the situation has not changed: there are only new grounds for speculation.

Thursday. The judge told counsel last night that it was worth the £1,000 it cost to send the jury to the hotel for yet another night to save the expense of a retrial. At 4.10 in the afternoon, after rather a number of big brains have gone into a sort of group trance, the final summons comes at last. The jury looks noticeably grim. The same rigmarole read out by the Court Clerk is answered with a slight variation on the same result: it is a majority verdict, eleven to one, finding Thomas A. Quigley guilty on nine counts. It is only since the 1967 Criminal Justice Act that majority verdicts have been permitted.

As the counts are individually read out and it is apparent that he has one friend over there, Quigley ferociously reads their faces, looking for the one, and nodding at each in turn. He will never know. Could it have been 'she'?

Natalino Vella's case was soon dispensed with. When he appeared in the dock with the others he seemed much younger than they did, though he was two years older. He was thin with floppy hair and a boyish look, and his stomach was in his face as he listened to his statement of confession being read out.

He'd got mixed up in this two years earlier when he joined the Provisionals in Dublin. He wasn't of much importance, he'd said, just 'a glorified chauffeur' – quarter-master, supplying arms to the Active Service Units, including Kavanagh's: 233 pounds of explosives in this case ('You know England always gets the best,' he'd told the police). But unlike the others he'd never been trained in anti-interrogation techniques since 'I was never supposed to go to the North or the mainland.' The mission he had made, however – during which he had been followed by seventeen men from the Special Branch – had come up suddenly because Kavanagh's unit had 'stepped outside its instructions' by bombing Harrods, and Vella was meant to 'find out what went wrong and to tell the unit to go back to Ireland,' as well as to learn the locations of their arms dumps so he could show them to the next ASU.

This was the first we'd heard of Harrods. Kavanagh had been under instructions to bomb only military targets, and the explosion outside the store just before Christmas 1983, resulting in six dead and ninety-one injured, had caused 'a lot of trouble. We didn't want all those people killed. We didn't know whether they gave a genuine 45-minute warning or not.'

There was no mention in the confession of Quigley.

It was the sentencing everyone was waiting for now. Newsmen beside me were writing up their stories in their laps with spaces left for the number of years each man would have to serve. The judge too had already written his statement.

When the time came Vella stood up but the others kept sitting. The judge seemed to realize this and didn't look at them, just read. Vella got fifteen years. Quigley and Kavanagh were given five life sentences each.

'In the light of the horror and carnage it may be that no Home Secretary will ever think it right to release you. Nonetheless I think it my duty to express what society will feel about the nature of these murders by making minimum recommendations. Society feels you are not fit to be at liberty for a very long time.' They would have to serve at least thirty-five years, he said.

Quigley was smiling to himself as he was led away. The papers next day said he had 'grinned' and 'smirked'. One paper pointed out they would be free in 2020, aged 64.

What will Belfast be like then?

9
Our Way

The first thought you have at Long Kesh is escape. The doors that lock behind you are so many, so solid – each with a guard, each with the definitive *thunk* that car makers pay fortunes for. You can't see a thing but the next door, or hear a thing but the clash of keys. Three outer walls stand twenty feet high, sheer metal, topped with billows of barbed wire, so that far up is a stripe of sky; otherwise no distance is ever available to the eye. Tunnels of cage, wall and wire, deeper and deeper into the airless depths you go. And that is only for a visitor – who first must be conveyed by prison van with painted windows to the fences for the meeting with the prisoner who himself has just been driven in another painted van from somewhere even deeper. Your response to the ingenuity of those who have succeeded in escaping goes beyond applause: you stop caring what they've done or why, so overpowering is the need to *get out*. I've visited prisons before and been locked up in one, but nothing compares to this, nothing gets near it.

Hester and I had caught the UDA bus, a Dodge so old it 'once carried the wounded in the blitz,' which now trundles off to the jail three times a week from the UDA office and the Shankill. There were hard benches along the sides and folding wooden chairs to put in the central aisle for the overflow of passengers. Most of them were women, a cross-section of the poor. It was bitter cold and the bus unheated but only one woman was dressed for it in a tatty old fur; the others, in their serious efforts to look nice, had put on pointed high heels and freshly ironed jeans with miserably inadequate, if gaily-coloured, jackets. In my new moonboots, heavy coat and two sets of tights I was still numb by the time we got there.

You couldn't see out the window, so fogged up and scratched it was, and our arrival at the prison took me unawares. We followed the others into a small room where, behind a window, men studied passes and IDs. Even though my pass and ID failed to match I was waved through. They all knew Hester. 'Hiya Hester!' – 'What about ye Hester?' 'I've been coming here so long,' she said, 'they think I'm an inmate.' The guards exchanged wise-cracks with her about the resemblance of her new haircut to a haystack. It was hard to imagine a similar greeting for Republican visitors.

While Hester went in to be searched I waited under a carefully painted sign: ANY CASH FOR SPECIAL CATAGORY [sic] PRISONERS MUST BE LEFT AT CASH DESK. We were in the special category compounds for prisoners of war, long termers who had been inside for at least ten years, most without a release date: life means life. And we were to see Joker Andrews, *triple* lifer. That meant how many he'd been caught for.

My search was more perfunctory than that I'd undergone at Heathrow to come to the North at all. Two women, not in uniform, gave me a pat and took my handbag, counted and enveloped the money and returned it to me. No conversation – my carefully rehearsed local-style accent never got a try-out. Then from a second waiting room, when everyone was searched, we were led past a guard patrolling with a huge Alsatian yanking at its lead to a minibus with windows painted white, and locked inside. Probably no prisoners on earth call on more sympathy from allies to collaborate on escape, so one is deprived where possible of the chance to learn the layout of the place. For all I knew we were driven straight back to where we came from. Wherever it was, it was a third waiting room. A longer wait. Regular visitors here are used to having to devote a day to it.

At last, a call for us. We followed a warder, navy blue and jangling like the rest, down a corridor with numbered doors on either side. As we entered ours, a tall handsome young man was being led in from the back – which had no rear wall, like a backless hospital gown. In a hall behind were regularly-spaced guards to listen and to look. The cubicles were painted a peculiarly disagreeable mustard colour. 'Mustard' is Northern Irish slang for anything peculiarly disagreeable. No relation.

The most obvious characteristic of Joker was his physical perfection. He was so splendid it was hard to feel sorry for him. I still felt sorry for him. His physique and head were perfect as if by Praxiteles, with thick brown hair cut apparently strand by strand. '*Did he look like a murderer?*' people asked later. What does a murderer look like? A brutal hint to the eyes? A sneering, twisted mouth? Dorian Gray without the picture? Joker's strong jaw and square gaze gave only the impression of an honest, upright citizen in a socialist realist painting. Well, Hester prefers to believe he's innocent, taking the rap for some higher-up. Anyway so go the rumours, she said later. When she once challenged him on this he wouldn't discuss it – not only didn't he do it, he won't even squeal. And the other murders he was charged with over the years – sure he got off, didn't he? As for the three he's in for, it's delicate. Two of them were women. Some bungled burglary, goes the story, the gun a panicked response, and anyway he wasn't even there.

The second most obvious characteristic about Joker was the tattoo job. Protruding from the beige sweater was one perfect right hand with the fingers individually etched L-O-V-E; and a left with fingers reading H-A-T-E. Beyond

LOVE, as well, were ALICE, PAULA, MUM and DAD. Above HATE, a bird in flight. I had time to study all this artistry as Hester and Joker were in conversation inaudible even on the other side of the table where I sat, and certainly behind me to the screw. Hester's new haystack hairdo that the guards had made much of was so voluminous they both could hide in it. I only heard the frequent word 'document'.

The heated talk between them stopped suddenly with Joker seeming to remember his manners to exchange pleasantries with me, as if at a dinner party where the guests politely distribute their attentions either side. I commented on his tattoos, whereupon he raised his pullover to reveal, written carefully across the muscles of his lower belly: 'YOUR SEXY LOVE'. 'Isn't that wrong?' I said with great tact. 'Wrong?' he asked, put out but not offended. 'How?' 'Shouldn't it be Y-O-U-apostrophe-R-E?' The answer didn't interest him and he raised his jumper higher. Emblazoned in an arc across the top of his perfect chest was 'UDA COMMANDO'. Then up came a sleeve, to show something about having been a POLITICAL PRISONER in 1972. I gathered he had been interned then. The warder showed no interest in this advancing nudity.

Nor did he comment when another prisoner, finished with his own visit, was hailed by Joker and Hester as he passed behind our cubicle and then entered it, kissed Hester, and stayed for a good five minutes' banter. Hester had told me in the third waiting room about the battle she'd had with the authorities here simply to be allowed to wear a Remembrance Day poppy. The rules seemed to be discretionary. So much so that I heard later about babies conceived in the Kesh. In this case, they'd been Republican babies.

'How on earth did you do that?'

'Oh it was simple. We just piled one chair on another

with coats on them to make a screen, and told the screw to shove off, or if he wanted to look it would be more embarrassing for him than for us.' But for some years now the line had been drawn short of that.

As the other prisoner moved away, Joker continued the tattoo tale. Who had administered the needles? The hands were done inside, he said, when he was interned in the early '70s. The prisoners from different paramilitary groups hadn't been segregated then for recreation. He'd got an IRA man to do his fingers.

Another ex-internee I talked to about those days of mass imprisonment told me that at first there had been Catholic–Protestant association for sport and games and they'd got on pretty well, some of them sitting together on the side – where Joker's tattooing may have taken place. 'It was like two dogs with a fence between them barking and yapping at each other, then when they come to a gap in the fence they don't know what to do.' *Not* knowing what to do, they made friends – to the extent that when the guards peed into the food of Republicans or put dirt or glass in it, the Loyalists would toss over some of their own uncontaminated cooked meat or fruit. 'They didn't like the Catholics being messed about.'

Meanwhile Joker described his three hours of workouts a day, 'what I live for.' He was proud of his low heartbeat and the intricate callisthenics he had mastered, looking to us both for reassurance that he was wonderful and that it was somehow worth it.

He was not a political prisoner, he said, but a prisoner of politics, and he had come to realize that progress was hardly the word for what was happening in Northern Ireland. 'The situation changes here every day. Every day it's dicey. Every day they crack an egg into the pan. Sometimes they break the yolk, sometimes they cook it too long. Sometimes a day without violence, sometimes not.

But you can never take it for granted that it's going to be all right.'

About violence: so, I'd lived in New York, had I? They knew a thing or two about violence, in New York. But it wasn't much like war there, was it? There they mug and bludgeon *anyone*. There they beat up *old ladies*.

Joker's third most marked characteristic was his lack of jokiness. Now he returned to Hester. The 'document' they had been discussing was the new set of guidelines issued by the NIO about long-term prisoners, both lifers and SOSPs – juveniles sentenced to serve at the Secretary of State's Pleasure. He and others in his plight had been poring over it in the few days since it was issued, misinterpreting it to mean that release dates might be forthcoming; Hester had been sadly setting him straight. The cubicles up and down the corridor must have been full of the same conversation. And another: the problem of special status, which Bobby Sands and nine other Republicans had died for, and which gave those still included in it the dignity of prisoners-of-war with privileges of sorts – their own recognized commanding officer, extra recreation time, no work, *pride*. Now it had been announced that with the completion of a new prison at Maghaberry and the reshuffle of inmates, special category might be ended. Joker was incensed.

'I'm not a criminal! I'm a political prisoner! That's what gives me my self-respect! My principles!' And if they took it away, he'd been telling Hester behind her hair, he didn't know what lengths he wouldn't go to. He wanted to explain to me.

'I'm here because of the politicians. What they decided, we did. They said "shoot to kill"; we did it. Now see them sitting in Stormont over hot coffee. *With* a taste of whiskey in it. And look at me! If it wasn't for the likes of her and

Andy Tyrie where would I be? They've stuck with us, they're the only ones.

'Do you know how I grew up? In a house up the Shankill with two bedrooms, eight kids, and we had £10.17.6 a week to live on.' He was leaning across the table talking at me feverishly, as taut of mind as of body. 'We wore hand-me-downs. We never had anything new me ma didn't knit for us.' He wanted me to know that he supported the striking miners in England, he knew what it was like, and all he had in the world was his pride at having stuck to his principles however much those principles had been betrayed by the people who had advanced them to begin with. *They* had already put him away forever: if now in a final act of betrayal *they* took away the one thing that made his life bearable, he didn't want that life.

A warder leaned in the door and warned that the visit was over. Joker saw us out, a smiling and gracious host, before following his guards back to his lock-up and a life about nothing but the passage of time. We got our bags back ('One suitcase for Hester! Another suitcase for Hester's mate!') and after tracking back through the three waiting rooms and the white painted van, through door after door after door, locked, locked, locked, we collected the others in the only waiting room run not by warders but by the Quakers. Protestants and Catholics together had hot snacks and the children tried out the stocks of toys. Without such a decompression chamber, it felt that we had gone so deep we were in danger of the bends. Some of the faces were tear-stained.

The last thought you have at Long Kesh is escape.

Later Hester talked some more about Joker. His father had been killed when the IRA bombed a Shankill pub, the Four-Step Inn – 'so you can see what started him off.' His mother died while he was in prison and he had not been allowed out even for her funeral. After that for a year and a half he'd refused all visits. A sister had committed suicide.

We were with her twenty-year-old daughter, Maria, among Joker's mates in a UDA club off the Shankill Road. Every paramilitary group had its own drinking clubs and, with strictly no cross-fertilization, the wonder was their similarity – particularly in the utilitarian concentration on getting plastered. This one, in a dead-end beside a vast empty tract of rubble, was very well defended, with no way of creeping up on it or taking cover; inside, a reception committee of large men with military titles vetted entrants. Live music played from a small, not too proficient band, who compensated with volume. The smoke matched the fog outside, dimly lit by red bulbs in lace shades at intervals in the ceiling. At quite a few of the tables women sat alone, mostly rather overweight and squeezed into yesteryears' black cocktail dresses.

They were waiting for the bingo. After it was over the compère announced a couple of birthdays. 'Many happy returns to Sam Campbell – c'mon up here, you muggy! C'mere, Summy! I got summing for ya!' 'Rayyyyy!' cheered the audience. (The atmosphere was a ringer for the last Republican club I'd been to when the compère had announced that 'Des Breslin is here, just released from jail where he was in on the paid perjurer Christopher Black. Welcome home, Dessy!' 'Rayyyyy!' yelled the audience.) Here, at any rate, the birthday boy stood, delighted and abashed, and looking to be celebrating something well into his fifth decade. The atmosphere, come to think of it, was distinctly middle-aged – from Maria's point of view, you might say has-been. In the cab on the way Hester and the driver had been lamenting the loss of many Loyalist clubs they'd known in their younger days, but Maria had interjected: 'You know, people now would rather be together in clubs in the centre. It's *natural* to be together.' She had mentioned friends with Celtic names like Niall and Sean, and I asked her where they could meet. 'Anywhere in the centre. But usually only on Fridays. They're all on the dole, like me. The only time I have any money is Friday, so other nights we usually go to each other's houses and talk.' It was money that worried her, not sect. She had a lovely way of speaking, typical of Belfast but her own even more so: every sentence ended on an up note. At first it sounded like questioning. Then it began to seem light and optimistic. Her words did too.

She'd missed her Friday night on the town this week to go with us to another UDA club in Ardoyne. The goings on there had been younger, louder and friendlier, as people they knew kept coming to sit with us and apply themselves to rows of pints whose combined volume rivalled their own. At the end of both evenings, something happened which absurdly outraged me: the playing of *God Save the Queen*, for which everybody rose. On the other side of town they played *The Soldier's Song* and I'd stood happily enough for that: it had involved respect for the customs of others. But this anthem was *mine*, and in London long ago people had mocked such symbols into oblivion. Hester, I noticed, stood to the Queen on both evenings with her head bowed, hands clasped. 'I stand in respect,' she explained afterwards. 'And I bow my head in disappointment at the same time, because of the Loyalist prisoners who are in for being British.' My objections to the whole performance sailed by her entirely. 'It's something that belongs to us in Ulster. Something that represents us. But I would like to stand one day and not bow my head.'

Nobody left afterwards, even though the bar was closed, music over, and severe bouncing efforts made: people had lined up ranks of pints for this contingency. I went to the ladies' room and in the mirror spied two plump women in their fifties wearing gold Stars of David. 'Are there Jews in the UDA?' I asked Hester back at the table. 'The only thing Jewish in this room is my name,' she said, meaning Esther. But many Loyalists wear Stars of David: she used to have one herself but passed it on when the man who gave it to her was had up for stealing and she began to suspect its provenance. 'It's no big deal about the Star of David. In Loyalist areas a lot of people wear them. Most of them wouldn't know why. It's just a fashional thing.' But to her it had more significance: a matter of identifying with Israel. 'They have the PLO just as we have the IRA, with terrorist methods similar to the boyos. In fact the PLO trains and finances the Provos.'

She knew nothing of anti-Semitism ('You mean people against the Jews? Where?') except as a long-gone phenomenon of Nazism. In the war she had felt fiercely about that, she said, and if she'd been old enough would have fought, because of what Hitler was doing to the Jews.

'See part of me says murder is wrong, wrong, wrong. Right? But then if you turn the other cheek, just sit back and get on with bringing your family up and doing absolutely nothing, believe in God and do what's right – the Jewish people obviously must have done this. And look what happened to them. So I'm afraid I couldn't do that.'

Staying with Hester's family in Ballybeen, at Belfast's eastern edge, was unlike staying with the Ryans in Andersonstown only in personal ways. The houses were mirror images of each other, and although John had work for the moment he had recently been through a long period of unemployment with nothing to do but sit in his armchair, 'an L-shaped daddy,' as Hester put it. There were only two little boys instead of the Ryans' swarm of eight, and there were particular tensions because Hester and John happened to be at odds – a situation not all that unfamiliar to a marriage veteran – but there was little real difference between the two households economically, in matters of taste, or when it came to meals.

Now Hester was making Sunday lunch. I had been whining about the amazing lack of adventurousness among the Belfast population – so bold (to say the least) in other aspects of life – over food. Baked beans and sausages and chips. Bacon. Maybe some stew or soup, the ingredients almost indistinguishable. A treat was an Ulster fry: egg and bacon and sausage and tomato fried with soda bread and potato bread. A painless way to die, considering the alternatives, and not unpalatable. On my own I subsisted on bread and apples; the bread is the best anywhere, but even that gets boring. I'd tried taking friends to foreign restaurants in town. At an Italian one a typical victim, who had never tasted veal or aubergine in her life, wasn't about to start now. Closest to the familiar on the menu was minestrone, since it was translated 'vegetable soup', so she stuck to that. When the waiter tried to sprinkle parmesan on it she had a fit. '*Cheese* on *soup*!' she said with disgust, as if she'd been offered chopped worms. In Chinese restaurants I'd described the novel system of ordering several dishes and everybody sharing. What a great idea, all agreed. Unfortunately there was nothing on the menu they liked, and they'd order chips with curry sauce. There was absolute unanimity between Catholics and Protestants on this. Hester herself, having stomached my food lecture in her local Chinese, was however not about to stomach wonton soup or even roast pork, though she did venture some scampi with her chips and curry sauce. I'd seen her cooking system, more or less the same as everyone's: one deep pot of dripping, one shallow pan of dripping. In the first went the chips, in the second the meat. When not in use the pot and the pan were kept on or in the cooker with their fat going white.

She'd had enough of my complaints and for Sunday lunch unwrapped several lovely steaks, putting them in the shallow pan. 'It's just plain and ordinary, it'll do ya. It's not fancy Italian. If you get bringing Italian in here no one else would eat it, only yourself.' The steak bubbled away in its broth of hot fat, John came in periodically for a can of beer, and sounds of the boys' space invaders zapped and zowied through the wall. I read out to Hester a story from the paper about that week's visit to the North of the Duchess of Kent and how (it said) they were being 'fobbed off with second-class royalty yet again.'

'We'd rather have the Queen Mum,' Hester said seriously. She was transforming potatoes into chips. I'd tried to help but was much too slow for her.

Another story was about George Seawright – a Belfast city councillor known as 'Burn-'em George' since his recommendation earlier in the year that Catholics and their priests be incinerated – starting a 'Protestant League' to 'oppose the activities of the so-called Fair Employment Agency.' His League would model itself after a similar organization in the 1930s 'which fought for Protestants to get jobs instead of Catholics.' Their policy had been 'Neither to talk with nor walk with nor buy nor sell, borrow nor lend, take nor give, nor have any dealings at all with Catholics nor for employers to employ them nor employees to work with them.' The modern version, Seawright stated, aimed to do the same thing. Any Protestant seventeen or over who paid £1 could join, he said.

'Lend us a pound, Sally,' said Hester. She opened a tin of peas. 'See – if somebody's completely nuts, the media shouldn't give them that coverage. It makes outside people think that's what we're like.'

From many different angles over the next hour as the meat cooked she approached the matter of what they were like: robbed of their history ('You have a *right* to your own history! We were taught *English* history!'), not filled with hate, violent only to defend themselves from those who wanted to exterminate them. 'If you're asking me is it wrong to shoot an IRA man who's been murdering and goading other people into murder and slapping other people on the back for murder – then I would say it's basically wrong to shoot anyone. But I wouldn't cry my eyes out if Gerry Adams was shot, or some of his henchmen. You notice I'm not referring to the guy who's sent out on a job and hasn't any option. Because to me he's maybe a murderer but he's also a victim. I don't think Gerry Adams is a victim. I think he is a reasonably smart, devious, evil bastard.'

She had 'no time for': Russians, Yanks, bombers (as opposed to assassins, 'because you can't guarantee you'll not kill one innocent person'), British politicians, most Unionist politicians, Noraid. 'The people at Noraid owe me one: they have done me a bad turn by giving people arms. If you don't have a gun you're not going to be able to shoot me. All you can do is thump me and I'll get better.' The Workers' Party: 'If it came to it, I couldn't see them sitting in the middle. Their aims are like the Provies': to overthrow the country. If someone's offering me a promise to fight for bread-and-butter issues, I'd agree, but if in the end that meant giving up my identity, it's not on. Because I will fight for my bread-and-butter issues *my* way.'

All roads led to the same chief dread: a united Ireland. 'That's one thing that most of the Loyalist community have in common.' Her view of the South was of 'the upper class, the money class – you don't seem to have many middle-of-the-roaders – and then the poor people running around begging in the streets. With nothing on their feet, some of the kids. You know I couldn't live in that and not do something.'

The ubiquitous ice-cream van pulled up outside, its music amplified to blot out the loudest manifestation from space; the two little boys plunged at their mother for cash. The fact that it was colder than ice cream outside furnished the content of Hester's side of the row that followed. When everything had returned to normal, the steaks still boiling in their oil, I asked Hester if her objections to a united Ireland were economic, then.

'No no no, I wouldn't say they are. What it really amounts to is the Church. Now I respect their religion. I mean I don't care if next door are worshipping burning sticks; if they want that, they want it. But I don't want to live in the sort of country where if I'm different I have to do it their way. And there's plenty of big deal about some bastard being out with an Armalite. I can't even consider a united Ireland. And I consider it even less because of the years of violence. An awful lot of people feel that way too.' She started to drain the chips. 'We're dealing with people who are fighting to have their society enlarged by taking in Ulster. This is what those people are supposedly fighting for – but sometimes I don't think they really know what they're fighting for except just to fight. They want the British out of Ireland and then they think the big rainbow will appear. It won't. Because we're still left with our way – the aggro. Look at the many scars. Look at the many crosses.'

She retrieved the steak and called the children. Lunch was ready.

It was a couple of months before I got back to UDA territory, and then directly from staying in Andersonstown: leaving one secure universe for another, with the strange leap that always involved. People warn you about it but what exactly you're supposed to be scared of isn't clear. If you take it in pieces there is nothing to it because each world in itself is so intact, and much the same as the other. But this, of course, is the situation for someone who is irrelevant as a target. Driving through a hostile part of town with a representative of the other side, either side, you find the doors are quickly locked and the windows rolled up. My only personal nightmare was the roadblock. It wasn't just the delay; the 'security forces' themselves were felt to be the enemy, the forces guaranteed to give most people the most serious insecurity, and it was contagious. When they stopped me I felt suspect without any reason. By accident I found a good way to deflect them, after I was pulled over by a camouflaged UDR man who, over my wildly thudding heartbeat, kindly informed me that my coat was hanging out the door. If I always left it hanging out the door they suspected me of nothing but stupidly leaving my coat hanging out the door, and you could see how gallant they felt as I fixed it and they waved me on.

There were changes at the UDA office since the Newry mortar-bombing. The grille inside the front door was now kept locked, and an extra TV monitor had been installed to vet entrants. Hester, smiling and warm, made little of it, although the chart she kept on her wall, TERRORIST MURDERS, showed twenty dead under February. The problem after Newry, she said, was 'appeasing the heavies' who would like some quick revenge, solving nothing: 'even shooting Gerry [Adams] would be like cutting a worm in half.' In general, and with little cause for it, she felt optimistic: maybe it was just spring coming but she had the distinct feeling that there was new hope and happiness in the air. 'The boyos don't like it,' she said. 'The boyos' was what she called the Provisionals.

The UDA had issued a press statement after Newry:

The despicable acts of terrorism which took the lives of ten [sic]

Ulster people yesterday continue to be possible only because the government refuses to accept that a war situation and not a giant crime-wave exists in Northern Ireland.

Republican terrorists, who are not interested in any solution but military victory, must be met with counter military strategy and action. It is not enough to wait in the hope of trapping terrorists in the act, they must be sought out and destroyed in their lair.

This is not a job for the police force whose role it is to deal with normal crime through a normal judicial process. Wars are fought by soldiers who are trained for that purpose.

Under such circumstances our membership is calling for a more para-military emphasis within the organization.

The fact that republican terrorists can train, store weapons, construct bombs and launch attacks from Eire almost with impunity and the refusal of Irish Nationalist politicians to seek a realistic political solution within Ulster lead us to believe that the likelihood of a political settlement within the foreseeable future is unrealistic.

In the light of recent terrorist and political events the Ulster Defence Association, will in the coming week, be considering its role in the present situation.

It was all a bit of a trick, Andy Tyrie explained. He was like a cat who'd just outmanoeuvred a coyote. 'We done it deliberately for a reaction from the Dublin government. If they thought for sure that we were considering bombing the people down South, it's up to them'uns to increase security along the border.' The result would be to curtail IRA, not UDA, activity. That was all he'd aimed for anyway, he said, and it had worked! Extra gardai were being moved into the border areas, surveillance increased, and security stepped up. 'They done everything we wanted. So we don't have to do anything about it.'

We were in his office where a new poster read THE DOWNFALL OF THE DICTATORS IS ASSURED; the oversize bullet was missing from his desk; and he talked about how tired and depressed he was. He didn't look very tired or depressed except as someone might who started at a higher threshold than most. For three years now he had been out on bail after some incendiary literature had been found in his desk in a police raid. He had to report in twice a week and was unable to go away. He wanted it over with. Another cause of the sleepless night was some complicated reshuffling in the organization. He had recently fired everyone, top to bottom, in various UDA businesses – specifically the clubs, like the ones I'd been to with Hester. According to outsiders they were hotbeds of corruption, extortion and graft. Tyrie had called in each man individually and asked him three questions: had he stolen money, taken booze, or given perks. When they all said unequivocal Noes to each question, he'd dismissed them. 'I'd *believe* a man who said he'd helped himself to a bottle here or there or done something for his friends – it's only *human*.' But to get rid of them had required a great deal of preparation, because he had had to be very sure, and ready with replacements. To be seen to be fair he had interviewed everybody for the positions, even inviting the dismissed men to be reinterviewed along with everyone else. Most of them hadn't availed themselves, I gathered.

Having agreed to ten minutes to answer questions about Newry, Tyrie sat back and reminisced for an hour and a half. He talked about leaving school at fourteen to become an apprentice landscape gardener. 'I *love* gardening. It was practically a calling.' At that, he went off into transports of loving detail about all the things he'd learned: 'to understand trees, roses, indoor plants, outdoor plants, herbaceous borders, bowling greens, lawns . . . I started off, would you believe, in the Falls Park. I even learned to play hurley up there!' But flowers were his special love. In Ballymurphy, where he'd grown up, there had been 'the people's pride in growing orange lilies and sweet william – the traditional Orange-type flowers here.' His own favourites were carnations. 'I love carnations.'

He had finished his apprenticeship, 'loving every minute of it,' so that he would 'always be able to go back to having that job.' But gardening didn't pay enough and when he got married he worked in a factory lifting hundredweight bags of oil cakes 'like a bear' for seven years. 'It was something out of Charlie Chaplin's fillum *Modern Times* – if you can't get the button switched off, you got complications.' He was involved with union work, 'and I was shop steward and I was convener and I was a general nuisance.' The factory had either to promote him to management or give him his bags, as they say in Belfast. 'But I had outstepped the usefulness of the job; and the dust – it would have killed you after a while.'

Next, he started training with Rolls-Royce, 'and, uh, I wasn't very good at it. There was this great wee book, *Engineering Calculations* they called it. Now to me as far as a plane was concerned, that was the plane up in the air or the plain where the cowboys went across, not the plane of a surface. It was difficult but I learned it, and I got the job.'

He might have remained in a factory for good if history hadn't started happening on the street outside. It was a matter of 'either ignoring the Troubles and working full-time, or packing the job in and seeing what the hell is going on. That was round about 1973, and I took over running this organization since that.

'There was a whole load of defence organizations from '69, and they all sort of came together under one chairmanship in about '71. But there was joint chairmen and chairmen, all sorts of nonsense, so we had a weekend conference to talk about the future of the UDA, how it should be run. They decided that I was about the most impartial person who held any command in the organization and they asked me would I chair the meeting. I was to control the whole thing over the weekend and keep the situation going till everybody became reasonably good friends and talked to each other and got their wee bits and pieces sorted out. And at the end of three days they were all to go away and vote between three people, for who would run the UDA – Tommy Herron, Jimmy Anderson, or a fella called Harding Smith. After the vote they come back in again and they says, "Well, something very strange happened. They voted that *you* are now the chairman of the UDA."

'So then I sort of way looked at them and I said, "You're asking a wee bit too much." They said, "Well then why don't you take the job on a temporary basis? Till everybody settles down." I said I'd do that. I says, "I'll keep things going and make changes where I possibly can and then we can get somebody else for to chair the job."

'Well, I hadn't told the wife. I hadn't told anyone really. And it used to appear in the papers: WHO IS MISTER X in charge of the UDA? My wife used to say to me "You sure you're not Mister X?" But I finished up taking the job in '73 temporary and I'm still here. Still temporary.'

Of the three men mentioned, Herron and Anderson were shot. Why didn't anybody shoot Tyrie? 'I don't know. I don't want them to shoot me . . . There have been attempts. I've always said I'd love to be shot in the coat. So I could show it to people and say "Look at that."'

He had had to give up many of the ingredients of normal life. 'I used to like a drink, socializing. But I stopped. You have a responsibility: you become owned by other people, you're representing other people. So you can't be drunk, gambling, and getting up to all sorts of divilment. You have to get your priorities right, so you have.

'I enjoy the job. To do it is pretty difficult at times. If I was doing it for money, it would be impossible. I have no respect for money. I just need enough to live. I enjoy the work. You know you asked about people trying to shoot me, and bomb me and blackmail me and do all sorts of things. People get up to all sorts of things. When them things happen you do realize your choices. You either get out or you stay in. When I leave this organization it'll be because I want to leave it.

'The biggest problem is getting settled, conscientious people within the organization. A lot of these people think they can change into soldiers overnight. But what they do is they go into battle and they win and then they go home. And the enemy gets stronger: the IRA has been constantly prepared for hundreds of years. We have to be able to train people to cope with any situation that arrives here, without necessarily having to run about like soldiers scaring the life out of people. Changes could come about without people shooting anyone. That can be difficult but it's possible. What we're looking for is a steady, good UDA person who would think and question things and plan – really give it a lot more effort, not to do things on impulses or emotions. Because that's how the Protestants react here, on emotions. The condition here is ULSTER WILL FIGHT AND ULSTER WILL BE RIGHT.

'There's a massive gap in this community, but the only way you can get it going is confidence. Our people live in fear. There's two nations in this island. Where the southern Irish became Roman in their outlook, we became British. They built their culture round the whole Roman bit, where we actually tried to become imitation Englishmen. And our identity was almost destroyed by the British government. We have people saying "But we are British". That's ridiculous! My problem is I'm a disloyal Loyalist. I have no allegiance whatsoever to the British government. I don't trust them. I don't think we are very important in anyone's eyes but our own. What scares the life out of me is the bulk of the people here, if the British government says something's right, they *believe* it.'

I asked whether he thought about going into politics himself. 'I am not ambitious,' he answered, dissolving into silence. 'I fit into any situation, but the role I avoid is politics. I always worry about the misuse of power. You see when Andy Tyrie wakes up he thinks: Who is Andy Tyrie?' He was quiet again for some time. 'I don't think I'd make a good politician,' he said as if it were a new conclusion.

Another problem, maybe, was priorities again. 'A lot of things just don't excite me any more.' What did? 'I love cooking,' he said. Hester had told me about his reputation as a cook. 'There's lots of things I feel are very important, extra-normal things. We have a blackbird comes to us every year. Not the same one but. There's nothing as nice as a thrush first thing in the morning. The crocuses in the garden this time of year. All them things. That's the point I'm making.'

It was hard to see him as some sort of Godfather figure. Perhaps he was still a gardener, but a gardener of men: cultivating, pruning, transplanting, weeding, and taking pride in the landscape he was creating. After all, and his fixation with nature notwithstanding, the word he most commonly used was *people*. The only beings who apparently didn't qualify for the name were politicians. But there are limits to the bucolic vision of Andy out there in his old boots with his secateurs, dead-heading the roses. This was the man who had said: 'Politicians are always worried the paramilitaries will shoot or bomb. Paramilitaries do not have to deal with the public, they are not worried about votes.' Power was what it was about, and what did sweet williams or carnations care for power? They only bloom or die.

At several points during our talk he asked me to turn off the tape recorder. Later when I tried to piece together what had been said in those intervals, apart from some off-the-record stuff about his family, I thought of several remarks that gave off a kind of menacing solicitousness. 'I have never known a visitor here to be hurt,' he'd thrown in, apropos of nothing. Later: 'People who come over and walk down the middle of the road are treading a difficult path. If they go too far one way or the other, it might end badly.' And: 'People in Belfast are treacherous con-men: you never know who's telling the truth.' Naturally he could not have been referring to himself, with his wide-open, amiable sincerity. 'But of course,' he'd mitigated it, 'there are different truths.'

His last words were unambiguous: 'Be careful.'

10
Other Trials

In Andersonstown, there is a context for this war that goes beyond the issues ostensibly involved. Once it becomes possible to assimilate, somehow, the constant shock of the army and other visible manifestations of conflict, there remain problems which I, at any rate, can hardly imagine having to cope with. The helplessness of being unemployed and completely dependent on the state – a state moreover in which one has no confidence whatever – must by any reckoning be chief among them. Add to this various aspects of a dominating and restrictive religion, and a system of law so contorted that it serves only to buttress injustice, and the war begins to seem almost like light relief. But of course nothing is entirely separable from the war, which leaks into every aspect of life.

For example, poverty has a special local twist. After internment, thirty thousand Nationalist households in the province went on a rent and rates strike in protest. The government, which was also the landlord, retaliated with what the Child Poverty Action Group called 'one of the most vicious pieces of legislation to be passed this century' – the Payment for Debt Act 1971, under which the money owed could be deducted at source from social security payments. Confiscated benefits included child allowance, even the compensation awarded for death or injury; and those penalized were not just the strikers for their rent and rates arrears but anyone overdue on a utility bill. Many years after the strike which caused it, the Act is still in place and causes great hardship, as well as tending to give an understandably Live Today quality to the disposition of resources.

'In Northern Ireland, thirty-five per cent of all households live below the official British poverty line and there is sixty per cent unemployment in Catholic areas,' says the *Guardian* (23 January 1985). There is very little connection between the statistics and the experience. Percentages give no idea of how cold it is when there isn't any money left for coal; or of how you get the baby to stop crying when his last bottle suddenly breaks and the social security has run out; or of how to cope at all the week the broo doesn't come through because the post office was robbed.

That's the situation at the Mullins' where the welcome, anyway, is the most opulent anywhere. In a home where you can't afford lavatory paper (special expedition to get it when I come) let alone food for tomorrow, what there is for material comfort is in the realm of dreams: the TV providing the vicarious luxuries of some other world; a giant doll's house the girls got for Christmas, where a Cindy doll reclines on a chaise in her shades after a session in her battery-powered sun-tanning apparatus; and for the grownups some alcohol to get 'paladic' on Saturday night and briefly beyond the realities. The children make up their calories with sweets. Their milk teeth are already brownish.

Kathy Mullin is prone, having just come out of hospital after a miscarriage (and anticipating the wrath of Father O'Hare for having had a D and C, even though the baby was dead). The same week, Brendan was told that the 'asthma' the doctors had diagnosed for years is tuberculosis, with one of his lungs past repair. But even these matters don't seem to weigh on them: TB is no reason for Brendan to pamper himself, even to stop smoking, and there is the usual deep if inexplicable happiness in the house. Constant touching and hugging for the children, an open door for friends to come in, adventures going by the window as the army patrols circle or the neighbours clobber each other on the pavement again (even more entertaining than *Dynasty*). Brendan may still be unemployed but he has plenty to do around the house, mopping the kitchen, making stew, doing laundry, shopping, walking the girls to school. Always a racket, loving chaos, the sound of laughter.

But the ends-meeting game is tricky, there is much pride involved, and appearances count. The money-lender, with his extortionate interest rates, is considered preferable to help from friends or relatives. Andersonstown has gone into colossal debt over Christmas presents for the children, never an economy here, so it was a bad week for the post office stick-up as the entire locality lives on dole cheques collected there. It can't re-open before an audit. Then again the post office is often held up, so there are schemes and schemes. Frugality, however, is a luxury: thrift is a matter of organizing priorities, something you have to be able to afford. This life is lived in the *present*. The left-over stew is thrown away, and no one would dream of asking for a doggy bag at their rare meals out. A short-lasting cheap new garment or piece of furniture is chosen over a good quality second-hand one; pride forbids fuss over something already acquired that turns out not to fit or to have something wrong with it. Confirmation outfits for the children set people back £70 to £100, but a little girl can't wear someone else's once-worn white dress, she must have her own new one, together with crown and veil.

The Mullins' daughter Josephine is even going to have a parasol. She takes a tangerine I offer her and before eating it becomes absorbed on the floor in spreading out its paper wrapping, then a border of peel, then the sections into an intricate flower pattern. It's a big week for her, as on Thursday she makes her first confession, prelude to confirmation. She is so enthusiastic about the world and herself, and is about to embark on life as a sinner. She is seven. At least she had thought out what to tell the priest: that she shouted at her baby brother. Pat down the road said she'd come into the kitchen one morning to find her daughter Clare crying into her cornflakes, and when she asked what was the matter Clare said 'I need a sin.' – 'You what?' – 'I need a sin! All the others have sins and I don't have any!' The mother suggested she say she'd used a bad word, which she hadn't. Clare ran off to school cheerful again, ready to lie to Father O'Hare.

The people's bond with the Church is real. There appears to be little recognition of the contradictions its teachings represent to the desired thirty-two-county socialist republic. A very few decide to take a stand, but they are stuck when their children are used as the Church's lever for their fealty: if the parents aren't married, or if they don't attend Mass regularly (which they may not do anyway if they are unmarried parents), great pressure is put on them to shape up or their child will be denied confirmation and eventually the right to go to the local Catholic school at all. An escape route of sorts had just presented itself: an Irish school opened nearby with lessons given entirely in Gaelic and religious education optional. It was even co-educational. Unfortunately it only went up to age eleven. I asked one father, a top Sinn Fein official whose three-year-old son was just due to start there, what they would do when the boy was eleven. 'Maybe we'll have won by then,' he said.

I went to Mass with Mairead, the eldest Ryan child. She was perhaps the brightest, most competent person of fourteen I'd ever met. Her family were deeply committed Sinn Feiners. It had never crossed her mind to doubt the Catholic Church. She certainly wasn't going to Mass out of duty, to see or be seen, or for any reason except her strong beliefs.

The service included the introduction of an Irish Bishops' pastoral on love and sexuality called *Love is for Life*, with free copies available afterwards. There was nothing particularly novel about the directives it preached, but how could people reconcile them to their professed politics? Sinn Fein women to whom the booklet was shown universally scoffed at it, though that didn't much affect their personal behaviour, which stayed more or less in line. If you have six or eight children, contraception presumably hasn't come into it and divorce is not an attractive option.

Beginning by defining sex as 'a means of communication', the bishops elaborate: 'By sexual union, a man and woman say to each other: "I love you. There is nobody else in all the world I love in the way I love you. I love you just for being you. I want you to become even more wonderful than you are. I want to share my life and my world with you. I want you to share your life and your world with me. I want us to build a new life together, a future together, which will be our future. I need you. I can't live without you."' And so on, as much again. 'Sexual union also speaks of man's willingness or readiness to give a child to a woman as ours and of a woman's readiness to bear his child.' They go on to define 'Christian marriage . . . as marriage restored to its original condition before the first sin, (and reflecting) Christ's love to the world.'

As for divorce, the Church cannot permit it, 'not because she is lacking in compassion and unwilling to do so. It is because she cannot do so. She cannot change the teaching entrusted to her by her Lord.' Here, although you wouldn't know it from a simple reading of the booklet, 'her Lord' has nothing to do with Christ. The supporting biblical citation is to 'the prophet Malachi (2: 14–16)' who, they say, 'puts it plainly: "Do not break faith with the wife of your youth; for I hate divorce, says the Lord, the God of Israel."' This comes from the Old Testament, seldom used as authority for anything in the Catholic Church; and if you look at the whole chapter of Malachi in the King James version, you realize it's about something different. Chapter 2 begins 'And now, O ye priests, this commandment is for you. If ye will not hear . . . I will send a curse upon you . . . and spread dung upon your faces.' It appears that Malachi was discussing the Lord's covenant with Levi [the priestly caste] and inveighing against corrupt priests in the Kingdom of Judah [Judea] who had taken to divorcing their first wives and marrying non-Israelites. 'Judah hath profaned the holiness of the Lord which he loved, and hath married the daughter of a strange god. The Lord will cut off the man that doeth this, the master and the scholar, out of the tabernacles of Jacob.' We then get to the verses in queston, which in the King James version read:

> Yet ye say, Wherefore? Because the Lord hath been witness between thee and the wife of thy youth, against whom thou has dealt treacherously: yet is she thy companion, and the wife of thy covenant. And did not he make one? Yet had he the residue of the spirit. And wherefore one? That he might seek a godly seed. Therefore take heed to your spirit, and let none deal treacherously against the wife of his youth. For the Lord, the God of Israel, saith that he hateth putting away . . .

It seems clear that the passage's concern was mixed marriages among the priesthood, to protect the 'godly seed' of Israel. Its misuse is unlikely to be challenged as Bible reading is not encouraged in Catholic Ireland, and certainly not Old Testament reading. No one I met in the Catholic community had an Old Testament, and there was not one in stock in the Church bookshop.

Deviations from the rules call down most opprobrium. 'All relationships which separate sex from marriage are against God's law of love,' reads the pamphlet ('Enough to make God turn in his grave,' commented a local cynic). No authority is cited in this case. The problem of homosexuality is viewed with 'compassion', which is also bestowed on unmarried pregnant girls, brutally treated wives, and the children of bad marriages. Not much compassion to spare for rape victims: 'Following rape, immediate interventions to remove semen and prevent fertilization are morally right . . . If, nevertheless, fertilization were to occur and pregnancy result following rape, there is a new and innocent human life present whose right to life must be respected.'

For those whose marriages lead to 'intolerable suffering', compassion is about all they can expect. Despite all the lip-service paid to Irish unity, the hierarchy continues its uncompromising disregard of the concerns of those who would have to be persuaded. Ireland forbids divorce not just by religious fiat but by state law, and a public referendum in the South some months later confirmed its illegality. But even in Paraguay, one of the very few other countries which ban divorce, the prohibition applies only to Catholic Paraguayans. There may be no great demand for it among Northern Ireland Protestants – all Unionists but one voted in the House of Commons against extending British divorce rights to Northern Ireland, reflecting the fundamentalism of their constituents – but 'they're such sanctimonious bullies' was a Protestant view of the Catholic Church. At all events, while acknowledging that special local problems mean 'legislators have to aim at creating a body of laws which as far as possible favours reconciliation between citizens and communities,' the bishops' view is that 'the legalization of civil divorce . . . builds up a social pressure, which for large numbers of people become [sic] stronger than moral or religious resistance.' So much for sectarian reconciliation.

Father O'Hare did not discuss any of this with his congregation, only waving the booklet about and entreating them to read it. After the service some of the people in his congregation told me that he was rather disapproved of because he had encouraged their children to go on RUC tours of Belfast: since the RUC are equated with the Brits, this made him 'pro-Brit'.

This judgement also satisfied Mairead in the matter of the nine RUC men and women who had been killed in the mortar bombing the week before in their tea hut in Newry: the implication was that as honorary Brits, they asked for it. The concept of Irish killing Irish was a wildly startling, brand-new idea to her. Her twelve-year-old brother Tony joked about the event as 'the Last Supper', and there was a new piece of graffiti up the road in giant red letters: RUC FOOD IS BAD FOR YOUR HEALTH. Their mother was upset about rumours that a man arrested in Newry might squeal, and that a 'successful military operation' could come to grief this way. She reported that the cheering in the streets after the Newry bombing had been almost as wild as after the time the thirty-eight men escaped from Long Kesh. Brendan, on the other hand, said, 'We don't gloat over death. It's horrible whoever it is.'

It wouldn't bother Brendan, though, if the Rah dealt with the supposed informer in jail; that went too for another man who was in custody after stabbing to death an old fellow who delivered groceries. Brendan himself the other day had chased and kicked to a pulp a joyrider who had run over and killed a three-year-old girl. The Rah had now fittingly punished the joyrider – a hammer to the hands, breaking all the bones, and breeze-blocking for the legs.

I had come downstairs in the morning to find Brendan

ironing three frilly dresses on top o
said there had been a big fight in th
before, so rowdy that he and Kathy ha
window half the night; then we were all wok
by an army helicopter. There is nothing like be
dozed out of sleep by a chopper a few feet above ur
head the other side of the roof, as if the world is breaking open. It was normal for them. Practically sleepless, Brendan had been out early to buy me an *Irish News* – he read the London *Mirror* himself ever since the *News* stopped printing the IRA Deaths in Action.

While I read the paper Kathy, with the baby crawling all over her, thumbed through *Love is for Life*. She thought it was quite a hoot. The Church wasn't all that rigid about failed marriages, she said. An uncle of hers had got an annulment because his wife had run off two days after the wedding. 'Only they were married twenty-five years ago,' she said, 'and the annulment came through last week.'

Rita Ryan had introduced me to her neighbour Pat, whose husband was one of the accused in a case based on the testimony of the supergrass Harry Kirkpatrick, now on at Crumlin Road. Having just been allocated the house, Pat was new to the neighbourhood and felt completely isolated because it was Provo territory and her husband was an Irp, an INLA man. After his arrest she'd spent days in tears, until one of the Ryan children had alerted Rita who'd gone to the rescue. Rita tolerated Irps; it was the Stickies she reviled.

Pat attended the trial, which was due to go on for months, every day, and I was going with her. She looked about sixteen but already had three children, one just born; disposing of the kids so she could go to court was only one of her chores. Her daily routine involved getting the eldest child (the sinless Clare) to school, grocery ıg with the other two, delivering the baby to her mother in another part of town, walking well over a mile to Crumlin Road, depositing the middle child in the Save the Children Fund Families' Centre next to the court, queuing at the jail with a food parcel or clean laundry for her husband, and sitting in the court all day where she couldn't hear anything anyway. Three times a week she also got visits with him afterwards. Then back to SCF, to her mother's for the baby, and home. Sometimes she didn't even start the tea until after seven, she said. This was her only complaint.

The weather was icy but Pat wore three-inch stilettos, like every other woman we passed who was under fifty, as she towed a four-year-old through puddles and rubble and tried to manage as well a huge bundle of clean clothes to be delivered for her husband. Of course she had help this day, but not as a rule. Frail and near the edge physically, she'd had to spend two months in hospital over the latest birth, and only three days later her husband – who had at first been granted bail, as his alleged offence was minor – was picked up again.

In the courthouse another trial was going on as well as the Kirkpatrick trial; I dropped in there first. In the dock were five young women and an old man who was the father of one of them, all acquaintances or neighbours of Rita's. The women had been found in his house with bombing gear. The trial was in the Foregone Conclusion Department, the only question being the degree of responsibility of the old man and his daughter – neither of whom, Rita assured me, had had anything to do with it. Everyone (apart from the court) always seemed to know who *had*.

'If the jury would apply its common sense . . .' the barrister was saying. I looked around for this jury but nothing looked like one. 'What I would submit to the jury

. . .' 'The totality of what he says must be taken into consideration by the jury . . .'

'But I'm afraid,' replied the judge, 'that the jury would draw adverse inferences which I wouldn't draw.' This was of course a Diplock Court and there was no jury – only speculations on what the jury would be thinking if there were a jury, with the judge doing half the speculating when he wasn't being the jury himself. And when was that? It was entirely up to him after all. The old man sat on, a pained expression on his face. It seemed he was opposed to violence and would never have let his home be used to further it; all he knew was that once in a while a group of his daughter's friends disappeared into her room. It never occurred to him they might be having Cumann na mBan cell meetings. When all this began he'd just come back from a two-week cycling trip round Ireland, and he was out buying a pot of marmalade one day when the police overran his place and the next thing he knew he was under arrest.

'Any reasonable jury would take into account . . .' the barrister was pleading as I left. I recalled Pat's remark as we'd entered the building: 'It doesn't seem to be like law at all any more.'

In the Crown Court, the scene seemed little different from the last supergrass event I'd attended there. Kirkpatrick wouldn't be turning up until after Easter, and most of the evidence now being heard was supposed to provide background to what he would say, but since no one knew what that would be, there wasn't much sense to be made of it.

The room was jammed to bursting, the banked pews up the back full of wives and mothers and, below, overflowing dockfuls of young men indistinguishable from the police except for their dress. Boys to bruisers, they filled every description of male youth, and it seemed a question of sheer chance which side any of them was on – witness, cop or culprit. The only visible difference between the right side of the law and the wrong was how clothed its upholders were and how naked the defendants, like a Goya painting of a courtroom. I counted forty-eight uniforms, eighteen RUC and thirty prison guards. They were muddled up together with the prisoners sitting in all sections, standing in the aisles, leaning in the doorways. The judge had no ermine here, but sported grey silk trim on his psychedelically red robe, and wore a wig like a sheep's bottom. It was hard to see how he or any judge could deal with this, obviously entirely his show. There were ten other wigs in the room, rows of various solicitors and legal staff in suits and a long box of witnesses and plainclothesmen. Only the legal people had padded seats, and only they could really make out what was going on – in the tall and echoing space the microphones merely amplified the mushy inaudibility of the proceedings.

The press box was in a favoured spot so I could hear quite a lot – although eavesdrop would be more the word, as it seemed to be a very exclusive three-way dialogue between counsel, judge and witness all of whom were quite indifferent to their audience. But the evidence was almost incredibly uninteresting, even for a recent Old Bailey alumnus. The last time I had been in this court this 'press box' had been a prisoners' dock, and those people must have found the proceedings as tedious then as I did now; the shelf before me was doodled over top to bottom with dates and initials, a Gothically lettered 'This is boring' and various other messages ranging from 'Not Guilty!' to 'Basil is a cunt'.

Picking out the defendants again in their different spots I saw they were all in their mid-twenties to mid-thirties – a generation of INLA men. The most interesting one to look at was Ta Power, who hadn't cut his hair since he had been arrested. He'd 'been under' five separate supergrasses. The others retracted and he was let loose, only to be rearrested on the courthouse steps. Having been in jail unconvicted of anything for almost three years, he was becoming famous as the longest remand prisoner ever in the British Isles. His red hair and beard came way past his shoulders and he looked very pale and spiritual. The men around him were of all kinds, but gave the impression of being boyish and eager – especially one of them, Gerard Steenson, strikingly angel-faced and innocent looking. In some circles he was known as 'Dr Death', said a neighbour in the press box, because he had usually done the killing.

One difficulty about 'criminalizing' these people was the question of individual responsibility. When a man murders another it is generally his idea, his act, his aberrant behaviour. In the case of these men, a whole section of society had risen up against their perceived oppressors. To have grown up among them and to have *avoided* joining them would have been aberrant behaviour. How could any of them be individually responsible for what they had done? It was literally a class action, a class of a nation on trial before another class of another nation who happened to share the same turf. How could the ordinary rules of criminal justice have anything to do with it? The absurdity of the operation was only equalled by its futility. When the responsibility is collective and on this scale, it becomes the kind of thing they invented war or politics to deal with, not courtrooms.

The greatest travesty was that all prosecution witnesses were in court at once and listening to one another. Two ex-British squaddies testified one after the other about some events which had occurred on the night of August 8th and 9th, 1980, and neither was asked to withdraw while the other spoke. I suddenly tuned in when the events – which seemed to involve someone having been shot –

were placed. 'Rossnareen Park', they said, and 'Shaw's Road'. This was where the Mullins lived, currently my address.

A Sergeant Clark was first, a handsome Scot with slightly wonky eyes. In the early hours of the morning, he said, his patrol was out in a pig accompanied by a ten-ton truck and a digger. Encountering a barricade, they attempted to plough straight through it but got caught and landed up balanced on top. The local populace took advantage by heaving bricks and bottles. The soldiers tried to protect themselves by firing some baton rounds, which broke up the crowd. At that point Sergeant Clark noticed a group crouched together by the side of the road and he got out of the pig to investigate, thinking they were preparing petrol bombs. But instead, 'a body' was lying there with the people surrounding it. It was up to the neck in a blanket and all he could make out for identification was an earring in the left ear and a medallion round the neck. He asked them for the name of the man but they wouldn't tell him. Then he asked them all for their names and they wouldn't tell him those either. When an ambulance came, the soldier tried to find out from the driver what hospital he was going to in order to pursue the matter, but the driver wouldn't speak to him. Eventually the squaddies got their pig unstuck and returned to base, where their ammunition was very carefully checked: nothing but baton rounds had been fired. The implication was that 'the body' had been harmed by his own side.

The next witness, another ex-Scots Guard, having been in court listening to his colleague's evidence, not surprisingly confirmed it. Just as nobody called the body 'dead', nobody mentioned that August 9th is Internment Day. Its eve must have been like the one I'd witnessed the summer before, with bonfires and barricades throughout the Nationalist areas of Belfast. The digger and the ten-ton truck were there presumably to clear these away. The rest of the story seemed plausible enough – especially the lonely detail about the people not speaking to the soldiers. But what Harry Kirkpatrick could have had to do with it was not clear, since Pat told me afterwards that he was in prison in the summer of 1980.

Late that night back at the Mullins', I mentioned the court case and asked if they remembered anything about somebody getting hurt up the road on Internment Night 1980. Brendan said he remembered very well because 'a young lad was killed by the army and he died in my arms.' Brendan's story was rather different from the version I had heard in court, but it was obviously the same story.

First the barricades went up, 'like every year', but in 1980 Brendan was involved in getting them there. With eighty other men, he had gone to a brewery early in the morning to commandeer some trucks. They were after empty trucks but, finding them already loaded with the day's liquor deliveries, they broke all the bottles and kegs 'so people wouldn't make a profit over it' and drove about three dozen of them to various barricades, dismantling the engines on site so the army couldn't move them away.

That night, 'the Saracens and pigs were trailing down the road and everybody throwing bottles or stones at them – the usual sporadic, you know, rioting? It's just a show of defiance, to let them know that people are not going to be ruled by them.' When the pig tried to break through their barrier it got caught, with army digger and ten-ton truck close behind, and the soldiers fired plastic bullets to disperse the crowd while they worked at freeing the pig. They'd almost accomplished this when, walking towards them, came a boy who 'had just been taking his girlfriend home and had nothing to do with it.' People shouted at him to get down because of the Brits, but 'he just kept walking right towards them, and that's when we heard the shots. It sounded to me like plastic bullets but other people said it was live rounds. Mrs O'Brien said she saw the two flashes. She said she knew the difference between flashes from a baton round and an SLR.

'We ran to the wee boy, we saw him falling. When we got up to him the blood was flowing out of his neck. So Mrs O'Brien knelt down and said the Act of Contrition in his ear.' Somebody got a blanket, another called for an ambulance. Then a third person 'found a plastic bullet lying in the green beside us. It was doctored, with piano wire up the middle of it. So it split the neck.'

At that point the pig was freed from the barricade, Brendan said, and 'the sergeant drove it right up on to the green where we were standing, right up to the dead body, and tried to ram us. But nobody would move. So about five of them got out wielding batons and tried to snatch the body away. But at that stage a bigger crowd had arrived and the soldiers were beat back.' The ambulance came then, the people laid the dead boy inside 'and they [the soldiers] tried to get the body back out but the ambulance man ushered them away and refused to say what hospital they were going to.

'Then the real rioting sparked off.'

An official version was published two days later, Brendan said. According to the army statement, 'they had been fired on by gunmen from them flats' (he gestured to a nearby block) 'and in their opinion the young fella was a gunman himself. Utter nonsense. He wasn't that kind of lad, he never got involved in any trouble.'

All night I kept thinking how punctilious the Old Bailey affair had been in retrospect, and waking intermittently in outrage. But outrage was scarce by now among the local people, who seemed just cynical. Brendan hadn't even shown surprise at my story of the court proceedings. As a social worker had said to me, 'The Catholic population has no confidence whatsoever in the security forces or the judicial system. And a large section of the Protestant population is now coming to realize that what [the Catholics] have said is true. The law is held in such disrepute in this place it's going to be very difficult to get people *ever* to have any respect for institutions.'

As for the legal participants, after the court had adjourned that afternoon, I had waylaid a defence barrister to ask him about this unique system of allowing prosecution witnesses to hear each other (a favour certainly not granted to the defence). 'It's an Irish custom,' he'd said dismissively. Before I could even reply that I thought this was meant to be *British*, after all, he gestured towards a crowd of more than a dozen men, among them the two Scots Guards, emerging from the depths of the courthouse. 'It makes no difference anyway,' he said. 'See that? They've all just been cooking up tomorrow's testimony.' He shrugged and walked off, the tiny pony tail on the back of his wig bobbing up and down.

11
'Peace'

Everywhere that night in Andersonstown the television sets were showing the same thing. The screen was green, with the sound of clicks as sticks hit balls, the occasional drone of a commentator, sprinkles of applause. It started to get on my nerves. The way the attention of Rita and Dermot and the children skipped like a light stone off me and back to the box made me think of moving on. At the next stop, Brendan and Kathy were watching their green square with such concentration that talk was impossible. Then to the mother of one of the women in the 'jury' trial I'd attended, who was looking at her set alone in her front room. She wanted to tell me about her daughter's sentencing (with time served on remand, they'd be back together in twenty-one months) – but her attention kept getting hooked back boxwards. Finally an expression akin to resentment flicked across her patient face as huge hurrahs burst from the telly and the announcer gasped, 'That was *impossible*!' Some crucial moment had been missed. I still couldn't see what the excitement was about.

'Do you play?' I asked.

'Play *snooker*! I couldn't play *snooker*!' said she aghast. It was useful to have the thing identified: it could have been golf for all the notice I'd been giving it. 'No, it's just, uh' – her eyes were on the screen – 'he was eight frames behind, and he caught up on them, and now he, u-uh . . .' she was lost to me.

Back at the Ryans', where I was to sleep, Mairead opened the door with a peremptory 'Sh!' The little ones having been sent to bed, Dermot and Rita, Mairead and twelve-year-old Tony were utterly engrossed. At long last it was explained to me: this was the end of the World Snooker Championship, and a squat fellow wearing very queer spectacles, called Denis Taylor, was neck and neck with a patrician-looking gent, Steve Davis, at the start of their very last frame. What counted was that Taylor, who had been desperately behind throughout the two-week match and might improbably still catch up, was a *Northern Ireland Catholic*, and the slim disdainful Davis, apparently in control not only of his cue but of his resolve, was a *Brit*. The whole shooting match was being played out on green baize in the corner of every living room in the North.

Could the likeable but unprepossessing underdog win the day? It seemed doubtful. The players showed no emotion, but the raging passions in the room compensated for their cool. Tony made a crack denigrating his fellow countryman for missing a shot. *'You're a scud, Anthony!'* Mairead blasted at him. (A scud 'puts bad luck on people', she told me next day, and Anthony is what she calls Tony to annoy.) Dermot, far from supine on the sofa, was bouncing up and down. 'Jammy bastard!' he shouted at a lucky shot from the Englishman. But the Brit sank another ball. 'Ya dirty English fuckpot!' bawled Dermot. As the tension grew Rita lowered her face to the arm of the couch. She couldn't watch. The children had theirs on their knees. Although the Irishman was getting in the odd shot it was inconceivable that he could take the title. But Davis made a mistake, then another. Finally not even Dermot was looking. I was the only one in the room with my eyes on the screen, having to tell them what was happening. I felt like a shabbas goy.

It was well past midnight when there was nothing left on the green table but one white ball and one black ball, with the commentator pointing out that if Taylor could sink this one, not only would he be world champ but it would be the first time in the entire two-week match that he would even have been ahead. He missed. No Ryan had breathed for some time now, only occasionally issuing forth a small trapped scream. Then Davis tried. He also missed. Tony was rolling around the floor clutching himself. Mairead was either praying or having a seizure. Rita and Dermot hadn't looked up at the screen for ages – Rita might have fainted. You could feel all of Northern Ireland in excruciating suspense as their man took his final shot – and potted it.

The Ryans were happier than I'd ever seen them, possibly as happy as they had ever been, but there wasn't a lot of noise, only a great grinning. It should all be so simple. It should all be so *vicarious*.

Next day the entire town was exhausted and *glad*. And there was nothing tribal about it: Denis Taylor wasn't a Catholic hero, he was a Northern Irish hero. A UDA man who normally referred to religion as 'all that shit' said he'd spent most of the final frame on his knees asking 'Please God let Denis Taylor win.' Taylor's first welcome-home celebration was on the Shankill, where he can't have spent much time heretofore and where no one was crass enough to mention his religion.

Less then six weeks later the whole performance was repeated when Barry McGuigan, another Northern Irish Catholic (although he comes from County Monaghan in the South), won the world featherweight boxing championship in London, before an almost wholly imported audience of every kind of Irishman. The streets of Belfast, deserted during the televised fight, were filled till morning with honking cars, cheering crowds. When the winner arrived home he got Belfast's equivalent of a ticker-tape parade: twenty thousand people watched and screamed from the streets and roofs and anywhere they could get a toehold as the new hero rode by on a float shaped like a boxing ring. Without a nod towards the war they usually fought in their columns, the *Shankill Bulletin* saluted him with stories of their readers whooping it up: 'It was out of this world . . . the greatest night in my life time . . . I'm not a boxing fan, but I'm a Barry McGuigan fan.' For anyone who might conceivably have missed the occasion, 'the Orange Cross is continuously re-running their RTE version of the fight.' The Orange Cross is a Loyalist club on the Shankill, and RTE is the state television company of the Republic, not normally their source of anything. I thought of how American blacks have been viewed historically by southern whites: victims or enemies if necessary, pets and children when they knew their place; and local hero too? Why not?

From his public statements, Barry McGuigan seemed to know his place all right, but this time the delight was less than universal. Married to a Protestant, McGuigan had gone so far as to mention the word 'peace', and to lend himself to the new slogan LEAVE THE FIGHTING TO MCGUIGAN. 'Peace' in this case wouldn't offend Loyalists because to them it simply meant the status quo ante, with them in charge and an absence of IRA. But Sinn Fein took exception. On the Falls Road some new graffiti went up. BARRY THE BRIT SOLD HIS SOUL FOR ENGLISH GOLD, said one, and O BARRY BOY, THE POUNDS, THE POUNDS ARE CALLING. 'What has galled Republicans,' explained a *Republican News* editorial, 'is McGuigan's apparent readiness to allow the Fleet Street gutter press to present him as a 1980s version of the so-called Peace People – an image which suits their portrayal of the war of national liberation as a glorified religious squabble.'

In Northern Ireland, peace has such a bad name that in order to achieve it they will have to call it something else.

The world might never have heard of the Peace People had it not been for their 1977 Nobel Peace Prize. The story of their origins moved everyone everywhere: how a Catholic mother, Anne Maguire, had been out walking with her four small children in Andersonstown when a car driven by two IRA men was shot at by the RUC and the driver killed; the car careered out of control and killed three of the children. It was the most senseless sacrifice of all. Both communities rose spontaneously in disgust. Ten thousand people went to the children's funeral. When Anne Maguire's sister Mairead – together with another local Catholic woman, Betty Williams, and journalist Ciaran McKeown – called for a protest demonstration, the town turned out. Protestant and Catholic linked arms. They marched up the Shankill, up the Falls, and they seemed unstoppable.

The people now working for peace, years later, are a small group, almost an endangered species. They meet often, though in different combinations, at the Friends' Meeting House or the People's College in Belfast, or at Corrymeela – a beautifully situated huddle of buildings, with a non-denominational chapel, above cliffs on the north coast. Representatives of each tradition are invited there for weekends or longer, to make friends and work out disputes together. Seminars are held to discuss means of reducing conflict. Groups of Catholics and Protestants hold hands and try to define and to bridge what holds them apart – everyone talking far into the night about the touchiest subjects, going to the local pub for drinks and songs, setting up psychodramas and role-playing sessions, attending ecumenical religious services, trying to conquer their animosities and project good feeling over the society as a whole. Then they return to their homes where most of what they've resolved is simply unreal. Many have no illusions about that. Alone among all the people who believe they are fighting God's war, no less, they admit to ambiguity and doubt. But so many in Northern Ireland belittle and discount their ideas, that while they are possibly the noblest in it, the rest have made a nonsense of them. 'Peace? We've tried it. It doesn't work.'

Details of the crumbling of the original movement are available, but there isn't much interest in the various political, sociological and sexual hypotheses brought out to explain its failure. It was taken over by the media, some say. It was taken over by men, others say. But most people dismiss the subject with some exaggerated gossip involving human frailty: Anne Maguire killed herself in 1980 and Mairead married Anne's husband; Mairead and Betty kept the Nobel money for themselves ('Sure it was the money they wanted'); Betty got herself fur coats and a Yank millionaire and moved to Florida. Some people didn't even bother to retail that much. For a refresher, all three of the original Peace People appeared on television in 1986, but refused to appear together. 'That may not have said it all,' as a friend in Belfast put it, 'but it said a lot.'

Meanwhile the peace people, lower case, carry on. One among them, rueful about himself, said, 'In some ways we have an even greater stake in the war than the people actually fighting it.' You could see his point. They were used to feeling odd-men-out; their struggle was so odd, in fact, that to maintain the spirit for it they had to become as obsessive in their dissidence as the extremists they opposed. 'We are terrorists for peace,' he also said.

At a conference at Corrymeela one weekend an assemblage of the good-hearted squabbled even about the first of their proposed ground-rules: 'We sit at this table as equals.' Most of them at least concurred that peace was unlikely to come about in the absence of 'talking to the man with the gun'; but it took two ex-men-with-guns – one Protestant, one Catholic, both from Derry – to come up with practical solutions. While the intellectuals sweated over lists of their side's demands and what they imagined the opposing group's demands to be, the two former paramilitaries worked it all out in minutes. Except for a united Ireland – over this the Catholic was prepared to concede to the Protestant – they agreed on: 'Brits out, jobs, bill of rights, amnesty for all prisoners, new police services, Irish language, new flag.'

Later the Derry men talked about the actual applications of their approach. After John Downes was killed in the Internment Day demonstration the previous August, there was a strong possibility of sectarian rioting in Derry. The two had rung up their friends there on both sides, and 'called in all our favours' to get it stopped. They had succeeded. But while their down-to-earth methods demonstrably worked, the rulers of the land didn't see fit to support or finance them: their peace office was manned by volunteers who lived on social security.

The others at the conference – capable of enjoying each other to the utmost at the pub after their working sessions – continually demonstrated the depth of the abyss between them by falling out over what seemed to an outsider quite ludicrously trivial issues. At several points they nearly came to blows over the problem of the Gaelic Athletic Association's ban on members of the security forces joining to play traditional Irish games; and at a final session two Protestants became apoplectic after the recitation in Gaelic (by a third Protestant) of 'Humpty Dumpty'. In pursuit of the more practical approach of the ex-paramilitaries (several were present, all wary of identification), I asked one of them how it was, if he'd managed with such courage to open the doors of peace, he couldn't publicize his efforts. 'Open doors?' he said. 'I don't want to die. All I'm doing is peeking through the mail slot.'

There was another peace conference at the Friends' Meeting House a few weeks later, on the theme BEYOND THE EUROPEAN CONVENTION. At issue was the question of a bill of rights – the possibilities of making into law, either in Britain as a whole or Northern Ireland in part, the European Convention of Human Rights, and if so whether to amend it to suit local circumstances. There was much discussion in American accents about the US Bill of Rights and American class-action suits.

During a coffee break I went outside and found a man there lighting his pipe. 'Unreal, isn't it?' he said. 'Listening to some of the arguments. Reconciliation – still people dying on the streets, still blood, and people talking about things that bear no relationship to it at all.'

He was strange, older than everybody there but not old, very firm and engaging, broad-boned but lean, and wearing a green suit that most of them wouldn't have been seen dead in. There was an air about him of a well-travelled sea captain not so used to land. I introduced myself and asked his name. 'Gusty Spence' nearly blew me down. He had just been released from Long Kesh on grounds of ill health, having been the longest serving prisoner of them all, and long-time head of the UVF in the compounds. At the time of his release the media called him 'founder of the UVF', 'a living Loyalist legend', and mentioned angina, ulcers, bronchitis and the recent removal of his gall bladder. I asked about his health. 'Not too bad, not too bad. They say I've had difficulties, you know? What difficulties could you possibly have after being eighteen and a half years in that place? You wouldn't have any other difficulties.'

His name had conjured up some brainless hit-man. He had been described to me as 'a hate-monger'. But he continued to contradict his image completely. 'Everyone talks about reconciliation,' he said, 'but there is none. Honestly. There are no roads to Damascus. It has to be a gradual process and you have to examine more, starting with yourself. You need to go some way on the road to peace, to accommodate someone on the opposite side. And there are very very few willing to do that.'

When I asked if I could come to see him another time, he said 'Certainly,' and gave an address between the Shankill and Crumlin Roads. One of those tiny kitchen houses? In a way, he said, but a modern version: 'When I went in they were all tiny wee houses, then they tore some down. We had a small poverty house, now it's a big poverty house.

'A chap was asking me about poverty – there's more poverty now than there was in '66. It's the worst type: poverty of the soul. He says to me, "Are you a Christian?" I says, "God protect me from 99.9 per cent of the Christians in Ulster."'

They summoned us back to the conference. 'It's a weird state of affairs,' he said, referring to the rather marked American presence within. 'Everybody outside has a solution. Even if they come across with an open mind, they have an ould bit of a solution in the back of their head: if these people worked together, did this, did that. But there's no solutions until people want solutions.'

When I arrived at his house the next day, two London journalists were there going through old photographs, which were piled in heaps about the floor. I was invited to glance through them as they finished. Most of the pictures, taken in prison, showed Gusty leading marching men, men in uniform, men with huge flags, men with *weapons*. They had obviously been snapped over many years with a variety of cameras. Gusty pointed out that to smuggle a camera into Long Kesh, you have to secrete it on your person, 'and your person's a very limited place.' As for the big banners and other props photographed in jail, 'look around this room: there's at least a hundred hiding places in this room.' I couldn't see them.

Gusty was wearing a blue track suit, appearing fit and athletic with a straight military bearing. I took him to be in his early sixties but someone later told me he was ten years younger. The house was modest, newish and comfortable, with signs of building work and sounds of domesticity coming from the kitchen. Cups of tea appeared mysteriously from within. It was his wife Louie, Gusty said, but she wouldn't come out: 'She hides, she's shy.'

After the English newspapermen left, Louie was finally persuaded to emerge. 'This is the woman here!' announced Gusty proudly. 'That's where you get the courage.' She was obviously some sort of indomitable mainstay – had waited for him for almost twenty years, brought up their children, and now had pulled the whole institution back together again. She called to mind what Elizabeth Taylor might have looked like if she hadn't turned to plastic, extraordinarily beautiful with huge dark fringed eyes, and dressed in worn jeans. 'When I went away,' Gusty said, 'my youngest wee fella was like this boy here.' A dirty-faced urchin had trailed in in Louie's wake. 'Our daughter was twelve the day I was sentenced. Louie had to start right from scratch.' Now their four children had eight children of their own, Louie said, all living nearby and coming in and out the whole time. 'Sometimes,' Gusty said, 'when you get the house to yourself, it's heaven.'

He wanted to bring Louie into the story, and told about how she'd dyed his hair once when he was on the run. 'Twice,' she corrected; 'blond, and then ginger.' And, said Gusty, she'd been shot twice. 'Three times,' she said. Two of the shots she got in crossfire in the Markets when 'the IRA and the police were shooting at each other.' She had scars on her back and said there were still pieces of lead in there, but 'It might work its way out.' Another time she'd been in a club when there was a knock at the door, 'and all I seen was a shotgun, two barrels in it, and all I heard was "Official IRA". When I turned round again all the men had disappeared. Then the gun went off.' A shot grazed her leg (more scars unveiled). All this with much laughter.

Shovelling up photographs, Gusty showed me an old postcard of the patriot hero John Mitchel and a quote: 'No man enters a prison cell with defiance on his lips for nothing.' Mitchel had been imprisoned in 1848 for treason, Gusty explained, and had written a famous jail journal. 'He happened to be a Protestant by religion, a Republican in sympathy. But at that time they weren't so much physical Republicans as theoretical Republicans. They were good, they knew exactly what they wanted and how to achieve it, not like some of the mindless violence of today.'

The jail photos were next. How had they managed to get hold of all those *things*? He said the flags were made out of towels – the prisoners had individually stripped the correctly coloured threads and rewoven them. 'Must is a great master.' As for the hats, the authorities had seized them so often that 'it ended up with the boys learning how to knit.' This called up rather a touching mental picture, but there wasn't a photo of it. Another, however, showed a great piece of ingenuity: a radio transmitter hidden in the base of a hot water boiler they used to make tea. 'Here's the wonderful part: we're dopey Irish people, you know. And we're Loyalists. If *we* were able to do that, what were the *Republicans* not able to do? We had a sympathy with the people who were keeping us in prison and they with us. But the Republicans, who identified the British as the enemy – what could they not get up to? And when Republicans escaped from prison, they had the South to go to, where there was no extradition. I could have escaped – I'm not saying that in a blasé manner, you know – but where was I going to go? I love this old place, you know. Half God-forsaken as it is. There's nowhere else for me to go.'

He was still flipping through photos. 'That's a wooden rifle, of course. But it's carved exactly the same as an SLR. The journalists were interested in using that picture for sensational impact, but I don't want that type of thing. See I've left all that behind.'

A shot of a church full of flowers: 'That was Joker Andrews' funeral. He was murdered when the IRA blew up the Four-Step Inn. It was only an ordinary pub. He was a street sweeper. He'd called in to have a couple of pints after his day's work.'

I told him about the Joker I'd met. 'That's his son, oh aye. That's how the son got involved, and ended up serving life imprisonment. He's not a bad big character. It's the same as everything else: he's beginning to wise up now. Same as I wised up.'

Among the photos was a copy of the current *Shankill Bulletin* with an interview of himself. 'Reveals that he did not create the modern-day UVF,' it said in a banner. I pointed at it. 'Why do you get the credit if you didn't?' He had been responsible for the Shankill, he said, but certainly not for the whole thing. 'I've removed myself, I'm outside this, you know? Whenever somebody talks about Gusty Spence, they're not talking about *me*, they're talking about another Gusty Spence.'

He asked a grandson who was hanging around to buy him some pipe tobacco, and was amazed to hear that the shops weren't open on the Shankill on a Sunday. 'Oh God, is that right? They're very very religious people. What about that wee shop down at Clifton Street – that's a Taig shop. Go down there.' The grandson was definitely not interested in going 'down past Unity flats' (a Catholic block with a ferocious reputation). Louie settled it by thinking of another shop and the boy went off. 'Good man.'

While this problem was being ironed out I was looking through the *Shankill Bulletin* interview. He had told them:

> 'For me there were no clocks, no days, no weeks, no calendars, no time. All you can do is think and reflect. What events led me to being in prison? What is the effect on my wife and family? How can I best help them?
>
> 'One November Saturday night, maybe twelve years ago, the young lads in the hut in the compound had a pop programme blaring out on the TV. I went outside to get my head showered. It was a stinking night and as I dandered towards the Provo compound, I saw a figure coming out of the mist about 70 yards away.
>
> "Is that you Gusty?" he asked.
>
> "It is," I said. I couldn't see who it was.
>
> "What the f. . . are we doing in here?" he asked.
>
> "Paddy, I don't know," I replied. It was one of the most profound moments of my life.'

'This word bridge-building,' Gusty said now. 'It's the only thing to be done now – trying to link hands with someone across the divide. Even then you have to do it clandestinely, because people of your own herd will invariably misunderstand you, instead of giving you some support, you know?

'The imposition of an all-Ireland at the moment is so unreal it's not even worth considering. People say "Withdraw the troops" – but look at the practicalities of the situation. Here we have the intelligentsia, or what passes for it, in the shape of the judiciary, and as you know the judiciary won't sit with the judges from the South. If it happens at that level, what can you expect at other levels? We're trying to educate the people, and those men should be giving the lead. They're not. But if you deal with reality – and believe me I had to deal with reality for all those years I was in prison, because *survival is reality*: and it's not just a question of survival, but how you survive. I have seen people going slowly insane, but I have survived all right, by adopting a real, practical, pragmatic approach to prison, and to the government since I have come out. So let's assume that Britain pulls out tomorrow. What are the practicalities of the situation? The Protestants go into a state of alarm. They are the majority. And perhaps in their alarm, in their fear, they strike out – as they did in 1969, only worse this time, because you don't have the British troops to maintain law. If you don't have the British troops, who do you have?'

'The UN?'

'*Every*body'd be shooting at the UN then. What could they possibly do? There would be repartition of this country. It's inevitable. Because even in '69, when there was a partial invasion of the Roman Catholic districts by Protestants, you had something like sixty thousand people moving – it was the biggest shift of population in Europe since the Second World War.'

A fantastic chef's salad appeared from Louie at this

point. They called it 'rough and ready'. A new small child coming in off the street looked yearningly at Gusty's plate and said, 'What d'ya get dem for?'

'You get those to eat,' said Gusty.

'Whar d'ya get dem?'

'Your Granny gives you them. Go see your Granny.' The child trotted off. Gusty acted as if he was used to it. 'After eighteen and a half years in prison, after extreme circumstances for so long, I don't fear an all-Ireland. It's the people who have been frightened for many years, like a kid: the dark, the dark, the dark. They scare the kid in order to control the kid. Then, when the kid grows up to fear the dark, they say "You bloody fool, what are you afraid of the dark for? There's nothing to be afraid of." At one time, for her own ends, Britain colonized the situation, and kept on frightening these people who held the fort for so long. And then Britain said, "Oh what have you got to fear? You've nothing to fear." But Britain's responsible for setting it up! They must not be allowed to abdicate their authority here.

'In many cases the settlers in Northern Ireland were forced here by British bayonets. The British killed two birds with one stone: they got rid of the people in Scotland who were giving them problems, and they sent them across to Northern Ireland, which they helped to colonize; if they were going to give anybody trouble, let them give the Irish Catholics trouble. It's what the British have done everywhere. I know because I ran into it in Cyprus. The effect is fear. And just because a fear is an unreasonable fear – or an unreasoning fear – doesn't mean that people aren't still afraid. They are.

'Thank God there were no more firearms in Northern Ireland in '69 than there were. If we had had as many as they had in Lebanon or Cyprus, the bloodshed and death here would have been phenomenal, and the situation would have been irreconcilable. There's still a ray of hope. However faint, there's still a ray of hope here in Northern Ireland that people can live together.

'But the situation will remain the same until such time as people want peace. There are very few people here who are prepared to make that extra effort at the moment. Anyone who is prepared to do it is looked on with suspicion.'

Yet another grandchild came in and gave huge hugs and kisses to Gusty before going home to bed. 'Goodnight, son.'

Gusty went on: 'If a person has an aspiration, that's fair. If people in Northern Ireland would recognize each other's aspirations, perhaps it might go some way towards ameliorating some of the problems. But the big Unionist parties are stupid, in my opinion. If you rule out mass evacuation or mass extermination of any section of the community, the only thing you have left is compromise. Logic! And in order to compromise there has to be some sharing of responsibility. If the Unionist parties would share responsibility with the SDLP, they would pull the carpet from under Sinn Fein, which in many instances have only got a protest vote. The sooner these big Unionists recognize that, the better.'

He stopped to pack and light his pipe – the tobacco had meanwhile appeared. I asked, 'Did you think this way in 1966?'

'No, not at all,' he said.

Louie, who had returned, said, 'He was shocking, Sally.'

'Shocking's the word,' acknowledged Gusty.

I asked Louie if she hadn't thought the same way as he had. 'No, I never thought the same as him,' she answered.

'Did you argue with him?'

'Yeah,' said Gusty. 'Often.'

Louie said, 'I was born down in a mixed community, you see. That you call the Falls now. Well – then I never thought anything of religion, you see. I couldn't get over *him*. But he's changed.'

'Too late,' said Gusty.

'Too late,' she echoed. 'He didn't change till he was inside.' They looked at each other.

'It was '71,' he said.

She went on: 'Really I didn't know what sort of way he was. I had a sister who married a Catholic, and her husband died. We lived in a house with her facing us. We had four children; she had three. Hers were Catholics. Now he never thought of putting his own children into church, but religiously every Sunday morning he went over and knocked them three children up to go to Mass. I used to say to him, "You're always going on about the Fenians! There's three of them you're getting up!" He'd say, "Oh but they're different." He had me really baffled then.'

'It wasn't a religious thing with me really,' he said. 'I was born and reared in a home where the British Army was a tradition – it was service to the Crown. When you're told to defend against Her Majesty's enemies, foreign and domestic, you take that literally because it's meant literally. You always prided yourself in service, and people of my age group who hadn't been in the army or navy were looked upon as some form of weird animal, half-cowards, you know. We're a fighting race – I've come away from all that, but the Ulster people are a warrior race. So when you come back to civilian life, you don't necessarily forsake that. Especially in your own country, if you think there's someone attempting to usurp your British rights – and then it was Irish Republicanism.

'Now I can look back and see that in '65 the IRA were

old men, with virtually no firepower. But at the time two things were coming up: there was a general election, and a month before that an IRA plot to murder the whole cabinet at Stormont was uncovered – of course there was no such thing as an IRA plot, but we didn't know that, and it frightened people; and secondly you had the fiftieth anniversary of the 1916 Republican rising, with marching men all over the place. When people saw that, different banners with rifles and all painted on them, there was alarm. There was really no need for alarm, but no one stopped to think about that.'

I asked if he went out marching on the Twelfth.

'No I do not indeed, no not under any circumstances, there's no chance of my ever doing that again. Although to be honest what I have noticed about the bands and demonstrations now – there's more of a carnival atmosphere. You've a younger element now, and the bands do play "Derry's Walls" and the "The Sash My Father Wore", but they're inclined to play more popular tunes too: "My Old Man Says Follow the Band", lovely tunes. But in the marching season tension is heightened, there's no question about it. A provocative march is a provocative march, it doesn't matter whose, and I decry that.'

What had happened in 1971 to make him start changing? 'At that time I had my first exposure to Republican prisoners. See in the schools here, there's no Irish history taught. You know all about the Tudor kings, the Reformation, but the 1916 rising never happened, just didn't exist. The kids in the state schools don't learn any Irish history to this day; it's just not on the curriculum. On the other hand, with Irish history being taught in the Nationalist schools, you have children in their formative years told about the British shooting Connolly and Pearse and

MacBride, and it leaves an impression on young minds that the British must be bad people.

'Catholic and Protestant kids go to separate kindergartens, separate schools, and separate higher schools, separate teacher training colleges. So the first time that a Protestant person might come in contact with a Catholic person would be when they sign on the dole together, and even then because of where you live there is dole for Protestants and dole for Catholics.

'But in Long Kesh, you see, what we had was very important: we had a microcosm of Ulster. The five COs of the Provisional IRA, Officials, INLA, the UDA, and the UVF went forward as a body to the NIO, i.e., the British government, and said, We want these conditions improved for our men; our conditions are bloody atrocious. And if you don't give us these conditions, we'll do A, B and C. As a body. And did do! And won!

'This was the only thing that brought prison reform about here in Northern Ireland. But one had to be very clandestine. I was in charge of all the Loyalist prisoners – and when I opted for political status, I couldn't be seen to be supporting the IRA, so I used the tactic of opting for segregation at the same time, which mollified the Protestants.

'With that microcosm in Long Kesh extended to the outside, going back and forth – Catholic and Protestant people saying we want better housing, we want better education, we want, we want, we want – then we'd get it.

'But no one can force change on ye. Change has to come within. It has to be a change of heart. That's what I had – a change of heart. Now it wasn't a road to Damascus thing, you know? I'm always very wary of road-to-Damascus conversions, because they're not sincere or people have sold out. See, this is important: I haven't . . . sold . . . out.

And most important too – this is a terrible, hard thing to say – I can't be bought. Money means nothing to me, you know? The only way people can buy me is to put a gun to my head and say "You must do this, or else." That's about the only way. There's no other way.'

Gusty thinks of himself as a socialist but 'there's no socialist outlet for me. With my political views, I'm a foreigner in my own land.' He has the reputation of a *bad* man, but he is obviously a *good* man. A fighter for the Protestants who, through studying Irish history, language and literature and reading 'vast amounts' in jail, has no stomach for the fight. 'They must grease up the guns and put them away. If I can do *any*thing to persuade them I'll do it.' Effectively what he did in prison for eighteen and a half years was social work, but he can't get a job because 'if you go anywhere they ask, "Qualified?"' For all his deep pockets of wisdom he had been deprived of all banal experience. But it was the deprivation which taught him the wisdom.

Above all Gusty is someone who couldn't possibly exist anywhere but in Northern Ireland, and knows it. He is sustained by his people. 'The people here – you've heard it often – they're rough and they're ready, and they come out with the most foulest language from time to time, and they'll fight at the drop of a hat – sometimes you don't need the hat – but they're good warm people. Oh they *are* good people!

'All we can do, we just have to keep on preaching, there's no other way.'

A demo had been in progress all weekend outside the Crumlin Road courthouse, a 'tent-in'. They had been sleeping there in the rain, the police redirecting traffic on either side of them, to protest the fact that their boys, accused by UVF supergrass Budgie Allen of various crimes, had been denied the counsel of their choice: Desmond Boal. Desmond Boal was the counsel of everyone's choice. There was such voodoo attached to his name that no one seemed to think they had a chance of getting off without him. Together with Ian Paisley, he had founded the Democratic Unionist Party in 1971, but was too busy for politics these days, defending everybody.

The reason that the UVF victims hadn't got 'Dessy' was simple enough, explained a man accompanied by a demonstrator dressed as a budgerigar: Budgie had said he would crack if he had to endure Dessy's cross-examination, and Dessy was getting ready to try to crack Harry Kirkpatrick. Of course, he knowingly continued, the two trials were deliberately scheduled simultaneously for this very purpose – if Dessy were unavailable then some lesser advocate would be all Budgie had to confront, so his story would have a chance to hold together and all their boys would go down. To begin with, therefore, the men accused by Budgie had refused counsel altogether, until the judge assured them it was their funeral. But there were a lot of irate and soggy characters bearing banners and importuning anyone who would listen about this grievance.

Inside on Monday, Harry Kirkpatrick himself was due to appear, the prosecution having finally finished producing – as one local wag put it – 'forensic evidence that wouldn't stand up if it was soaked in starch.' The lobby was filled with equal representations of INLA people and the law waiting to go in. Searching was far more rigorous than usual, and people talked about the difficulties of hearing anything at all now that a screen had been put up in front of the public gallery. They said Harry had an awful twitch these days.

The court was packed. The glass curtain which had sprouted between the gallery and the accused must have cut down the audibility behind it to nil, but its frame had already been match-painted the noxious two-tone greys and greens of the rest of the room. You'd never know it hadn't always been there. It obviously always would be.

Harry swaggered in surrounded by guards, but as soon as he was in his box he started to betray his anxiety, placing himself not sideways as the seat suggested but in an unnatural quarter-turn towards Judge Carswell and away from the audience whose every look accused him. The *informer*. His discomfort, despite the steady rehearsed voice, was horribly marked in the twitch, which took over his face in the middle of nowhere like some obscene wink. ('It gets worse as the day progresses,' a woman in the press box said, 'as the Valium wears off.') He was dressed in a double-breasted grey suit which, they said, concealed a bullet-proof vest, but it hung awkwardly and his collar was too small. He was still the best dressed fellow among his erstwhile chums – all in the T-shirts and jeans he must have once worn too – and coiffed and moustached like a poor man's Burt Reynolds.

The British Labour Pary's Tony Benn sat opposite, observing, in the box which on last sight housed witnesses and now appeared to contain plainclothesmen. The funny thing about plainclothesmen is that they do not wear plain clothes, but ties and suits like Harry; and, like him, this lot looked as if they'd never wear ties and suits if they weren't another sort of uniform.

A helicopter hovered feet above the courthouse drowning out much of Harry's monotone. He was talking about a robbery at the Twinbrook post office and, in testifying against one of his accomplices, was asked to identify him. He scanned twenty-nine hating faces until he found the one, before pointing himself at the judge again. It was difficult to understand, this one: betrayal on such a scale as to isolate you from your entire past. One of the best graffiti on the Falls was THANK GOD I WAS NOT AT HARRY'S WEDDING, since most of the people who had been there sat accused by him now. I have heard that being a murderer is the loneliest of life's experiences, but it couldn't be a patch on this one. Harry's reward for informing, having been convicted of five murders himself and sentenced to 999 years, was the lack of a judge's recommendation for a minimum prison term: if he performed properly he would be released at some point well short of the designated period that was given to 'stips'. Four years, they said. But released to what? The Secretary of State had recently announced that £1.3 million had been spent on supergrass payments, living expenses and resettlement. Harry would be fitted out with a new identity in Australia or South Africa. But his wife had left him, his blood relations wouldn't speak to him, and what would a new life mean without a single friend? Feeling, and being, hunted for the rest of his days: they could change the name and face but what could they do with the accent? It was the most pitiable situation and yet there was no way to pity it. These thoughts were unendurable, and I was hit by a bout of hysterical coughing which wouldn't go away until I left the courtroom.

Pat, who was in court as usual, saw me leave and followed, finding me in the searching antechamber, where a policewoman was asking where I got my shoes. We went to the court café. Pat told me that in 1981 her husband Tommy, during a seven-day arrest, was beaten in Castlereagh in an effort to make him inform, beaten so badly his eardrums were perforated. I thought the beatings had ended, I said, after the introduction of closed-circuit television in the interrogation rooms. 'But sure they *do* it on television,' she said. 'They're all *watch*ing.' They'd offered him £100 a week to report to them, she said, 'or more for information about guns,' and assured him 'your wife and family won't have to know.' He'd replied, 'They'd soon know if I was ten foot under.' Tommy had left a note with Pat to be used in the event of his arrest requesting that a solicitor call at Castlereagh. She took the note to Paddy McGrory, who went to the interrogation centre, in whose bowels somewhere Tommy was being 'kicked off the chair', and asked to see him. An obliging policeman replied that they would ask Tommy if indeed he wanted a lawyer and went into the next room where, within earshot of McGrory, he put the question to Tommy, who was heard to say 'No'. McGrory was very angry, Pat told me, when he found out it hadn't been Tommy's voice at all.

12
Papa Doc and Politicking

By the time I'd gone the ninth time to Belfast – for two supergrass trials and some elections – it was almost possible to meet a friend there every time I went outside. Londoners still said 'Be careful' before I left, not really accepting that I felt safer in Belfast than in many parts of London. I was getting used to that, but not yet to being in a city of such manageable size. A friend was buying a paper ahead of me at the newsagent's; another hooted driving past up the Newtownards Road; a woman I had tea with one night was in a bus queue the next morning at City Hall. Like its museum, which can be visited in one afternoon and doesn't overwhelm you with a lifetime's surfeit of magnificence, Belfast is a place you can handle and feel a part of – its official as well as informal self. People were faces, not numbers, and the warmth and kindness on the ones who weren't familiar suggested they ought to be or soon might be.

People often acted as if they knew you already. Like an old woman on a Ligoniel bus who suddenly announced 'I've felt worse many times when I was half as bad,' and asked me to unwrap her cough-drop. I had some too and offered her one. 'An exchange is no robbery,' she agreed – on condition we swap – and, tasting mine, which was vile, 'What hurts is best!' She grumbled about the health service and the government cuts that had reduced her and her husband, after a lifetime's hard work, to penury. We were passing lamp-posts decked out with election posters: who would she be voting for? 'Sure none of them'uns ever helped,' she shrugged.

It was local election time all over the province, and the people of Belfast were about to choose fifty-one city councillors. Fanfare and banners and beanos. Sound trucks howled VOTE THIS! OPPOSE THAT! on every other street, and candidates – surviving accusations that they never seemed to be seen except at such a time – blithely knocked on doors and made vague promises. By night they were out again sticking posters higher and higher up the lamp-posts; by day boys shinnied up and tore the other side's down.

The local councils have had no power since 1972, when everything from health and education to street lighting and dustbins went into the hands of Westminster as part of Direct Rule. Practically all they have left is environment control (pests, noise, dogs), inspection of housing, ships and airports. Undeterred, people vied in their hundreds for the thankless task of being a councillor. 'More people are running than voting,' commented one man who was doing neither. And since there was very little concretely to run for, most had found something to run against. It was the first local election in which Sinn Fein had candidates, which gave Unionists an obvious against. For the Democratic Unionist Party it was 'Smash Sinn Fein' whereas the Official Unionists wanted to 'Put Sinn Fein Out of Business'. By contrast the Ulster Loyalist Democratic Party was 'pledged to oppose Sinn Fein, Nationalists and their political cohorts in their insidious strive for a United Ireland', and the Independent Unionists were determined to 'oppose the advance of Republicanism . . . and defeat the IRA'. Sinn Fein itself promised to 'fight to end the repression of nationalists', the Alliance Party to 'remove sectarianism' and the SDLP to 'resist further devolution of power'. Even the Ecology Party, caught up in this wave of negativity, stood for 'resistance to pollution, nuclear power and chemical farming'. Only the Workers' Party put forward a platform without a smash, stop, resist, defeat, end, or remove in it, not even an oppose – talking instead about creating jobs, improving the environment and the public transport system, and developing leisure centres. But their practical suggestions to meet people's real needs seemed so alien to what voters regarded those needs to be that their share of the poll would no doubt again be derisory.

Rita was canvassing her part of Andersonstown for Sinn Fein, in a friend's car on which a PA system had been mounted. The trees were all in bloom, and a blanket of hugely amplified and passionate Republican songs was as thick as the clouds that covered the mountains. The car was full, mainly of kids, even Tony in the boot, and other children followed on their bikes, trikes, roller skates and legs, with their dogs and yoyos. Now and then the loudspeaker was turned off, haphazardly as in musical chairs, on 'There was war and death, plundering and killing – ' or 'God's curse on you, England – ' for Rita to bellow out *'Sinn Fein calling on the people of Edenmore Gardens: on May 15th vote Sinn Fein! Show your opposition to British rule in Ireland, the use of plastic bullets, the degrading strip searching of our women in Armagh jail, and the injustice of the supergrass system!'* Passersby smiled, clenched their fists, made V-signs and wisecracks – 'Up the Sticks!' – or stuck a tongue out ('That's me uncle,' said Dermot, 'six votes out of that house'). *'Vote Sinn Fein – show your opposition to those who seek to destroy us!'* We covered only certain streets, but from the mood of the people we passed, it seemed Sinn Fein had it sewn up.

'Och hello Rita!' said a man who looked about 150, tottering up to the car. 'Gettin' down to business again . . . surely, surely . . . I'll be doin' the Masses in the mornin'.'

'He's only out of jail,' Rita said as we drove off. 'He got bail.'

'For what?' I asked.

'Hidin' stuff,' said Dermot.

Rita had no campaigning on Sunday – others were 'doin' the Masses' – and I more or less dared her to go with me to hear Ian Paisley preach at his Martyrs' Memorial Church. It was hard to find a challenge Rita wouldn't take up, though she was agonizing lest she give the game away by genuflecting or crossing herself by mistake. As we parked outside and she got a look at all the women in their nifty spring hats and white gloves, she said 'You do the talkin'.' She expected to be interrogated at the entrance. But although we were the only non-hatted females in the place, no one but our immediate neighbours in the packed church was snoopy. 'Have you come from afar to visit us?' chirped a woman behind us. 'London? How nice. And your friend?' Rita just beamed.

The congregation, more than 1,500 of them, loudly and merrily sang a hymn which included the verse:

> Behold I in iniquity
> Was formed the womb within;
> My mother also me conceiv'd
> In guiltiness and sin.

Other hymns were sung with equal gusto, even extra verses not in the hymnal, causing some difficulty for me and Rita. Most of them seemed to do with being washed from sin. But all the congregation together sounded merely insipid when Paisley took to his pulpit. The temple must have been constructed specifically for his voice and its echoes: holy thunder vibrating and reverberating as though it came from within the self. He reminded me of the southern American preacher-demagogue in his mastery of his tools, the incantatory effect of repetition with the full range of voice, from the faintest whisper leading suddenly into a frightful fortissimo, with the occasional 'Halleluiah!' from the flock. But this kind of oratory was very Irish as well. A Belfast Catholic had said to me: 'Paisley is the most Irish person I've ever seen in my life – not to mention the best recruiting sergeant the IRA could hope for. I'd hate to think what would be in store for the ASU that knocked him off.'

To much of the world Paisley is almost synonymous with Northern Ireland, as the voice of Unionist paranoia. With his bluster, threats and apocalyptic predictions, his manipulation of every crisis to his own self-aggrandizement, and the extraordinary street theatre he has made of local politics, he has always managed to grab headlines. Often he uses imaginative incitements to violence which, when provoked, is notable for his absence. Wherever there is controversy, there is Ian Paisley, howling and roaring and fighting dirty, destroying any hope of compromise or settlement. He does the work of several men, is scrupulously conscientious to his constituents, and above all articulates what his followers feel – aided by their perception of him, which he doesn't discourage, as God's appointee in the struggle with the antichrist.

Unable to compromise with any existing church, in 1951 he started his own, the Free Presbyterian Church. Unable to compromise with any existing political party, in 1971 he started his own, the Democratic Unionist Party. For years he was complete autocrat in both, but finally has had to share some of his power in the DUP with his indispensable vote-getter, sidekick and probable successor, Peter Robinson. In his Church, however, he remains the absolute temporal authority – the spiritual authority being the Bible taken literally.

Behind the 'Big Man' in his church was not a cross but a brass-lettered 'We Preach Christ Crucified', which seemed to amount to the same thing. But half his hellfire rhetoric goes against Republicans and the other half against the Pope and his devices – 'Old Redsocks' and 'the wine of the Roman whore's fornication'. Today it was the political threat. Beginning his blood-and-thunder on the theme: 'MAY OUR ENEMIES BE DRIVEN BACK!' he spoke with all the burning conviction of the negative right. DOWN WITH! The council election was going to be 'the most crucial election in our history'. He alluded to Sinn Fein's 'highpocrisy' and other offences; taking God-is-on-our-side to new heights, 'I believe on Wednesday we shall see something startling in the history of this province: divine intervention! It will be a miracle when the votes are counted!' He told of people who had never before come near his Democratic Unionist Party, like some he had visited in their house in the 'two-hundred-*thousand* bracket' who 'said to me, "Big Man, we are with you!"' Only at the end could you be sure you were at a revival meeting, not an election rally: 'Hands up for people coming to Christ.' There seemed to be two takers (female) who disappeared inside a door below him for a private audience.

As we left, the man next to me, who'd been bellowing out the hymns without reference to texts, leaned over and – Rita glancing at him apprehensively – whispered, 'Thank you for sharing your fellowship with us.'

* * *

There was a chance to see the Big Man at closer quarters next day, when he was helping out his DUP candidates by taking turns in their loudspeaker cars. The current High Sheriff of Belfast, Pauline Whittley, had him for the 3.30 slot – his famous voice had already boomed out to more than half the city and would cover all of it before the day was out.

Pauline Whittley was an incongruity, often mentioned but never without a nudge-nudge and a wink-wink, referring to her previous career as a go-go dancer. Since most of Paisley's party were born-again Christians, her past caused even more public glee. Her Newtownabbey home was the only one I'd seen in Northern Ireland with just one child and a television of modest size which actually wasn't on. She appeared with a towel round her head, a nice relaxed woman with no airs. Packing me into a taxi, her hair still wet, she fretted about being late for 'Papa Doc'. '*Papa Doc?*' I repeated, not sure I'd heard right. She seemed to know no other reference for the name, taking my question to indicate some lack of respect and answering, 'Of course we don't call him that to his face.' There are many names for Paisley, only 'Big Man' being strictly accurate. Certainly the 'Doctor' is dubious, an honorary degree from Bob Jones University in South Carolina (which lost its US federal funding for refusing blacks).

Pauline talked about being High Sheriff – a largely ceremonial role – having won the internal council vote for the position 21–12 with the help of the SDLP and Alliance, 'and then they all called me a *liberal*!' The council job itself had come her way three and a half years earlier thanks to a by-election caused by the shooting dead of the incumbent, a Republican. Her district, with a 26,000 electorate, was more than half Republican. She wouldn't campaign in the Catholic areas: 'I did before, but I got the car wrecked.' She talked about 'young fellas jumping on the bonnet' as if it were a throwaway funny story. But this election she thought was pretty calm. 'There's leaflets going through doors about people's backgrounds,' she said, alluding to her dancing past, but it didn't worry her because she thought it redounded badly on the leafleteers. (The dancing, it turned out, had been disco dancing, and an allegedly smutty photograph that was circulating, which I saw at the *Ulster* magazine offices, was of a very pretty and decently clad Pauline of a decade earlier.) She didn't seem to care much if she won, in fact at an earlier point had withdrawn her nomination, but then 'the Doc talked me round'. A possible bonus was becoming the next Lord Mayor of Belfast, customary for ex-High Sheriffs.

I told her about the divine intervention predicted in church. 'He's never far wrong,' she said, shaking her head in wonder, then said it again. 'You know, he can nearly tell you who's going to get in and how many votes they'll get. He talks to everyone, and he works it all out on paper. He was able to tell me there's 1.9 seats for the DUP in my area. That's why they put me in, to try to draw the others and get two seats.'

As the taxi drew up to the rendezvous we could see Papa Doc already waiting. 'He never stops,' she said as we got out to meet him. 'He goes continuously.' His voice was showing the strain. She introduced us and he heaved his sixteen-stone bulk, clad in a wornout overcoat, out of the car to shake hands, looked extremely displeased to have me there, and addressed not another word or look in my direction.

As we drove around with Paisley enthralling the passersby with his amplified campaign on behalf of 'Whittley and Lunn, Lunn and Whittley in order of your choice,' the candidates themselves sat on either side of me in the back seat, grinning at voters. Pauline chattered about her husband, who was running in another district, and 'how great it is when people say "You're that woman's husband" instead of the other way round'; about her new home perm; about the pointlessness of actually doing anything for your constituents since the way they voted had nothing to do with it; and how her dancer-image no longer counted now that she had proved herself a serious politician.

Meanwhile the other local candidate, Peter Lunn, a pale young man, was having difficulties with the PA system. The mechanism, on the floor between his feet, kept making excruciating feedback. A theory developed that this was exacerbated by open windows, so while the weather was exceptionally cold for May the atmosphere inside the car was like a swimming pool locker room and with five of us breathing it – one of them several times larger than life – soon containing a marked dearth of oxygen. Paisley maybe lives on something else than air. To the background of a flute-and-drum band playing 'Red River Valley' and 'What a Friend We Have in Jesus', and accompanied by the occasional shriek of the system, The Voice boomed: *'This is Ian Paisley, the leader of the Ulster Democratic Unionist Party at this election. Make it a solid vote for the DUP, Whittley and Lunn, Lunn and Whittley, one and two, in order of your choice. Smash Sinn Fein! Hello there dear! Make it a solid vote for the DUP at this election. Thank you.'* Turning down the volume: 'Put up your winda, fella, and it'll not be squeakin' then. It's yer winda makes it squeak' . . . up volume: *'This is Ian Paisley, your own friend . . .'* The pale young man had obliged and the system behaved for a minute or two '. . . *visiting* (where are we?) *Torrens Parade today and asking for your first preference votes . . . Hello ladies!'* The PA system was not so much shrieking now as gonging. I'd gong too with that racket going through me. 'Get you out and hear what it's like,' said the loud speaker about the loudspeaker. The pale young man obliged again.

Knots of people gathered at corners when they heard us coming. *'Howya doin' man? You know what to do for us!'* To a woman with a load of shopping: *'I hope you've plenty of votes for us in that bag, dear!'* To another: *'Be sure and vote for us now, dear! And give us that hap-py smile!'* Another: *'Hello dear! I see you've got your hair in curlers for me!'* Another: *'Hope we can count on you, dear!'* This woman, alarmed, crossed herself. Much laughter in the car. Paisley: 'She must be scared of gettin' . . . con-*tam*inated.' The fifes and drums were playing 'Yo, Ho, and Up She Rises'. Whittley advised the driver where to turn, skirting Republican areas. We were getting near a street where I'd seen painted on a wall PAISLEY'S MA IS A VIRGIN but turned off short of it.

Luckily some people actually stopped the car to talk to their MP, which meant the window got rolled down – a very old woman, for instance, who limped painfully towards us to thank him for 'helping me that time'. Not that he could have remembered who she was or what favour he'd done her, but he acknowledged it with grace and 'You know what to do!' The feeling the people had for him was palpable. I thought of what a Belfast Protestant barrister had observed of him: 'The Irish say, "You know exactly where you are with Paisley" – they like extremists. The people they can't understand are the gentle liberals . . . because they are not used to being treated kindly.'

Three more constituents came to the car now to complain about a Sinn Fein sign in Irish, although from where they lived it would seem they had more realistic worries. It was one of those streets with endless warrens of tiny nineteenth-century houses, every other one bricked up, the children playing on the ususal teetering piles of rubble. Old shops and pubs were gone or sealed, the landscape desolate. It looked, indeed, about as threadbare as Paisley's overcoat – in his case an eccentricity, as he was said to earn at least £50,000 a year as MP, Euro MP, local Assemblyman, and founder of a church with fifty-nine congregations, mainly in Northern Ireland but also as far away as Australia and the US Bible Belt.

Inside the car, between broadcasts, the talk was optimistic. Among the candidates for Whittley's and Lunn's seats (Sinn Fein never mentioned except on the loudspeaker) were 'two Paddys' – Devlin, with his new Labour Party of Northern Ireland, and Bird, whose Ulster Independents were, they said, a front for the UVF. Neither worried them. 'At least I've been seen anyway,' said Paisley. 'We must be the only party that's really done a canvass. How're things going up the Shankill?' They decided that there, in the next-door constituency, the UDA, UVF and George Seawright would all cancel each other out. 'Burn 'em George's' posters had been pulled down, Pauline reported, and Paisley said, 'He's lazy. He never goes to the Assembly. I haven't seen him there for weeks.' Loudspeaker on. *'Help us smash Sinn Fein at this election by voting One-Two-Three for the D-U-P!'* The flutes whistled 'Waltzing Matilda'.

Meanwhile the pale young man said nothing, just smiled out at the people responding to the Big Man – who, his forty-five minutes up, left to go campaign elsewhere. Paisley's own bullet-proofed Ford, which had been following us, tailed in turn by a police Land-Rover to protect him, scooped him up and off. Peter Lunn took over the driving and delivered Pauline home. Still obliging, he then turned back to take me where I wanted to go. A cassette was playing heavenly music sung by a women's choir, and as we pounded down the motorway I noticed a Bible on the dashboard. I asked if Paisley had left it behind. Oh no! said Peter Lunn, it was his own, and he had it with him at all times to read whenever he had a minute. He was a born-again believer, he said, and everything he needed to know was in the Gospels. I asked if he were a member of 'the Martyrs', as they call Paisley's church. He was – and his campaign leaflet revealed that he was the church's pianist and assistant organist, as well as an insurance salesman; but it didn't say what I heard later, that he was engaged to Paisley's daughter (who was also running in the election). His leaflet finished with a bit of doggerel:

For a man that's dedicated
with you at heart
vote for Lunn
and prove yourself smart!

He was eager to talk now, about how God had chosen him at age nine to reveal that man is born in sin and only being washed in the blood of the Lamb could guarantee a place next to God in heaven. As he spoke more and more excitedly, turning to flourish his Bible at me in the back seat, I began to worry that he might have to use his heavenly guarantee sooner rather than later. On the other hand, he went on, God might come again. Meanwhile he spent a lot of time at prayer meetings and Bible classes.

He spoke with the believer's zeal, his whole slight frame thrilling to the import of the message, and his eyes so fiery with light they seemed transparent. The angelic chorus still accompanied him in the background. '"Gospel" means "Good News!"' he wanted me to know, turning around to waggle it at me again.

I thought I might change the subject. 'How do you put

all this together with politics?' I asked. This seemed to stun him. 'A good question,' he said, 'a *very* good question,' as if amazed at its novelty; but it got his eyes pointing forward again. In the DUP, 'a lot of the people who are standing are born-again believers. You'll find that a lot of them will freely admit to you that they're Christians!'

'How are you going to smash Sinn Fein?' I asked. 'That's another *very* good question,' he said in awe. After some thought he explained that all this smashing business should not be taken too literally – something people tended to do after seeing 'an interview done on the TV whereby Dr Paisley actually had a sledge-hammer in his hand.' But it wasn't like that of course; 'it's not by brutal force.' They really only meant smashing them in the election. Sinn Fein, having 'tried all sorts of means, bombings and bullets and shooting and all the rest of it, all sorts of thugs running about the streets and so forth,' now had 'totally warped schemes to worm their way into places of authority so they can use it for their own ends, which are wicked and evil and totally *wrong*.' But 'we will endeavour to muster as many votes as we can so that the votes of the Sinn Fein party will look derogatory.'

He was a member of the Apprentice Boys of Derry, he told me, and as an example of the threat they were facing, 'the Roman Catholic Council down there' had changed the name Londonderry to Derry. Why, then, I wondered, wasn't the name the Apprentice Boys of Londonderry? 'Well it *was* called Derry once. And then it was changed to Londonderry by a charter from one of the queens – I can't remember who she was but one of the queens. Now, the Roman Catholics want to do away with the name London because it reminds them of the British connection. So you can imagine what would happen if a majority of Roman Catholics, namely Sinn Fein and so forth, got into the council in Belfast. They would want to do *away* with things. Already they're talking about doing away with Royal in the title that we have for our police, Royal Ulster Constabulary. And indeed they're not going to want to call it *Ulster* any more.' All sorts of menacing possibilities loomed: 'They want to do away with the name Queen's University! They want to call it some *other* sort of university! So if they get into places of power, we're snookered. In behind the black, snookered, finished, see?'

After he had stopped the car Peter Lunn picked up a little flag from the dashboard and gave it to me. 'I'm going to let you have that,' he said. 'That's an Ulster flag.' Red bars crossing on white, the flag also features a severed hand in a six-pointed star surmounted by a crown. It was the red bars he wanted to show me: 'Now I don't need to tell you, that forms part of the Union Jack. And the rest of the Union Jack is made up by the flag of England, the flag of Wales, the flag of Scotland, you see? But the Ulster flag you'll find is a major part of the Union Jack, right? And the Union Jack means Union, that Northern Ireland is united with Great Britain, you see? And if *we* have any say in the matter we're going to fight to keep it that way!'

There was one more question: what did he think about independence for Ulster? He didn't want to make a comment on that, he said, having not been in politics long enough. But how did he feel personally? 'Personally speaking, yes, I think we could go it alone.'

'With Dr Paisley in charge?'

'Oh aye, most definitely!' For the first time since we'd turned to politics his pale brow unfurrowed and he laughed. 'Most definitely!'

'Would you prefer that to the current situation?'

He would, he said, yes, because 'there are many things that the British government do not allow us to do.' He was talking about dealing with the IRA. 'Because we're in the front line, it's our kith and kin that are being shot and bombed and killed, so therefore we would be harder on them and quite rightly so. Amen.'

He didn't say goodbye, he said 'Amen.'

I went on two more bouts of campaigning – one with Official Unionists, one with an SDLP candidate – both in lower-middle-class neighbourhoods unfamiliar to me, of different religions but very similar. The houses were set in green patches, semi-detached brick and stucco, neatly tended, the sort of place where small shopowners or minor civil servants might live, conservative, clinging to their relative prosperity.

Dorothy Dunlop, whose surname was accented on the second syllable, looked and spoke like an English lady. 'Secetreh,' she said, and 'temprereh.' 'Are you English?' I asked, and she was put out. She was born in Dublin, she said, but had lived in Belfast since the age of three. She had the professionally direct, open gaze of the successful politician. An Official Unionist member of the NI Assembly as well as a councillor, she got paid for being the former, with an allowance for an office on the Newtownards Road.

According to Mrs Dunlop, the DUP had been weeding out all the non-born-agains. The difference between the DUP and the OUP, she explained, was that the DUP's priority was Protestantism and anti-Romanism, and her own party's was the British connection and anti-Republicanism. 'We're not concerned, really, with people's religion. To me being a Protestant is something transcendent of nationality – I can be Protestant wherever I am, but I can only be British within the UK. It's very important to us that we should be able to take a large section of the

Roman Catholic population with us.' A poll had come out the day before: 'Thirty-four per cent of the Roman Catholic population said they wanted to remain British citizens, to preserve the link and remain part of the UK.'

'Will they be voting for you?' I asked.

'I would think a number will. It has been shown in every election that the number of people voting for the Union exceeds the Protestant population.'

We were canvassing a neighbourhood called Orangefield, and though at half the houses no one was home, she could drop off leaflets to show she'd been there. When a door was opened she said, 'Hello I'm Dorothy Dunlop, I'm one of your candidates in the election – do you want to ask me anything?' The people never did want to ask her anything. With us were two men – one very old party groupie, and the other a hearty outgoing fellow who was also a candidate, John McCrea, who actually did get involved in conversations of some length with everyone he could, even a coal delivery man who wasn't a voter ('His father used to deliver milk,' said Mrs Dunlop, 'so he knows all that sort of people'). As a result of her different approach, she got way ahead of McCrea and had to keep circling back.

An Official Unionist election poster, displayed all over Protestant Belfast, was seen around Orangefield too: CARELESS TALK COSTS LIVES, with pictures of Mrs Thatcher and Irish Prime Minister Garret FitzGerald. It referred to the current London-Dublin talks ('STOP THE SUMMITS' said another poster) preparing the way for what turned out to be the Anglo-Irish Agreement, which would for the first time allow the South a say in the North's affairs. Smelling a rat, the Official Unionist leader James Molyneux had in an election address scoffed at accusations of 'paranoia and so on', stating that 'summits between London and Dublin should be abolished because no good thing ever comes out of them.' I asked Mrs Dunlop if she thought there was some sort of conspiracy afoot against Ulster. 'Oh there's plenty of proof of that,' she said. She thought a bargain was being made to sell out the Unionists in return for American aid and the Republic joining NATO. 'We'd be delighted if they would join NATO, as long as we weren't used as a bargaining counter.'

McCrea was being berated (in good humour) by a constituent: 'You never see these fellas except around election time. Never see one the whole year round!' They got involved in a long conversation and meanwhile Mrs Dunlop put a dozen more leaflets through mailslots. McCrea, she told me, was Belfast County Grand Master of the Orange Order, the local Masonic-style secret society which had been promoting Protestant superiority since 1796, and this was his first electoral campaign. I asked her about the place of women in the Orange Order. 'They have a sort of women's equivalent,' she said, 'um, what's it called? The Purple Star or something. I've never had anything to do with it. If I was a man I would certainly want to be in the Orange Order. You couldn't get a better person than the best Orangeman.' A door answered. 'Hello I'm Dorothy Dunlop I'm one of your candidates in the election do you want to ask me anything?' she said without drawing breath. For once someone did: an old man wanted her to 'get them to put the rent control on again. This house started off at seven shillings and ninepence a week, do you know what it is now? It's over twelve pound. And us pensioners have to pay that.' She made various limp suggestions before moving on to meet McCrea again. He was at a door having a great laugh with a woman he'd known in the past: 'You meet more people when you're electioneering that you haven't met for years!' The woman said, 'I'm trying to make a bargain here, I'll vote for you if you'll put the carpet down for me.'

McCrea was agreeable: 'Number one vote and I'll come and put your carpet down!'

'Witness thar!' said the woman, pointing at me. 'Keep up the good work!'

I walked along with McCrea for a while, enjoying his rapport with the people. Knock, knock. 'Good afternoon, sorry to disturb ye, John McCrea is my name now' (laughter of recognition) 'and I'm one of the Official Unionist candidates.' – 'I never vote anything else,' was the reply. 'A good traditional Unionist!' said McCrea. 'Well we'll look forward to seein' ya. It's a good country isn't it?' – 'It is!' This was the general theme, rather than issues. 'I always felt we had a lovely country in Northern Ireland,' he said to someone else, 'if they would just let us live in peace to enjoy it.'

Between calls he answered a question about his position in the Orange Order: 'It's a part-time job, it can be quite exacting but. There's a fair degree of work in it. The run-of-the-mill correspondence, dealing with problems, the demonstrations on the Twelfth of July. I organized those for ten years.' He rang some door chimes. 'Hello, I'm John McCrea, I'm one of the Unionist candidates.' With a woman whom he spotted as being from Fermanagh he was in no time deep in rhapsodies about the lakes around Enniskillen, 'where the fisher–men go,' and how lucky anybody would be to live there if only the IRA wouldn't 'try to upset the fishing festival with bombs.'

Another first-time candidate, a young solicitor called Alex Attwood, was trying for an SDLP seat in the Upper Falls, the same district where Rita was campaigning for Sinn Fein; but this part of it was bijou and house-proud and I didn't recognize it at all. Here was where free enterprise worked, and there was where it didn't.

I had run into Alex Attwood at a demonstration against plastic bullets, when I asked if I could canvass with him. He was a bright, single-minded party activist, energetic and dedicated, and his looks were right – straightforward-cleancut. We met at the SDLP headquarters on the Falls, as dilapidated as its rivals, with a broken, dripping drain-pipe and an amazing assortment of rubbish in a stinking mess in the alleyway outside. A poster showed through the wired-up window: SOLIDARITY IS STRENGTH.

With a carload of volunteers to whom Attwood gave a pep talk, we drove in another loudspeaker car to Gransha, a relatively posh part of Andersonstown, and they all spread out among their allocated streets. It was teatime, so people would be at home. 'The issues are justice and equality,' said he to me as we walked to his bit. 'The SDLP has made them their own. Others may talk about justice and equality, but it is justice and equality for "ourselves alone" – which is what "Sinn Fein" means. That's what Unionism has represented for sixty years too – except they wouldn't translate it into Irish.'

He opened a creaking gate and knocked on a door. A middle-aged man with a doubtful expression answered. 'Good evening to you, sir. My name is Alex Attwood, I'm one of the SDLP candidates.' The man nodded neutrally. 'It's very late to canvass your vote, but if you are voting the SDLP, we'd appreciate it if you'd vote early. Secondly, if you're votin' SDLP make sure you vote the team one, two, three and four. And if you're lookin' for an experienced candidate, who's a solicitor who can represent people and get things done, who's the chairperson of Belfast in the party at age 26, I'd appreciate your first preference vote.' He was very sincere and good-humoured without ever being humorous, but the man kept on looking doubtful. 'I'll think about it anyway, so I will.' He nodded and shook his head at the same time. 'No problem. Right?'

'I like going into hard-line areas,' said Attwood as he closed the gate again. 'People there are much more honest – they tell you yes or no, but in a lot of the middle-class areas they just say "I'll think about it." That's my experience anyway.'

It was his twenty-third day of canvassing, he said, rattling another letterbox, and 'I'd say there's no more than two or three hundred houses at most that we haven't been to – Hello there, sir, how're ya keepin'? My name is Alex Attwood, I'm one of the SDLP candidates. Have you thought which way you're votin' yet?' He went on to say that he'd been one of the few Nationalists ever to be elected president of the Queen's University Students' Union, so he had political experience, and 'you might give one of the lesser known but up-and-coming young fellas a chance.' This voter, charmed, said 'Oh definitely.'

As we rounded a corner we saw an army patrol out, the third one in as many streets. Attwood said there had been three Sinn Fein candidates arrested already – 'they're playing right into Sinn Fein's hands.' One SF candidate had been picked up for disorderly behaviour in a demonstration the day before. 'Disorderly behaviour – it's the only place in the so-called United Kingdom where that offence exists. It's used deliberately to harass the Nationalist people in the most insignificant and subtle ways. I'm in the courts every day, and the number of Nationalists that are up on so-called disorderly behaviour charges – for saying "F-off" to the police or spitting on the ground in front of them – idiotic offences, just a constant systematic harassment.'

‘Do you get them off?’ I asked.

‘You never contest a disorderly charge. If the police down in those courts say you’re guilty, you’re guilty. Usually a fine – twenty, thirty pound up to £150. But if you’re getting closer to the big fines then the police’ll also prosecute you for a bigger offence, like for touching somebody or pushing somebody.’ He was looking for a specific door now, where lived a woman who one of his canvassers had said wanted to meet him. He found it and, ‘Good evening to you, madam. One of our people says – ’

‘That’s right,’ said the woman, a quick and cheerful person in her fifties, ‘they were trying to convert me.’ She had a specific complaint about a burnt-out building nearby that ought to be demolished, she said, and Attwood carefully outlined how it should be done and said that he would address himself to it even if he wasn’t elected. ‘I’m only standin’ because I am committed to the residents of the area. I’ll be back whether I’m a councillor or an ordinary SDLP member – I’m makin’ that personal guarantee.’

The woman was drawn in. ‘What does your party really think of a united Ireland?’ she asked.

‘Well, our constitution has three objectives – and one of them is that we will work towards a united Ireland. We believe that unity of the people of this country will only come through the unity of this country.’

And what was the SDLP position on the supergrass system? the woman wanted to know.

‘We’re completely opposed to it. The legal system can’t change unless the political system changes, because the legal system reflects the values and priorities of the political system. And if the political system is geared to shoot-to-kill, plastic bullets, harassment on the streets, the courts will just do the same. If you can get change in the political system, then you'll have the chance of getting principles of law established for the first time in the courts of the North.'

'I was definitely votin' Sinn Fein,' the woman said, 'and my sister, she lives over there where that banner is, she's votin' SDLP.'

'Well are you still votin' Sinn Fein?' asked the candidate.

She looked at him. 'I don't think so,' she said. Then: 'It's this supergrass system I'm really against. And I'd like the army out of here.'

'You'll only get the troops withdrawn,' said Alex, 'if you get politics back in. That sounds a cliché but that's accurate.'

The woman said, 'Honest to God, I think I'll vote SDLP.'

They parted allies. It was hard to believe that all this rhetoric was on behalf of winning a post with marginally more power than dog-catcher.

He went to door after door, and his patience never flagged; nor did he repeat himself. How did he do it? I asked. He was 'very very tired,' he said, 'and I've been getting confused,' but 'I'm always thinking up new stories because it's all a bit of story-making when you're standing up in court.'

After a dizzying succession of opened gates, knocks, spiels, we were back in the sound car with Alex indefatigably broadcasting through the streets (to no background music): '. . . *either the leadership of the SDLP, with their policies of justice and equality, or the leadership of extremism, with their shared policies of domination and discrimination. This is Alex Attwood, your SDLP candidate in Wednesday's election asking you to vote SDLP one, two, three and four . . . the people of this area have a choice between the SDLP leadership and the leadership of extremism . . .'*

Although the main thrust of this election was to defeat Sinn Fein, with 11.8 per cent of the vote they made a stronger showing than they themselves had predicted, and the OUP and DUP immediately announced a pact to thwart them in the councils where they had a voice. An SF candidate in Derry was elected to sit in the Guildhall he had bombed thirteen years earlier. Two of the three Sinn Feiners for whom Rita was campaigning got in. The SDLP won two in the Upper Falls as well, and out of thirteen contestants there, Alex Attwood scored the biggest single vote.

The Unionist parties between them won more than half the overall votes – the OUP with 29.4 per cent and the DUP 24.3 per cent, the latter 75,000 votes down province-wide from the election to the European Parliament when Paisley had carried them with his huge personal poll. Dorothy Dunlop was elected; John McCrea was not; Pauline Whittley lost too, but Peter Lunn got in on the twelfth count. (Two SF candidates also won in their Oldpark district, including a man who had served five years for firearms offences.) In the neighbouring constituency, George Seawright won hands down, scoring twice as many votes as his nearest competitor.

The Workers' Party got altogether 1.6 per cent of the vote.

Subsequent Unionist attempts to smash Sinn Fein in the councils met with less than total success. Incensed that Westminster representatives still boycotted SF – 'They expect us to sit down with murderers but they won't do it themselves' – Unionists stood rather than sat, expelled SF members illegally and selected decision-making committees which omitted them. A rigged election for council chairman in the town of Omagh led to a mix-up in which a Republican, Seamus Kerr, was chosen by mistake, followed by rowdy scenes with shouts from the gallery: 'You want your throat cut, Kerr,' and 'No pope here!' A Belfast Unionist who made an apoplectic speech about 'evil gunmen who have crawled out of the ghettos of West Belfast, evil human pus and part of the Republican poison in this city' was corrected by one of the Sinn Feiners, who said that actually he came from North Belfast.

The week before the election had finally been cross-examination time for Harry Kirkpatrick. The courthouse lobby was jammed with people queuing for admission: half the visitors' gallery was closed in the interest of 'crowd control'.

The legendary Desmond Boal had begun his part this week, and the question of whether he could crack Harry might have accounted for the crowd. (And, after all, Boal was going to get to try to crack UVF supergrass Budgie Allen, too: the trials were staggered to suit him.) Boal stopped the proceedings to argue that Kirkpatrick had been coached by the prosecution during the course of the trial (coaching in advance of the trial was S.O.P.) and therefore that the case should be thrown out. He argued that when Harry's contradictions of existing police evidence had become exceptionally flagrant, the prosecution had requested a week's adjournment on grounds of illness and then had spent the week smoothing out Harry. Prosecutor Appleton insisted it had all been quite above board. Between skirmishes Boal and Appleton sat side-by-side comfortably enough – parry vicious accusation and innuendo as they might, the customs and institutions of their profession kept the conflict civil. The fact that the twenty-nine young men spilling out of various docks had other less refined ways of settling scores was one reason why they were there.

But the matter would not be resolved today: the judge postponed his decision until morning. Hopes were so high that some prisoners' wives went straight home to wash curtains and spring clean for their men's return tomorrow, while others had a kind of bated-breath pre-ceremonial at an INLA club.

The next day the trial started more than forty minutes late: 'a screws' go-slow' was the rumour. The prisoners' families couldn't even begin to be searched and processed until the court was in session, so most of them dribbled in singly and too late to hear the news: 'I have given considerable care,' said Mr Justice Carswell – to his negative decision. Accepting that 'consultation did take place' between the witness and the law, he deemed it 'not unusual or exceptional' and 'not sufficient in itself to stop the case.' Furthermore, he didn't want 'to usurp the function of the jury' or 'withdraw the case from the jury if I were sitting with one.' Finally, 'Mr Boal, are you ready to proceed?' was the signal for the instant evacuation of the press box, as reporters went off to file the unamazing news.

Boal was evidently not amazed either. Harry was brought in, and the treatment began. Harry looked awful: blinking to concentrate, he seemed a haunted, hunted, twitching wreck. Never once did he look at Boal – who presented not a threatening but rather a discrepant appearance, his white wig worn low on the forehead giving him a pugnacious look, above bearish fuzzy white sideburns and twinkly eyes. A small, pot-bellied man, he yet aimed like a slithery arrow directly at the dead centre of his victim – an arrow that could twist and curve around corners and obstacles if necessary. A heat-seeking missile.

His method was mostly to confuse Harry by throwing his own words back at him. 'How can you say "It didn't seem important to me" when you don't remember what "*it*" was?' 'If that was the first question asked then you would *expect* to remember it wouldn't you?' 'Do you know of any *reason* you would have to lie?' Harry's squirms were all inward, his answers directed exclusively to the judge. 'No milord,' 'Yes milord.' 'I am not too sure about the question milord.' Demonstrating his double-tracked mind, Boal beckoned to his clerk while continuing to question Harry, conveyed a message and sent the clerk scurrying off to return a moment later with a ledger open to a page which Boal – still conducting another line of questioning – read at the same time and then smoothly incorporated into his next thrust.

What interested him was that Kirkpatrick had been locked up with Budgie Allen from April 1984 to February 1985. What had they talked about? They never discussed anything whatsoever about their cases, Harry insisted, or about the fact that each was getting ready to testify against all his former mates. But surely that was all they had in common? Were they not friendly? Was he not aware that his friend Budgie Allen answered the same questions in the same way? Harry kept doggedly facing only the judge, his voice a kind of automatic monotone, only his eyes looking frantically about as if for some way to get out of his face. But never at Boal. 'Have you any objection to looking at me?' asked Boal. 'No milord,' replied Harry, looking at the judge. Court laughter. 'Why don't you? Have you been told not to? Do you know that you have never looked at me once since I started?' 'Milord,' said Harry, 'I have on occasion glanced in Mr Boal's direction and I have seen Mr Boal smiling at me.' The crowd was loving this. For the first time, with Boal in charge, the proceedings were actually entertaining, and audible.

But not getting anywhere. The lawyer hacked away on two levels. First, he tried to induce his victim to acknowledge that he discussed all this with his cellmate, which obviously he must have done but could not admit because of the questions this might raise about their motivation for testifying ('Did it occur to you that you would be asked how you came to be in the witness box at all giving evidence against people who had been your friends?'). And then directly on the matter of the rewards and inducements themselves. Harry, it seemed, was recorded as having said in one of his initial sessions with the police, 'Look, what's the score here?' Boal pointed his arrow. 'What does the word "score" mean?' Harry ventured something disingenuous about scoring dope. Then he tried a reference to knowing the score. When he finally floundered, Boal interjected that in this context, it quite obviously meant 'What are the essential facts of the situation?' or 'What's the best they could do for you?' and what Harry was after was a deal.

But Harry wouldn't yield, and the brief session – on Fridays the court only sat until 1, having normally begun at 11 – was soon up, apparently to be carried over to the following Monday. Some American lawyers, in court to view the trial, were scandalized at the brevity of the proceedings: at home, they huffed, they worked a full day and they couldn't understand how it was possible to get anything done in four hours (Mondays to Thursdays) and two (Fridays, except in the event of a go-slow when it was less than an hour and a half). But now someone in the defence mentioned that as next Wednesday was election day the police would be busy elsewhere and they couldn't sit then. Judge Carswell added that he was unable to be there next Friday. Prosecutor Appleton contributed that unfortunately other business precluded his attendance on Monday and Tuesday. The defence pointed out that sitting merely on Thursday would affect Mr Boal's momentum so they might as well call it quits next week altogether. Finally Boal himself put in that he was due to begin on the Budgie Allen case at the end of next week and that he might well not be available on Monday week, although Tuesday week was a possibility. So satisfied, the legal profession excused themselves for a minimum of ten days. The American lawyers were speechless.

But that was before the prisoners got a chance to delay things. After what turned into a twelve-day recess, there was a fight in Crumlin Road jail among nine of them which ended with one having his nose bitten off. The trial was adjourned until he got better.

A week later. On the other side of the lobby from Court One, where Harry Kirkpatrick & Co were occasionally sitting, was its absolute mirror image, Court Two, where Budgie Allen & Co were ditto – both at the pleasure, it would seem, of the one-man band of Crumlin Road, Desmond Boal. The Catholics in the Kirkpatrick trial had a Protestant judge; the Protestants in the Allen trial a Catholic. Almost to the smallest detail this room was the reverse of the other, including the men in the dock. The twenty-five defendants, watched over by fifty-two constables and prison guards, were smoking (that was different) until the appearance of Mr Justice Higgins. Boal staggered in, balancing a foot-tall stack of papers, books and folders, his Archbold on top full of markers, very much the man who means business. Sizing up the judge, Boal peered at him expressionlessly over his half-glasses, and the judge peered expressionlessly back at Boal over his.

Budgie looked bluish with apprehension, a little man with faded ginger hair and beard and pursed lips. His stance, turned unnaturally away from the court, was just like Harry's – but unlike Harry, he couldn't resist a furtive glance at Boal now and then. Even less like Harry, he was unable to maintain the pose of the trained tough cookie. Boal kept shooting questions at him with the speed of an SLR, never needing to stop and reload, and Budgie, who had a long career of trying to weasel out of things before he got religion in 1982, had to take the course of admitting to previous deceptions. It couldn't but discredit him now. He reminded me of Harvey Matusow, who as a perjurer in the 1950s American witchhunt had implicated countless innocent people; later feeling remorse, he owned up and was sentenced for his pains to five years for lying when he said he had lied.

Boal's ferocity exceeded normal courtroom bounds, but, masquerading as a genuine public spirited enquiry, it went unchallenged. Who would dare, anyway? The real test came after he had extracted a history of mendacity from Budgie and then began the identical line of questioning he'd used on Harry: Did you ever discuss with Kirkpatrick the facts of your case? Your court appearances? The fact that you were giving evidence? What might happen in cross-examination? What your attitude should be? The effect of your giving evidence on your sentence? Your hope to get a reduction by giving evidence? Rat-a-tat-tat-tat-tat. No, said Budgie, clutching the rail of the witness box, no, no, no, no, no. 'The very thing that brings you together,' said Boal, 'that's the very thing you don't discuss! I would suggest that there is precious little else that you would have in common.' One man came from the Shankill, he pointed out, and one from the Falls; they attended different churches, their 'criminal activities were directed to contrary objects,' they patronized different bars, did different reading. 'What had you in common?'

'Just friendship,' mumbled Budgie feebly. Budgie wasn't a good enough liar, it was clear. His weakness if not his new-found morality led him to take the easier path of candour (if lying badly is a species of candour) and, like Matusow, his very honesty was his downfall. He couldn't even resist Boal's next shot – predictable if only from the scenario across the lobby: 'Is there any reason why you don't look at me? Kirkpatrick sits the same way.'

Fatal error: Budgie *looked*.

Whether Budgie's inadequacies as a witness were to blame or whether the judge in his case was a more discriminating jury, all the UVF men got off, and all of Kirkpatrick's victims were convicted. Most of the latter, however, were finally freed on appeal a year and a half later.

More cynicism, if not light, was shed on the supergrass phenomenon in a conversation I had afterwards with an ex-paramilitary. According to him, 'the only injustice is that one fella gets let off, gets a big sum of money and gets sent away.' The accused are all guilty of something, he said, and if the security forces didn't have serious evidence against them, the organizations could easily wreck the system's credibility by sending along people with cast-iron alibis to volunteer their informing services and then in court make a mockery of it all by producing the alibis. Some corroboration is implicit in the very accusation, therefore, although it is seldom if ever brought out; and what is brought out instead may be perjury from start to finish. 'They want to get someone for a murder, say. They can either shoot him, catch him doing something else, or take him off the board (jail him). The only rule is, "Do it to him before he does it to you." There is a Geneva Convention about how to conduct wars but everybody ignores it. There can be no rules in a conflict situation. It's a nonsense! Anything goes. But the ones that really think about it don't get upset by things like that.'

13
Wyatt Earp and the OK Corral

In late spring in Belfast, the night comes so gently it hardly comes at all, and by midnight there is still a fringe of light along the mountains, with the rest of the sky a rich, clear indigo. It's the reward in the far north for the winter of the long night; though people didn't seem to be out enjoying it much. On this particular June evening the stars were especially bright in the great deep blue and the street lamps in Andersonstown too dim to interfere. I thought I'd see if the Ryan children were interested in the constellations. 'Come outside and I'll show you something' – and all eight of them, with or without shoes, some in pyjamas, dropped everything (a TV film, painting-by-numbers, dish-washing, homework) to race each other to the door. On the pavement I asked if they knew where the Big Dipper was and they looked up past my pointed finger, then down at me again as if I were daft. They didn't, no; what about it? I showed them how to find the North Star, Orion, the Pleiades. Three of them drifted back inside. Martin said, 'But what are you going to show us?' I said the sight they were seeing no longer existed, that that was what the stars had looked like millions of years ago. Mairead said she had to get back to the dishes. The last three followed her in. 'I thought you were going to show us something,' Tony grumbled.

An American friend had taken two of them, Martin and 'wee Rita', out of their packed living room on a drive up the mountain behind the estate. Halfway up she'd looked back at the extraordinary view: in no time you are out of the city and can see Belfast cuddled round its lough with the shipyard gantries – toytown. She continued to drive on up into the isolated countryside with its small, attractive farms and country lanes – the view better yet – her plan to go to the top and circle back round. 'Isn't it interesting? Isn't it beautiful?' she said. Martin and Rita, having sat silently, suddenly panicked. 'Turn back! Turn back!' She couldn't make it out, but they were so insistent she obliged, made a U-turn and drove down again. Now, what was that all about? she asked as they pulled up outside home. They just didn't like being in a place without any *people*, they said.

What's interesting in Belfast is not necessarily what's interesting anywhere else. I thought about that again next morning, when in the dazzling weather I met a freelance journalist setting out unenthusiastically on the hour's drive to Armagh to look into the archaeological site at Emain Macha, threatened by undermining from a nearby quarry. It wasn't much of a story, she said, but pickings were scarce these days. I asked if she were going to a Women's Health Fair that was on at the moment at the Ulster Hall. 'Oh no,' she said, 'I only go to things that make me money.' I'd seen her during the past year at all the big newsworthy events, almost able to gauge by her presence if I were at the right place at the right time. 'What I need now is a big bomb, as a matter of fact,' she went on. 'They're money makers, no doubt about it.'

The big bomb went off without her at ten past one, an isolated thunder boom in the clear sky. I dismissed it at once as some aberrant act of God. The natives, less sanguine, appeared at their doors and windows and soon clumps of people formed to chat about the explosion which didn't put *them* in any doubt. Quite a few started walking towards where the sound had come from. The going became rather difficult as the RUC stopped traffic and tied off bits of the city centre with white ribbon. A young man walking near me volunteered that usually a bomb set off phone calls giving other bomb warnings and no way of knowing which, if any, were hoaxes. He was eager to get to the action. 'When there's a bomb in Belfast,' he said, 'once the ribbons go up, everybody just stands and watches and waits and they just hope to get one goin' off, ya know? It's like sport, ya know? If you're lucky, it misses you.'

The buses had stopped running and only a helicopter and police cars showing off their sirens disturbed the weird quiet. Mobs of evacuated shop assistants basked in the sun on the lawn around City Hall, making splodges of colour like synthetic flower beds in their uniforms of cherry red, bottle green, pink. Shoppers loaded with bags were stranded, either for lack of public transport or because their cars were parked inside beribboned areas. Crowds of the curious gathered at the ribbon from all directions, relaxed and engaged at once. 'Gettin' back to normal,' said one elderly woman, viewing it with what seemed a common sentiment: 'Things have been so calm lately you'd be wonderin' if we'd dreamt the whole thing.' You couldn't tell if she was resigned or pleased or both. Rhetorically she asked the nearest cop, 'Can you give an idea about time, can you?' – 'Not really, no,' the cop said, as if he'd actually been pondering it. Gazing past him at a burnt-out car down the street, she went on, 'That would have been a controlled explosion, would it?' I didn't know what she meant. She explained that the army blew up all the parked cars in there in case they, too, contained bombs. Firemen were hosing down the hulks.

The converging people seemed to view the event as an excuse to down tools and stand in the sun. The only ones obviously perturbed were those who'd parked their cars within the white ribbons, like the young man approaching the same policeman to ask, 'What's the crack then?' – 'It's a weddin',' replied the policeman. 'Give over,' said the young man, irritated. He was needing to get to the parking lot down there. Another bystander told him not to bother, he was parked there too and he'd just bumped into the attendant. 'I asked him if he'd need paid if the car had to stay all day. "Och," says he, "I'll have to get a rulin' on that."' They both laughed knowingly, then continued their friendly conversation – which took in everyone nearby as well – for at least half an hour, when I moved on.

Rumours flew about: there was a bomb on Great Victoria Street, another on Linenhall Street, and it was all roped off round Shaftesbury Square. Meanwhile the whole world communicated, joked and consoled each other. It must have been like this in London in the blitz. A woman heaving an enormous bagful of cabbages sighed stoically: 'I'd walk but I just got a new hip and this is the first time I been out without me stick.' Not that she seemed vexed. She set down her bag on the warm pavement and prepared to wait. 'Me cabbage'll be cooked by the time I get home.'

Three executive-looking gents stood together soberly assessing structural damage, or what they could make out of it down Chichester Street, with a view either to rebuilding or perhaps insurance, it was hard to tell. A middle-class travelling salesman, Protestant (he made clear) was telling stories to a building worker, Catholic (he made clear) about his problems with his car, now parked down there too and who knew in what condition? It seemed he'd had his car hijacked twice in as many months. The first time it was retrieved on the motorway, out of fuel, and the second time it turned up in Twinbrook in someone's garden wrapped around a tree. The police had come to get him at 3 A.M. to go fetch the remains, and why couldn't it have waited till morning? How was he supposed to get there? Finally the same police, after suggesting that it was his problem, had grudgingly agreed to take him to the scene, but on arrival they had dropped him two hundred yards short of the car – because, he reckoned, they thought it might be booby-trapped and he, not they, was going to have to be the booby. It was a write-off anyway; at this point he'd only just got the insurance and bought another and *now* what? The building worker commiserated, though out of mechanical friendliness more than need as the salesman couldn't have been more cheerful. 'Maybe the fella's watching,' he said, delighted with the idea. 'Maybe he only made a phone call after the big bomb with a story about more of them, and now he's watching all this crack and enjoying himself.' They laughed together.

The ribbons were little deterrent to the shoppers in the centre, who rerouted themselves straight through the front and rear doors of the large stores to bypass obstructions, as if they were mere building or sewage works. A mall being repaved with criss-crossed bricks was still being repaved, despite its unfortunate location beyond a white ribbon. A UDR man in a camouflage jacket was standing guard on a pile of the bricks and cradling his SLR like a new baby.

Winding back towards the Ulster Hall I decided to go where I'd been headed in the first place, the Women's Health Fair. But that street, too, was cordoned off and guarded with another big crowd spectating at the edge and chatting together as far away could be seen, directly outside the Hall, the fire brigade dousing the carcass of something that not long ago must have driven there. No women's fair that day. 'We're lucky in the weather, aren't we, love?' said an old man leaning on a lamp-post.

* * *

By 7 that evening it seemed possible to try again. On the news it had been said that the bomb, an estimated thousand pounds of explosives, was claimed by the IRA; a warning was given and nobody hurt, but millions of pounds' worth of commercial property was destroyed. The streets were now accessible almost all the way to the blast centre. Windows for blocks around had smashed and sweepers were brushing up the bits with a musical tinkling in all directions. The street was looking lovely, being carefully brushed spotless. The crowds had gone home; apart from the law and the clean-up squad, only the odd knot of people were still gazing at the destruction, and gangs of small boys, who in Belfast always seemed to favour piles of rubble to play on, were trying out the new ones. Suddenly around a corner there was more of a mess than mere shards of glass. An entire building had collapsed in a heap, its neighbours listing this way and that. Chichester Street was paved in broken glass; catching the oblique evening sun it glinted like diamonds. A tall square modern block had all its windows out with what looked like stacks of newspapers inside each hole: crumpled blinds. I asked several people what the building was. 'The IDB.' – 'What's that stand for?' Nobody knew, beyond it having to do with 'that ad on the telly, you know, I'm Doing Better.' The building that no longer existed at all except as a heap of debris had housed the Directorate of Public Prosecutions. Everyone knew what that was, and none seemed to lament it.

A broken pipe was spilling out a waterfall, the only sound apart from brooms-on-glass. Nearer the scene, though still a hundred yards from the epicentre, were scattered springs, a blackened hubcap and other bits of the car which had exploded to cause it all. Other cars were suddenly visible in a parking lot. I thought of the poor cheerful hijack victim. The cars gave the impression of being concussed, oddly injured, with their bonnets sprung open and a strange sagging quality to their posture. Some of them looked less obviously hurt than others but it was clear they'd never drive again.

A camera crew was trying to film the jewelled street but the reflected light was too strong and they had to settle for an artful shot of Her Majesty's Stationery Office with spoilt books strewn everywhere. Two cars drew up and out of one of them unfolded Ian Paisley, grim-looking, come to survey the damage. He was dressed in a snappy Burberry with mirror-polished shoes, quite another sight from the shabby Papa Doc who went campaigning. 'This will go on until they determine to stop it,' he growled at the camera. 'They're doing everything to encourage it. No one in the world would put up with this.'

The crew got a better quote out of the kids. Three urchins were beckoned over and they ducked and blushed at the idea of being on TV. Finally the bravest agreed to speak. 'Tell me,' he was asked, 'if you'd seen someone plant that bomb, would you have told the police?'

'No,' said the urchin.

'Say it,' said the director.

'NO I WOULD NOT TELL THE PEELERS,' said the boy obediently.

'Why not?' asked the director.

'Because they're dickheads,' the boy said.

I was on my way with Jack, an American professor of political science who was making a film on the supergrass system, to see the Binghams. It had been almost a year since I had interviewed Dora Bingham; now her husband John, who had been jailed for twenty years on the testimony of supergrass Joe Bennett, was free after serving two. Fourteen of Bennett's sixteen victims had been released when the appeal court decided to doubt his word. When we had first visited him less than a week after his release, John had already framed his pardon from the Queen and hung it on the wall above the mantelpiece.

Dora, so self-possessed as John languished in the Kesh, was different with him out of it. He did all the talking: a powerful personality all round. A heavy, fair fellow with quick wits and emotions and decisive movements, he had wasted no time after getting out but had already signed up as George Seawright's election agent.

As Dora had told me, John was a pigeon fancier and his current troubles had begun in 1976, when 'I lived in a confrontation area in Ardoyne and they burnt my pigeon shed down.' They had gone after him in particular, he thought, 'on the principle of getting rid of the one who'll stand up and fight: since my philosophy is, "If someone hits you in the gub, hit him back."' He was definitely not, of course, a member of the UVF (one of the charges). 'I'm a well-known Loyalist, not a terrorist. But I support their aims. My grandfather, who died at the Battle of the Somme, was a member of the UVF. My granda handed down to my father and my father handed down to me.' Strictly speaking, his forebears had not been members of quite the same UVF: originally founded in 1912 to fight the imposition from Westminster of Irish Home Rule, they had later been sent to the Somme where nearly all perished in one day. The name was revived in 1966 for what became one of the most ruthless organizations in the province's history.

John's childhood was full of the memory of his father, a policeman, 'drawing his gun every time the door was knocked.' It left him with almost a genetic duty to defend his Britishness: 'I want to hold on to what I have. There's nobody can take away this. The Provies can believe what they believe . . . drive sixty miles and you're in a different country. It's the threat of a Loyalist backlash that prevents a united Ireland.'

The perceptions of people who had served time with their opposite numbers have an interesting quality. There is a kind of adversarial honour, the feeling that an enemy in war is like a rival in love – the greater the stature of the other, the more it enhances your own. No one hated the IRA more than John, but his respect for them was real enough. 'I have come through a hell of a lot this weather,' he said, 'but the Provies have suffered the same things we suffer. I've talked to a lot of them in jail. There's no difference between them and me.'

On the other hand, 'Republicans are killing people you went to school with, people you came up with. Religion has nothing to do with it. What I'm trying to say to you is I'm not sectarian.'

Jack asked a question about discrimination in employment. John didn't see how it could be called discrimination. Look at it this way: 'For a Catholic to go down to the shipyard, he's taking his life in his hands because he's going to the British Empire that he wants so badly out of.'

Not that the British were doing very well by John at the moment. He had lost not just two years out of his life but his job as an electrician, and the prospect for his family was bleak, but even that was nothing compared to the process he'd just lived through: 'a way of sickening the people that was prepared to come out on the street and do a bit of flag-waving – putting us away and trying to stop us fighting for them.'

How had he got mixed up in the Bennett case to begin with? 'I'd met boys who supposedly murdered people along with Joe Bennett.' But he certainly wasn't involved himself and was 'always a speaker against the violent end of it. I can't name one death that has forwarded anyone's cause.

'But there's two kinds of terrorists: the kind who wants to take away the constitutional right and the terrorist who just wants to hold on to what he has. I see *him* as right. The man that has it in his heart is the man who thinks it's right. The man who thinks it's wrong is the totally wrong one.'

Who could he mean? By their own standards they were all right. It was the maniacs: take the Shankill butchers. In the 1970s a gang of them, led by a real butcher called Willie Moore, had gone in for killing random Catholics, mutilating them before, during and after. Brendan had told me about how he grew up with Willie Moore on the Shankill – 'Ach, we knocked about together,' he'd said, 'used to go to the disco together. Moore was the quietest wee lad you ever met.' John now said Moore had been 'caught when he was found trying to decapitate his fourteenth victim. He was a butcher, but he was drunk and he had a bad knife – it had done thirteen and never been sharpened.' Gales of laughter. 'They're mustard men!'

Then there were UDA people who, according to John, didn't measure up either. 'Some of their crimes were unbelievable. But they haven't got the guts to go into a Republican area and kill Gerry Adams.' The UDA was populated with gangsters and extortionists, he said, who threatened building sites for protection money. They even had the nerve to extort money from businesses using the UVF's name. The UVF was a group of dedicated and upright men by contrast, according to John, citing as evidence that 'many UDR men have been UVF as well, statistics show.' The UDA 'can't even get their Prisoners' Aid together: the UVF gets each man in jail eight pounds a week – ten if they're married – plus newspapers, free buses for visitors. The UDA men end up having to share the UVF papers, and sometimes their money doesn't come through, while the boys above are driving their brand-new Mercedes.' I didn't mention Tyrie's Renault.

More statistics: John claimed that '98 to 99.9 per cent of the people in prison has signed statements that they did it. In my wing only one guy I ever met was completely innocent.' He showed us a letter he'd just received from a prisoner friend. 'He has 35 stip. He's a Christian. He would do it again.' [35 stip = 35-year stipulated, or minimum, sentence.] His own case had revolved around alleged arms-running from two uncles in the US who were supposed to have sent in for the guns through a mail-order catalogue. 'I wanted to get into the witness box and say, "Wait'll I *tell* ya, judge, I don't *have* uncles in America."' Not only that but some warheads he was accused of acquiring by this exotic route were for an RPG-7 which, being Russian, were unlikely to be available through Sears-Roebuck. There had been no evidence to support these charges, he said; but the defence, as with the other supergrass cases, had been conducted on the gamble of discrediting Bennett entirely rather than singling out individual lies and discrepancies, and the judge had decided that 'because he accepted Joe Bennett's word he was going to send me down. Dessy Boal, my barrister, had said "Don't you worry, you're going home . . ." Twenty years!'

'How did you feel when that happened?' asked Jack.

'I felt fuckin sick.'

Jack was setting up appointments to film people involved in these cases on all sides and, while John was relevant as a victim, he wasn't, he said, UVF enough. 'I'm just an unemployed grassroots electrician and the supergrass system has me in debt and danger. But I'm not innocent: if there's going to be a showdown I can go get Wyatt Earp and find the OK Corral.'

Jack called him on that and John immediately offered to help him meet Wyatt Earp – or the OC of Belfast. 'No trouble, though he'll have to be hooded, of course.'

It didn't seem too likely that Wyatt Earp would come through and if so at a time when I could go along, but John was true to his word and when Jack's Californian cameraman turned up, the meeting was arranged. This was the day the big bomb had gone off in town and, when we arrived at the Binghams', bombs were the subject of conversation. John reminisced about Bloody Friday, in July 1972, when in one hour there were twenty explosions throughout Belfast, with nine people killed and 130 maimed. 'I was standing around and I suddenly looked up at the pigeon loft and the pigeons took off as I was watching them. Then I heard the sound of the bomb. So I run up the stairs and the city was all around you – you could see the big pall of smoke rising. Two seconds later Boof! another one. And then Boof! the next. I says, Fuck me! It was down along York Street direction. Boof! and Boof! coming closer. Boof! fuckin closer. There was just constant explosions. If you had a camera that day you'da caught it fantastic. Actually destroyin' the fuckin city, a minute or two apart. Fantastic. You could actually see the bombs goin' off and there was people getting killed in them. They were no-warning car bombs, you know?

'Another time I lived just up from the peace line. The Provies jumped out at the bar at the top of the street, out of a hijacked post office van, and away they went and left it. The army had already told us there was a bomb scare and got us out of the houses. Well once we were in the street, away she went, boy! And there was this woman beside us, Rosie McNeice you called her. And you could see a bumper, a fender, coming down the fuckin street, boy, in slow motion and you could see who it was going to hit and everything. It's wonderful, see, when you're in a thing like that there, you could actually see it tumbling, it was going like a propeller, and it come down and it whacked her. It hit her side on and actually embedded itself right intil her. I think at the end of the day they took her leg off – the gangrene started settin' in. But it's wonderful, them sort of things, you know? It's unbelievable like.'

Eventually there was a rap at the door and a hefty bald man, 'Billy', came in to take us to the meeting with the UVF. We were to take two cars, leaving Jack's behind. Almost in silence, we drove for a long time. I was trying to memorize the route, as Jack and the cameraman had started to scare me with their last-minute requests to a friend to 'do something' (what?) if they hadn't returned by tomorrow. I thought: I can't remember all this, I'll have to be hypnotized. In the event we were taken to an ordinary neighbourhood drinking club with no particular attempt to deceive us. But as we entered a side-road the driver waved at a man sitting casually on a hillside nearby. Other men sat around on hills as if they were just out enjoying the late afternoon weather. There were seven lookouts, it seemed. Later someone told me two of his friends were buried in those hills.

The club was like many others – pool tables, video games, the smell of stale booze, heavily male – with nothing very paramilitary about it. But since every paramilitary organization ran such clubs, and any young man might be a paramilitary, that wasn't saying much. A pool game was in progress and the players ignored us, but John and Billy were hospitable with beer and bonhomie. We were given drinks and asked to wait. John wanted us to know that interviews of this sort were 'never done' and the men we were to see might be nervous. He wasn't trying to be funny. He told Jack to ask the same questions he'd submitted previously and 'he'll answer; he won't elaborate.' 'These boys have never done this before,' he said again. Jack wanted to know if they would have weapons. 'I don't know,' said John, 'but if they have, then you'll know it's the real thing.'

'Why do you think they want to do this?' asked Jack.

'I dunno,' John answered. 'Ask them. Don't supergrass me.'

At a signal we were taken out to another small building and locked inside. Three black-hooded men were seated under spotlights at a table with a UVF banner on it; pinned to a blue arras which divided the room in two, obscuring the rear, were four artistically draped flags: a Union Jack, an Ulster flag and the banners of the UVF and the YCV (Young Citizens' Volunteers, the UVF's junior wing).

The men not only wore black balaclavas, but were dressed in black from scalp to toe apart from UVF badges on their foreheads. Even black gloves – a masked UDA man had once been identified from a photograph by the freckles on his hands. All three were very thin and slight, with ginger moustaches showing through the mouth-holes of the masks of two of them. Six blue eyes showed through the helmet holes. The convivial atmosphere of the bar was gone: no more smiles, no more drinks. Then I noticed the table again.

The display was arranged with a view to cinematic appeal, a machine gun placed diagonally between two pistols with their chambers (loaded) sticking out. More bullets showed at the bottom of the handle of the machine gun.

Jack introduced himself, chatting away disarmingly about his film 'for educational TV in the States,' and asking them please to speak slowly because of the accent problem. Of course you couldn't see how the men were reacting. The UVF badges on their brows were exactly the size and oval shape of the holes for their eyes and mouths, giving them the appearance of four-eyed, paralysed, noseless black monkeys. It must have been awfully hot and prickly inside those masks and woolly gloves under the bright lights, but of course you couldn't even see them sweating either.

While the camera was being fine-tuned Jack told them he'd filmed people in all the areas and from each of the paramilitary organizations (maybe they'd put on this show because they thought the others had?) and about his purpose – to assess the impact of the supergrass system on the UVF. He said he'd like to make it 'informal.' John had advised Jack to relax the men first, but Jack kept clearing his throat and, being locked up with all that gunpower, how relaxed could you get?

Camera. Action. Jack began by asking the men to 'explain to an American audience who you are; tell them a little of the background of your organization?'

The man in the middle, who did all the talking, said 'We three who sit in front of you now are members of the Ulster Volunteer Force. The Ulster Volunteer Force [like UDA members, they don't use the initials] was formed some seventy-odd years ago. That basically is it.' His voice was quite pleasant and the accent not strong enough to cause trouble, but speaking through a small woollen hole he wasn't always audible.

Jack asked him to 'explain the strength of your membership; how you recruit; what sort of people you try to bring into your organization; what sort of training you might offer them?'

His hopes for a long narrative response were dashed. 'Which of those questions would you like answered first?'

Jack: 'What the size of your organization is.'

UVF: 'I'm sorry I can't answer that. For security reasons.'

Jack: 'The reason I'm asking is that the RUC claim they've been successful in lowering levels of violence and that slowly but surely the paramilitary groups are being defeated.'

UVF: 'The RUC are drastically wrong. The UVF did scale operations down at the request of the RUC, because they felt they would have more time to spend defeating the IRA. There was no other reason for it. If at any time we wish to upscale it again, we will.'

Jack: 'Can you envision the circumstances in which your organization would become more active?'

UVF: 'Yes, of course. If the British government tried to force down the throats of the Ulster people a solution to their troubles – that is, a united Ireland, a federal Ireland – then by all means we would go out in force.'

When Jack asked how the supergrass system had affected the UVF, the man spoke at more length, if with less clarity, about the British intention to 'take people off the streets, incarcerate them and hope they'd be in prison for lengthy terms. They hoped it would weaken the UVF's determination' and the public would turn against them; but people could see through this and 'nobody views an informer with anything other than disdain.' In fact 'ordinary civilians' had come forward with sympathy, offers of help and information and 'the volunteers, instead of running, actually stood their ground, showed more grit, more enthusiasm simply because of the informer system.'

So what, Jack wanted to know, was the organization's policy on touts? If they found someone who they thought to be employed by the police, then what? The bottom hole in the middle mask mumbled something about 'extreme measures' and Jack pursued it. 'Have you had to do that?'

'Yes.'

'How many times?'

'I'm sorry, I can't divulge that. Some are already well-known to the police; some will never be discovered.'

A convoluted question followed with the clear aim of finding out whether a UVF member had to be prepared to kill. 'Of course,' was the reply.

What did they look for in a recruit? was a question that got a largely inaudible answer about a number of qualities, first among them conscience.

And how did the UVF differ from the UDA? The shrouded mouth seemed almost to chuckle. 'We're not in it for the money. We're in it for beliefs.'

Jack wanted to know about the guns. 'The one on my right, the one on my left, they are two .38 specials. And any weapon, regardless of what it is, they're manufactured to kill . . . something. The weapon you see in the middle is a Sterling submachine gun, produced obviously for the same reason.'

At this point Jack started treading on more delicate territory. 'In the past,' he said, 'the UVF has engaged in sectarian killing, random killing of Catholics who are not involved in the military forces. Is this an accurate description of UVF policy in the past? And is it to date?' The hackles rose on the very wool of the balaclavas. '*Cut!*' said the man in the middle; and proceeded to give Jack a dressing down about abusing their agreement to stick to the subject of supergrasses. I was starting to wish that Jack would consider moderating his normal behaviour, but he wasn't like that. In the times I'd seen him he'd always spoken his mind, expecting absolute candour in return. He was full of choice, if unverifiable, statistics ('Fourteen per cent of the income of the Irish home goes on booze. Second is Holland, with four per cent'), and questions asked with apparent imperviousness to fear and embarrassment. It was a very American form of communication, short on tact but long on spreading indiscriminate goodwill. Usually it had a miraculous effect. But he was quite capable of making a jest to some obvious killer to get a rise out of him, about 'topping people', say, so that you couldn't decide if he'd just made his very last blunder or if conceivably he knew what he was doing. A Belfast man said of him: 'Definitely a suicide pilot, that chappie.' But he got away with it, and learned a great deal on the way. Today it was a question of whether his never-say-die approach was altogether appropriate with all those loaded guns pointing at him.

However, at this stage he reverted to a sober question about the aims of the UVF and we heard: 'There's no other Loyalist paramilitary organization as dangerous. There's no other Loyalist paramilitary organization willing to go just quite as far as we will. We will take any measures that we deem necessary to defeat the IRA, to retain our link with Britain. If anyone in any part of the world gives support to the IRA that's going to cost lives in this country, then we're going to take action against them. Your country is one in particular in which this will happen. If it ever comes that we have to take to the streets, then we won't be satisfied with the IRA. Militarily we will attack those groups like Noraid who more than any other organization has supported them.'

Since this subject, too, was hardly connected to supergrasses, the emphasis on it seemed puzzling. 'Noraid is a very, very dangerous organization,' the masked man continued. 'It supplies money, weapons and safe havens to IRA men on the run. No one can expect to give such help with impunity.'

How did they know who was in Noraid? Jack asked. A thick sheaf of papers suddenly materialized among the guns. They were, it seemed, the membership lists of 'the Derry Society of Philadelphia, the Irish-American Club, the Ancient Order of Hibernians, the Irish Social and Cultural Society, Anglo-Celtic Cultural Society . . . do you wish to hear more?' And the UVF, its representative said, had already taken action against Noraid members who 'filter money into Ulster to give to the IRA to purchase guns. They were executed.'

The cameraman was allowed to film some names (and addresses) of Americans. It suddenly appeared that the purpose of this event, from the UVF's point of view, was fulfilled.

Back to the beer and the pool in the hospitality room. I set my tape recorder on the table among the glasses, openly but with little hope because of a neighbouring video game and a television.

John and Billy began telling war stories to Jack. There had been the assassination squad sent one night to kill Gerard Steenson (the angel-faced 'Dr Death' of the Kirkpatrick trial), and because Steenson had a washing machine against the door they couldn't get in. They tried instead to hit another target, but got the wrong house and shot an old-age pensioner instead. 'Them sort of things, we'd put them down to what you'd call a casualty of war,' John said. 'It just happens, accidentally. But I wouldn't try to excuse the death of an innocent person.'

There is something about overexposure to horror which makes you fix on the insignificant. I wanted to know if they couldn't get in, how could they tell it was a washing machine? For that matter, did Steenson know they were coming or did he always keep the washing machine at the door?

'Always,' said John. 'When you go to bed at night in Belfast that's what you do – put *every*thing in front of the fuckin door.'

Someone else told a story about an event the past Friday night when a man who was 'involved with prostitutes' got a 'warning from the Officials', disregarded it, and had gone into a café when he saw two men following him. 'He sensed there was something wrong, so he walked out and the guys kept following, so yer mon began to run. They shot after him but the bullet missed, by the whole width of the street but! It hit a lamp-post and ricocheted right into the guy's head. Killed him anyway.'

As with all these stories, there was no sense of ally or enemy, only individual luck and derring-do. Luck played the main role in another yarn about a target of some group (unidentified) who had been to a dance and picked up a girl. The gunmen were waiting for him outside, 'put the gun to his head and pulled the trigger. Click! – it didn't fire. Click! again. The girl began to run and to scream, and the gunmen aimed at her to keep her quiet and blew her head off.' After that apparently they had continued to shoot at 'yer mon' but 'it never worked, only when he pointed it at *her* it worked. It was just what you call fate.'

The cameraman asked if the UVF would retaliate for the big IRA bomb in the city centre that day. He was told that since there was 'no body count, it's not an emotive thing.' Dismissed, in favour of another story with a body count. We never got to the action, though, because it was said to have happened in 'Derry', and since Protestants generally make such a palaver about 'Londonderry' I stopped him.

'It *is* Derry! Don't make any mistake about it: if you go to Derry City and speak to Loyalists, they say Derry. Unionists just say Londonderry for effect.'

I asked them about sectarianism – how they saw themselves in relation to people who were anti-Catholic or others who were anti-Republican.

'We're anti-Republican. We're not sectarian.'

'No problems about Catholicism?'

Lots of them answered at once: 'No no no, sure.' 'My brother's a Catholic.' 'I have Catholic relatives.' The one with the Catholic brother (a convert by marriage) said, 'My brother's the bigot.'

'UVFers aren't bigots?' asked Jack.

'No no.'

'Catholics aren't different from you?'

'No difference whatsoever.'

Several conversations started going at once. Jack asked John one of his favourite questions: 'What do you think you'll be doing ten years from now?'

Without hesitation John said, 'Life, probably.'

Jack pursued this, probing into John's 'goals', and asking why he didn't go to college.

'That's just bettering yourself at a lot of other people's expense,' replied John. 'What I'd love is to be a farmer. Have a wee plot of ground. Smallholder, wee bit of ground, couple of pigs, couple horses, not too many people about. That's my ambition, I've thought about it all the time.'

A few moments later, Billy was telling Jack about Long Kesh, and a couple of friends of his who, because they were one month apart in age – as it happened, one under age, one over – got different sentences for the same crime. The older was now out and the younger was an SOSP and might never be.

Jack's voice rose as he addressed the table. He wanted to ask again, he said, if that was the British system, 'why do you want to have anything to do with it? In the United States when this happened to us we declared a revolution. Jesus Christ, they're fucking you over!'

'Well, we want to be part of the system,' John said.

'What for? They're fucking you over left and right!'

'They're not.'

'You guys keep giving the party line like a bunch of Communists. You've got your whole life to live and you have kids . . .'

'The miners in England didn't say they didn't want to be British,' said John. 'They didn't say Hang on, we want out of it.'

Jack: 'I don't see why in hell you guys are grabbing on to it so tight, always wanting to maintain this British identity. I can't convince Americans of that. You guys are not convincing, let me tell you.'

John: 'We don't have to convince Americans.'

Jack: 'I do though. I have to convince them that you guys are for real and not just a bunch of phoney baloneys.'

Billy: 'You want me to quote the Provies on it? "To those who understand, no explanation is necessary. To those who will not understand, no explanation is possible."' The graffiti on the Falls Road.

At that moment the BBC news came on with footage of the Queen's youngest grandson, Prince Harry. Jack pointed up at it. 'There he is! Stand up Billy, bow your head. You guys revere the British bullshit so much you might as well bow your head.'

John was angry. 'You're insultin' us now. You're fuckin insultin' us!'

'He's just making mock,' I said, modestly trying to save our lives.

The men paid no attention to me. 'It *is* pretty ridiculous, John!' said Jack.

John was now furious. 'You're insultin'! You're gettin fuckin my hackles up!'

Oh God. Here we were in the middle of who knew where, wall-to-wall UVF, and Jack has to start. The UVF motto, after all, was DEATH BEFORE DISHONOUR. 'John,' I had another try, 'how do you stand when the national anthem is played?' I was thinking of the UDA style, as Hester had it, 'standing in respect, with the head bowed in sorrow for the prisoners who are inside just for being British.'

'On the floor,' said John. 'On my feet.' He'd never heard about their way of doing it.

Meanwhile the news showed an item about that day's bomb, and the room went silent. When it was over Jack said he'd counted and the item had lasted for twenty-four seconds. 'That's how important you guys are to the rest of the world! Twenty-four seconds! No body count!'

'Jack's got what he fuckin wanted,' John was shouting. 'Now he doesn't care. He's got his fuckin fillum.'

Jack: 'John, I'm givin' you my best personal view of this whole – after bein' here six months – is that all it's worth, twenty-four seconds on the fuckin news? Every man has an obligation to live his own life and promote his own and his family's life . . .'

John: 'I believe in the thing! No way will you, or anybody in the fuckin world, tell me I'm wrong! As long as I'm convinced, both in my heart and my conscience, that I'm right! Hundreds of thousands went to Vietnam to fight – they were wrong. They were even more wrong when they knew at the start they were wrong but they went ahead and took life and lost their lives . . .'

Jack: 'Well it's time to stop dyin' for flags and symbols, and start askin' what's in it for me?'

John: 'We're not a selfish race!'

Jack: 'Maybe it's time to be a bit more selfish.'

John: 'If people are prepared to risk their lives and their freedom for what they believe, what right has anybody else got to tell you you're wrong?'

Billy: 'Exactly.'

Jack: 'No one's tellin' you you're wrong, I'm just sayin' what I would do.'

John: 'There's people who say "I'm goin' to look after Number One and I'm goin' to get what I can fuckin get." If you can get a wee bit you're not satisfied with a wee bit, Jack, you want a wee bit fuckin more and a wee bit more till you have every fuckin thing!'

Jack: 'What's a country? Why do we have to have countries? Why can't we be citizens of the world?'

John was practically speechless with rage. 'I – I'm – All I have to *show*, all that my fuckin people have *left* me, my grandfather and father have *left* me, was a country to live in where I was brought up in – '

Jack: 'They left you a mind and a body and they'd expect you to use it, not just follow along in their footsteps!'

I thought: now they're going to hit him, at least. But Billy, in a clear attempt at reasonableness, turned to Jack and said: 'If you lived in Belfast, and you'd a wife and a family, and lived in a house in an interface area, and you were lying in bed at night and your family's in the next room, and suddenly in the middle of the night comes a petrol bomb through your window to evacuate you from that place, right? A grave risk of you and your family being burnt to death in bed, and the next night because you don't move out they fire through your windows, through your doors – what do you do?'

Maybe nobody was going to get hurt after all. But if not, it wasn't Jack's doing. 'That's not happening now!' he said. 'It *has* happened, but are we going to be captives of the past, or can we move on?'

Billy was determined to keep things calm. 'There's been a cessation of Loyalist violence in this country for some considerable time now. So what are you supposed to do? You can only go so far along the road to peace. A man spits in your face and he walks away. Do you chase after him to shake hands? How far do you go? Compromise to me means going halfway. That's necessary. We've gone beyond halfway. The only people who've compromised in this country since 1969 have been Loyalists.'

'But what compromise is there? As long as you want to be British, what compromise is there with people who want to be Irish?'

Billy: 'Most of the people who are pretending to be Irish are not. Look at the names. They're no more Irish than what you are.'

'They see the island to be Ireland and you see this part of it as being Britain. How is there a way between?'

Billy said, 'Geographically it's British.'

They got up to leave. The bonhomie was quite, quite gone, and while they weren't going to give someone a hammering, at least they could stop paying for drinks. As we threaded through corridors, Jack was still trying to persuade John to go to college. 'That's shit,' said John. 'That's bullshit.' Then he burst out: 'See the way I want to explain til ye. See the crowd the other day bringin' Barry McGuigan home? All Catholics and Protestants, all cheerin' and all that. I was one of that crowd! I was there in the middle of them, wait'll I tell ya! That's normal life here! People fuckin stand there, I don't not stand beside you because you're a Catholic. But then sure a couple of days later a bomb explosion – the same people won't let us have our natural . . . It's not me! It's them people!'

Another man said: 'You can't shake hands with someone who's got their foot on your neck.'

The paramilitary aspects of the struggle in Belfast were starting to remind me of the Knights and the Angels, two gangs of boys who fought each other in my part of New York when we were teenagers. What's it all about? I used to ask a Knight who sometimes let me wear his green jacket with the tribal name on the back. He never could answer me. As the Belfast mod said when asked why they fight the skinheads: 'Have to, don't we?' In a way I accepted it as one of those mysteries forever beyond my understanding: something about being a boy, about establishing and asserting an identity among men, about power and aggressiveness, about belonging. Virginia Woolf, addressing men, wrote: 'Obviously there is for you some glory, some necessity, some satisfaction in fighting which we have never felt or enjoyed.' Her 'never' would be disputed by Belfast women, and I would be hard put to say I *entirely* lack *all* such feelings myself. But constitutionally, maybe, I'd have bad trouble acting on them. And to the extent I have them, I wish I didn't.

At any rate those impulses are certainly powerful in Belfast, and while the gang-warfare parallel comes up regularly, with people saying, 'The paramilitaries are just boys who never grew up,' this judgement ignores the fact that such behaviour, particularly among men, is seldom outgrown, and world power politics is fought out in the same way. Only the language is more sophisticated, the

P.R. attended to more efficiently, and responsibility for the actual violence delegated to others, to obscure what hasn't changed since cavemen were at it with stones and cudgels. 'War is just more fun than peace,' said one paramilitary.

What is certainly neither male nor female is nationalism, the impulse behind the behaviour. If this is the issue, not violence itself but the nationalism that gives rise to it, could nationalism itself have to do with not growing up? As a baby you are completely centred in yourself, your mother, then your family; then it becomes your school and a few groups of friends; your circle – your clan – expands with the capacities of your imagination until it's your country. Feelings of group-loyalty often end there. While more and more people sense a need to grow beyond that now, in Northern Ireland any such development has been arrested by the war and their history. In this way they are all victims. The idea is not the least new to the Irish – in 1926 Sean O'Casey had one of his characters say: 'Look here, comrade, there's no such thing as an Irishman, or an Englishman, or a German or a Turk; we're all only human bein's. Scientifically speakin', it's all a question of the accidental gatherin' together of mollycewels an' atoms.'

Within three days the city centre was cleaned up and even most of the windows replaced. The gap made quite a tasteful space in the middle of some pretty boring urbanity. In fact, you had to hand it to the IRA about the target and the aesthetics of the thing: the blasted buildings had all been square, squat glass boxes. It was an answer of sorts to the developers, who just that month had screwed up their nerve after some years' pause to do what they do so well in modern cities: schedule the demolition of some historic buildings to replace them with an enormous new shopping complex. In Belfast this seemed rather more pointless than in other cities since there were so many available bombsites, but the authorities had been bragging about how safe and secure from criminal wreckers their city had lately become, and how better to demonstrate that than to wreck it officially?

At 1 A.M. on 14 September 1986, John Bingham was shot dead in his home by the IRA. According to the *Republican News*,

> three IRA Volunteers, two of them armed with automatic rifles and the third with a .38 Special, sledge-hammered their way through Bingham's front door in the staunchly Loyalist Ballysillan area of North Belfast. While one Volunteer, armed with a rifle, stood at the front door, the two others went upstairs [where] the security door was locked, blocking their way. One Volunteer fired several rounds at the lock, smashing it, and they then systematically searched the bedrooms. Bingham was found hiding in the darkness and was shot nine or ten times in the chest and head. The Volunteer with the .38 Special then stepped forward and shot Bingham.

The paper quoted a statement form the IRA's Belfast Brigade:

> We shall avail of every opportunity to remove from the face of the earth those who callously gun down and murder our people. We are satisfied that Bingham fell into this category, as he had a long history of UVF membership. Following his release from prison, he became the UVF's 'operations officer', a position previously held by Shankill Butcher Lenny Murphy, and in this capacity he sanctioned and actively organized the murder of a number of Catholics in the Belfast area.

The murders in question – of six men and a Protestant woman married to a Catholic – had taken place over the previous few months in response to the Anglo-Irish Agreement.

In the *Belfast Telegraph*, there were three-and-a-half columns of personal death notices from John's friends and relations, including 'Aunt Agnes and Gladys (USA)', various bars and social clubs, 'all the lads in H6, 1 and 3 Maze', and his Orange Lodge. Several of them said: 'He died as he lived, everyone's friend.' Some contained bits of home-made verse such as 'No farewell was spoken, no time to say goodbye, you were gone before we knew and only God knows why.' Another read: 'Some day, if God's in Heaven overlooking His preserve, I know the men that shot him down will get what they deserve.' And: 'Here dead we lie because we did not choose to live and shame the land from which we sprung, life to be sure is nothing much to lose but young men think it is and we were young.' The man I have called 'Billy' was represented, as was George Seawright, who wrote: 'Your friendship was a priceless gift, that could not be bought or sold, its value was far greater than a mountain made of gold, for gold is cold and lifeless, it can never see or hear, but in times of trouble, John, you were always near. God bless, dear Friend.'

14
The Glorious Twelfth

'It's an experience you *never, ever,* get over.'

There was a young Belfast Protestant in exile in London and in mourning for missing 'the Twelfth'. He didn't mind exile, though he thought little of English hospitality and he missed his friends at home (both sides), and it wasn't as if the patriotic part of the celebration was important – he'd never even marched in the parade himself. But he was still wretched about being away for the day, and tried to explain. 'When those drums come past, beatin' away, and that music and everything, you just can't help – everybody just gets – ' he made some kind of bubbling-over noise. 'It's like all-friends-together, everything perfect for a couple of days, people offerin' ya a drink and all, you're all out for the bonies [bonfires] on the Eleventh night and watching the bands on the Twelfth. It's just – it's *everything.*' He was almost crying. 'The saddest thing I can *think* of is being here, coming out of work and watching it all on TV. It'll be desperate. *Awwwwkh,*' he howled. 'Like separated from your mother.'

Above the Irish Sea, the British Airways pilot announced that the temperature in Belfast was 60 degrees and the local time was 1690. Landing, the only visible excitement to begin with was another bomb, this one in the Loyalist stronghold of Sandy Row. The street had a huge arch erected in permanent concrete mountings for the holiday, with a painted '1690' and '1912', a picture of a crown on a Bible, and a motto: 'This we will maintain'. The arch was intact, but the rest of Sandy Row's decorations lay mixed with broken glass around the street. The inhabitants, not the least put out, were sweeping it up. A pub had been the target, its Twelfth banners now dragging on the ground, broken beer barrels scattered, plastic furniture toppled and torn, bits of sound equipment littered about with glass and ragged red, white and blue bunting. Beyond, once neatly-stacked boxes cascaded down from the remains of a shoeshop. Mixed up with the rubble were some poster fragments:

Presenting
the Champion of Champions
JESUS
Hear a message of deliverance
for Ulster

Women were tut-tutting at the nuisance of having to walk around all the mess, gathering to discuss how no one seemed to have heard the 3 A.M. explosion except the 'wains'. I asked one shop proprietor whose display windows were shattered and merchandise wrecked, what he was going to do. 'Ach, the glass'll be here within the hour,' he said brightly, sweeping his pavement. 'By lunchtime the sale will be on, customers in. Back to normal tomorrow. What's the point of worrying? There's always someone worse off. Look at the shoeshop – totally banjaxed.' I asked if he were insured. 'Hope so,' he said. 'Can I lend you a broom?'

The Orange Order was having its first press conference in the history of the world. Outside the beflagged Ballymacarrett Orange Hall stood two guards, ushering all comers (with credentials) to a room 'dedicated to the memory of Brother John Hume' (deceased 1 October 1934). Outside the room was a coat rack with swords and bowler hats hanging on it. Inside were portraits of ex-grand masters and a large tin under each chair. Spittoons?

Statements were made about the Belfast parade, about the twenty-six bands coming from Scotland and 'guest brethren' from around the world. They hoped the Secretary of State would enjoy it. It was 'customary for the Secretary of State to watch from a vantage point in the city.' All the Orangemen would be marching, apart from those on duty serving Queen and Country.

But the pressmen weren't interested in this. They wanted to ask about the forthcoming Portadown march, which the RUC intended to reroute to avoid a Nationalist area. The local MP, Harold McCusker, had complained in the House of Commons earlier in the week: 'When the men walk into Portadown over the route their forefathers walked in 1796, they are not motivated by any desire to break the laws of their country, but by a sense of historic necessity to express, as they have always done, their legitimate pride in the possession of their lands and traditions.'

The brethren beefed about it now: 'Republicans might object but not ordinary Roman Catholics, who enjoy it and will be present along the parade route.' Then again 'some people will go out of their way and travel some distance to be provoked.' They said alternative routes were more inflammatory than traditional ones, and this was all the 'bungling stupidity' of the Secretary of State and the Chief Constable of the RUC, 'who manipulate the situation; but we will not fall into their trap.' Although some concern was expressed about certain 'coat-trailers' who intended to defy the police, there would be no split within the Order, they maintained, and it would be perfectly safe; after all, 'why are our brethren coming from as far off as

French-speaking Togo?' Anyway, 'How far does civilization back down?'

After the conference I met Cecil Reid, an Orangeman since 1936. A grizzled old man with an outdoor face and worn, bumpy hands, he had been a milk roundsman and was now retired after thirty-four years – 'the first man in the Co-op Milk that ever got a send-off in the dairy office. I was the first to get that privilege. The bosses supplied all the eats.' He said there was no class distinction in the Order: 'Street sweepers to factory managers, we all march together.' And no church distinction, either, although 'the Orange Order is opposed to the principle of the Roman Catholic Church.' (Orangemen are not allowed to attend Catholic services on pain of expulsion.) But 'I myself have many Roman Catholic friends.'

At the Orange initiation, he said, 'you get the Obligation, to do your best to preserve the Protestant way of life. You lead by showing an example. A lot of fellas runnin' about now, to me they don't know their Obligation. Having the odd drink seems the norm now. It's hard to get new members.' Their Loyal Orange Lodge 747 was 'the only total abstinence lodge in East Belfast at the minute.' Other lodges only observed temperance, which meant they could drink outside but not in the hall's social functions.

Apart from not drink, what did they do? He mentioned levels to be attained, 'plain purple degree, royal arch purple degree – from the Bible. The exact chapters I can't quote, but everything in the Orange Order is based on the Bible.' He himself had been master of LOL 747 in 1963 'and a very pleasant year it was, too.' The men marched to church on Sundays and met the ladies there. 'The work of the Ladies' Orange Order is based on the Bible too. Mainly fund-raising.'

It seemed that the Twelfth was not just the high point of their year, but very nearly the only point. Reid himself had never missed a Twelfth in his life except in the war. He marches but doesn't play an instrument. 'When I was a nipper I always fancied having a go at the accordion. But I never had the opportunity,' he said.

Before we could get any further I was swept off by another lodge member who was well-dressed and spoke in educated tones: 'We're in every walk of life. We don't have a class problem. We're a pan-Protestant organization.'

I thought I'd take some time out from the Twelfth and go to Andersonstown. It had taken a dozen trips for me to find my way around there, so identical are the houses and the Crescents, Gardens, Parks, Parades and Drives. The knack lay in following the murals. Turn left at YOU ARE NOW ENTERING FREE A-TOWN past FOUR GREEN FIELDS and FREE OUR COUNTRY, along by VICTORY IS OURS and PROVO'S RULE and, two roads past KEEP IRELAND TIDY, BRITS OUT is the Ryans'. There, large numbers of arms waited, not the shooting kind but those that enveloped you in warmth, inner and outer. A big plate of sausages and thickly buttered bread was put in my lap, with at least an hour or two of everyone's news, in no special order as they talked around and past and over each other to fill me in.

Pat, who still went on attending the Kirkpatrick trial until the day it stopped for the judge to be jury, had been burgled in the night a few weeks earlier, all her rings stolen and the food in her kitchen dumped on the floor and mixed into a disgusting porridge. She was forced to call the police – highly unusual, Rita conceded – because the vandals had torn up her supplementary benefit and child allowance books and she couldn't get replacements without recourse to the law.

There was news about the kids' progress at school. In Mairead's home economics class, she had been taught how to make tea, two boiled eggs and orange juice. The fact that at home she routinely cooked elaborate meals for ten was neither here nor there; nor was the blouse she had to make to a useless pattern, standard and compulsory for all and never worn. So coming up was the annual St Louise's blouse-burning party.

There was as usual news of someone's son arrested or someone's daughter just released from Armagh. There were first communions, ceilis, demonstrations, weddings – one of Rita's sisters, a nun, was soon to be ceremonially wed to Christ, and wee Rita was to be the bridesmaid and carry the ring. Two more blocks of Divis were to come down, according to a rumour. A little girl had been run over in the street just outside and her life saved by rushing her to the Royal Victoria Hospital. This led to tales of the latest joyriding incidents and stick-ups by the hoods at the local shops; then to how Tony had got the family a whole leg of lamb for their Sunday dinner from the butcher where he apprenticed after school; Dermot's latest futile efforts to find a job; Rita's chance to go on holiday to Belgium escorting a couple of dozen children. A new passport was needed because the one she had, from the South, was for both her and Dermot and was unusable by her alone without a letter signed by two people saying he had given permission. She refused this insult, but a new single Irish passport was too expensive, so now – almost as bad as Pat having called in the police for her robbery – Rita was actually applying for a British one. (All citizens of Northern Ireland qualify for both.)

The letterbox rattled to announce a visitor; one of the

children got up to answer. Pat came in silently with a fistful of something which she deposited in Rita's lap. It was her stolen rings. She had just been out, she said, and coming back had found them on the floor inside the door. Who or what or how was a mystery not to be solved, but it clearly had to do with pressure from the local law enforcers.

What was furthest from all this was any reference to the celebrations in the rest of town for the Twelfth. But that 'rest of town' had very little reality in Andytown, most of whose inhabitants have never been there in their lives and many of whom went for months without going so far as the city centre. There was plenty to do within walking distance: friends and relatives to visit or, if there was any kind of windfall, an evening out at a Republican club.

There is little in my life's experience, except maybe singing round a campfire as a child, that makes me feel so fully a part of the people of the planet as a night in an Irish Republican club. It has a lot to do with the music. G. K. Chesterton wrote:

> For the great Gaels of Ireland
> Are the men that God made mad,
> For all their wars are merry
> And all their songs are sad.

Many of the songs are about the mother who has lost her sons to Ireland, or about heroism in death; but they are sung not just with sadness and longing but with a rousing spirit that the lyrics alone can't convey. Everyone joins in, but when it comes to *A Nation Once Again* they really get going; and any excuse will do to bellow out 'Up the Rah, Up the Rah, Up the Rah!' The noise is frenetic but it subsides for conversation now and then.

A woman I'd come to know who was sitting at our table

was telling about the Exclusion Order she'd just managed to get against her husband. She was suing for divorce and he was counter-suing, she said, 'charging cruelty – thirteen years of marriage and I never once asked him to go to bed. I'm thinking of doing a survey how many women have. I do know a few who've asked, mind you, but not their husbands.' Everybody was laughing and laughing, the men rather hollowly. 'My father said to me that he had twelve children, and if he'd waited for me mammy to ask he wouldn't have had *one*.'

Me Little Armalite, they sang, *The Belfast Brigade, The H-Block Song*: '. . . I'll wear no convict's uniform / Nor meekly serve my time / That Britain might brand Ireland's fight / Eight hundred years of crime.' Looking around at all the young courting couples, I wondered what the words meant to them. If I were a young man hearing these electrifying anthems, and considering my political inheritance, I might well be inspired to try to do what my fathers had failed to do. But somehow it seemed to me that if I were one of the young women, I might more likely feel fed up that this political inheritance doomed me to probable early widowhood, grass or otherwise; and to my own dead sons.

But there are cracks in the madonna monument by now, and not only in the casual talk of divorce, let alone sex, at our table. In the ladies' room I found three women sitting on the sinks having a smoke. As they made room for me one of them dropped her bag, and among the contents scattered around the floor were her contraceptive pills. 'Oh!' said one of her friends, startled, 'the Pope doesn't let you take those!'

'The Pope,' said the woman sweeping up her belongings, 'doesn't get a say, since he doesn't play the game.'

The third of them spoke up then. 'I keep mine behind

the holy picture. I stick them there with Blu-Tack. Because whenever my mother-in-law comes I know she rummages through the drawers, but she wouldn't dare touch the holy picture.'

Back at the table, the opening chords of *A Soldier's Song* began and everyone stood and joined in with fervour. It marked the end of the evening. As I left, the man at the door said solicitously to me: 'Watch out at the corner for the peelers, love.'

July or no July, it was only 59 degrees at midday in Belfast, grey and clammy. 'Oh it's shockin'! Who turned the rain on anyway?' Huge annoyance among the populace. In the UDA office John McMichael said they were being punished for fighting. While Hester drew distinctions about which flags were flying, Union Jacks or Ulster flags, McMichael commented that it didn't matter anyway since the only concern was the border, and keeping it that way. 'If people really cared about social and economic issues,' he said, 'they'd vote for the Workers' Party.'

While I waited for Hester I read people's tattoos, presumably on display for the sake of its being July. One man's arm said 'UDA/Our Only Crime is Loyalty.' A picture of King Billy on his horse, '1690'. A red hand of Ulster. A UDA emblem and 'Quis Separabit', their motto. An Ulster flag. 'FTP.' A Union Jack. 'Keep Scotland Protestant'. A big red arch with '2½' in the middle. 'Two and a half what?' I asked. 'Secret,' the man said. Then he got self-conscious and walked out. I hadn't read his other arm yet.

But my notebook was still open to where I'd been copying the decor of the first. One young lout, very deadpan, wanted to know what I was writing. 'Secrets,' he accused. 'I must have at least . . . seven pounds' worth of secrets.' I only wanted to know about the presumably thriving tattoo parlours of Belfast. He scoffed – sure they do it to each other, he said, in the long winter evenings. 'You just get hold of the stencil and the needle and anybody can do it.' Everybody did.

More than the usual number of men were hobnobbing in the halls and tramping up and down in their great black boots. They ended on the top floor, where they were warming up for the drinking of the Eleventh night by having a few drinks. Sober Andy Tyrie gave his opinions about my latest encounters. The bomb on Sandy Row? Insurance. 'There's nothing like having a new building and not being able to pay for it. All you need is a gas cylinder and a candle. The *Irish News* says that pub was bombed because the owner refused to pay protection money to the Protestant paramilitaries. Ninety per cent of the things said of us is a load of shit. The money from these "protection rackets" – it's not coming to UDA Central. We are far from innocent, but we are not guilty of everything that is put on til us.' He said there were RUC members responsible for a lot of 'robberies, shootings, you name it. You don't notice them because they're the RUC. Bigger print for the UDA.'

He talked about the different Ulster groups. With the UVF it was 'a problem of regimental rivalry.' They fancied themselves as soldiers, 'pipe-smoking people' involved only in procurements, not robberies; assassinations, not murders. They were 'heavily penetrated by the security forces,' but the worst he could say of them had to do with their 'long association with the Provisionals' in dividing up territory and organizing rackets like the black taxis. What with all the racketeering, 'sectarian conflict has almost been wiped out.'

As for the Orange Order, 'This society is full of perverts.' Supposedly they stand by the philosophy of giving 'not an inch', but when the police reroute their marches they're just 'nice wee men who say "Yes, sir," and "You are absolutely right, sir: we are not marching up that street because we are too respectable." Respectability will kill them. The Orange Order has been living a myth since 1690. The siege of Londonderry – the apprentices were all thugs.' The Orangemen 'hide behind the paramilitaries, and the police let them through for fear of violence', but the men of the Order themselves are 'wriggling: they "can't attack the Crown." They're dodo birds: haven't the sense to fight back. All they can do is march, and they will continue marching until we are taken off this island in boats and dumped somewhere else.'

On his wall was a new poster, saying 'Somewhere on an alien planet, deep in the universe in a galaxy far, far away, there is a government that really knows what it is doing.'

'Actually they wouldn't have me in the Orange Order when I tried to join,' Andy said. 'I tried for divilment.' He went teetotalling out to join the revellers.

In his office was another non-drinker who had been telling Andy about his book on Ulster history which was being published. Michael Hall was very tall and thin and looked like a cleaned-up ex-hippy. He did social work on both sides of the divide for the National Society for the Prevention of Cruelty to Children. His book dealt with the people's collective origins, and he had written it partly 'to avoid the concept of an independent Ulster being hijacked by UDI-ers in the Paisley camp. I have no time for Loyalists or Republicans. All I am interested in is our children's future. The Bible, the Koran, all those – they're only pieces of paper for all the effect they have. St Patrick should have left the snakes and got rid of the clergy.'

He said he found young people on both sides not bored but frustrated, and he worried that soon they wouldn't be under the control of anybody. Young Protestants threw stones at the Orange Order; the Provos had their hoods. 'Every organization here was established at least fifteen, sixteen years ago, and they're now run by people seen as Establishment by the seventeen- and eighteen-year-olds. They see not only the state and the police as authoritarian, but the IRA, the UDA, all of them. They feel frustration and alienation at the poor conditions, and these groups don't offer anything to challenge and change that.

'The way to save Ulster is to change it.'

He thought the best hope lay in self-help groups and 'the Sinn Fein community approach.' He took young people across the line in both directions, and organized trips abroad where for the first time they could meet one another. 'People here are beginning to see they have class problems in common. Identity and fear are motivating them, not sectarianism or bigotry. There are people on both sides who are basically socialists and this situation doesn't allow them to act on their beliefs. The trouble in Northern Ireland is not bad people hating bad people, but good people hating good people.' But he found them very open and with a great ability to express themselves. 'Maybe even the violence is a result of people being so open. It's an open gesture as well.'

Writing was his other occupation to the same end. His book, *Ulster – the Hidden History*, traced the people's common identity, centuries back, to the Cruthin. 'I don't see it as a book, I see it as a weapon. I'm not trying to reconcile; all I'm trying to do is pinpoint what this society needs. I'm agitating without wanting to be a public agitator. "Be a realist: demand the impossible" – that was one of the Sorbonne graffiti in '68. That's how I look at it.' He smiled broadly. 'At the beginning I was all for changing the world overnight, but now I realize it takes a week at least.'

He also wrote an irregular column in *Ulster* magazine, and plays, as yet unproduced. 'What motivates me is the desire to see fundamental social change. The people I meet every day who are warm and humane give me hope. The fact that they can't do anything gives me no hope. Hope against hope.'

Hester and I had a standard conversation about smoking. Since I'd seen her last she'd been taken in hand by an American feminist psychiatrist who had tried to hypnotize her to stop smoking. It worked for a day or two. The pressures are harder in a place where most people have more to worry about than lung cancer and don't even consider giving up. What had really got to Hester was the American's remonstrances about the need to be invulnerable in situations in which she found herself in someone's power. This hit her hard because of the time she'd been under questioning for a week at Castlereagh and reached the point where she'd almost longed for her interrogators because they gave her a cigarette. When she'd finally been released, 'I couldn't get myself together and I kept gettin' up at half 4, 5 in the morning, sitting on the step in the sun – lovely, you know that early morning sun that's not too warm? I was sittin' on the step with this horrible man's cardy over the top of a frilly nightie – *smokin' my brains out*. Fuckin brilliant it was. I was on a high for about a week, and literally couldn't stop talking, as if someone had wound me up like one of those dolls.'

We had another conversation which was turning into a

standard too. Since we met I'd been engaged by her interest in the women on the other side of town. She loved to hear homey details of their lives: their domestic situations, their children, how they coped. There was no question ever of getting her and, say, Rita together and I wouldn't have broached it, but a meeting with Catholics who had transcended their tribalism seemed a possibility. She was willing; they were willing. Then, when it came to it, nerves on both sides took over. First of all, *where*? 'If it could be somewhere neutral . . .' I invited her to occasional feminist events, but she always had an excuse. There were pubs in the town centre. 'But are you quite sure they haven't got connections with Sinn Fein?' she'd ask.

In West Belfast, I encountered the same thing. Catholics in the women's movement had seen Hester's column in *Ulster* and were fascinated that a feminist lurked within the ranks of the UDA. What kind of woman was she? They wanted to know about her life, to meet her. But when there might have been a chance, somehow nothing seemed convenient.

I was to spend the 11th and 12th with Hester to see the 'bonies' and the marching. While the two-day event celebrates the anniversary of the 1690 Battle of the Boyne, when the Catholic James II was beaten by the Protestant William of Orange (with the Pope's support, as Catholics never tire of telling you – though Dorothy Elliott, Protestant ex-principal of Finiston, went them several better with the information that 'King Billy was gay, had piles, wasn't English, hadn't a white horse, *and* was supported by the Pope'), there was less anti-Catholicism about it than sheer self-indulgence. Traditionally it's 'kick the Pope' time and somehow you expect the bonfires to burn effigies like the Guy Fawkes ones in England. A few did: not of the

Pope but of Lundy, a Protestant turncoat in the siege of Derry. There were huge teetering stacks of scrap wood set up to begin all over East Belfast, most made of old doors and furniture, usually augmented with still useful fork-lift truck platforms. The only concern of their makers was to guard them lest people from their own side steal the wood for their own fires. Fulminations against Papists were few. Not that there wasn't mention of war and death, the IRA and Loyalist prisoners – as in the UDA and UVF records Hester played when we got back to her place, 'dedicated to those who've fought and died for the loyal cause of Ulster, those who are still fighting, and to those loyal Protestants who are incarcerated in Crumlin Road, Long Kesh, and other concentration camps . . . The message is: No Surrender!' But after this lugubrious start the record launched into a frantic rendition of 'The Sash':

> It is old but it is beautiful
> And its colours they are fine
> It was worn in Derry, Aughrin,
> Enniskillen and the Boyne.
> Sure my father wore it in his youth
> In bygone days of yore
> And it's on the Twelfth I love to wear
> The sash my father wore.

The next record celebrated UVF victories against the IRA, a male voice too syrupy to credit, with sentimental accordion accompaniment, crooning 'Death to all the IRA'. One verse went:

> And when Ulster once more is free
> And rids itself of Popery
> And all the dead are laid to rest
> Remember the men of the UVF.

While the music played and friends and neighbours came by, the television was on noiselessly showing pictures of maimed and blinded Indians outside Union Carbide in Bhopal. Running short of good tunes – a problem for Loyalists – the next songs were set to familiar melodies not at all Irish: first 'Silent Night' in a slow waltz tempo showed to new effect, with 'Sleep in heavenly peace' becoming 'Remember the Loyalist prisoners'; then 'The Cowboy's Lament' turned into

> And still on the walls of our old city Derry
> Our boul' leader Andy he stepped to the fore
> He says come and join us you true sons of Ulster . . .

Among Hester and John's friends there was some bombastic bantering about joining the fray the next day at Portadown where the Orange march was due to be rerouted, but no one seemed to take it seriously, and it was hardly an issue as the real point of the entire business emerged – an excuse for everyone to become totally, colossally, uproariously, staggeringly drunk. In the UDA everyone but Tyrie, McMichael and Hester had been quite legless by 4 o'clock that afternoon, and I'd been interested to consider how they would get home; less interested in sharing the roads with them that night.

The domestic atmosphere at Hester's was immeasurably improved since my last visit – John had accepted a job in England and was soon to move. Meanwhile they were quite forbearing with each other. John showed me the purple short-jacketed uniform he would be parading in tomorrow and his Lambeg drum, with paintings on the sides and ropes to tighten the skin. It was huge; I could only just heave it off the floor. How could anyone carry and beat it for sixteen miles? 'See those wee lads, you'd never think they could even pick one *up*,' he said. But he explained that if the weather was poor the big drums couldn't come out because the dampness burst the skins. Considering Belfast's normal climate, I shouldn't have thought there were that many Lambegs from year to year. 'Pity really: they make that much noise they break the windows.' He claimed you could play a tune on it, 'you could play Tchaikovsky's 1812 Overture on it,' though I had a little trouble with this. But John was not yet half seas over: other men in the room were well away – and this six hours before the bonies would be lit. Fires were not their priority. They were certainly all going to march the next day, somehow.

Hester's friend Joan dropped in, very spruced up ('I'm spotless. Toes and all painted. *Got* to paint me toes for the Twelfth') and with an air of anticipation about the events which seemed so far unwarranted. Very intensely she said: 'Whenever I was anywhere else on the Twelfth I cried my eyes out. This is our heritage, you know.'

We left and went to pub after pub. At one on the Shankill decorated with handmade collages of boxers, with pride of place to Barry McGuigan, someone was still coherent enough to talk – a thin, rather touching man with an elfin sweetness who suddenly said: 'I hate Fenians.'

'Why?' I asked.

'They smell.' He looked at me challengingly. 'I hate Chinese and blacks too.'

He had spent his life in the army and the Kesh, he said, though there had been an interesting gap in the middle when, for example, 'They wouldn't serve me in a bar, so I bombed it.' Then and there, I gathered.

'Where did you get the bomb?'

'Och I carried stuff with me.'

He went on to say that he'd once bombed a Fenian pub

and shot all the survivors. How many? 'Three,' he said. How many people were in the pub to begin with? '*I* don't know,' he said, getting annoyed. He was drinking double vodkas, and was on his third since we'd arrived.

Raucous bonhomie took over. Everyone was hugely friendly. Entering any new pub we were immediately claimed by a mob of Hester's mates, overcrowded at their tables in the first place. Smoke, crush and din. Someone would start a song, and everybody knew it and loudly joined in:

> Now the IRA, they came upon us
> We returned their fire that August
> Shot the bastards all around us
> Derry rules the Falls!
> No surrender was it
> No surrender was it
> We're proud to fight
> We're proud to die
> Like our fathers did before us.

The next song had a noteworthy couplet: 'For we won't be mastered / By no Fenian bastard . . .'

While the singing flowed, at the other end of our table half a dozen elderly people sat looking at us pleasantly but didn't join in. I don't know why I found this surprising – they were the pub's real regulars, and they must have been through all this many times before. Maybe that was why they didn't sing. But after the anti-IRA repertoire was exhausted, they were asked for a number. They stuck in with a will – 'Bye Bye Blackbird'. Then, when we got up to leave, I was summoned to them for a private song. A very old man, at least eighty-five, held my hand and put his whole heart into 'When Irish Eyes are Smiling'.

In the last pub, room was made at a table with, among

others, a gangster of such renown that no one had yet dared testify against him except in a mask, which didn't go down well with the judge, so he was still free. He was the most personally powerful man I had ever met, with an air of animal force that inspired awe at the idea of its ever being let loose. He was also as drunk as I had seen anyone in my life who could still more or less negotiate a sentence and a sequence of steps. The sentences he negotiated with me were memorable. 'Can I say something rude to you?' he asked, and without waiting for an answer, propositioned me. I turned him down on the grounds that I wanted to go to the bonfires. Flabbergasted (which must be an Irish word), he said, 'What? You'd rather watch a *fire*?' I said I'd never seen an Eleventh bonfire before. This struck him as so hilarious that he nearly fell off his chair. Then to prove his superhumanity he lurched to the microphone and led the whole room in 'The Sash'. Afterwards he sat down again just in time to catch a young woman who did fall off her chair.

We had some trouble leaving and it was nearly midnight: Hester was fraught about getting home in time to be with her sons at her local bonfire. Luckily the management called a halt with 'God Save the Queen'. Hester bowed her head and clenched her fists, as always, but most others had all they could do to remain on their feet. The woman who had fallen over had to be held upright by each elbow.

On the drive back we passed fire after fire lighting up the night, each surrounded with the silhouettes of the celebrators, and somehow made it back in time for Hester's. John had constructed it with the local children's help, and with great pride had just lit it. An enormous fire is like a magnet, and the whole neighbourhood was there, drinks in hand, clustered in groups and silent, the faces rapt in the light. Windows nearby were boarded up to prevent damage from the heat, which was so strong the circle of people expanded outwards to the nearest walls.

After seeing that his own fire was going well, John walked up to the crest of a hill to look at the next one – reputed to be Dundonald's biggest, but not, in fact, a patch on his. He was saddened at the idea of leaving. 'See these people, they're the best in the world. They would give you anything. They would take you into their home even if they didn't know you. I love these people. But their lives are futile. For all their love of life and their Twelfth of Julys and that, they have nothing. They've been trodden on and walked on and still they bounce back – still they love the Queen and still they support the British government: you just can't make sense at them. When will they stand up and say "enough"? Should have said it in 1912, and what did the British government do to them? Put them at the Battle of the Somme, wiped the whole regiment out in one day. They should have said that's enough in 1939 and what happened? They all joined up. I mean there was never conscription over here! It was all volunteers! There were volunteers from the South as well.'

He looked reflectively at his neighbours standing in the light. 'It's lovely seeing them enjoy themselves. It's one night they really can. There's so much poverty. No more than a third of them are working, if that. See all the mates I run about with? The guys I drink with – nine or ten of them – I'm the only one who's working.'

You always seem to have to get up early for large events like the Glorious Twelfth. The larger they are, the earlier. Hester had John and their elder son roused, uniformed, breakfasted and out by dawn; she and I and seven-year-old James staggered out at dawn plus one. The idea was to find a decent vantage point on the parade; none of us was keen to follow it the whole way to 'the field'. ('The field' is the destination of any Twelfth parade, from whatever town it's marching; after resting and eating and hearing Orange speeches there, everyone marches back again.) We found a good spot near Shaftesbury Square as the bleary-eyed assembled with folding chairs and the paraphernalia for a day's outing, mainly beer cans and bottles. Children wore No Surrender rosettes and Union Jack hats and PROUD TO BE PROD T-shirts and carried banners and 'bandsticks' – red, white and blue poles with knobs on top. James had one, plus a hat saying 'Boys in blue, loyal and true.' Hester had a special shirt on too: 'I wear this T-shirt for badness every Twelfth,' she said. It had a circular motif with three prison compounds inside a barbed-wire enclosure surrounded by the motto: IMPRISONED FOR LOYALTY, LONG KESH and, underneath, the letters L P O W (a common tattoo, as well – Loyalist Prisoners-of-War). This was the only shirt of its kind, she said, and everyone always took her picture in it. It had been made in the Kesh by the pixie-faced man who hated Fenians.

If we stood in the right place, she said, we might get on TV. Of itself this didn't interest her, but she said the prisoners watched it inside on the Twelfth as they drank home brew. What did they make it from? I asked. 'Everything barring their socks,' she said.

People were lined up three and four deep behind the folding chairs and babies' prams, and it seemed the march was about to begin when a procession passed with banners reading THE COMING OF THE LORD DRAWETH NIGH and THE WICKED SHALL RETURN INTO HELL, AND ALL THE NATIONS THAT FORGET GOD. But it was only a teaser, and more time elapsed before the unmistakable music approached.

It was a special kind of music, with flute bands interspersed with accordions and drums, but the real point was the Lambegs, their martial pounding so penetrating I didn't doubt it was audible in Andytown. The noise had an eerie physical effect: you could feel the vibrations overpowering – as if replacing – your heartbeat, and after a couple of hours of it my body lost its bearings and I began to feel ill. I had never heard of such an effect and found it frightening.

The most important Orangemen led the procession, McCrea and other spokesmen from the press conference at the head. Besides 'the sash my father wore' – actually an orange collarette, the sash being outmoded – each wore a dark suit with bowler hat and white gloves and carried a folded umbrella. Except for the white gloves, this was the identical outfit which had stopped being standard attire for the City of London gent at just around the time the Troubles were beginning. Because one seldom sees such dress in England any more, it reinforced the idea that time had passed these people by: If this was the Britain they pined to belong to, did they know it no longer exists?

Rat-a-tat-tat came the drummers, crash boom boom the Lambegs, then the flutes, the baton twirlers, the girls in short skirts playing concertinas, the banners. Each banner – lush, fringed, heavy, ornately painted – was slung from one pole suspended from two others, with four guy ropes to steady it in the breeze. Obviously a centuries-old institution, the banners predated the time when someone thought of putting flaps in the things to let the air through and keep them from being blown down. As it was they seemed like huge sails made of old brocade fourposter-bed canopies, and carrying them was clearly desperate work. The complicated pictures they bore, different front and back, often showed King Billy on his white horse or the standard Bible on a cushion with a crown on top 'for God and Ulster', but some had elaborate portraits of deceased Orange greats: the Late George Thompson, Angelo Davison, Brother Alfred Downey P.M., whoever they might have been. Others in the pantheon included The Duke of York, Martin Luther, The Lord Salisbury, Oliver Cromwell, 'Prince Albert, The Late Prince Consort'. Canon Irvine Memorial Temperance. MARTYRS OF THE GRASSMARKET. A turbaned black man kneeling to a young Queen Victoria with the motto: 'The Secret of England's Greatness'. Lots of angels with books, and Jacob's Dream. It was all starting to seem emblematic of another place as well as another time, with an aura of the Deep South: brotherhoods of men in funny clothes ritually promoting the cause of their superiority, and grounded in fundamentalist Christianity.

The format was soon predictable: a block of Orangemen with a banner, a drum major leading a band in brightly coloured uniforms (none the same, few fitting the occupant), another Orange Lodge, another banner. Many lodges advertised their temperance or abstinence, and all their love of their true God. The men in a few lodges wore sweet williams in their bowlers, or even homburgs, or little velvet aprons with tassels under their suit jackets; some carried upraised swords, wooden gavels or antique pikes. But however varied the marchers were, the main impression was of how many there were and how much the same. They came on, and on, and on, if not playing then whistling the tunes – the same tunes from band to band, Sash and more Sash, The Green Grassy Slopes of the Boyne, We Are the Billy Boys, My Old Man Says Follow the Band, Pack Up Your Troubles. All marchers were very practised and in step: a flock of birds passing overhead was not more united. Dedication on all faces, doggedness, we're marching the way we've always marched and our fathers always marched, even the halt and the lame keeping step. Only the truly feeble and the biggest wigs got to ride in limousines and black taxis. One, a huge Cadillac, bore an almost Brechtian capitalist fatcat from Chicago. He had masses of chins and was very solemn. They all were; it seemed half a gala event and a half a religious duty.

The gala part was on the pavement, where the spectators were having some rare crack. Up front there was much attentive watching, but behind the place was awash in beer and booze. At a nearby pub pushing people got refills and then tried to manoeuvre their way up front again. Soon many gave up trying. By 11 A.M. they had set up picnics outside shopfronts behind the shove, obviously having a marvellous time which bore no relation to the marchers. A drunk in a doorway behind us yelled 'Shurrup' and pranced in time to the drums, then stopped and yelled 'Shurrup' again. A girl in orange, head to foot, teetered lopsidedly on enormous high heels and clutched a Coke bottle she told friends was 'mostly Bacardi'. It had been an Eleventh night to remember, she said; she hadn't gone to bed at all. 'Enjoy yourself?' a friend asked. 'Och greatly! I was sick twice!' Across the road three boys were making guttural rowdy noises from the top of a bus-stop shelter, occasionally giving the finger to marchers they knew. The three boys became seven became ten then became thirteen: how many boys could fit on a bus shelter?

Such speculations began to dominate as the monotony of the procession, and the problem of the war drums' effect on my organic rhythms, threatened to get the better of me. My heart was still palpitating to catch up to the beat. Maybe you had to be used to it to enjoy it. Hester grew more not less enthusiastic, especially as she saw her friends go by. I noticed a few men I'd met: an Orangeman familiar from LOL 747 staggering under a huge banner depicting a bearded Edwardian, nameless, with the motto NO POPERY. Peter Lunn in a pale grey suit with his pale grey smile affixed to his face. The pixie-faced bomber in a blue and white uniform beating a wee drum. A UDA contingent in blinding orangy-red; the UVF in red and black. I scrutinized the latter hard, hoping to find a familiar set of mouth and eyes last seen masked in black. No luck, though one man had an interesting knife pattern on his face. All men. The only women who marched were under twenty and with suitable thighs for short skirts. Along the edge an occasional older woman from the Ladies' Orange Order jingled a collection tin for the Orange Widows. But it was a male thing. Or a boy thing. Protestant Boys from Glasgow, Apprentice Boys from everywhere. Why did they style themselves boys, even limping old gents of seventy-five or eighty? This perverse insistence on their childishness seemed especially jarring considering the gravity of their expressions – but it's an Irish tradition, from the White-boys and the Rightboys through the Peep o'Day Boys and the Oakboys and the Steelboys. Like the thin man buried in the fat man and trying to get out, there seemed to be a boy inside the oldest codger released for the day, and only incidentally wearing the disguise of age.

The parade eventually went by three hours after it had begun, the most massive physical demonstration I had witnessed, relative to the population, outside Peking or Havana. But with quite another flavour. There, when the people had come out to see Mao or Fidel, what pressed them was the present and the future. This had to do with tradition, with the present only insofar as it contained and continued the past: let's keep it that way. I remember after about a million people had gone by the plinth in Peking someone near me shouting 'Stop the parade! I'm convinced!' I didn't need all three of those hours to feel the same way in Belfast. As they were locked in step, so they were locked in an idea, and there were too many of them, far too many of them, to discount. What made it all the stranger and the stronger was that this idea they were locked in was such a myth. They were patriots without a patria.

While the marchers continued on to the field where, temperance or no temperance, most would consume a liquid lunch, Hester and James and I decided to go home for a rest. The pavements were thick with rubbish and among it lay drunken boys, flat out, their knees in the air. One group that was still perpendicular was bellowing out, to the tune of 'The Men of Harlech': 'We are the boys from Derry / Fuck the Pope and the Virgin Mary . . .' The parade would be returning later in the day, and all those people would get out all those folding chairs and the rest muster what remained of their legs to go through the whole thing all over again: and that before a long night's drinking. The stamina was other-worldly. But since we had a tired seven-year-old with us, there was an excuse to drop out for a while.

The seven-year-old was the only one completely uninterested in this project. Hester slept, I slept, and when I came downstairs James was watching television and waiting for us. He and I had tea. He decided to try his mixed with orange drink. It was delicious, he said.

'What do you think the parade was for?' I asked him.

'Nuthin',' he said, stirring his brew.

'What about King William?'

'He's dead.'

'Do you know anything about him?'

'He was popular,' said James.

'Who with?'

'With the Queen.'

'What was her name?'

'I dunno. Maybe Queen William of Orange.'

'Oh. Do you know anything else about him?'

'He owned all the orange things. Every single thing. All them bands belonged to him. He owned them clothes the bands was wearing.'

'But some of the suits were different colours. Your dad's is purple.'

'He doesn't own me *da's*.' He looked at me as if I were a half-wit. 'He only owns the bands with *orange* suits. Everything in this world what is orange he owns. He could tell me to give him that bottle,' he said, pointing at the source of half the concoction he was drinking. 'And he could tell you to give him that pen. And that,' he said, 'is all I know about him.'

Orange March Part II: Rub-it-in Dept. The scene resembled the morning's but the drinkers seemed finally to have flagged or stayed in the pub. We waited with the patient crowd several deep with push chairs, wheel chairs, folding chairs to the fore. Friends greeted one another, admired babies, gossiped and ate chips and sweets and ice creams: the standard diet, not a festive matter. In a crowd, and in their crisp white and pastel holiday clothes, you could see what such food did to them – stunning bright-eyed youth and radiant adolescence suddenly gave way to early old age. Young mothers were depleted, grey and slack, as if the very act of replacing themselves had made them redundant except to continue to be drained in the service of the new generation.

Jaunty music began to be heard down the road. Everyone thought the parade was coming, but this was from the wrong direction. Besides, there were no drums. Then into view came a dozen rows of men in blue and red uniforms with plumes in their hats marching in perfect step without instruments but mimicking a band. They were unspeakably drunk. The crowd loved it.

When the real parade arrived, the man at the head bore before him an actual crown on a Bible on a purple cushion. Some of the men were sweaty and unkempt but what was remarkable was that their spirits and energy seemed to have increased. Hester at my side was so proud of them, so joyous at the marvel they were still performing – in the strength (and length) of their commitment and the skill the years had given them at showing it; and an equal feeling of worth and happiness was apparent in the faces of all the spectators reprieved for an instant from their pinched lives. It was hard not to respond to them, even knowing that the very feelings evoked in them now were what helped keep them in their poverty.

The shattering din of the Lambeg drums was confusing my heart again, and I thought of other confusions I'd got into in London the week before. There, people jeered at these ludicrous joy-boys and the massive show they made of the world's most lethal sentiment: their patriotism. It was when they made allowances and excuses for manifestations of Republicanism that I had to see that to most, it was not patriotism itself which was disgusting; it all depended on whose patriotism, or on whether it could be justified as defensive. ('Our own,' when called upon, is always defensive.) The beleaguered Republicans in Northern Ireland had every right, in much of the world's eyes, to work their spirits up. Because the Loyalists employed the epithets of superiority they obscured a view of their behaviour as, in fact, more defensive than anybody's. The drums could not drown out the fact that they were the ones with everything to lose, and they were scared. The annual exhibit of bravery was more a matter of bravado. That didn't make it any more agreeable. But I had an uneasy feeling that what I was witnessing was a genuine people's festival, an entertainment very much by, of, and for the people. A look at the class composition here was to see overwhelmingly the poor, albeit with the gentry to the fore, and it ill-became middle-class snobs to sneer at this celebration of who they were. At any rate, the replay of the morning seemed designed to drum the point further home: They may be misled, but there's an awful lot of them and they are not, it is violently clear, going to go away.

James was dying to go to a pub, an unheard-of treat because of its illegality, and in the event more than that: the merrymakers in the bar were so unutterably plastered that they were actually quite ashamed of themselves, and compensated for their other inadequacies by giving James cokes, crisps, cuddles, conversation and cash. One man who fell over twice claimed to have got to the field and back on his bicycle. In moments of intelligibility he would mumble: 'Fee fi fo fum, I smell the blood of a Republican bastard.' This man felt impelled to say to me: 'We are not cruel. We deal in the bomb and the bullet, but we are never cruel.' Wasn't taking life cruel? I said. 'We all have to die,' he shrugged, then tried to get up and fell on the floor again. I don't think I've ever seen so many people having trouble with the floor.

There was an oddly penitential atmosphere to the scene as more of them seized the opportunity of being in their cups to make remarks to me which only partly veiled guilt. But they seemed trapped in this impasse: because of their condition wanting to relieve themselves of some burden, but unable to because of their condition.

I thought of a Republican song about an IRA volunteer who shoots a soldier on patrol and ultimately resists giving him the *coup de grâce* in memory of his mother, to whom he keeps singing the refrain:

> Oh mama, oh mama comfort me
> For I know these awful things have got to be
> And when the war of freedom has been won
> I promise you I'll put away my gun.

I felt a little like mama.

15
Four Men

A LABOURER

'I now hate Catholics and I hate Protestants. I've heard so much bullshit from both bloody sides. It all should have been stamped out before this. The organizations are like the Mafia – they're all collecting money every week. I'm not against anybody else – a lot of coloured people who come over here seem great. They're not involved in any of the nonsense. I'm just fed up with the whole heap of it, you know?

'I worked for a company and the UDA burnt the offices down. It's a big firm, spread out all over the UK, and the UDA were collecting money from the local branch. One of them said to me, "I believe your store was burnt last night?" I says, "I heard something, aye." He says, "It's terrible what these kids get up til nowadays – if you hadda seen us that maybe wouldn't have happened." But they actually done it. They actually done it.

'At one time I was a taxi driver. One of the guys I worked with used to have his own firm. He had a row with the IRA and they trailed the big radio master set – the dispatcher radio – out of his depot and burnt it in the middle of the Falls Road.

'I know for a fact that the IRA built De Lorean. Some of it was stolen, I reckon – they stole the scaffolding. Now if I know that, how the hell does British Intelligence and everybody else not know it? They offered me a job and I was going to take it, only as me being from the top of the Shankill some fellas that were workin' on the site mightn't have liked that. This guy says, "It could be dangerous, somethin' might happen til ye, somebody might take a dislike because of your religion." So I never took the job. I'm afraid to say too much. But how the hell doesn't British Intelligence know what I know? So I'm wonderin' if *they're* gettin' – somebody *there* is makin' money out of it too.

'See a lot of people bring up these things about discrimination in the shipyard and that. But there are so many Catholic businesses that haven't a Protestant in them. And nobody wants to look into the Catholic side and see how bigoted they are.

'And then they complain as well about the Prods gettin' all the business. Well that's very true but a man's not goin' to set up a business in the Falls Road when he knows he's got to shell out protection money for the building of the place, for the running of the place, a split of the profits, and he's goin' to get bombed out if he doesn't. That's not a proposition to any businessman. Whereas the Prods, whereas they do charge their own protection, usually do it in a different way like, through a legitimate security firm. Okay it's legal blackmailing, but you can report it legally and it's cheaper.

'There are an awful lot of people who try their best not to have the Troubles stop. They're makin' too much personal profit out of it. Not just security. Burglaries, petty theft. Someone's got to do the fencing – and if you've got the guns, you do the fencing. Same on both sides. No one's allowed to commit crime. But if you're in the Provos it's okay, or if you're selling to the Provos it's okay. As soon as somebody else starts getting in on the action, they're elbowed out with the Provos sayin', "We've done our best, we're protectin' the people of this area." That looks good on world coverage. Nobody can prove any different.

Nobody's goin' to speak up. Happens in all areas, and that's why people will not let the Troubles rest.

'You think of the money they make – there's no way on *earth* they're goin' to let things rest. Both sides. The people makin' all the money out of it would just be out of work. Okay, you'd get a lot more investment from companies and that, but if the investment didn't run equal to the redundancies, the money that the Brits bring in, the soldiers, and the money the policemen get paid – we may even be better off.

'They try to keep the communities divided. If the communities started mixin' they'd lose their control, lose their grip. But everybody's Irish, you know, in my opinion. Sure this guy I know's a Provie. That guy's good to me. He's got that old-fashioned friendship quality about him. If I'm ever up near his house, he welcomes me in. Says, "You can have your dinner with us." Lovely gesture, you know. Very few people like that these days.

'My mother's dead but she would have been horrified at some of the friends I keep. I mix with everybody. I walk wherever I want in this city. If somebody wants to take exception, wants to smash me teeth out or shoot me or beat my face up with a glass, that's up to them, but they're not goin' to stop me goin' where I feel like. It's my city. Had my birthday party up in Turf Lodge. Never had a party like it. Everybody there, a cake and all for me, and they presented the cake at midnight. Lucky the lights were down, it brought tears to me eyes.

'But I wouldn't like an all-Ireland. Say, for example, when I was a taxi driver, I went through an experimental phase – I wasn't sure if it was goin' to pay for me, since it's a pretty hard struggle, taxi-in', though I liked it – and to make sure I was safe, I went off the dole. 'Cause you're too easy caught that way. So I worked away for two years, then the tax man started catchin' up on me, sent me letters. So I went and got an accountant, and I told him, "For the last two years, I've been down South." So I didn't have to pay employment stamps, which was £4.75 a week. I was able to escape that – the reason why is because the border's there. Now if it was all one country I couldn't have done that. I'm better off. I'm not a hypocrite you see, I'm bein' honest.

'I've a friend who's a labourer for the Housing Executive. I tried to get work with them – repairs, you know. They go in in the morning, start about half past nine, knock off about half two. The reason why they knock off – if it's rainin': "It's a terrible bad day lads, have the day off." And if it's a sunny day, "Wonderful day, be a shame to waste it." The H.E. is lethal for it. That's why nothin' ever gets done.

'I've had twelve jobs since I left school. I was sixteen then, twenty-five now. Of the twenty guys I used to knock about with, there's only five of us that haven't done time. Petty crimes. But people don't get hurt in Belfast like in London. Very few people get stabbed. Muggings are virtually unheard of in Belfast. Because if somebody mugs somebody, the mugger's eventually caught and shot, before the police get him. It's not worth it for a handbag.

'There are a few sensible people in Belfast. But kids now – gettin' really cheeky, younger and younger. Used to be a brat was givin' you trouble, you'd say, "Right, I'm bringin' you down to the peelers' station," and they'd start cryin' so you'd let them go, say, "Don't get into any more trouble." Now they just throw stones at you.'

A PRIEST

'We live here on the peace line between the Falls and the Shankill. You've the two sides here and it sums up the situation. On this side a Catholic community, fairly Republican, whereas on the other side it's Unionist, Loyalist, Protestant. Now you've people on this side in Long Kesh for IRA activities and people on the other side in Long Kesh for UVF activities. The tragedy of the North is that if you come to know the people on the other side, ninety-five per cent of them are very good people. Same as with the people this side. An awful lot of their concerns are the same.

'A fair amount of what a priest here in this situation does is what a priest does anywhere: saying mass, hearing confessions, preaching, visiting people. You can live here as a priest and not really get involved, except indirectly, in the Troubles. Some of the problems here have some relation to the Troubles – problems of joyriders, the young people, a kind of wildness which is at least partly caused by the Troubles. You have drink problems, marriage problems which are indirectly caused by them. You'd be involved with prisoners' parents, their wives, their children. The problems of wives separated from their husbands for long years. Sometimes these wives are not politically minded themselves, you know, and couldn't care less whether there's a united Ireland; they just happened to marry someone who was very committed. Then they're faced with the fact that their husband's got fifteen years or something, after maybe only two or three years' marriage.

'There's the whole dimension of suffering, fighting this kind of war. Everybody is to some extent under threat, everybody's in danger of being shot or blown up – maybe not so much now as they used to be. You live in this kind of uncertainty, you don't know what's going to happen. Catholics for quite a long time lived in fear of assassination. Catholic wives whose husbands every day were going out to work down at the shipyard, or anywhere practically, there was always the danger . . . not so much now.

'An individual Churchman may have his own personal political opinions, but the priest as a representative of the Church really can't take sides on political issues – only insofar as moral issues are involved, or issues of justice. The Church must be concerned with the human side of the situation, where there's suffering – it doesn't matter who the people are. The Church must respond and say what can be done about stopping the suffering. The Church has to do its best to get the situation away from violent confrontation. But not take sides or intervene politically. The Church tries to avoid giving the impression of being a Nationalist church or a Republican church – because it isn't really. All the more so here because it doesn't want the Unionist people to get that impression. So with issues like the hunger strike or strip searching in Armagh, the Church is afraid to mobilize all its resources, I think.

'From the Church's point of view a hunger strike is immoral because it's a form of suicide. But some Irish theologians have argued that in certain circumstances it can be justified, for a higher good, as a form of self-sacrifice. The basic problem was that these men believed they were fighting for Irish freedom, that they were soldiers fighting a war who had been captured by the enemy.

'I used to go to the prison regularly. I went every Sunday all through the time of the blanket protest and the hunger strike. I knew Bobby Sands and all those ones. We used to get around the cells; we'd be hearing confessions. It was very shocking all right. Unbelievable really, a kind of nightmare thing really. I've been back there since in those corridors and cells and it's normal now and you have to stop and think for a moment . . . You'd wonder how they would come through it. Psychologically survive it. But they did, very well.

'The day they burnt down Bombay Street I saw the whole set-up. If you ever saw those films with Red Indians attacking settlers, it was that kind of situation. But the fact is that ninety-five per cent of the people over there wouldn't be involved in that kind of thing. They felt very threatened and frightened, and it was basically fear that inspired all that. I've had the experience of getting to know people who at one time epitomized the whole anti-Catholic sectarian attitude and when I've got to know them personally I've found they were very easy people to deal with, who would admit that because of their upbringing and the kind of ideas they had, they were very violent. But then having begun to live through the situation – usually through prison – they'd rethought their whole position. Most of the Loyalist paramilitaries now are not sectarian. They've lived through experiences which have taught them that the Catholics were not their enemies – they were fighting enemies that didn't exist. But in their own minds they thought they were protecting themselves.

'The Church has to be careful about getting into a political thing: the Church would be interested in having a society that's just, that's fair. An individual speaking privately might himself believe that the best solution was some form of united Ireland, but the Church couldn't actively promote that. From the point of view of political realities, you'll never have peace as long as you have the situation you have at the moment, with the majority of the people in Ireland opposed to partition, and a sizeable minority in the North here opposed to partition. You can only maintain partition by force, basically. The problem then is that people are going to use force against you. Continual conflict. The minority who are up here are having to use various forms of discrimination in order to maintain their position. They can't allow the Nationalist people to get into positions of authority, because they're enemies, in a sense, of the state: therefore you have to keep them down, keep them at bay, keep harassing them. It was a very bad solution to a problem. It was a bad solution on the first day, and all the problems were in it. It's bound to cause conflict, violence, discrimination. You'll have to go back to 1921 or '22 and rethink the thing again, because it hasn't worked, and it's not going to work.

'You don't have this kind of experience, but if you belong to a poor people, a people who have been evicted, with all the consciousness that the Irish people have of the misery, the terrible basic things they had to suffer – you have a sense that here are people that are trying to get up off their knees, to fight back, to assert their basic rights against forces that are a thousand times stronger than they. If you grow up in that kind of community, belong to that kind of community, well, you're going to side with that community.

'The Unionist people never really had to think, because all they had to do was to say to Britain, "You're going to back us, aren't you?" and they'd say, "We are" and that's it, "Well then, all we have to do is say No." In order to be put in a situation where they're going to have to make a new arrangement, whatever that new arrangement is, they're going to have to start thinking. Once they realize that they have to create a new situation, you'll find that they'll be very very good at it. Maybe this is the first stage where they're beginning to realize they're going to have to start thinking for themselves. And at the moment they're making the point that nobody is going to make arrangements which affect their future without involving them. I would support them, insofar as people *were* making decisions behind their backs and railroading them in directions they didn't want to go, insofar as they were protesting in terms of their rights. I would be much more sympathetic towards the Unionists and the Loyalists than I would have been in former times.

'Nobody would say that if the Protestants were coming into a united Ireland, any freedoms they have now should be interfered with. You'd have a completely new situation. You'd have to have a new constitution that would take into account that a million people don't think along certain lines – a quarter of the population – and therefore you'd have to provide for them. They have been told that if they would talk in terms of a united Ireland, everything would be up for discussion and their point of view would be embodied in a new constitution. But they're not interested; they believe that the best way to maintain their identity is under the UK, and there's no way to persuade them. What the British are doing now are saying to the Unionists, "Look, you're not going to have it all your own way; you're going to have to make adjustments." The British haven't really faced up to their responsibilities before; I think they're beginning to face up to them now.

'As a people the Unionist people are good people. They're Irish in a lot of ways, much more Irish than they'd admit, and would be much more Irish if they didn't feel as threatened or feel it would be misunderstood.

'This is a situation where you have to be very patient. You have to use your faith. If you really keep at it in the spirit of trust in God and work on the principle of trying to get people to talk to one another, to be prepared to grant basic rights to each other, to wish each other well, you can solve any problem.

'The basic weakness in the whole situation is that people on both sides who tend to express the problem violently have been ostracized and have become more violent. Nobody will talk to the paramilitaries, on either side, and they have a very significant role in the situation, since they represent a lot of the feelings of the ordinary people, especially the poorer people. Condemning them or oppressing them doesn't work. The only way you can deal with them is to try to engage them in some kind of meaningful discussion. And if you do you'd find they wouldn't be as unreasonable as people fear.

'If you want to resolve the conflict you have to sit down with the people involved and make sure you understand how they feel and think. I believe that if you do that and if you're patient, you begin to see where there is common ground and you can build on it and develop it; you can bring them out of the area where the conflict has been expressed in violence.

'This is the tragedy of Northern Ireland. It's like a jigsaw puzzle: all the pieces are there to make peace, and make a very wonderful peace in Ireland – and please God they will one day make it.'

AN ODC

'I keep me ears open and I keep me eyes open. You have to see what's what but, know what I mean? See when I see the crock like I have to make a move on it you know. So a fella come up to me the other day – honest to God, if you hadda seen it, it was so fuckin big, heavy whaddaya call them chains? – charm bracelets. Solid gold and must have been fourteen, fifteen charms hangin' on it. It was an ugly lookin' thing, a big dangly lookin' thing, every link on the chain was stamped and every charm was stamped. Jesus –

I don't know if you know ounces of gold is different from ounces of whatever, you know. Thirty-seven grammes to a fuckin ounce of gold, it's called a troy ounce. The gold's in a different category altoge'er, like, you know? Anyway I had these wee lads up from Lisburn, and there was no way I could get rid of it for a fuckin two hundred quid, no way, you know? I got them £120 for it, I think I done all right, simple as that. And fuck me, I have to take me cut. Done all right.

'I was a lazy cunt, I never would have worked. Still doin' me own thing. You get whaddaya call it, throw a bad fuckin card or whatever, you go in and you do your wee bit of – but that's what I'm sayin', you do six months whatever, you come out, don't give a fuck, it's an occupational hazard. But that's all I draw like, no more, no crazy stunts like you know? Ach they've enough crazies runnin' puttin' the fire among the fuckin sticks. Now and again you have to, know what I mean, go and wake 'em up like a bit you know? You have to, like.

'They'd kill me over there if they fuckin thought they could. Married a Taig, well fuckin so what, who didn't, so what. I honestly don't give a fuck, I've four great kids, and that does me. It's not allegiance to the IRA or somethin'. I don't give a bally, I don't care what they think anyway so I don't.

'But get a job? *Do* a good job like. *I* wouldn't work for no bastard, honest to God I wouldn't, I wouldn't even work for Shorts. Application forms and all down there. Now, managin' director's job or something – call the shots. Sell them Arabs a lotta missiles, bomb Maggie Thatcher out. I don't give a ballocks honest to God. I'm into property at the minute. Speculatin' like fuck. Speculatin' and accumulatin'. Want to see the job I done last week. No problem. I got three things to show for it. I took the family and kitted them out. I'm not that fuckin bad like you know? They get fuckin well seen to you know?

'I'm goin' to buy a packet of fags. See that there [a cigarette being rolled], that there reminds me of jail, and I hate jail, honest to God. See all the rest of these fuckin men comin' out of jail smokin' them things? I would have to be doin' life before I'd smoke them, fuckin bastards.'

The hood talks with a friend about the South: the hood loves it. The dope is good but too much heroin is going around, making people crazy. The IRA has kept heroin out of the North – 'one good thing the Rah's done.' Even down South, their tactic, he says, is to nail dealers to the floor by their hands. He talked about a friend arrested for three weights of hash, 'bang in joy' (imprisoned in Mountjoy, Dublin), who had now been caught in Holland with heroin, expecting to be extradited back and facing a life sentence. "Somebody better tell him to fuckin start makin' escape fuckin preparations, 'cause when he gets back they'll kill him, nail him to the floor or something".'

'Can you get dope in prison down there?' I ask.

'Dublin is a different fuckin world altoge'er. Dublin is crazy. You're in jail – it's like fuckin bein' out in the street. Everythin's available. But there are fuckin crackers on the go too like, you know, wantin' to bust heads and all. I was in with this cunt, he's a Taig from the Falls Road. One time in the joy suddenly yer mon stood up because he didn't know what I was talkin' about, but see when everybody knew, like, what the crack was, the whole fuckin jail was buttin' heads backin' me up against these 'uns. Half of them was scared 'cause they thought I was a mad Prod, then when they knew what the crack was . . . we near wrecked the fuckin place. I'm a Prod you know and you get kilt. But soon as you know what's what, you're sound, you're took by the hand. Great city, Dublin.

'I've met a lotta people there like you know. I go down, I remember them all and they're great til me. Once, couple Taigs started on me. And these Dubs just fuckin jumped in and says, "What? What are you slobberin' about?" Taig says, "What? He's a Prod!" "He's an all right bloke as far as we're concerned" – and didn't want to know like, Prod or Taig or what. These fuckin guys from the North sayin' "He's a Prod" like, you know, "tryin' to mix"? And they got kilt. And that's no joke. All the Dubs took my side: "He's fuckin one of *us*!' And that was it. End of story. They're fuckin brilliant fellas, honest to God. They're like us. There's no tribism among them. They're good lads.'

AN ENGLISH SOLDIER

'I had a lot of fun in Northern Ireland. Hilarious things happened. You've got to cultivate an abnormal sense of humour. It's difficult to explain. People join the army for various reasons. And after you've finished your training you spend X months or years with your regiment and you don't do anything that you're trained to do. You work 9 to 5, and you go out at night and get drunk and people pick fights with you because you're a soldier. It's dead easy to recognize a soldier because he's the guy with no hair.

'And it goes on like this and suddenly, you get to Northern Ireland. And you're actually being a soldier. I was terrified at first. But I was being a soldier for the first time.

'Lots of the men just cracked up in Belfast; people you'd have thought would have been good there just couldn't take the strain. We did eighteen hours on patrol, four and a half hours on guard and seven hours' rest. And four days off in the middle of your shift for R & R. There weren't enough men. Generally we patrolled the streets on foot. If

I walked a thousand miles in Belfast I walked 999 of them backwards, because I have the good eyesight: I was a sniper.

'If you started at lunch time you'd go out to a couple of patrols; then you'd do a mobile patrol with a local RUC guy who knew the area. But he couldn't walk around, so we used to put him in the back of a pig and drive him everywhere. You'd come in, have your tea, hang around, then you'd go on a sneakie-beakie. You'd sneak out en masse, a lot of people, and you'd lose pairs of them on the way. You'd get like ten people walking down the road, and two would disappear into a garden. You'd constantly move around, trying to make it look as if everyone was still there; go around a corner, then split up. These two people would have night-scopes and things like that. Image intensifiers – good for looking through windows. You can see right through lace curtains. I know exactly, I used to carry the bastard. Then you'd come back half an hour later and they'd join you.

'Almost straight after that, you'd go out and do your usual pub patrols with the intelligence officer. The idea was for him to chat to the people. You knew who all the baddies were in your area. And you knew the local PIRA leader of the ASU in your area. You knew his 2-i-c [second-in-command], his bomb-maker, his snipers. Trouble is, you couldn't prove anything, you just knew who they were. Everybody knows. You'd walk into the pub, leave two guys at the door. Then the intelligence officer would go up to someone he recognized – say the local bomb-maker. There'd been a bomb gone off in Belfast that day. He'd go up and say, "Hello Seamus, how are you? How's the wife, the kids? What do you know about what happened in town today?" And he'd say "I don't know anything, I was in Lisburn and I can prove it." But you had to go through the motions. Even if you knew it was him that did it. You had to go through the motions until you had enough evidence on him to arrest him.

'Then say about midnight you'd go out and do another sneakie-beakie. Except by this time you wouldn't do it with so many men.

'I was *terrified* for the first month. Nothing happened. Nothing happened for about four months. But then it does and you start getting addicted to adrenalin surges: you *want* something to happen, so you can get that swooping feeling in your stomach and your pulse – you feel like Superman, you feel invulnerable, it's not going to happen to me and if they did shoot at me it would just bounce off me anyway.

'We used to draw straws to see who'd arrest somebody – because it would guarantee you at least six hours off the streets to rest. So I won this particular lottery, and we were going to arrest a guy at half past 4 in the morning. They sent out the foot patrols early and surrounded the house, and I was at the back of the Land-Rover. I was supposed to be the first person in the house. So the Land-Rover skids to a stop in front of this little terraced house. I ran out to the door: I was going to shoulder-charge it open, like you see in the films. I threw myself at this door and bounced right off it. Just about dislocated my shoulder. And everybody thought it was so funny that we just all got back in the Land-Rover and went away.

'Next day I was told how to kick a door in. Big lecture. What you do is, you run up to the door and you aim for the lock, you kick it where the lock is and it just flies open. So the next morning, half past 4, out we go. Run up to the door, flying leap at it, kicked it where the lock was, and the door didn't budge. I'm lying there on the pavement moaning "Oh! God! OH!" So they picked me up again, back in the Land-Rover.

'The third night, third time lucky. They got this huge guy to kick the door in. And I went in, arrested the man and took him away. He was just a young guy from the Fianna, the PIRA youth division. I don't know what he was arrested for. Probably because he was in the Fianna.

'What they do is every so often they say, "Oh we haven't had Seamus O'Toole in for a couple of weeks: go arrest him and we'll give him a hard time." Just to let them know, you know, that we're still here. Obviously they'd get their wires crossed sometimes but I don't know if we ever arrested anyone that was innocent. You'd take them in, handcuff them with those plastic handcuffs, put them in the back of the Land-Rover, read them their rights – "As a member of HM forces I arrest you," et cetera. You've got to look them in the eye as you say that so they know who they're talking to. And you take them to your regimental intelligence, who has first crack at them. They say, "We know you did this." "No, bollocks, I was at my auntie's, she'll prove it,' you know. Then you take them to the RUC, who take them down to Castlereagh. A few days later they're back on the streets. It's the way the game is played.

'I think everyone has their own personal enemy in Northern Ireland and I had this guy. He used to play tricks on me. Like as I was walking backwards he'd move a dustbin – the guy in front of me is twenty yards ahead, so he'd just move it in between. Then you'd fall over backwards. Lying in somebody's garbage, flopping around, trying to get up, and the people all standing around laughing at you: "Look at the British squaddy!" And it gets to you. He held a riot specially for me. I came round a corner and there it was: twenty of them. I had my gun but you don't shoot somebody for having a riot. I could have asked for my rubber bullet guy to come to the front, but I didn't have enough time. Ten guys in front of us and ten guys behind and we didn't stand a chance. Beat the crap out of me. And they weren't after anything, didn't take anything, didn't even beat up the other guys all that much.

'He was another Fianna guy. I like to think I'm a mild-mannered person, but if someone said, "Okay, if you shoot him tomorrow we'll let you get off with three years in jail," I'd shoot that little bastard. All I could do was, if I was P-checking him – and I must admit I used to look for him sometimes – it was "What's your name?' then "Right, spell it." Then you'd say "Okay, spell it backwards." This is harassment. Then "Where'd you come from?" so he'd tell you. "Okay, spell it. Spell it backwards." But that was just an attitude I got because of the way he treated me. I was really terrified when I first went out there and I wouldn't have said boo to a goose. And I think he knew that about me.

'One guy carries the plastic bullet gun and six rounds. He's got an SLR and a baton gun slung over his back. Awesome weapon, you know, the baton gun. That's one of the reasons why I never ever wanted to shoot it. Before we went to Belfast, we did six months' training, and we fired these things on the ranges, at a wooden target of a man with a two-by-three fence stub holding it up. One of the guys fired a baton round at it and it snapped in half. You're supposed to fire them at the ground, so they come up. But I think that's worse because if they bounce off a rough tarmac surface you've got no control: it starts to spin, and it could hit anyone at all.

'And the SLR, which we all carried, that's overkill. You can stop a charging bull elephant with an SLR. You can shoot somebody through a brick wall. If a sniper shoots at you through a window and you see him going behind the brick wall, you just shoot at the wall and it'll go right through and kill him. I never actually shot my gun at all.

'We had seventeen car bombs in one afternoon. Worst day of my life. Every time a car stopped somebody got out of it and said, "There's a bomb in my car." What happens is the IRA – or whoever – go to somebody's home and hold the wife or children hostage, and they put the bomb in the car and get the man of the house and say, "Okay, this bomb will not go off for X hours. We want you to drive the car, park it next to Y building, get out and walk away." Usually these people will stop at the nearest army patrol. That happens a lot. Once a double-decker bus drew up and the driver gets out and says, "There's a bomb in my bus." So we got everyone off the bus and the troop leader says to me, "Get on the bus, show him where to go." There was a bit of waste ground, and we used to park them in the middle of it because if they blew up all it did was put a hole in the waste ground. I looked at him and I said, "You've got to be fucking joking. I'm eighteen, and you want me to get in a bus that's about to blow up?" We had a big argument in the street and eventually we both got on the bus. But with a car what you do is, if a guy says there's a bomb, you cock your gun, you point it at him and say, 'Get back in." And you just walk him along to where it's safe and say "Right, get out now." Get him out the way, arrest him, cordon off the area, evacuate the houses, call in Felix – the bomb disposal people. They have Felix the Cat on the sides of their cars.

'Raids were a common occurrence. Almost daily. We used to raid the head of the local ASU once every three days, search his house once every two weeks. There's another kind of sneakie-beakie patrol, again. An OP section, just four guys. What you'd do is, you'd go into the house to search it, and you'd search three houses, his and the two houses next to it. You'd send as many guys as you could possibly fit into that house. People'd be walking in and out all the time, up the stairs and everything. And when you left, there'd be four guys in the attic. With all the James Bond kit, you know, microphones screwed into the floor, mikes underneath his carpet. And they'd sit in there for a week, four hours on, eight hours off. They had food, and if you wanted to go for a crap you did it in a plastic bag. Then next week, *wham*, it would happen again – you'd get all these people in there searching the house, and they'd come out. It's a good game.

'There were photographs of wanted men everywhere you went. In the hall, A4 size. Patrol commanders had a notebook. Passport-size photos stuck on the butt of your rifle. Inside the pigs. Everywhere. You got to know the faces. An ASU in the IRA is only about seven guys. Allied to that you've got the Fianna, the girls, the women. You knew them better than your brothers and sisters. You could recognize them quickly, that was the idea.

'I remember – I can't remember her surname but her first name was Brenda. She was the wife of one of the men who blew up the gas towers. This little three-man section had planted the bomb but the fuse had gone wrong and as they ran away it exploded and the gas tank blew up. The force of the explosion pushed them through this chicken-wire fence. Brenda gave us a hard time – she would spit on us, or you'd walk past her house in the street and the top window would open and she'd empty her potty over you. Not very nice, to walk around the streets stinking, trying to get the bits of shit out of your hair. Kind of puts you in a bad mood. We sent her photographs of the pieces of bodies that had come through the fence. That shut her up.

'I have no personal feelings about the IRA at all. They're okay. I can sympathize with them more if they just killed soldiers and policemen. I disagree with them bombing indiscriminately, be it on mainland Britain or Northern Ireland. Warning bombs? Okay – if they want to blow up their own homes. They're frightening away business. They're just making their own lives a misery. If they want to live in shit, that's up to them. I don't mind the fact that they want Ireland to be whole. But I also sympathize with the Protestants that don't want that. I'm in the middle: I don't hate them, I don't love them. None of them ever actually done anything to me.

'You know, I wasn't even particularly offended that they shot at me twice. That was part of the game. It's not a war. Well I justify it in my mind as a game – I can live with that. And there's certain rules that you play to and if you know the rules then you don't get hurt so often.

'It's always the same families that continually feed the ranks. Great-grandfather, grandfather, father, son, and cousins of one family. The way I think it works – you get Seamus, whose father is already in the Maze, and that is what has made Seamus actively join the IRA. So he thinks, "I don't like my father being treated like this, the British bastards," talks to someone, goes away to the South, does his training: he's one of the boyos. So you know all about Seamus, you catch him one day, bang to rights, thrown in jail, goes to the Maze, gets the same sort of treatment as his father. So then Seamus's younger brother becomes active, or maybe two of his cousins. For every martyr – as they call themselves, and quite rightly, they are, in a way, or so the rest of the Catholic population see them – for every one you lock away, five take exception. And it goes in spurts: sometimes they have a large active service personnel within the IRA – maybe five or six hundred in

Belfast involving themselves in terrorist activity; or it dies down a bit and maybe there's only three hundred, or people are locked away or get bored or are forced South into exile so it dies down except for the nucleus of people who are always in it, not the "casual labour" but the committed boyos.

'But can you ever drop out of an organization like that? Say a wounded gunman came knocking at 3 o'clock in the morning. There are some moderate people who'd turn him away if they could but they're frightened: the guy from the ASU is going to come knocking the next day. Kneecapping, something like that, because they turned away "a hero". I think the IRA is like the Mafia – you're in, you're in. I admire them in a way, because they're so committed. And the good ones in the IRA or the INLA are very good. The bad ones or even the indifferent ones are laughable.

'They're very technical now. They're very clever as well. Photosensitive cells. Take two bricks out of a wall, pack in two pounds of plastic explosive, couple of pounds of nails in the hole, detonators, and wire it all up to a photosensitive cell. Then put a poster on it slagging off British squaddies or the RUC. You come out on patrol and see it and think "the bastards" and rip it off. Light on photosensitive cell – KABOOM. The ones that are clever are very clever. They're the ones that are never caught. "Most Wanted Man in Northern Ireland" – you know who he is, but you can't prove it. There are about five or six *most* Most Wanted, and probably fifteen that everybody would like to get. I'm talking about gunmen or bombers. That's not counting the general staff.

'I'm neutral about the whole . . . I think actually I'm more anti-Protestant-terrorist organization than Catholic. I can't understand why they have to have terrorist organizations when it's commonly accepted that the British

Army is there to protect the Protestants, no matter what anyone says. And I think the average British squaddy sympathizes with the Protestant point of view, so he's more lenient towards them.

'They think they have to fight fire with fire, but they're more part-time terrorists than the IRA, and also they don't have the expertise to call on that the IRA has. So a lot of their terrorist acts go wrong and they kill innocent bystanders. They would be more likely to indiscriminately bomb Catholic areas without warning. That's the only thing I really hold against them: they involve innocent people, children.

'It's like the riots. Rioting in Belfast is an art. It's always little children right at the front, then your teenagers, then people who think, "Oh, a riot! That'd be good fun!" Then right at the back, your three or four guys who are running it, who are boyos. They say, "Okay, let's go" and it's all over. Or they say, "Get the petrol bombs out now." Or they give the signal to the sniper. On a really good riot that's how it's worked. It's the guys at the back you're after. Get them and there's no control and it disperses, everyone loses interest.

'It's a game, a game. I wouldn't say I was very good at it but it was a game I enjoyed playing. I enjoyed myself in Belfast, not because I was being mean, or because I felt "I'm walking the streets with a gun and the power of life and death." If you think about that you become frightened. So I never really used to think about it. Before I went out there, you had to ask yourself these questions: could I kill a woman if she was endangering my life, or a child? How will I react? Will I just start to cry? Will I be frightened? Especially when you're young. A lot of us were very very young.'

16
Living With War

The voices I have included here are to me the archetypal ones, or the most affecting, or both. But they are not representative of a place where many more people are outside the conflict – or try to be – than are in it. A poll conducted by the *Belfast Telegraph* in 1986 showed that only 21.2 per cent of Catholics favoured a united Ireland; of these, only a few are willing to fight for it. And of those who reject change on the Loyalist side, the same applies. But because the militants have forced a way of life on all their compatriots, they obviously attract the most attention.

Many images crowd in when I try to pin down anything about Belfast, and so many people who seemed crucial to understanding:

– The Workers' Party man with such savage commitment that he cried as he talked about the suffering endured during the 1920s, and his overwhelming horror when he watched the Catholic houses burn in 1970 – not so much because he was homeless but because he knew it meant 'it was beginning all over again'.

– The social scientist, an amateur military strategist and an admirer of Marshal Zhukov, who feverishly drew maps on the inside of her windscreen as she drove her car in the rain, to demonstrate that the Catholics were effectively pinned down in three enclaves and no amount of help from the South could save them if civil war came, unless there emerged a Zhukov who could devise the right pincer movement. 'And that is why to my mind the war is lost.

They cannot win it militarily, they won't win it politically, and they have lost it long ago morally.'

– The terror of the man on the run in Belfast, not because of paramilitary activities but because he was gay, and his own family were after him with their guns. He was Catholic, but he could as well have been Protestant.

– The middle-class Orangeman, a passionate patriot who despised even Irish music, reacting to the Anglo-Irish Agreement with philosophical optimism: 'After all, in 1685 things were bad, but five years later we had a changed situation!' After the RUC had stopped an Orange march on the grounds that it was provocative he said, 'As of today, I can truly say we have a definite affinity with the people of the Warsaw ghetto.'

– The surgeon who believed that 'a new Ireland is about all the people participating in, creating and welcoming the fact that there *are* so many different traditions. We could create a society with a message far beyond our shores if we resolved our ancient conflict.' He was nearly isolated in Protestant society through his efforts, for 'to fire a question in your own community takes far more courage than to fire a bullet in somebody else's. But I sometimes wonder if I have the psychological strength to continue to be odd man out.'

– The fearless Provo woman who once was caught carrying two .45s in her jeans. Her attitude about the prospect of a fourteen-year sentence was 'Wee buns' (no problem), but she called off an interview because *'We have a crisis here!'* after a mouse ran across her kitchen floor.

– The city councillor who believed that 'There are only three hundred Provies in Northern Ireland, guys with guns. Arrest them, put them away, until you get consensus.' Official Unionist? No, SDLP. 'If the SDLP prevails, the

Provisionals will wither and die.' If the SDLP did not prevail, he planned to move to France.

– Sinn Fein's Danny Morrison on television: 'You can put us in jail but still we are going to come back and we will *bleed you white.*'

– The women at a mother-toddler group in Divis (half of whose husbands were in Long Kesh) who, when asked what Northern Ireland needs, answered: 'More pay to the workers. More grants from the assistance. Cheaper bus fares. Cheaper dinners. Cheaper drink. And cheaper electric and coal.' End of list.

– The sprightliest of Irish reels played in a pub, whose title, said the flautist, was 'My Mother was Drowned in the Pool at Lourdes'.

– The worker for the Northern Ireland Association for the Care and Rehabilitation of Offenders, whose particular concern was the isolation of the wives of ODCs: 'It's acceptable in the ghettos that your husband's doing time for political offences – murder's all right – but some poor guy's in for nicking and you're ostracized because it's criminal.'

– The low self-esteem in which so many hold themselves, from the educated Protestant woman who confessed to feeling shame every time she had to open her mouth to speak in England, to the Catholic shop in the city centre which sold 'Irish pencils' with erasers at both ends, 'Irish mugs' with the handles inside, and 'Irish alarm clocks' which each consisted of a candle with instructions to 'stick it up your arse'.

– A man connected to the UVF talking about how they punish their own. 'They just shoot them and dump them or cut their fingers off. They're not corrupt.' – 'Cut their fingers off?' I said. 'Which ones?' – 'One every week. Start with the little finger. With a blunt knife. "Hold it out.

Right. We'll be back next week."' – 'What's the most fingers anybody's lost?' I asked. 'One,' he said.

– The residents at a battered wives' refuge, Protestant and Catholic living together not only contentedly but with a sense of true, almost miraculous discovery of each other. When presented with the notion that they might try to find permanent housing together, they vetoed it solidly: 'I feel safer in me own area.'

– An outraged Angloperson, after the Brighton bombing: 'That's the trouble with the IRA! They missed! I mean, what happens, they get into this Grand Hotel weeks in advance, intelligence A-OK, amazing computerized bomb, and then they fucking blow it! So that *she* comes out of it fucking *coiffed*, Boadicea on her charger! If she had been *behind* it she couldn't have planned it better. I mean they're Micks when you get down to it.'

And the most enduring image of all, because it is seen everywhere and often in Belfast: a snotty faced child trying hard to be a man in the only way a boy knows how there, by shooting his friends with a stick.

When I first went to Belfast I believed people would choose peace, but that violence has its reasons and is sometimes justified. There is no choice in South Africa or anywhere else where injustice is institutionalized beyond the means of peaceful confrontation to affect. There are those, particularly in America and England, who see the Catholic plight in Northern Ireland in the same way, a view encouraged in West Belfast where a Sinn Fein mural links African National Congress and IRA insignia under the sign APARTHEID FREE ZONE. But only a few weeks in Belfast made me feel the parallel to be inappropriate. There is no way to gloss over the horrors and injustices that have been endured by Catholics, but it also seemed an insult to the ANC *and* the IRA to see the Northern Catholic experience now as equivalent to the black South African one, or the Protestants as Afrikaners. Racism is racism wherever it is, but the degrees of power exercised in its name obviously differ. The Minister of Justice of South Africa is said to have expressed envy of the powers available to the Northern Ireland security forces; but most governments now have no difficulty in waiving constitutional restraints when they are inconvenient, particularly if they cry 'emergency' and can carry (or coerce) public opinion to assent. In a 'democracy' it is enough to manipulate the opinions of the voters, having first selected the voters.

But in Northern Ireland while the authority to abuse power is available and in use, the trappings of a free society still exist. It is the best illustration I've seen of the old riddle: freedom for all, or freedom for all except the enemies of freedom. The British view of who are 'the enemies of freedom' is what the insurgents have to contend with. Still, in Northern Ireland anyone who doesn't make waves can live a life that is light years away from the life of *everyone* in Soweto.

People in the Catholic ghettos do not deserve to be harassed by troops in the streets or forced constantly to endure guns pointed at them. But by and large some of their activities might be expected to earn as much from any military-police state. I met many people who claimed to have been, say, locked up for nothing, but the same people – and those who are familiar with the imprisoned – admit that although people are often sentenced for a crime they didn't do, or for something that to them is not a crime at all, very few are in fact inside for nothing.

What is a crime in this situation? For some in Sinn Fein, the greatest crime is silence. The history of suffering in

Ireland, inherited by and perpetuated in Catholic Northern Ireland, has produced a feeling of passionate righteousness in their cause which makes them see their lot as the same as that of black South Africa's – and this perception, not an outsider's view, is the reality to be reckoned with. Not least among those accused of silence are the people of the South. 'I never fought alongside anybody but a Belfast man,' said a Belfast fighter. 'And that goes for down there too. Not a fuckin one. I never seen one. The only accent I ever heard was a Belfast accent.' And here is a typical voice from the Republic: 'We never mention the North in Cork. They give us *the dry gawks*.'

There may be numerous Belfast Protestants who base their politics on an assessment of Catholics as subhuman, but I met few of them. Apart from Paisley frothing over about Papists whoring with the devil – and, presumably, his substantial congregation – the Protestants I met who spoke of their problems with Catholicism were often more rational than prejudiced. Many of the charges they levelled against the Church and its influence in the Republic I also heard from some Sinn Feiners, most feminists, and radicals of all stripes. As early as 1814 Daniel O'Connell was calling for 'An eternal separation' between church and state and 'the eternal right to freedom of conscience – a right which would . . . bury in oblivion the bloody orange flag of dissension in Ireland.' A BBC political commentator who has studied the situation for years said, simply enough, 'Britain can't leave until Ireland is tolerable for the other side to join.'

During the months I was travelling to Belfast, the 'Kerry Babies' trial was proceeding in the South, its details exciting public relish and rage in the local papers daily. A young woman was accused of stabbing to death her newborn baby, despite its being shown the child was not hers. Her own baby had died at birth in a field outside her farmhouse. Therefore the stabbed baby, found twenty miles away, was advanced as having been the other half of twins, and since its bloodgroup was neither hers nor her lover's, it must have been fathered by another man. The police, in attempting to justify both the twins-by-two-men theory and the extraction of dubious confessions, felt free to torment her publicly and piously, presumably on the assumption that she deserved no better because she had become pregnant by a married man.

None of this could have happened as it did without the influence of the Church, whose practical stranglehold on the regulation of morality in the South is nearly complete. 'In the name of the Most Holy Trinity, from Whom all authority flows and to Whom as our first end all actions both of men and states must be referred . . .' states the preamble to the Republic's constitution. These words were never taken lightly by the Church, which has from the beginning influenced legislation, imposed censorship, and suppressed any trend towards a secular pluralist state. They carry on. In March 1984, a referendum heavily influenced by the Church hierarchy made abortion, already illegal, unconstitutional as well. (Sinn Fein meanwhile deleted the 'totally' from 'We are totally against abortion' in their platform. The following year they voted for 'a woman's right to choose'. The year after that, they rescinded it.) In March 1985 by a narrow vote in the Dail the sale of condoms (not of the pill, the coil, or the diaphragm) was finally made legal in the South – though since selling them is discretionary for the individual pharmacist, the vote didn't greatly affect accessibility. In June 1986 another referendum, again influenced by the Church, ended in defeat for the possibility of divorce. No options had been open to the woman in Kerry or her lover. Non-

Catholics in the South are also governed by the Church's rules to the extent that a secular education for their children is virtually unobtainable. Even the principal Protestant graveyard has had to close down. All this and *Ne Temere* too – the decree whereby children of mixed marriages must be brought up Catholic. The Southern Protestant population has been reduced since partition by over two-thirds.

Matters like these are important to poor and powerless people who cannot easily circumvent the law, and it is not all that surprising that to many Northerners the South seems to be a place of benighted retrogression. You don't need to be prejudiced, or even Protestant, to feel wary of the 'ecclesiastical imperialism' of the Catholic Church in Ireland. You don't need to be anything at all to wonder why, if the South wants the unification of the island, it makes no concessions towards those it would absorb. 'For me not to be allowed a diaphragm in the Republic is on the same level as not allowing infidels to have a drink in Saudi Arabia,' a Catholic woman said. 'I'm not fussed what their rules are, but why inflict them on me?' In November 1985, just after the Anglo-Irish Accord had provoked the overwhelming anger of Protestants in the streets of Belfast a dissenting Protestant said, 'If the Unionists would cool down and think with their heads, they could cause serious problems for the Southern government. No one has challenged Southern bigotry yet. There's plenty of it – not necessarily against Northern Prods, but against the minorities in their own society. They've got to be made to face their own bigotry.'

In the North, I found Protestant bigotry more marked among the middle than the working class. The latter were quite likely to express envy of the Catholics' ability to play the system more effectively, of their greater articulateness, of their talent for life ('They've got all the best songs!' –

'Our graffiti is so stupid next to theirs'); old saws about Catholic shiftlessness and dirt were too evidently untrue to persist among people who used their senses.

But bigotry does exist, and on both sides: it is the reverse of the patriotism on which both rely for political energy. With life on an unemployment handout a mean affair from every point of view, drive and purpose are to be found in the glorious cause of Us v. Them. The 'Us' is based not on class but entirely on tribal identity with a religious label. 'This is not a religious war,' everyone said; but fear and suspicion flourish in churches, nurtured by the smugness of those who consider themselves Saved, with the implication that the lives of the un-Saved are less valuable. And there is bigotry beyond mere attitudes of mind in killing a fellow Irishman because of what amounts to a disagreement about who is Us.

Louis MacNeice, born in Belfast, wrote:

> I come from an island, Ireland, a nation
> Built upon violence and morose vendettas.
> My diehard countrymen like drayhorses
> Drag their ruin behind them.
> Shooting straight in the cause of crooked thinking
> Their greed is sugared with pretence of public spirit.

It seems unkind for an outsider even to read these words, let alone quote them, especially since they tell only one side of the story. But that side exists.

Outsiders have been more polite and amusing about this aspect of Ireland. In 1873 Mark Twain and his wife visited Belfast. Mrs Clemens wrote to her mother that the food was 'unbearable'. Her husband observed the following:

> Belfast is a peculiarly religious community. This may be said of the whole of the North of Ireland. About one-half of the people

are Protestants and the other half Catholics. Each party does all it can to make its own doctrines popular and draw the affections of the irreligious toward them. One hears constantly of the most touching instances of this zeal. A week ago a vast concourse of Catholics assembled at Armagh to dedicate a new Cathedral; and when they started home again the roadways were lined with groups of meek and lowly Protestants who stoned them till all the region round about was marked with blood. I thought that only Catholics argued in that way, but it seems to be a mistake.

It worried me how, if peace ever came, people could live together again after becoming so used to violence. More precisely, it worried me that the people supporting violence didn't seem to worry about the lessons in means they were bequeathing their children on the way to their noble ends. This question was usually regarded as irrelevant. 'Think, say, of the Second World War,' a Republican woman said. 'You didn't find people who killed in wartime incorporating that violence into their civilian lives later: they understood the difference.' Yes, but the Second World War lasted for six years and the present Troubles have already gone on three times as long, not counting the inheritance of centuries, and have penetrated communities in a permanent kind of way. What of those who have grown up knowing nothing else? To distinguish between permissible and impermissible violence must ultimately depend on a strong moral sense, very hard to maintain when your battlefield is civilian life and your acts of heroism are defined in courts of law as criminal activity.

I introduced an ex-paramilitary friend to my daughter, who wanted no part of it: 'Those kinds of people really frighten me.' What she sensed in him, she said, was that 'he's crossed a line. He's done something immoral. I don't mean illegal. It's like what I'm reading at school. When Hamlet kills Polonius and overcomes all his inhibitions, somehow his principles have lost their original meaning. And he's so proud of himself; he screams, I've done it! I've done it!' She thought that if people could kill so readily for a cause, they might 'lose the grip they have over themselves, over right and wrong. They could kill their family. They could kill you. It would mean nothing.'

I told the paramilitary, after some thought, what she had said. 'She's right,' was his answer.

One of the most painful of all the conversations I had in Belfast was with the mother of an IRA volunteer, who said she foresaw only two ends for him: a life sentence, or coming home in a box. 'I don't think he will scratch many grey hairs.' She waited; she did nothing but wait. She was completely bewildered by him, because his morality was no longer hers. 'His eyes have changed,' she kept saying. 'I try to tell him that I don't want him to hurt anybody, I don't care who they are or what for. But he won't listen, his eyes have changed. Sometimes I think it would be better if it was all over and he was dead.'

Yet the effort to make sure people 'understood the difference' still goes on. One way is to impose a rigid orthodoxy on beliefs and behaviour. There is no compromise in holy war; dogma rules in Belfast. On the Protestant side it often seems to be dogma for its own sake. They just say 'No'. The Catholics back their dogma up with one of the world's most attractive traditions, with song and romantic history, and with a comprehensible political rationale that has clearly defined angels and devils. But despite the Republicans' meticulous theoretical analyses of their war of liberation, they don't have much to say about the Protestants. The Protestants don't fit in. They aren't even dignified with the name of enemy; the Brits are the enemy. Some Loyalist fighters seem to feel perversely humiliated at being so inconsiderable as adversaries; all of them who think about it must feel rejected and excluded by the absolute lack of attention paid them in the Catholic scheme of things. 'Look at me' is half their battle.

Another way to keep ends and means separate is through culture. For the Nationalists, war and cultural activity reinforce each other. They are far more interested in Irish language classes (often taught by men who learned Gaelic in prison) and traditional music and sport, than are people in the South. The sense of Irish identity derived from the culture feeds a political consciousness that drives the war; the war creates a heightened nationalism that feeds an urgency for the language and music.

Meanwhile the Loyalists who are omitted from Republican calculations have a hard time constructing a tradition of their own. As an aspect of their culture-envy they take on the enemy form without its content: the brutal and dogmatic features of the war unattached to a solid base in culture or history. They end up with no more than a meagre structure for their behaviour – marching to commemorate the Battle of the Boyne (a river which isn't even in the North) three hundred years ago, or the siege of the Apprentice Boys of Derry, the No Surrender of the Unionists in 1912, the Battle of the Somme. Those events are just about the sum of their past; without them they don't know who they are, but only who they aren't (or, more accurately, who they don't want to be). Dorothy Elliott said: 'Loads and loads of people call themselves Prods not because they're Prods but because they're not Catholics. I think Protestants have no identity. Catholics know who they are; we don't. So we try to be more British than the British, like the old Anglo-Indian.' People such as Andy Tyrie speak of their having been robbed of their history, anxious to put together more. Without it Loyalist fighters too easily slide into gangsterism, brainlessly copying only the symptoms of a consciousness bred into the very blood of Republicans. It will be very difficult ever to tame those Loyalists. When their policemen are killed by Republicans for being British stooges, the Loyalists are determined to avenge what they see merely as Protestant deaths without knowing any other reason why. Killing without a reason can be a very simple and attractive solution to conflict. After the Anglo-Irish Agreement, Loyalists took to attacking their policemen themselves. When they want to fight, who is there to fight? 'Whoever comes in front of you,' said one who'd left fighting behind.

Those Protestants who have transcended violence have a tendency to see all the fighting in the light of their own side's. They don't understand Republicanism. Republicans have never made efforts to be understood by them. It is easier for someone in London or New York to tune into the Irish cultural and political tradition than for a Protestant in Belfast. A maverick from Loyalism, thinking of the hollow, lurid battles he once fought, has little sense of that tradition of freedom struggle compelling his Catholic fellow citizens. He sees the abuses, like the petty racketeering the Republicans have now to cope with too, as grounds for dismissing their struggle as he has dismissed his own former one. I met dozens of such Protestants, people of overwhelming pacifist goodwill who had developed a contempt for flags and fights in defence of them. Catholics in the same position were few (like their equivalents, they had generally lived or travelled lengthily abroad); and while they might see the futility in continuing violence as a method, they never doubted the decent motives of most of the people on their own side who were still fighting. The Catholics have a corner on decent motives. Individual Republican mavericks seldom seem maverick enough to embrace world citizenship. The Catholics have *suffered;*

there is a score to settle. The Protestants as a whole have not; they can afford magnanimity.

But the Republicans' refusal to consider seriously the Protestant mentality is creating potential havoc. The Protestant anarchy let loose after the Anglo-Irish Agreement, leading from protest to intimidation to rioting to a renewal of sectarian assassination – all symptomatic of a profound disaffection among the larger group – is lethal for the society as a whole. Republicans have little to say about this; they just hope the anarchy will help them further to destabilize the situation to a point where it is intolerable to the British. But destabilization can work against them, too.

And for all their ideas about a socialist republic, Sinn Fein forgets about socialism when it comes to the Protestants. In a contribution to a book called *Ireland After Britain*, Gerry Adams has extraordinarily little to say on the subject. 'I presume that if partition goes as part of a British withdrawal,' he writes, 'then regardless of what sort of institutions are left, there will be a coming together of people who have the same class interests over the whole of Ireland.' But 'class interests' don't play a part in people's thinking. Adams goes on to say (in his only specific reference to Protestants), 'When Britain goes, the whole ballgame changes. We would have a new 32 County Ireland. That would mean for one thing having a sizeable national minority – that is, the Protestants – who would need to have their understandable but misguided fears about civil and religious liberties answered.' Why can't somebody start answering these misguided fears now? Why wait? Why can't their concerns be addressed?

By the same token, when Loyalists discuss a future independent Ulster with Protestant and Catholic living happily ever after, they spare not one thought for Catholic fears *now*, making only vague suggestions that in their own brand of socialism, whatever that is, the interests of all the people will be protected. What are they waiting for? How about, for a start, letting Catholics work beside them? Or not killing them?

It doesn't require much imagination to come up with such questions, and yet in Belfast one is looked upon as some sort of freak if one voices them. The irresistible conclusion is that neither group takes its own proposals very seriously. A further conclusion is that most plans for peace are mirages: only plans for war occupy these people's minds. Maurice James Craig's famous couplet 'It's to hell with the future and live on the past / May the Lord in his mercy be kind to Belfast' seems only partly true: everyone lives thoroughly in the present, as it is informed by the past. But Craig certainly had it right about the future.

The overwhelming feeling I got in Northern Ireland was that the war was going to continue because so many people had a stake in it. For some the stake is idealism, for some it's personal profit, for some it's power, for some it's their version of Ireland-for-the-Irish, or of socialism. For a kid-rioter of my acquaintance, it's just the crack. Some fight for the status it gives them in the fight; even the people obsessed with peace would be out of a job if it came. And ironically, the status quo, if not the war, means survival for many. If Britain left, it would take away the social security structure. Public expenditure now accounts for more than 70 per cent of the gross domestic product (48 per cent in the UK as a whole); 45 per cent of those in work at all are employed in the public sector, i.e. paid by the Exchequer. Large numbers of jobholders, from prison warders to glaziers, are direct beneficiaries of the Troubles. Others owe their employment to the need for duplication in a divided society, such as two lots of teachers, doctors, lawyers; not to mention any number of positions that have to be filled both North and South. This can work in the most mundane spheres.

Richard Ferguson, QC, a Unionist MP in the 1970s, talked about his efforts at that time simply to organize one soccer team – Rugby is already united – for the island. Neither side would have it. 'Both football associations had formed little hierarchies of their own, and if you had a fusion there could only be, for example, one chairman, so one man's going to lose his job. Two of everything: that's now built into the structure of the country. And that's only a small, non-doctrinaire impediment. Partition is now institutionalized. It suits people.' He thought it was necessary to 'recognize the fact that the present situation really is what the majority of people want. They may not say they want it, they may not even know they want it, but it has a better chance of working than any alternative I can see. That's the policy of despair – but maybe not. Maybe if that could be acknowledged and recognized and built upon they might come out a better state.'

Failing such recognition, choices still exist for people caught in the situation. Indisputably the most awful hardship and misery are to be found, almost all of it the place's fault. Why not move away? Many young people are forced to go to England seeking work, but no one you talk to wants to leave to either of the countries which offer them citizenship. Of other, more general choices, there is no mass movement to integrate education, the most obvious way to halt the handing down of hatred from generation to generation. State schools are almost entirely Protestant; the same state supports the Catholic schools attended by virtually all Catholic children. The Catholic hierarchy led the battle against uniting the two teacher-training colleges as the first step in overcoming the children's segregation; but you find few people of either side who lament the situation, let alone work to change it. If the war oppresses them so much, it is hard to think why. But all the political and religious alternatives available seem to lack popular appeal.

Adding this up, there seems little to be said for the never-ending procession of experts seeking a 'solution'. Everyone who is not terminally bored with Northern Ireland (admittedly a large group) seems to be trying to devise a way to help the people there out of their plight. Is it not presumptuous to do their thinking for them? Any citizen who wants to get out of this 'plight' has to change the way he acts or votes. No one does. Therefore it seems sensible to assume he can't see how to or doesn't want to. It is a strange place where peace is simply unknown in the lifetime of almost half the population, but Northern Ireland fills the bill; and like everyone else, they prefer the familiar. 'The people do not believe in change,' wrote one experienced correspondent, 'neither in its possibility, nor in its desirability.' Living in perpetual war may seem unthinkable to someone who knows it only in the abstract; but the particular, especially if it is your own, has something to be said for it.

'Let me have war, say I,' wrote Shakespeare in *Coriolanus*; 'it exceeds peace, as far as day does night; it's sprightly, waking, audible, and full of vent. Peace is a very apoplexy, lethargy; mulled, deaf, sleepy, insensible . . . and it makes men hate one another.' 'The man who has renounced war has renounced a grand life,' wrote Nietzsche. Nostalgia for the blitz is still nearly universal among Londoners old enough to have lived through it; the Falklands War had all the flags out for a week or two. Fighting a war is certainly a much more exciting *raison d'être* than none at all, which is what confronts so many people in the British Isles of the 1980s; what is so enviable about the 'peace' the rest of us live in? What is preferable about sharing the unemployment, riots, crime, welfare cuts and economic hopelessness of the Northern Irish but without their reasons for getting up in the morning? Their grand cause, their commitment, sense of purpose, *clarity*. 'Something *great* got hold of you,' said an eighty-year-old Englishman of World War II. 'Even clear-cut suffering is better than long-term depression – it gives you something to kick off against.' Being in Belfast is like being in a magnetic field: everything points one way or the other and lines up. At home we are all in such a demoralized, disorganized tumult that even an asinine adventure like the Falklands War is welcomed.

War on a parochial scale is also a great preoccupation in a world where death looms over all of us together and at once, whatever the colour of our passports. The Northern Irish war seems to have concentrated minds well away from such nightmares. Reading a thoughtful piece by Michael Hall, Ulster's popular historian, I encounter this passage: '. . . isn't it totally farcical, given the dangerous state our society is now in, that the question of how we avoid the possible catastrophe isn't being tackled at all by the educational establishments?' To me, reading this in London, the only 'possible catastrophe' is nuclear annihilation. I had to go much further before realizing he was talking about something else. At most, only three or four of all the people I met in Belfast alluded to nuclear war as a concern, and then only glancingly. A Sinn Feiner, pushed, said 'At the end of the day it would solve our problem anyway, 'cause it would fuckin wipe out the Brits.' It may well be a delusion to avoid the problem, but it's certainly a relief.

Another aspect of war is how significant it can make you feel in the world picture. People in Northern Ireland feel they really count and, considering there are only a million and a half of them, the attention their altercation earns in the media is preposterous. Belfast is chock-a-block with journalists, academics, social scientists, photographers, every kind of pundit. Interviewing the most out-of-the-way people, I got used to the idea that I was the fourth interviewer they'd had that week. Sometimes I felt as if I were on a delegation to China, where at every enterprise you visit the seats are still warm from the last group. But China contains a quarter of the world's population.

None of this can be held against the people of Belfast: who wouldn't enjoy being in such demand? If you have to be unemployed, it is a great help to have experts on your doorstep forever asking you how it feels (among other things) – like the victim of a disease who, given only a placebo, thrives anyway from the attention. An old man in Divis said, 'People need us to live in these conditions or else they couldn't come up and research us.' He meant, of course, the economic conditions, but the researchers are there because of the war.

Another angle, for those who enjoy that sort of thing, is the excitement of participating in an atrocity and then going home to watch it replayed on the 6 o'clock news. Does anyone watch television news the way they do in Belfast? Even if there isn't enough to eat there is always a very large colour TV on in the corner of every living room. That way people are always ready for a local flash. As for the flashers, you get the sensation that Northern Irish events are almost designed to be civilized and precision-targeted enough not to panic the cameramen and sufficiently imaginative to continue to attract their interest. What are conflicts about any more if not coverage? Yet the very word *coverage* is so new it isn't in the twelve-volume Oxford Dictionary.

My conclusions about the Northern Ireland war are actually on the bright side, from the point of view of those caught in it. One of the more ghoulish sets of statistics to emerge from the Troubles shows an inverse ratio between the homicide and suicide rates – make of this what one will. Incidence of suicide fell by half in the early 1970s and has only very gradually grown again. The same is true of the rate of depressive illness. On a more positive scale the people, when asked, turn out to be, incredible though it seems, the happiest on earth. According to a Gallup Poll 'values survey' conducted world-wide in the mid-1980s, 39 per cent of the people of Northern Ireland define themselves as 'very happy' (compared, for example, to 15 per cent of West Germans and Italians, 10 per cent of Japanese). Perhaps what makes them happy is a fierce commitment to a cause transcending themselves. The world of my own dreams has no war in it. But what if we are stuck between war, and a peace with no dreams?

Appendix
The Background

Northern Ireland is the one-fifth of Ireland at the top right-hand corner which remained part of the United Kingdom when the rest of the island got independence in 1921. About 600,000 of the Northern population are Catholic, think of themselves as Irish, and many of them want a united Ireland. About 900,000 are Protestant, think of themselves as British, and most want to remain as they are. The British government is pledged to support this desire so long as it is reflected in an electoral majority within the province.

There is no neutral name for the place. The British call it 'Northern Ireland', but the Protestants say 'Ulster' – which the Catholics reject because the boundaries include only six of the nine counties of true Ulster, one of the four ancient provinces of the island. Catholics often refer to 'the Six Counties' or 'the North of Ireland' and call the Republic of Ireland 'the Twenty-six Counties' or 'the Free State'. 'Eire' is unacceptable unless the speaker is using the Irish language, because the name is meant to refer to the whole island, and in hostile British mouths suggests that their truncated country is in fact complete.

The British have been in Ireland, in one form or another, for eight hundred years. Resistance, often confused and mistimed, sprang up occasionally from different quarters, most notably from the United Irishmen in 1798 and half a century later from the Fenians (still used as a term of abuse by Protestants of Catholics). The 1916 Easter Rising in Dublin, followed by a war of independence, led to the limited victory of partition and freedom for the South; it also led to a demoralizing civil war fought partly over the issue of this very concession to Britain. But ultimately partition reduced the area of conflict and diluted its force. Nevertheless in each succeeding decade there were outbreaks of sectarian fighting, put down in months or years but contributing to the alienation of Catholics and a sense of siege among Protestants.

In 1968, civil-rights marchers in Northern Ireland, modelling their movement after the one in the American South, tried to gain equal voting, housing, and employment rights for Catholics from the Protestant regime at Stormont (the province's then seat of power in the capital, Belfast). Their demands were resisted by the Protestants with most of the apparatus of the state, and serious rioting began. The British sent the army, initially to protect the Catholics from sectarian violence but very soon to protect the status quo. The Provisional IRA (Irish Republican Army) came into being and the Protestants later began constructing their own paramilitary setup.

In the summer of 1971 the British arrested, and subsequently interned without charge or trial, hundreds of alleged IRA men – many of them innocent. Such mass incarcerations had been periodically used in the 1920s, 1940s and 1950s; but this time virtually the entire Catholic community erupted in violence. IRA recruitment soared. In 1972, in a period of apparently endless sectarian carnage, the British suspended the Stormont government and instituted Direct Rule. Since then almost every phase of life has been run by Westminster, as represented by the Northern Ireland Office (NIO) and a British Secretary of State in residence at Stormont. Most of the petty injustices to Catholics have been, belatedly, removed, but the major grievance – that the British are there at all – remains, and while it remains the fighting continues.

After the first decade of killing, the conflict began to develop the characteristics of an institution, almost with rules. Thus for instance it has never taken to the air, and is conducted almost wholly with the gun, home-made mortar, and carefully targeted car bomb (a Northern Irish invention). More than 2,500 people have died, but by now little of the violence is random. Each side has its paramilitary organizations: the Irish Republican Army attacks the British security forces – or their local Protestant representatives; and the Protestant paramilitaries fight the IRA (and also, sporadically, the security forces, or simply Catholics).

It is not a religious war, nor is religious tolerance strictly an issue. Religion is more a badge of identification to distinguish two traditions, two perceptions of the past, two views of cultural superiority, two sets of mind about the border dividing Ireland, two kinds of fear. Both groups are minorities: one within the province, one within the island. Because their arguments are usually mutually exclusive, it is necessary to look at them separately.

Most of the Protestants in Northern Ireland descend from Presbyterian Scots brought over by the British in the 'Ulster Plantation' of 1609–10 to farm land taken from the native Irish. Others have come down from the Ascendancy, the ruling British land-owning class who were high-church Anglicans. There was Protestant–Catholic conflict from the start, allegiances called upon by one faction or another fighting for power in Britain and Europe and playing out the struggle across the Irish Sea. At a pivotal point in 1690 the Protestant (Dutch) William of Orange defeated the Catholic (English) King James II at the Battle of the Boyne.

To this day Protestants celebrate the Orange victory on the Twelfth of July.

Their side, however, was once less single-minded than is today recognized. The Presbyterians too were victims, though never so much as the Catholics, of Westminster and the Ascendancy – which passed a law in 1704 repudiating their clergy and prohibiting Presbyterians from serving in the law, the army, the civil service, or education. As a result a flood of Ulster Presbyterians left for North America, where (known as the Scotch-Irish) they became the staunchest revolutionaries, western frontiersmen, and Indian fighters, and contributed ten presidents to the United States. (It may be worth reminding Americans who question the legitimacy of the Protestants' claim to Ulster that they have been there since before the *Mayflower* set sail.) Those Presbyterians who were left behind maintained a tradition of dissent which led some, by the end of the eighteenth century, to found, with Catholics, the Society of United Irishmen – to 'break the connection with England, the never failing source of all our political evils,' as Wolfe Tone, Protestant leader, put it in 1798. The rebellion was savagely crushed by the English. On a few occasions since, Protestants and Catholics have found common cause, though never for long. Most Ulster Protestants would now disavow anything of the sort and claim to have been at one then as now: firm in their opposition to the threat of Gaelic infringement on their institutions and absorption by a foreign power. To them Northern Ireland is as much a part of the 'United Kingdom of Great Britain and Northern Ireland' as Scotland or Wales (although their status, as the title indicates, is not in fact the same), and calling themselves 'Irish', as some do, means no more than 'Welsh' or 'English'. Essentially they are the British who remained loyal when the South broke away, and only the British guarantee protects their survival. They view Dublin's territorial claims on them as an imperialist affront – Article 2 of the Republic's 1937 Constitution insists that 'the national territory consists of the whole island of Ireland' – and view the Northern Catholics as subversives.

As most Catholics see it, Ireland is their island, all of it, and having been the first colony of England they are now the last. In the North their dispossession by invading planters was only another injustice England visited upon Ireland over the centuries in which any attempt to assert their independence was brutally overpowered. The English banned their religion and culture, prevented them from owning land, forbade their schools, forced the Church underground, and protected English interests by discriminatory trade practices which impoverished Ireland. In the great famine of 1845–9, English absentee landlords shipped home grain and meat while the Irish starved, died in epidemics or emigrated, ultimately reducing the population by half. After partition, Protestant agents of the colonizers encouraged continuing Catholic emigration by refusing Catholics work, taking the best housing, populating the forces of the law, and gerrymandering voting districts to ensure their continuing power. The border had been arbitrarily drawn in any case, specifically to assure a perpetual Protestant majority. The gerrymandering of the smaller districts may since have been abolished, but to many Catholics the whole province is one monstrous gerrymander. They feel they belong with the South, their flag is its green-white-and-orange tricolour, their anthem its 'Soldier's Song', and their goal: 'A Nation Once Again'.

To the Ulster Protestants, Ireland was never a nation anyway, but a land of warring chieftains, not once united except under the British in the nineteenth century. It was

Protestant money and Protestant industry (if not exclusively Protestant muscle) with which Belfast became one of the richest cities in the British Isles. Having given their all in Britain's defence in two world wars, believing in the Protestant work ethic and upholding 'the good old-fashioned honest Anglo-Saxon virtues,' they feel profoundly misunderstood and betrayed. While many of them decry the discrimination and injustice which led to the present 'Troubles', they remain steadfast subjects of the Crown embattled against its enemies. Many also are apprehensive of Catholicism (though not necessarily of Catholics) and have contempt for and fear of 'Roman' rituals and what they regard as the Church's interference in every sphere of life in the South. Having been stripped of their privilege since the early 1970s with nothing to show for it but an anarchic society and the continuing deaths of their people at the hands of gunmen whose tacit, if not legal, support from the South enables them to train and hide, they see concessions to Catholics as appeasements, sops to disguise what the Catholics really want: a united Ireland, and for Protestants to disappear. Deprived of 'their' Stormont government and 'their' police force (the 'B' Specials, disbanded by Britain in 1970), they see any further compromise as part of an inexorable process to divest them of what they hold dear: the Crown, *God Save the Queen,* the Union Jack and their Protestant heritage. 'We will fight anybody to remain British, even the British.' NO SURRENDER. NOT AN INCH.

There has been some talk of forming an independent Ulster. A history supports this, of a time B.C. when a people called the Cruthin ruled the area and were at continual war with people of the south. At one point there was a mass exodus across the thirteen miles of open sea to Scotland – a simple enough voyage undertaken since prehistory – thus providing its name, since the Romans there called the new arrivals Scotti. The Ulster Plantation many centuries later was therefore a matter of native Ulstermen *returning home* – divided now by war and the Reformation from their ethnic countrymen.

The Catholics react to the Cruthin story with some disdain. It is unprovable and irrelevant and doesn't interest them. Their sense of the past resides more securely in living folk memory. In any case the enemy to them is not the Protestants but the British, the fight directed against the armed representatives of the Crown, even (or all the more) if they happen to be Irish. Catholics say that those Protestants who acknowledge their own Irishness are welcome to share in a future united Ireland. To this the Protestants reply that even if they did so willingly, they are in danger of being culturally dominated and absorbed – as has happened in the Republic, where since 1921 the proportion of Protestants has gone from 10 per cent to 3 per cent.

The names they call themselves can be hard to follow. Most Catholics in Northern Ireland are 'Nationalists' or 'Republicans', and most Protestants are 'Unionists' or 'Loyalists'. It is not as simple as Protestants being loyal to the Union with Britain and Catholics nationalist about an all-Ireland republic. While most Catholics are Nationalists, Sinn Fein (pronounced Shin Fane – the political wing of the IRA) reserves to itself the term Republican, leaving the broader classification, Nationalist, to the moderate party of the majority of Catholics, the Social Democratic and Labour Party (SDLP). Protestants are 'Unionists' through their allegiance to various Unionist parties, particularly the Official Unionists and the Democratic Unionists (led by Ian Paisley). 'Loyalist' can be equivalent to 'Republican' since it is how the more extreme Protestant groupings describe themselves.

Each side has its own fighters who not only take on the enemy but police their own people with their own brand of vigilante law. Paramilitarism is a big and proliferating business. The initials of different groups are thrown at one at such a rate that it helps to realize that if the letters contain an 'I' for Ireland the organization is Catholic, and if they have a 'U' for Ulster it is Protestant.

On the Catholic side, the IRA, correctly the *Provisional* IRA (colloquially 'the Provisionals', 'Provos', 'Provies' or just 'the Rah'), which is the military wing of *Provisional* Sinn Fein, split, in 1970, from what then became known as the *Official* IRA, over the latter's emphasis on a political rather than a military campaign. The 'Officials' have since mostly been absorbed into the Workers' Party, which condemns violence, and have turned to class politics. This move created another split: the Irish Republican Socialist Party (IRSP, known as 'the Irps'), whose own military wing, the Irish National Liberation Army (INLA), pursues armed conflict. As well, the IRA has a women's auxiliary, Cumann na Mban (pronounced almost like 'common-a-man'), with a similar military structure. The IRA, Cumann na Mban, and INLA are illegal, with membership alone earning seven years' imprisonment.

For the other side, as well as the overwhelmingly Protestant Ulster Defence Regiment (UDR), a locally recruited unit attached to the British Army, and the Royal Ulster Constabulary (RUC), the police, there are the paramilitary Ulster Defence Association (UDA) and Ulster Volunteer Force (UVF). The UDA is legal and the UVF illegal. But the UDA has an illegal cover, the Ulster Freedom Fighters. New groups are constantly being formed, or new/old groups, such as the Protestant Action Force, the Ulster Defence Force, Ulster Clubs.

* * *

Because so many people live on the 'broo' (social security), there is the peculiarity of the British government paying the upkeep (such as it is) of people who seek to destroy it. In another anomaly, compensation is paid to victims of violence, not just their own but each other's, and while British soldiers are seldom held legally accountable for killing and maiming, nonetheless the British government often gives compensation to the victims or their families. There are other knots. While the IRA is banned, Sinn Fein is not; but representatives of the British government will not speak to Sinn Feiners. There is a major contradiction in the law: although paramilitaries who are caught by the authorities are no longer given prisoner-of-war status – as they were before 1976 – but are considered mere criminals, they are tried in special 'Diplock Courts' which allow uncorroborated evidence and have dispensed with juries. At the same time the 'ODC', or Ordinary Decent Criminal, receives traditional British justice. Also, despite British insistence that Northern Ireland is part of the same country, there are Northerners who are prohibited from setting foot on the mainland, and hundreds have been detained, under the Prevention of Terrorism Act – a 'temporary' piece of legislation enacted in 1974 which cancels many democratic rights of the Irish on both sides of the water.

Sixty-one per cent of the mainland British, in a February 1987 poll, advocated withdrawal of the British Army from Northern Ireland. But all British political parties still believe that Northern Ireland is a cross they have to bear: that despite the province's costing up to £4 billion a year, there is an obligation to hold to the 'Loyalist veto', the bargain made with the Ulster Protestants at the time of partition in which the government promised to maintain their position so long as the voters of Northern Ireland request it. Some people argue that Northern Ireland has an essential strategic significance to NATO, and that Britain will not withdraw except in exchange for the South's giving up its neutrality.

Meanwhile every few years a new initiative to address the problem is tried. In 1982 the latest of many efforts to get the local parties to cooperate with each other in a new Assembly at Stormont failed when Sinn Fein was barred and the SDLP refused to attend. In 1984 the New Ireland Forum in Dublin recommended as possible solutions a unitary state, a federal state, or joint authority. 'Out, out, out!' said Mrs Thatcher, rejecting any diminution of British sovereignty in the North. But in 1985 an Anglo-Irish Agreement at last gave the South some input in the North's affairs – and by so doing united the Unionists in an opposition as profound as that of the Nationalists.

The basic political asymmetry of the Irish island persuades some outsiders that the British are colonialists pure and simple, that the war is against British oppression and for self-determination, and that the British must withdraw. Parallels are constantly found, from Algeria to Israel-Palestine to South Africa. Moral rights are cited, which leave out of consideration the fact that the 'right' to any land has generally depended historically on how much of the indigenous population the colonizers have managed to exterminate. Otherwise talk of such rights suggests a last-in first-out solution, as if the Northern Irish were a factory work-force subject to redundancies. Most simply viewed, Britain ought to hand over the North to Dublin, and the Northern Protestants might either lump it or somehow return to the homeland they left three centuries ago.

The most obvious difficulty with this analysis is the refusal of the Protestants to accede to it, and the dedication of their paramilitary forces to defending their actual homeland, never mind Scotland – threatening a far bloodier civil war than anything seen yet. At the end of 1985 there were 123,169 licensed firearms in NI; this leaves out the guns in illegal paramilitary hands. Another problem is the South's commitment to unification and its ability to implement it. Dominated by the Catholic hierarchy and proudly so, Dublin has on the one hand been able to concede nothing in the way of legislation or constitutional change to conciliate Northern Protestants, and on the other has cracked down as hard as the British on the IRA and Sinn Fein. 'Re-unification' may be the declared objective of both main parties in the South, but with the highest unemployment rate in Europe and a chaotic economy, the Republic is in a poor position to fight a civil war, take on the North's subsidy or the cost of bringing Southern social benefits up to par, and to assimilate nearly a million hostile citizens into its own three and a half million population.

These difficulties are not lost on the Irish: the Southern interst in unification, according to various polls, is vague and unenthusiastic the moment it goes beyond the simple statement of an aspiration. In a 1979 survey, 68 per cent of the Irish wanted the island united, but only 45.9 per cent were prepared to pay any extra taxes for it. In addition, 60 per cent believed that loyalist paramilitaries would be more of a problem in a united Ireland than the IRA is today in the North. In another poll, a majority in the South thought Northern Catholics had more in common with Northern Protestants than with themselves, and that both sides in the North were 'extreme and unreasonable'. In general, however, the Southern Irish are more interested in maintaining their homogeneous Roman Catholic quality of life than in risking change. Asked in 1982 to list the problems facing their country, just one per cent mentioned the North.

The Anglo-Irish Agreement can be seen as an attempt by Mrs Thatcher to placate world opinion in its virtually universal censure of British moral shortcomings in Northern Ireland. The 'embarrassment factor' came from all sides: the Washington Irish lobby, representing forty million US citizens of Irish descent, would not let the issue rest; the Soviet Union rebutted western criticism of its own human rights behaviour by bringing up Northern Ireland. For its part, the Republic of Ireland could not go on tolerating British inactivity in the North, reflected in so much lawlessness and alienation spilling across a three-hundred mile border to infect them too. A year and a half after the Agreement was signed, nothing of any substance had changed; whether it will have any real effect on the war or on the lives of the Northern Irish remains to be seen.